Why Didn't Nietzsche
Get His Act Together?

Why Didn't Nietzsche Get His Act Together?

ELIJAH MILLGRAM

OXFORD
UNIVERSITY PRESS

Oxford University Press is a department of the University of Oxford.
It furthers the University's objective of excellence in research, scholarship,
and education by publishing worldwide. Oxford is a registered trade mark of
Oxford University Press in the UK and in certain other countries.

Published in the United States of America by Oxford University Press
198 Madison Avenue, New York, NY 10016, United States of America.

© Oxford University Press 2023

All rights reserved. No part of this publication may be reproduced, stored in a retrieval system,
or transmitted, in any form or by any means, without the prior permission in writing of Oxford
University Press, or as expressly permitted by law, by license or under terms agreed with the
appropriate reprographics rights organization. Inquiries concerning reproduction outside the scope
of the above should be sent to the Rights Department, Oxford University Press, at the address above.

You must not circulate this work in any other form and you must impose this same condition on any acquirer

Library of Congress Cataloging-in-Publication Data

Names: Millgram, Elijah, author.
Title: Why didn't Nietzsche get his act together? / Elijah Millgram.
Description: New York, NY : Oxford University Press, [2023] |
Includes bibliographical references and index.
Identifiers: LCCN 2023019463 (print) | LCCN 2023019464 (ebook) |
ISBN 9780197669303 (hardback) | ISBN 9780197669327 (epub)
Subjects: LCSH: Nietzsche, Friedrich Wilhelm, 1844–1900. |
Philosophy, German—19th century.
Classification: LCC B3317 .M57195 2023 (print) | LCC B3317 (ebook) |
DDC 193—dc23/eng/20230512
LC record available at https://lccn.loc.gov/2023019463
LC ebook record available at https://lccn.loc.gov/2023019464

DOI: 10.1093/oso/9780197669303.001.0001

Printed by Integrated Books International, United States of America

For Alasdair MacIntyre

Contents

Acknowledgments	ix
1. Why Read *about* Nietzsche, Instead of Just Reading Nietzsche Himself?	1
2. Who Was Nietzsche's Genealogist?	15
3. Who Was the Author of Nietzsche's *Zarathustra*?	31
First Interlude: What Was Nietzsche's Genealogy?	65
4. Who Was Nietzsche's "Good European"? (How to Read *Beyond Good and Evil*)	72
Appendix: Unpacking BGE §15	106
Second Interlude: Was Nietzsche a Nazi?	108
5. Who Was Nietzsche's Convalescent? (How to Read *The Gay Science*)	112
6. Who Was Nietzsche's Psychologist? (How to Read *Twilight of the Idols*)	139
Third Interlude: Are We Interpreting Nietzsche the Right Way?	153
7. Who Was Nietzsche's Antichrist?	158
8. Who Wrote Nietzsche's Autobiography?	187
9. What Was Nietzsche's Perspectivism?	213
Appendix: Truth and Lie	241
10. What Was Nietzsche's Tragedy?	245
11. What Is the Meaning of Life?	259
Notes	279
Bibliography	353
Index	365

Acknowledgments

I've gotten a lot of help along the way, and I'd like to express my appreciation.

I'm enormously grateful to the people who put in the time to read and give me comments on drafts of one or more chapters: Ron Aboodi, Chrisoula Andreou, Dani Attas, Jonathan Bendor, Alyssa Bernstein, Stephen Buckle, Sarah Buss, Xi Chen, Ben Crowe, Robert Engleman, David Enoch, Luca Ferrero, Leslie Francis, Ken Gemes, Svantje Guinebert, Bernard Harrison, Brooke Hopkins, Chris Janaway, Buket Korkut-Raptis, Brian Leiter, Alasdair MacIntyre, Hillel Millgram, Stephen Mulhall, C. Thi Nguyen, Madeleine Parkinson, Matt Potolsky, Rachel Shuh, Neil Sinhababu, Lauren Tillinghast, and Dar Triffonres—as well as an anonymous reviewer of a previously published chapter. R. Lanier Anderson, Michael Ridge, and a further anonymous reviewer read through the manuscript as a whole. In addition, Avigail Millgram helped with the chemistry vocabulary.

There was much conversation along the way, for which I'd like to thank especially Lori Alward, Konstanze Ballueer, Margaret Bowman, Pepe Chang, Nadeem Hussain, Amy Johnson, Kathrin Koslicki, Jonathan Lear, Gloria Park, Madeleine Parkinson, Nathan Porter, John Richardson, Sherri Roush, Jan Schiller, Aubrey Spivey, Valerie Tiberius, and Candace Vogler.

The work-in-progress was much improved by feedback from audiences at the Western Humanities Alliance's 22nd Annual Conference, a conference on Moral Theory after Nietzsche hosted by the University of Texas, the University of Utah's Philosophy Club and its Tanner Humanities Center, the University of the Saarland, Boston University, the University of Arizona, the University of Waterloo, Utah Valley University, Salt Lake Community College, the University of Canterbury, the University of Otago, the University of Auckland, Oxford University, UNC/Chapel Hill, the University of Tennessee/Knoxville, a panel hosted by the North American Nietzsche Society, Dartmouth College, the Hebrew University, Macquarie University, the University of Melbourne, the Australian National University, the University of Washington, Simon Fraser University, the University of British Columbia, Ohio University, Tel Aviv University, and Vanderbilt University. Belated thanks to Robert Solomon for serving as a commentator at one of these venues.

X ACKNOWLEDGMENTS

I would also like to thank the Klassik Stiftung Weimar for a residential fellowship; the Herzogin Anna Amalia Bibliothek for access to material from Nietzsche's personal library; the Hebrew University, for a Lady Davis Fellowship; the Sackler Institute of Advanced Studies, for a Sackler Lectureship; Keble College, for having me as Senior Research Visitor; the University of Utah's College of Humanities for research travel funding; and its Philosophy Department for a Sterling M. McMurrin Esteemed Faculty Award.

Some material in this book has previously appeared in other venues, and I'm grateful for permisson to incorporate it in revised form here:

Who Was Nietzsche's Genealogist? *Philosophy and Phenomenological Research* 75(1), July 2007, pp. 92–110. © 2007 International Phenomenological Society.

Who Is a Meaning of Life For? *The Philosophers' Magazine* 89 (2nd Quarter): 50–54. 2020.

Who Wrote Nietzsche's Autobiography? In J. Ulatowski and L. van Zyl, *Virtue, Narrative, and Self* (New York: Routledge, 2020): 185–213.

Finally, I want to express my appreciation for the patience of the students in a couple decades of classes on Nietzsche, who put up with the many false starts that got me to the train of thought I'm about to lay out here.

1

Why Read *about* Nietzsche, Instead of Just Reading Nietzsche Himself?

1.1

There aren't many philosophers who have a widely familiar musical work named after one of their books, but Richard Strauss's *Thus Spoke Zarathustra* both borrowed its title from Friedrich Nietzsche, and went on to be appropriated as the sound track for the opening moments of Stanley Kubrick's *2001: A Space Odyssey*. If you buttonhole a pedestrian on some sidewalk, and ask them for a quote from any other philosopher, you're liable to come up empty handed; for Nietzsche, however, you can almost count on getting one of two: either "God is dead" or "What does not kill you makes you stronger."[1] Politicians, pretty much of whatever stripe, don't usually want to be seen paying attention to philosophers, but Adolph Hitler went out of his way to be photographed contemplating the bust of Nietzsche in the Villa Silberblick.[2] Milan Kundera's *The Unbearable Lightness of Being*, a novel so popular it was made into a mainstream movie, is a thoughtful response to Nietzsche's work. And I could go on in this vein indefinitely, which is to say that for a philosopher, Nietzsche gets a great deal of uptake both in the popular culture and in the academic culture as well.

But when you look at that uptake, to see what his readers and admirers thought he was about, Nietzsche starts to look like a Rorschach inkblot in text. For as long as people have been reading Nietzsche, whoever they were, they were sure that Nietzsche was speaking to *them*. I've just gestured at the National Socialist adoption of Nietzsche as *their* great philosopher— and because, when you discuss Nietzsche, somehow Nazis keep coming up, again and again, we'll have to face up to that in the course of our discussion. But there were Nietzschean socialists, and Nietzschean feminists, and even Nietzschean Zionists. Martin Heidegger, who for some time was actually a member of the Nazi party, took Nietzsche as his foil, presenting him as the last metaphysician; Michel Foucault, a philosopher who has been

---

Why Didn't Nietzsche Get His Act Together? Elijah Millgram, Oxford University Press. © Oxford University Press 2023.
DOI: 10.1093/oso/9780197669303.003.0001

2 WHY DIDN'T NIETZSCHE GET HIS ACT TOGETHER?

an inspiration to the political left, understood his metaphysics-dissolving critical methods to be a development of a technique he had learned from Nietzsche, that of genealogies.[3] Among the mainstream historians of philosophy, Nietzsche is announced to have one after another view; somehow they often turn out to be familiar positions taken by philosophers today.[4] And somehow the various claims ascribed to him frequently contradict one another; whoever is reading him right, we can be confident that other interpreters with contrary views are flat out wrong. It's also not too early to observe that, almost without exception, there's a test these glosses don't pass. When I'm teaching Nietzsche, and I lay out for the class one of these reconstructions of some theory or other Nietzsche is supposed to have thought up, I conclude the students' discussion by asking them to vote: if someone nowadays, say, a professor at a respectable university elsewhere, had written a book defending this theory, would it be worth devoting a significant amount of your semester to it? And when the time comes for *no*, I find myself looking out on a small sea of raised hands.

Although intelligent readers very, very often find Nietzsche compelling, absolutely worth reading, and even enormously *fun*, this sort of track record shows that we don't know *how* to read him, and one side of the slightly complicated agenda of this book is very practical: I want to show you how to read Nietzsche for yourself.

This means that you won't find anything like a systematic and exhaustive overview or synopsis of his theories here. There is a book titled *What Nietzsche **Really** Said*, and there are a great many other books that could sincerely have given themselves that title, but not this one.[5] Call the sort of treatments by professional historians of philosophy I was gesturing at a moment ago *straight readings*; they purport to tell you what the dead philosopher believed on one point or another or, more ambitiously, what he believed about everything. (A marker of straight readings—although there are a few exceptions—is that they ignore the elephant in the room, which is that, and let's opt to be direct about this, Nietzsche *writes funny*.) As we'll see, straight readings of Nietzsche are deeply misguided, because there *wasn't* anything he "really said," there was no systematic view that he believed, and trying to say what it was isn't how you engage Nietzsche.

Having announced that a little baldly, I do need to qualify it. Let's divide up Nietzsche's writing into periods: *early* will cover his first book, *The Birth of Tragedy*, as well as the series of essays collected into the *Untimely Meditations*; *middle* is to include the books from then on, up through the first edition of

The Gay Science; mature or *late* will mean everything he wrote from *Thus Spoke Zarathustra* until the end of his working life. (Nietzsche collapsed about ten years before he finally died, a decade he spent first as a psychiatric patient, then under the care of his mother, and eventually as the paralyzed ward of his sister.) During his early and middle periods, Nietzsche did have opinions that were fully attributable to him in the normal manner but, and this is one way of saying what the topic of this book will be, his late period was devoted to a much more indirect, much trickier philosophical and literary enterprise; to a very first approximation, a self-portrait reflecting his own psychological state, that of being the sort of mess where, asked what someone in that state thinks, you realize there's no straight answer—an observation that will bring us in a few moments to the next part of the agenda of this book.

Here I'll be showing you how to navigate the works belonging to that late period—although *The Birth of Tragedy* will come in for discussion in our final chapter, and there will be a brief explanation of what went into some of the middle-period works in ch. 5. While a great many of the responses to those later writings can, as I suggested a few moments back, strike a spectator as an orgy of free association, Nietzsche does provide reading instructions, and because he's quite heavy-handed about them, it's remarkable that they're generally not noticed and not followed.

For reasons we'll get to shortly, approaching those later-period books properly means making a fresh start on each one. So the book you're holding is organized with that in mind: chs. 2–8 take up one after another of those works, stepping through the framing and orientation that Nietzsche is providing his reader, and then demoing how to do what Nietzsche is asking. You can read these chapters as standalones, you can read them in any order, and you can use them to accompany whichever of those books you're reading. However, the final three chapters, which tie together the parts of the argument I'll have been putting in place, do presuppose that you've read through the previous chapters.

Each of those chapters will pick out and develop some of the ideas in the book that it accompanies—of course, those I'll need for the philosophical train of thought I want to develop—but Nietzsche was an enormously rich author. There's always more going on, and always further surprises hidden inside one passage or another. (In the vocabulary of video games, Nietzsche plants Easter eggs everywhere.) So, again, the objective is not to give you coverage of everything Nietzsche thought, but rather to equip you to engage

4   WHY DIDN'T NIETZSCHE GET HIS ACT TOGETHER?

Nietzsche on whichever topics he takes up that you find interesting or important.

1.2

Nietzsche was the philosopher of the disintegrating self, or as analytic philosophers say it nowadays, of disunified agency. Within analytic philosophy—and just to be up front, that's the tribe I was raised in, and the intellectual background I'll be bringing to bear here—unity of agency provides the frame within which people are understood. But it's not just professionals in one division of an academic specialization, and here's a quick way to say what it looks like for people in the real world to take unity of agency for granted.

A little too often for comfort, I'll be sitting in a coffeeshop, or on a ferry, and I'll find myself overhearing a conversation in which one of the parties asks a rhetorical question about a member of the opposite sex: *I don't understand, what does he—or she—*want? The question expresses frustration, and you'll have noticed that there's no shortage of magazine articles and popular books purporting to tell you what women in general, or men in general, really want. Now of course there are several dubious assumptions built into the notion that this is a kind of question you can answer as is; in those magazines, for instance, it's blandly presumed that when it comes to motivation, there isn't a lot of individual variation. But the assumption we want to notice here is that what a person does is *explained* by what he wants— that is, that he implements an organized process for making decisions, that his desires, which are states of mind attributable to him as a whole, are inputs into that process, and so that, if you only understood what those desires were, you would be able to anticipate and, in the right circumstances, influence or control his behavior.

When I say that this is the frame we use to make sense not just of other people, but of ourselves, I don't mean that we always assume that everything that everyone does is accounted for as a coherent and deliberate choice on the basis of what the person as a whole thinks, wants, hopes, and so on. But we treat the occasions on which the schema fails as exceptions and lapses. We don't have an alternative schema we can use to describe people's psychologies, and so we cast those occasions as *deviations*, which means we have a picture of an organized self there in the background, in which attitudes

WHY READ *ABOUT* NIETZSCHE? 5

have their place and mostly pull the weight assigned to them by their roles. (So you assume, modulo the exceptions, that what someone does is explained by what he believes, by what his goals are, and so on.) Being wedded to this descriptive technique has theoretical consequences: philosophers can't get away from the thought that those failures are somehow paradoxical. Under this heading, for instance, *akrasia*, or weakness of will, is when you know you really ought to do one thing, but you end up doing something else. Inside the default unified-agency schema, philosophers inevitably ask: How can that *be*? And so attempts to unravel the perceived paradox go as far back as Plato, which is why the word I used for it just now is inherited from the Greek.

There are ethical consequences as well. Philosophers emphasize the disadvantages of disunity of agency: if your thinking and decisions aren't coordinated in centralized fashion, you'll end up tripping over your own feet, your activities will be self-frustrating, and so on. And so, almost always, they treat disunity of the self as a grave personal defect.

However, Nietzsche experienced himself as a disunified agent, and he philosophized to address personal and urgent needs; the self-understanding he pursued in order to manage—and to rescue—his own life required facing up to one after another philosophical question. In doing so, he not only worked out distinctive and original takes on a great many of them, but displayed someone who can't be made sense of by trying to force him into that default schema. So this book is both an experiment in reading a philosopher who is so disorganized as to block a straight reading, and an occasion to think philosophically—together with Nietzsche—about how to make sense of such a person.

Nietzsche himself had ideas about what interpretation was, and what it is to go about it. Since we'll need to be thinking out our own views of interpretation—in particular, how is it reasonable to go about interpreting someone like *him*?—it would be unreasonable to ignore what he has to say about it. (Which isn't to say that we're necessarily going to adopt his ideas for our own; I mean our engagement with Nietzsche to be respectful, but neither worshipful nor obsequious.) On the other hand, figuring out what Nietzsche thought about interpretation isn't on the main track of the organizing theme I'll introduce in the next lap, and it won't neatly fit the organizational scheme I'll describe momentarily. So you'll find, folded in between the chapters, three interludes: as the material we are going to need to sort out that topic falls into place, they'll fill you in on what you need to know

6 WHY DIDN'T NIETZSCHE GET HIS ACT TOGETHER?

to take our next steps, while also covering that awkward issue I mentioned earlier: what *is* it about Nietzsche and the Nazis?[6]

Nietzsche, we'll see, was disunified in more than one way. An especially important side of his lack of overall integration took the form of living through, or occupying, a sequence of personalities. These personae—or, as we'll see, *perspectives*: this turns out to be a technical term for Nietzsche—largely share their psychic raw materials (ideas, gut feelings, even and especially their drives), but solidify them into very different arrangements or configurations. (So as you read along, you'll encounter those ideas, many of which are fascinating; but please remember that what we're after is not simply a survey.) Each of his later books is a product of yet another character in this display of what used to be called Multiple Personality Disorder, and because figuring them out requires that you let a new author introduce himself to you, it's best to make a fresh start each time you open one of the volumes. And this is why I've written the corresponding chapters so that they can be read as standalone guides.

This is a good point at which to mention another of Nietzsche's readers. Alexander Nehamas has noticed that Nietzsche's writings are in the business of presenting an author to his readers, and I'll be using his approach to some extent as a foil—if you read the footnotes, you'll see that there's an ongoing engagement with his interpretation, and it's not just in the footnotes. So here's a first pass at keeping our respective takes on Nietzsche distinct.

I agree with Nehamas that a productive way to approach Nietzsche's later writings is to ask who the authorial personae they project are supposed to be. But I differ with Nehamas on other points; for one thing, in his view, the approach has nothing to do with Nietzsche in particular, but as a matter of general methodology is how we're to approach all literary texts. I think it works well for some texts but not others, and in particular for some of Nietzsche's writings (the later ones) and not for others (his productions up through the first edition of *The Gay Science*). More importantly, Nehamas thinks that all of Nietzsche's texts jointly belong to—or rather, *induce*—a single author. Moreover, he insists that the authorial persona is, in a nontrivial sense, a unified and coherent character. That is, Nehamas wants to construe all of Nietzsche's body of work as the fully intentional action of such an author; but as we'll see, not all of Nietzsche's implicit authors are fully or even nearly up to the demands of a complex intentional action. And finally for just now, Nehamas takes it that the "postulated author" is always—as a matter of, roughly, conceptual necessity—distinct from the "writer," that is, the human being who has produced the texts.[7] We'll return to his views repeatedly, so consider yourself alerted.

Philosophy nowadays is treated as a theoretical enterprise, one which doesn't have much to do with the philosopher himself; in the university, what professors of philosophy are paid for is producing and teaching philosophical theories, and their own personalities and lives are supposed to remain in the background. But it hasn't always been that way; for the Stoics, or the ancient Skeptics, or for that matter more recent figures such as Montaigne, philosophizing was in the service of one's own life: the product of philosophizing—and the reason you do it—is *you*. For Nietzsche, who became a professor at an extraordinarily young age, and who walked away from the job on the nineteenth-century version of a disability pension, also at an extraordinarily young age, philosophy became personal in this way, and that brings us to the third and final aspect of the agenda we're previewing, namely, the meaning of life.

1.3

If you let a coffeeshop conversation with whoever was at the next table drift onto the topic of philosophy—or anyway, this is what seems to happen to me—it emerges often enough that your interlocutor thinks that what philosophers spend their time on is the meaning of life, and that that's their proper occupation. To professionals, that seems naive and uninformed, and certainly within analytic philosophy it's a topic that has been pushed to the far periphery of the field. But for what it's worth, that response seems to me to be naivete on the part of the professionals: the laymen are right, and the professionals have lost track of something that it is very important for philosophers in particular to be thinking about.

It's not that it's the business of philosophers to tell you what the meaning of your life is; that's plausibly either something you have to settle for yourself or something that your very particular circumstances make inevitable, and settle for you. But settling it, or recognizing what your fate has become, aren't made any easier by the inchoateness of the very notion as we have it, and that's marked by the surface of the phrase: is your life supposed to be like a sentence, with a sense that you could paraphrase? If you could give such

8   WHY DIDN'T NIETZSCHE GET HIS ACT TOGETHER?

a paraphrase—if lives had meanings *that* way—we probably wouldn't take them very seriously, and many of us, at least when we pull our heads up out of our to-do lists and look around, feel it to be a failing if we don't take the meaningfulness of our lives seriously. Philosophers help out by making it clearer what's at stake, what you're after, and what the meaning of your life does for you.

Now in the school of philosophers I belong to, there's a traditional way of taking on tasks like this one, which is just as traditionally called "conceptual analysis"—and that's not on the agenda here.[8] If you wanted a label for what I think is a better approach, *cognitive-function analysis* might do: the question it's most helpful to speak to is, What role would a meaning for your life play *in* your life—and in the first place, in your mental life? In the usual way of imagining our mental lives, which I'm not sure I share, the role of desires is to set your objectives; the role of beliefs is to enable you to draw conclusions, including conclusions about what to do.[9] Analogously, we can ask: what role would the meaning of your life play?

If you expect that people come with different cognitive architectures—although we can already wonder whether a term like "architecture" over-states the structural rigidity in Nietzsche's case—then you should also expect that the question I've just posed won't have just one answer that's supposed to be good for everyone. On the contrary, personalities with different archi-tectures will be built out of different elements, and assign different roles to similar-seeming elements; what the meaning of your life does for you ought to depend on how you're put together. Taking what looks to be the opposite end of the spectrum from Nietzsche's own personality, if you're very tightly wired, a unified self who plans things out, makes decisions, and then executes them, the meaning of your life can be called upon to direct your choices, and while there are various shapes that sort of meaning might take, a very natural version is the life project, that is, an ongoing, openended endeavor which all—or almost all—of your energies are devoted to promoting.

I've explored that sort of life, and that function for the meaning of such a life, by making the career of another philosopher, John Stuart Mill, out to be an argument—one arriving at the conclusion that it doesn't really work out.[10] Here we'll be considering the other extreme, someone who is so loosely held together that there's no point in even attempting that sort of decision-making. (So I'm leaving for another time the personalities that live in the happy medium; that's probably most of us, but we get clarity for the middling cases, in my view, by figuring out the extreme ones first.) What

WHY READ *ABOUT* NIETZSCHE? 9

we're going to see is someone inventing a remarkably ingenious meaning for his life as a way of managing an out-of-control self.

The meaning that Nietzsche came up with for his life was, along multiple dimensions, innovative enough that I won't be able to tell you what it was until we've seen more of the moving parts. But by way of a teaser, it involved not only the idea that we can invent values, but that that's a job which some of us should throw ourselves into—and if it's something you'd like to try your hand at, I'll be pairing off Nietzsche's perhaps overdramatic illustrations with down-home, real-life examples. If, on the other hand, your interest in this proposal is theoretical rather than practical, you should be aware that his take on what inventing a value amounts to doesn't fit any of the standard positions in metaethics today, and that, even now, over a century later, it's—still—a new approach, and one from which we can learn.

Because Nietzsche was thoroughly creative about it, and because we want to see the nuts and bolts of this mode of personality management, we'll lay out a good many of the ideas, arguments, and—this is a bit unusual for a philosopher—the *visions* he came up with, alongside one after another story that he confabulated about who he was. Although their intended consumer was most importantly Nietzsche himself, they've proved to be of interest to a great many other people, and they're what has gotten most of the attention of his interpreters. Since I both need to correct some misapprehensions about them, and because a good many of Nietzsche's innovations, especially in what we now call metaethics, have not been properly appreciated, I'll be giving a somewhat different take on them than you might get elsewhere, and you should be aware of that going in. Moreover, because the focus is on what those ideas and so on *did* for Nietzsche, and because, as I suggested a couple of laps back, in my view straight readings of Nietzsche are misguided, and bound to come out wrong, I won't be engaging the scholarly literature in the normal way.

So, and now pulling together the tripartite agenda of the book, I want to put you in a position to read and engage Nietzsche's writing, without getting lost in the welter of apparently all-over-the-place fragments. I want to use Nietzsche as a testbed for thinking with and about a disunified agent—a disintegrated self—and I hope to convince you that we need a reset on the way we approach and understand disunified agency. And last but not least, I want you to be well placed to consider whether you would want a Nietzschean meaning of life—that is, for your life to have a meaning with the function that Nietzsche assigned to the meaning he invented for his own life.

1.4

Normally books don't come with a user guide; their readers are assumed to have the drill down already. But Nietzsche does provide a good deal of direction, and reasonably, because his books aren't meant to be read in the standard manner. And for a somewhat similar reason—but a much less extreme version of it!—some orientation on my part, presented much more explicitly than Nietzsche's, may be helpful.

These days, academics write either for one another or for the general public, but almost never both at the same time. When it's the former, what they produce is generally inaccessible to nonspecialists, partly because a great deal of background is presupposed, and partly because the norm is an artificial and stilted prose style. When it's the latter, it's usually condescending: the ideas are thinned down, the arguments are omitted, and the content is sloganized. Both audiences have for the most part internalized the signaling. When the experts see the sort of explanations that are necessary to bring a nonspecialist up to speed and on board, they infer that it's not meant for them, and put the book down. When the broader audiences encounter the marks of scholarly prose—footnotes, bibliographies and other such apparatus, but also demanding and extended argumentation—they take it as a warning that the author is going to be talking over their heads...and likewise put the book down.

However, I make a point of writing for both kinds of audience at the same time, and when what's being discussed is how Nietzsche invented a meaning of life for himself, in the service of managing his chaotic personality, doing so is appropriate for more than one reason.

In my view, it's good practice generally. For one thing, philosophy isn't a laboratory science, and so philosophers need other reality checks. Even when it seems to have the most technical, esoteric subject matter, you should be able to talk a philosophical idea through to someone coming to it with no professional background, and if you can't, there's almost certainly something wrong with what you're thinking. So I write for a general public in part as a matter of self-interest: explaining what you're thinking about to someone who doesn't know anything about it is normally a decent reality check.

For another thing, and now from the reader's perspective, you can no more get the benefits of philosophy from an expert's summary than you can get the benefits of art by delegating the job of looking at it to someone else, and asking him to report back.[11] When it's philosophy, if you can't see the *why* for yourself, you haven't gotten anything at all, and so I need to lay out reasons, rather than just conclusions.

But over and above generic best practices for philosophers and generic advice for nonphilosophers reading philosophy, on the one hand, we're going to be discussing what are challenging problems for the full-time philosophers—for instance, what is it to invent a value? how do we make sense of a disintegrating mind? On the other hand, we're going to be drawing practical lessons from Nietzsche's struggle to master his own life, and his experience in producing a meaning of life for it, which are scarcely of interest to any but a handful of philosophers in their professional capacity.[12] These lessons are of immediate and personal import to those of us who, first and foremost as human beings living our lives, and hoping to be thoughtful about it, want to consider what Nietzsche came up with.

All that means that I have to ask both kinds of readers to cut me more slack than usual. If you're a moral philosopher or an epistemologist or a Nietzsche scholar, please bear with my reintroducing concepts that, in our lines of work, we're assumed to have under our belts. Some of the material I'll rehearse, however, I expect will be necessary even for professionals; one subtask, when you're making sense of Nietzsche, is filling in his intellectual background, and because it's no longer the nineteenth century, a good deal of that will be unfamiliar to almost everyone. And please also bear with my attempts to write readably.

If you're a nonacademic, be assured that this book is written for you as well—and not just *as well*, but in the first place. The ideas and arguments we find in Nietzsche, not to mention his literary staging, are demanding, and I won't water them down; but there shouldn't be anywhere you get lost. However, because this is also for the scholars, please bear with the scholarly apparatus—citations, footnotes, and the like—as well as with discussion that engages other philosophers and scholars, and let me say just a little more about that.

To appreciate what Nietzsche was doing, it helps to see how it pushes against and moves beyond the state of play in various subfields of philosophy today. So while I won't be doing it exhaustively, I will be engaging some of the secondary literature on Nietzsche, and invoking some of the views you find today in, especially, metaethics, moral psychology, and theory of agency. Again, I won't be complying with the scholarly norm, which is to respond to each and every one of the participants; if I introduce some current theorizing

12 WHY DIDN'T NIETZSCHE GET HIS ACT TOGETHER?

or commentary, it's because we need it and there's a payoff, not just because it's there.

Apropos citations, here's how to read them. I'll refer to Nietzsche's writings by volume:page in the *Kritische Studienausgabe* (1988), which is the more widely available of two versions of the standard edition of his works. But it's in German, which I don't assume my readers have, so where it's possible (which is mostly), I'll follow it with book and section, which are uniform across the many and much more widely available editions; you'll find a table of the abbreviations for Nietzsche's writings after this paragraph, followed by sample references, with explanations. Where I can, I'll be using Walter Kaufmann's translations, because he's better than anyone else in the Nietzsche business at matching certain aspects of English to German style. Kaufmann's renderings both get the sound of Nietzsche's prose right, and reproduce the literary failings of his German remarkably well, and both will turn out to matter a great deal. The price is sometimes minor deviations from a literal translation, and when that matters, I'll provide the needed corrections.

	Guide to Abbreviations
A:	The Antichrist
BGE:	Beyond Good and Evil
BT:	The Birth of Tragedy
CW:	The Case of Wagner
D:	Daybreak
EH:	Ecce Homo
GS:	The Gay Science
GM:	On the Genealogy of Morals
HTH:	Human, All-too-Human
NCW:	Nietzsche Contra Wagner
TW:	Twilight of the Idols
UM:	Untimely Meditations
WEN:	Writings from the Early Notebooks
WLN:	Writings from the Late Notebooks
WP:	The Will to Power
Z:	Thus Spoke Zarathustra

WHY READ *ABOUT* NIETZSCHE? 13

Thus, 3:480–82/GS 125 refers to volume 3, pages 480ff of the *Kritische Studienausgabe*, the famous section 125 of *The Gay Science*, in which Nietzsche, or his "madman," proclaims that God is dead. When Nietzsche asks you how you would feel if you learned that you were going to relive your life, over and over again, with no changes at all—this is the *Eternal Return*, sometimes also called *Eternal Recurrence*, which we'll have something to say about both in ch. 3 and in the final chapter—that's at 3:570/GS 341, i.e., page 570 of that same volume, still *The Gay Science*, now at section 341.

Now for a little bit of messiness. First, Nietzsche's books often have, not only parts and sections, but subsections. For instance, that other easy-to-elicit quote I started out with, that what doesn't kill you makes you stronger, comes from 6:60/TI 1.8, that is, section 8 of part 1 of *Twilight of the Idols* (now in volume 6). There's a passage in *Thus Spoke Zarathustra*, where Nietzsche (or maybe his prophet) tells you that people who think that even though everything empirical is in flux, concepts and values are firm—those people are "blockheads". The passage is at 4:252/Z III.12.8, that is, part III, section 12, subsection 8.

Then there are a good many often belatedly added prefaces, postscripts, afterwords, and the like, which can get confusing. I'll use "P" for prefaces and prologues; Z P.2 points you to the second section of the Prologue where Zarathustra seems amazed that a saint living in a forest could be *so* isolated that God's death would come as news to him. I'll use A for the "Attempt at a Self-Criticism" in *The Birth of Tragedy*, and by way of keeping them easy to distinguish, N1, N2, and E for the Postscripts and Epilogue to *The Case of Wagner* ("N" for "*Nachschrift*").

Then some parts of *Ecce Homo* have Nietzsche's earlier books as their titles, and for those I'll also use the abbreviations above in specifying the references. Nietzsche tells you that when he talks about Wagner and Schopenhauer, he's really talking about himself; that's at 6:320/EH III.UM.3, that is, part III, the chapter on the *Untimely Meditations*, section 3.

Finally, when I refer to his *Nachlass*—his posthumously published writing—when possible, I'll give the notebook and entry: when Nietzsche worries, at 7:423/WEN 19[21], about a "terrible danger," the "fusion of the American type of political wheeling and dealing with the unstable culture of scholars," that's in *Writings from the Early Notebooks*, specifically from Notebook 19, entry 21.

14 WHY DIDN'T NIETZSCHE GET HIS ACT TOGETHER?

If you're looking to read along, and don't yet have Nietzsche's works on your bookshelf, the best starter package currently out there is Kaufmann's *Basic Writings*, together with his *The Portable Nietzsche* and his translation of *The Gay Science* (1974, 1954, 2000). And although we'll be discussing the middle-period works somewhat less, when Kaufmann's translation isn't available, I'll default to R. J. Hollingdale's renderings of *Human, All-Too-Human* (1996) and *Daybreak* (1982).

If you have those editions, the table of contents at pp. 112–114 of *The Portable Nietzsche* will let you match up section numbers and titles in *Zarathustra* with page numbers, and spare you counting them off.

2

Who Was Nietzsche's Genealogist?

I want to begin with Nietzsche's *Genealogy of Morals*. While it is part of the ethical canon, and deservedly, it also receives disproportionate attention, both in the classroom and in academic publications. That's due, I think, to its being apparently straightforward; it comes off, anyway initially, as the sort of writing that both professors and students are used to, namely, a scholarly treatise, developing a sustained argument on a much-discussed topic. And that makes it a good entry point into Nietzsche's later works.

However, appearances are deceiving: the book is also enormously and insistently absent-minded, and I'm going to first present, as a textual puzzle, a handful of forgetful moments in the first two Essays of the *Genealogy*. To address the puzzle, I'll take up a familiar idea, that the *Genealogy* is both a subversive account of ethics and of what it is to be an intellectual. But as I introduce our strategy for reading the text, I'll make these out to be differently and more closely connected than they're usually taken to be.

Along the way, I'll explain how the *Genealogy*'s criticism of morality can be something other than an instance of the genetic fallacy, yet also not lapse into one or another form of moralism. But all that will be happening as I try to warm you up to the suggestion that you shouldn't be approaching this book as you would a middle-of-the-road scholarly treatise. And that in turn will be warmup for one of the arguments I'll be advancing over the next several chapters, to the effect that Nietzsche's later writings come with the reading instructions that are needed to make sense of them.

2.1

First, the puzzle. Nietzsche commences the argument of the *Genealogy of Morals* by criticizing another account of the origin of morality, attributed to "English psychologists": " '[o]riginally ... one approved unegoistic actions and called them good from the point of view of those to whom they were done, that is to say, those to whom they were *useful*; later one *forgot* how

---

Why Didn't Nietzsche Get His Act Together? Elijah Millgram, Oxford University Press. © Oxford University Press 2023.
DOI: 10.1093/oso/9780197669303.003.0002

16 WHY DIDN'T NIETZSCHE GET HIS ACT TOGETHER?

this approval originated and...felt them to be...good in themselves.'"
Nietzsche objects that this account "suffers from an inherent psychological
absurdity...how is this forgetting *possible*?...this utility has...been an
everyday experience at all times...consequently, instead of fading from
consciousness, instead of becoming easily forgotten, it must have been
impressed on the consciousness more and more clearly." Forgetting,
Nietzsche is telling us, is harder than the British Empiricists and their
intellectual descendants think.[1]

Now if you've already encountered the *Genealogy*, possibly in the classroom, you may recall Nietzsche's account of the origin of what he calls
slave morality: very briefly, that the priestly classes of the ancient world
invented an evaluative system for the downtrodden, according to which what
their masters considered virtues (think of the virtues of Homeric heros)
are evil, and the postures the slaves have no choice but to adopt (servility,
submissiveness, willingness to tolerate abuse, and so on) are made out
to be virtues—specifically, Christian virtues. The new evaluative structure
was supplemented by a fantasied afterlife, in which the slaves were to be
rewarded, and their enemies punished.

This account presents a couple of related problems. The first is that the
slaves compensate themselves for their suffering by inventing hell. But if the
slaves have invented their revenge, why don't they know it's imaginary? And
if they do, how can they find it satisfying? The account only makes sense if
the slaves have forgotten.[2]

The second is that of explaining how the masters could have been taken
in by slave morality. One way or another, the masters have to forget an awful
lot that's perfectly obvious to them: that they've never seen hell or any reason
to believe in it, that the slaves or priests who are telling them about it are
(they think) dishonest and untrustworthy, and that it's obviously some kind
of revenge fantasy.[3]

Apparently, in the short space between criticizing the "English psychologists" and presenting his own alternative, Nietzsche has forgotten how hard
forgetting is supposed to be. Nietzsche rubs it in by later referring back to
the discussion of his predecessors: "To say it again—or haven't I said it yet?
[i.e., I've already *forgotten*]—they are worthless" (5:297/GM 2.4). And why
worthless? Because they've *forgotten* the history of morality.

The swerve isn't a one-off lapse. The *Genealogy*'s second Essay starts out
by announcing that "*forgetfulness*...is...an active and in the strictest sense
positive faculty of repression," and that Nietzsche is going to describe how

"one create[d] a memory for the human animal" (5:291, 295/GM 2.1, 3). But that description is itself incoherent. Humans are supposed to acquire a memory by being painfully trained into it. But if you don't have a memory, you can't be trained: it doesn't matter how painful it was if, next time around, you don't remember the pain.[4] That is, by the time he gets to the second Essay, Nietzsche has forgotten his criticisms of the "English psychologists"; and by the time he gets to his explanation of memory, he's forgotten what it was that needed to be explained.

Perhaps the most interesting phenomemon in this neighborhood is that, while readers occasionally notice the local problems, they almost never keep track of the commitments Nietzsche assumes in addressing them—that is, keep track of them long enough to notice the pattern of inconsistencies. I can confirm this anecdotally: I've taught the *Genealogy* a fair number of times, occasionally to classes of over a hundred students; there have been some very bright people in these classes, and they've been quite willing to point out difficulties in Nietzsche's view. I've never had someone raise their hand and ask, apropos the trail of breadcrumbs I've just pointed out, "But didn't Nietzsche say, just a few pages back, that...?" And the record isn't merely anecdotal; none of the professional Nietzsche scholars seem to have noticed that Nietzsche is dangling before his readers a series of inconsistencies having to do with memory and forgetting. Nietzsche has not only forgotten; he's managed to make his readers forget, too. What are we to make of this?[5]

There are a great many such tensions and inconsistencies in Nietzsche's text. I'll remark on some of those we encounter in the course of the coming argument, and in just a moment I'll provide pointers to a handful of them, so you don't have the impression that the fits of absentmindedness I've been treating as our entry point into the work are all there are. But the puzzle I've laid out makes the contradictions unmistakably *pointed*: this is an author standing up, waving a large, brightly colored flag, and practically shouting to the skies, "I'm contradicting myself!"

2.2

At the beginning of the chapter, I gave a nod to the attention the *Genealogy* has gotten from ethics teachers and of course historians of philosophy. As I'll explain in a lap or two, philosophers are trained to read away apparent

18 WHY DIDN'T NIETZSCHE GET HIS ACT TOGETHER?

contradictions in canonical texts they're working on, in something like the way that, formerly, interpreters of the Bible were supposed to provide explanations that smoothed over inconsistencies. And so, first, the professional response to the puzzle I just raised is bound to be a kind of champing at the bit: *give me just a moment, and I'll explain that away!* And second, there's already been a good deal of this sort of work done on the *Genealogy*. As you'll already have realized, I think this is the wrong way to read Nietzsche, and to help you keep an open mind about it, what comes next is a list—not an exhaustive list!—of similarly blatant inconsistencies. If there were just one or two, it might be reasonable to make them out to be only apparent, but what we're seeing is part of a pattern.

In the very first phrase of the book, its author tells us that "we are unknown to ourselves," and immediately follows the first-person plural pronouncement with a bit of intellectual autobiography that purports to exhibit considerable self-knowledge. Or again, the Preface emphasizes the importance of "what is documented, what can actually be confirmed and has actually existed, in short the entire long heiroglyphic record, so hard to decipher, of the moral past of mankind" (5:254/GM P.7), and thus leads a first-time reader to expect carefully substantiated historical scholarship—as opposed to the Just So story which Nietzsche has attributed to English psychologists and dismissed. As frequent readers know, what follows is not historical scholarship at all, but another Just So story. Or again in the Preface, the author asks rhetorically, "what have I to do with refutations"—and he means, of Paul Rée's work. As we've already noticed, the first Essay starts right off with a refutation (and of course, it's of Rée).

As Nietzsche's genealogy is put in place, the force of the demand for documentation ought only to escalate. Nietzsche purports to explain the development of the value of truth; so at the outset of his reconstructed history, truth is hardly a concern at all; so Nietzsche has systematically impugned the veracity of his own primary sources. Worse, much of Nietzsche's story is placed in what he repeatedly and insistently refers to as prehistory.[6] Prehistory is the period from which we have no historical records, and protohumans are not to be expected to have done much in the way of creating reliable documentation. Given the methodological problems such a view poses, you'd think that *especially* cautious and rigorous scholarly treatment would be in order.[7]

The note at the end of the first Essay further emphasizes the tension. In it, Nietzsche proposes a series of academic prize essays (a common institution at the time), and suggests that "perhaps this present book will serve to provide a powerful impetus in this direction." He doesn't quite go as far as suggesting his own writing as a model, but it's striking that no work that allowed itself as many historiographical liberties as the *Genealogy* could be in the running for such a prize.

Nietzsche even provides us with a version of the Liar Paradox: an interlocutor's query, as to just what Nietzsche thinks he's doing, receives the response that erecting an ideal requires misunderstanding and slandering reality, and sanctifying lies (5:335/GM 2.24); since Nietzsche is clearly on the way to new ideals himself (and the point of his remark is that his new ideals will involve destroying older ones), this is tantamount to applying those descriptions to the *Genealogy* itself.

Just in case you're *still* inclined to take the text at face value, rather than as riddled with contradictions that function as—to borrow Bernard Williams's astute characterization—booby-traps, let's pause on a further, longish example, one that I think will show that what we're seeing can't possibly be inadvertent. In a famous passage, Nietzsche claims that we tend to misrepresent a great many phenomena to ourselves as the operation of a prior or underlying cause, where that cause is merely the phenomenon imagined as present for a second time: we distinguish between the lightning and the flash it causes, but there's just one lightning flash.[8] We likewise distinguish between the force and its effects, and—importantly—the person and the actions we imagine him to stand behind and produce. That is, just as we "redouble" or "reduplicate" the lightning (we have no conception of the lightning behind the flash, except as yet another flash), the person is similarly copied over, as his own soul. This is a metaphysical mistake (there's no such substratum), but Nietzsche suggests further that it's also motivated self-deception: distinguishing the person from his actions allows the resentful and injured to blame others for their actions. After all, since you're not simply the sum of your actions, you could have done things other than you did.

In the immediately following section (the so-called "Tour of the Workshop," that is, the workshop where ideals are fabricated), ideals (the effects) are distinguished from their cause: the men of *ressentiment*, probably a conspiracy of priests, who are being graphically blamed. The juxtaposition of the two sections amounts to announcing that we're to take Nietzsche's own presentation as motivated self-deception of the sort he's just described: what seems to be a conspiracy of priests can only be an impersonal sociological process, which is being "redoubled" in the manner of the lightning and its

20 WHY DIDN'T NIETZSCHE GET HIS ACT TOGETHER?

flash, or a person and his soul (5:278–283/GM 1.13f). That is, we're seeing Nietzsche staking out a position about the origins of our morality in a manner that he has just moments before disavowed.

As this quick parade shows, once you start looking for his assorted inconsistencies, incoherences, and pragmatic contradictions, they're all over the place. And what we're finding in the *Genealogy*, we'll see much, much more of in the other books we're going to be taking up; the local pattern is part of a much more extensive pattern. Nonetheless, analytically trained philosophers will want to object at this point that attributing contradictions to a philosophical text is uncharitable, and should be allowed only as a very last resort. (The reading isn't "noticed" because it's a *bad* reading.) Surely we haven't yet run out of resources for construing Nietzsche as consistent, and isn't becoming adept at reading Nietzsche a matter of learning to find thoughtful organization in what looks to his popular audience like exuberant chaos? So, before settling on this reading, I must consider and dispose of a great many—maybe *all*—alternative readings that smooth away the inconsistencies I'm seeing.

Since that would be an unending task, the right tactical choice is to circumvent it. And so instead I'll shortly discuss the application of the Principle of Charity, and later on, I'll consider a Nietzschean strategy for short-circuiting the objection. But first, I want to take up the more textual question, of what the relation between the form and the content of the *Genealogy* is supposed to be.

2.3

The third Essay of the *Genealogy* purports to explain the ascetic ideal, and its most refined and extreme form, the scientific—*wissenschaftlich*, scholarly or academic—aspiration to truth. I don't think it's an accident or coincidence that the *Genealogy* is the only one of Nietzsche's mature works that looks, more or less, like traditional academic writing. (But only more or less: it *is* a series of three essays—*Abhandlungen*, better rendered as "treatises"[9]—but the tone is off, and it's full of odd parenthetical digressions, eruptions of emotion, segues from topic to topic managed by ellipses, and the like.[10]) The *Genealogy* has a subtitle: it's a *Streitschrift*, a polemic, that is, writing akin to the popular books written on, for instance, the different sides of the nineteenth-century materialism debate (*Streit*).[11] (We don't have quite this term in English, but think of some of the popular writing addressed to the general public by, in the last generation, Stephen Jay Gould or, more recently, Daniel Dennett.) That is, it announces itself as a product of the class of persons introduced by the very first sentence of the book's Preface.

"We are unknown to ourselves, we men of knowledge"—"knowers" would be a less awkward translation, and "intelligentsia" or "knowledge workers" might be reasonable renderings in more recent idiom—"and with good reason."[12] This announcement, at the very outset of the book, tells us that Nietzsche's agenda has to do with understanding the "knowers," and it identifies the narrator of the volume as one of the intellectuals or knowledge workers: "*we* men of knowledge," it says. To be sure, the agenda of the *Genealogy* is also to provide a critique of moral values (5:252f/GM P.6), and somehow these two agendas must be connected, or turn out to be the same thing. But without yet seeing how that's the case, we can adopt as our working assumption the idea that the *Genealogy* is meant to *exhibit* the workings of a "man of knowledge," and let's call the character it's portraying *Nietzsche's Genealogist*.

If the narrative voice of the *Genealogy* is pointedly absent-minded, and if the *Genealogy* is intended to put on display the mind of perhaps a scholar, perhaps an intellectual, then we need to ask why "men of knowledge" are as forgetful as all that.[13]

Suppose you've come to value what Nietzsche calls "intellectual cleanliness" (5:398/GM 3.24), and it's very important to you to understand yourself to be consistent. There are, if you think about it, two ways to achieve that self-understanding. One is actually to *be* consistent. But this is difficult. For one thing, it requires a lot of what we might today imagine as processor time: in order to adjust your intellectual assertions and commitments when they conflict, you have to keep track of them, and check them against each other, one by one, and in combinations; all in all, it requires you to spend limited intellectual resources on searching out and correcting obvious and unobvious inconsistencies. More importantly, from Nietzsche's perspective, it involves regimenting your internal emotional life. Nietzsche represents the person as composed of drives, and drives express themselves not merely as urges to the more visible bodily actions, but as opinion, utterance, and evaluation. Resentment will exhibit itself not only as an urge to kick its object, but in a lower opinion of its object, as when an artist develops dismissive responses toward hostile reviewers—and perhaps adopts a new set of standards on which he does well, and the reviewers and competitors do badly. If conflicting drives express themselves in conflicting opinions, then to make your theoretical views consistent, one of your drives will have to take control of the others. Overcoming this difficulty requires strength (Nietzsche's metaphor, which I'm leaving undischarged), and so we can call this *consistency through strength*.[14]

The other way to achieve consistency as far as you're concerned, that is, to achieve the *appearance* of consistency, is simply to lose track of your commitments: to forget what you said earlier. This is in some ways much easier than the first option, especially if forgetting, as Nietzsche suggests in the second Essay, comes naturally. And we can now see why it does. If (certain) opinions are tied to particular drives, then when one drive surges forward with its opinion, it's also pushing competing drives (along with their associated opinions) into the background: as Nietzsche remarks, apropos the ascetic priests' not unrelated use of the affects, "the chamber of human consciousness is *small!*"[15] Failure to regiment your drives ruthlessly and completely (or, what in Nietzsche's view comes to the same thing, failure of one drive to subordinate the others) produces forgetting as a side effect. Call this *consistency through weakness*.

Now which route to the appearance of consistency (to consistency as far as one is oneself concerned) can we expect the professional knowledge worker to take? According to Nietzsche, the man of knowledge is the current incarnation of the ascetic ideal, and

> *the ascetic ideal springs from the protective instinct of a degenerating life* ...
> it indicates a partial physiological obstruction and exhaustion ...
>
> (5:366/GM 3.13)
>
> science rests on the same foundation as the ascetic ideal: a certain *impoverishment of life* ... the scholar steps into the foreground [during] ... ages of exhaustion ...   (5:403/GM 3.25)

The ascetic ideal can be accounted for as a form of medication (possibly self-medication) improvised to cope with suffering, sickness, and overall depletion (5:387–392/GM 3.20f); in fact, one of the therapeutic techniques Nietzsche mentions is "self-forgetfulness" (5:382/GM 3.18). What's more, Christianity is presented as two millenia of training in forgetting (as when you learn to forget that you don't love your neighbor, but, rather, hate him),[16] and a contemporary scholar is an inheritor of that training: roughly, a monk in secular garb. So we should expect intellectuals to be quite adept at forgetting, and we shouldn't be surprised if, by and large, the form of consistency exhibited by the "men of knowledge" is consistency though weakness: managing the appearance of consistency by forgetting what one said earlier.

To be sure, the appearance of consistency isn't exhausted by having fooled *oneself*. But recall that Nietzsche's readers by and large also fail to notice the pattern of inconsistencies having to do with forgetting. How is that managed? Let's grant that the recurring outbursts of emotion in the text are Nietzsche showing us what the scientific or scholarly personality is really like: not nearly as impersonal and objective as the publicity has it. In so doing, he's also reminding those of us who eventually notice what's going on how we succeed in slipping consistency through weakness past our own audiences.

If Nietzsche's inconsistencies aren't noticed, that's because his readers are swept along by one emotion after another. Nietzsche's drives are put on display in his prose: think of that odd moment when he announces that "Negros...taken as representatives of prehistoric man," scarcely feel pain, and that, for his own part, "[he] has no doubt that the combined suffering of all the animals ever subjected to the knife for scientific ends is utterly negligible compared with *one* painful night of a single hysterical bluestocking" (5:303/GM 2.7). Vivisection was a hot-button subject at the time, gender roles and social class have long been touchy topics, and race was becoming an intensely emotional issue during the period Nietzsche was writing.[17]

Or again, consider one of the many moments at which the author seems to be doing precisely what he seems to be condemning, the point in the text where the priests' ingenuity in revaluing earlier values is described as motivated by poisonous hatred (5:266–268/GM 1.7). The language in which that description is given is itself vitriolic; poisonous hatred would be a pretty good characterization of the tone of that very passage. And of course the project, or one of them, of the *Genealogy* is a revaluation of values (a notion we'll attend to in the coming chapters). But just where the juxtaposition of what the author is saying with how he's saying it could be expected to make the reader wonder how far he can really take the text at face value, Nietzsche swerves into the rhetoric of then-contemporary political antisemitism: "All that has been done on earth against 'the noble,' 'the powerful,' 'the masters,' 'the rulers,' fades into nothing compared with what the *Jews* have done against them."[18] Antisemitism was a politically explosive movement at the time, which is to say that it was able to evoke powerful affective responses— pro and con—from a surprisingly broad public.

24 WHY DIDN'T NIETZSCHE GET HIS ACT TOGETHER?

Nietzsche is pushing his reader's buttons. When he invokes his drives, they (frequently enough) resonate in his readers, bringing their analogous drives to the forefront. Those drives foreground the opinions associated with them, and so displace the opinions associated with previously foregrounded drives. That is, his audiences can be induced to forget because they too lack emotional self-control. As Nietzsche reminds us in the second Essay: "On the average, a small dose of aggression, malice, or insinuation certainly suffices to drive the blood into the eyes—and fairness out of the eyes—of even the most upright people" (5:311/GM 2.11). And now we're in a position to notice a further reason for giving the *Genealogy* the shape of an academic treatise, packed to the brim with complicated historical narrative: men of knowledge, we're told at the outset, are easily distracted by *knowledge* (5:247/GM P.1).

2.4

Recall the objection to my reading that proceeds from the Principle of Charity. Texts are correctly interpreted when they're charitably interpreted, and the Principle of Charity requires you not to impute contradictions to a text whenever that's at all avoidable. We're now in a position to explain why that response is a mistake, and to do so we need to ask a question that has almost entirely dropped out of our collective philosophical awareness: Why be charitable? While philosophers are trained to apply and invoke the Principle, if you ask almost any professional philosopher for a justification, you'll get reiterated insistence, but not an argument.[19] But we shouldn't apply the methods we were taught in graduate school merely by reflex.

The Principle of Charity was reintroduced into our literary tradition in the Middle Ages, as an interpretive methodology developed for one text in particular. The Bible came with a theological guarantee of infallibility, and so here the exegetical technique was warranted by prior knowledge that the word of God couldn't contain errors, and consequently couldn't contain contradictions. That is, originally, the use of the Principle was warranted by a feature of the text that made it appropriate, namely, its divine authorship.[20]

I've just argued that we have in front of us a text constructed to exhibit a particular personality type at work. That personality type, we know from the historical account Nietzsche is providing us, is one for whom actual consistency should be nearly impossible, and the illusion of consistency almost inevitable. That is, the very sort of justification that originally accompanied the Principle of Charity (a view about the fabrication of the text to which it is to be applied) justifies, in this case, *not* applying the Principle. For a text fabricated to exhibit the tendency of a personality type to inconsistency should be expected to exhibit inconsistencies, and we shouldn't count it against the interpretation of such a text that they're found.[21]

Let me emphasize that the reading of the *Genealogy* which I've been developing isn't exhaustive or complete; of course there's much more going on, most notably, the ethical theorizing that has attracted the attention of, by now, several generations of commentators. However, because the theory is presented to us by what I've been arguing is intended as an erratic narrator, and because the theory makes up the backstory of that narrator, we're complicating the task of making out Nietzsche's theoretical claims, and so further complicating our understanding of the author himself. I remarked earlier that Nietzsche offers us in passing something on the order of a Liar Paradox, and what we have here looks to be a still larger and more elaborate variation on one: the body of theory with which we're presented explains why we should understand the narrator to be extremely unreliable, and defuses appeals to the Principle of Charity; but the theory is presented to us by that very narrator, and if he's as unreliable as all that, how much of it can we believe? I don't want to try to settle the question of whether there is a stable reading to be had, or if the *Genealogy* is, on the contrary, constructed in order to preempt one.[22] For our purposes it suffices that, once the theoretical backstory is in play, we have enough to make bracketing the Principle of Charity no more than respect for the text in front of us.

2.5

Earlier on, I put to one side the question of how an investigation that begins with a worry about the self-understanding of knowers could be a critique of morality. That question should by now be considerably more urgent. How could a treatise that exhibits a moment-to-moment inability to remember what it's saying be a compelling critique of *anything*? If the argument is as shoddy as that, why should we take its conclusion seriously, whatever it is?

In answering this question, I hope to explain how Nietzsche's critique of morality can avoid falling into either of two apparent traps. On the one hand, Nietzsche's commentators have been concerned that the problem with morality evidently has to do, somehow, with the people who invented it and who use it; but in that case, why isn't it just an *ad hominem* or genetic argument—both, we were all taught in school, fallacies?[23]

In fact, this will turn out to be a more complicated question than it seems at first. Leaving to one side a special class of cases, for which *ad hominem* arguments are clearly legitimate, as we'll see, Nietzsche himself—or one of his authorial characters—recommends what looks very like *ad hominem* argument, but as a *change* to our methods of evaluation and assessment.[24] So think of the line I'm now taking as a stopgap, not yet the complete story, but something that will do until we can get more of Nietzsche's ideas out in front of us.

On the other hand, his interpreters worry about what we can call *moralism*, that is, making the reconstructed critique depend on the very moral evaluations that it's attacking. We can illustrate the worry with two proposals, floated not that long ago, for explaining the force of his criticism. Suppose it's suggested that the problem with morality is that its producers or consumers are self-deceiving. Why isn't the negative evaluation of self-deception that the criticism is inviting one to evince a moral one? (This is a point that Nietzsche makes himself, at 3:574f/GS 344.) Suppose it's suggested that the problem with morality is that the *ressentiment*-driven agent is engaged in a self-frustrating course of action. Why isn't a preoccupation with efficiency and effectiveness merely a marker of some personality types and social strata—and not necessarily the ones Nietzsche seems to have found admirable? (The *nobility* don't worry themselves about such things: "what," Nietzsche asks rhetorically, "had they to do with utility!")[25] And there's a related issue we'll want to keep track of: Nietzsche complains that morality is one-size-fits-all; why won't the negative assessment of morality be subject to just such a complaint itself?

Recall that drives, according to the *Genealogy*, express themselves not only in action and opinion, but in producing systems of evaluation. I remarked that garden-variety resentment colors your evaluations of the people you resent; on a larger scale, *ressentiment*, Nietzsche claims, has given rise to the system of evaluations that we call morality. Nietzsche attributes a very important part of the invention of morality to the priestly classes, and the priests, the third Essay of the *Genealogy* explains to us, are the predecessors of contemporary intellectuals and their scholarship.[26] Science is just the "latest and noblest" form of the ascetic ideal cultivated by the priestly class (5:396f/GM 3.23).

Once we see how systems of moral and intellectual standards are produced and held together, we should expect the earlier evaluative inventions of the religious castes to have been no less shoddy than the productions of contemporary "men of knowledge."[27] This point appeals to the origin of morality without committing a genetic fallacy, that is, without confusing the value of the source with the value of the product: examining the origin of morality shows how its mode of production predictably leaves its imprint on the product. There's all the difference in the world between treating a dismissive assessment of an opponent as itself a refutation of his views, and constructing a plausible argument from that assessment to the inevitable inadequacy or unsatisfactoriness of whatever views he comes up with.[28]

Recall who the *Genealogy* is addressing: "*we* men of knowledge." If you're a product of the line of historical development Nietzsche has been describing, you care about intellectual cleanliness. Once you see how shoddy the system of moral values is bound to be, you have all the answer *you* need to the question posed in Nietzsche's Preface, What value do the value judgements good and evil possess?[29] A Nietzschean critique of the value of values won't forget whose values it's invoking as a standard.

If Nietzsche meant to address his criticisms of morality not just to a class of overeducated intellectuals, if his critiques operate by exhibiting the implied authors or narrators of his books, and if the critique developed in the *Genealogy* appeals to and turns on values that are shared primarily by overeducated intellectuals, then we should expect Nietzsche's mature writings to project *different* authorial personae—personae capable of supporting critiques addressed to different audiences. The *Genealogy of Morals* is a very sophisticated critique of morality—*for intellectuals*, and that's because it is, at the same time, an exposé of the intellectuals themselves.

2.6

It remains to take up the very indirect and apparently patchy form of the argument as I've reconstructed it. Allow that the heart of the argument really is this: that the fabricators of our moral and intellectual values can't have been expected to deliver a product that lives up to standards such as internal consistency and coherence; that intellectuals such as yourself, the reader, care about niceties of this sort; and consequently that you have reason to reject our moral and intellectual values. Then why doesn't Nietzsche just *say* that? Furthermore, why bother with the roundabout argument that our moral and intellectual values must almost certainly be internally incoherent, etc.? Why not just demonstrate directly that they *are*? And finally, even if some intellectuals (and their priestly predecessors) are as scatterbrained as I'm claiming the author makes himself out to be, how can he be so sure that his own readers are?

I don't think I can tie the suggestion I'm about to make nearly as closely to the text as I have the argument up to this point. Nonetheless, not only does the answer I'm about to give tie up some loose ends, it's a stepping stone on our way to the other books we're about to take up. I've already alluded to Nietzsche's complaint that morality prescribes the same medicine for everybody, and drawn the conclusion that we shouldn't expect him to prescribe the same philosophical medication for everybody. We have to let the *Genealogy* tell us who it's written for: as it turns out, not just any "men of knowledge," but those who will respond to a particular sort of shock treatment.

Nietzsche was quite aware that there's only so much you can do with straight philosophical argumentation.[30] If he's correctly anticipated his readers' intellectual failings, nothing on the order of ordinary argument will suffice: his readers will be all too prone to forget the conclusion itself, or crucial bits and pieces of the argument, or the failings of an unsatisfactory counterargument. In particular, Nietzsche would have been aware that inconsistencies can be explained away. Intellectuals are very good at this, partly because they're often trained in it; so when you try to insist on inconsistencies in their system of values, you get not acknowledgement, but theologizing, and centuries of it.[31] (Indeed, you may have experienced the impulse that Nietzsche is trying to preempt. When I presented what I've been claiming are pointed contradictions in Nietzsche's text, did you find yourself looking around for explanations that would make them out to be not really inconsistencies after all?) If I'm right, Nietzsche hopes to bypass this response, and the way he seems to think he can do that is to catch the reader out: you're set up, and when you finally notice what's been going on, your sudden awareness of your own lack of intellectual acuity is supposed to bring you up short. That is, in order to make his conclusion stick, Nietzsche is attempting to elicit an *emotional* response.

Nietzsche's writing is often read smugly, as an attempt to partition its audience into a sophisticated elite and naive outsiders. But if I'm right, we shouldn't take Nietzsche to be exempting readers of the *Genealogy* from the shortcomings of run-of-the-mill "men of knowledge." If the *Genealogy* works as I've been suggesting, the audience for whom the book is in the first place written must be just those who *are* liable to fall into the trap: those who fail, at the outset, to notice the pattern of inconsistencies; who eventually do notice; and who are embarrassed enough to acquiesce in the point that's being made about them.[32]

For related reasons, we ought not to take Nietzsche to be exempting himself from those shortcomings. Nietzsche has every strategic incentive to avoid making himself out to be holier-than-thou (and responsiveness to those incentives is exhibited when, for instance, he includes himself among the "tame domestic animals," at 5:301/GM 2.6). In catching his audience with its pants down, Nietzsche had better not prompt the wrong emotional responses. This particular audience's psyches are supposed to be built around *ressentiment*. If he were just to manipulate his readers into tripping over their own feet, but present himself the way that academic authors normally do (as fully in control of their own prose, and above clumsy mistakes in reasoning), he would be all too likely to elicit resentful rejection. So Nietzsche presents himself as intellectually fallible partly in order to disarm a certain kind of resistance, and this is a further reason for his use of the first-person plural in that opening line: "We are unknown to ourselves, *we* men of knowledge."

2.7

Let's pull together some of what we've been gleaning about how to read the later Nietzsche.

First, we've been emphasizing that when we spot a contradiction, we shouldn't be too quick to look for a way of glossing it that makes it vanish. It may well be meant as, precisely, an inconsistency, one that reveals something about the authorial character we're encountering—typically, as we'll see soon enough, in the first place that he's incoherent in one way or another.

And second, while at this early stage we can only advance this as a hypothesis, to be confirmed or disconfirmed as we proceed to his further publications, the recommendation is to read Nietzsche's books for their authors, and to do so by asking a pair of questions: What is the book's genre? And what kind of person writes books in that genre?

If what we've seen so far is any indication, you can expect to be given the answers fairly directly. We saw that the *Genealogy* identified itself as

30 WHY DIDN'T NIETZSCHE GET HIS ACT TOGETHER?

a *Streitschrift* in its subtitle, and flagged the author of such a book as an intellectual in its very first sentence. And likewise, you can further expect the philosophical agenda of the book to fall into place around the answers to those questions.

Nietzsche was an enormously rich writer, and what you're led to by the acknowledgedly too-pat formula I've just offered won't be more than a small fraction—even if a structurally central fraction—of the content of whichever book you are reading. Just to make that vivid: the book is titled *On the Genealogy of Morals*, and there's been a good deal of interest in exactly what a genealogy is supposed to be, and in whether Nietzsche invented a distinctive genealogical methodology; we made our way to the end of our own discussion without so much as touching on that topic. (I'll say what I think about it in the first Interlude, but since it won't make sense until after you've read the next chapter, that's where I'll place it.) This is one reason why I'm not trying to survey what Nietzsche said, but rather giving you equipment to read him for yourself; once you're oriented and have your bearings within one of his books, it should cease to function as a Rorschach inkblot—or anyway that's been my classroom experience—and you'll be wrestling with the further material you find on your own.

And I addressed the pushback the reading is likely to get from Nietzsche scholars, who have a century of practice in smoothing out apparent contradictions in this particular text, by emphasizing the way they're *staged*. But that raises a question we'll have to face up to as we proceed: how can an author who is as forgetful as *that* manage all of the careful staging? Mustn't he be completely on the ball and at the top of his game to simulate the incoherent character he's pretending to be?

In the meantime, and to reiterate, the claim we just put on the table, about the right entry point to those later books, is one where the proof of the pudding can only be in the eating. So let's turn next to what is, outside the academic world, Nietzsche's most popular book, and see what happens when we try out the instructions I've just proposed to you.

3

Who Was the Author of
Nietzsche's *Zarathustra*?

The title of this chapter sounds like an unfunny children's joke ("Who is buried in Grant's Tomb?"), but I am going to try to answer the question anyway. As we're already seeing, I agree with Alexander Nehamas that a productive avenue of approach to Nietzsche's texts—anyway, his later texts—is to ask who their "postulated author" is, and I think that pressing this question can make *Thus Spoke Zarathustra* philosophically readable, which thus far it hasn't been. Although it's perhaps Nietzsche's best-known and most admired work among the general public, and although Nietzsche seems to insist that this is a piece of writing that we should take very seriously, philosophers for the most part do not know what to make of it, and with occasional exceptions find it frankly embarrassing.[1]

That's unfortunate, because the book advances, develops, and critically explores ideas that, despite speaking directly and very interestingly to concerns and positions at the center of current ethics and metaethics, have yet to be assimilated by moral philosophy. Let's borrow from Joseph Raz a rough and ready characterization of what philosophers have in mind when we discuss one such concern: we "will generally agree that whatever else people having value in themselves, or being ends in themselves, means it means that, other things being equal, their interests should count." And he continues: "Many will say that an essential element of the idea that people have value in themselves is that they must be respected." Nietzsche notoriously had what is among philosophers today an unusual view of the value of humanity, namely, that it has scarcely any at all, and is likely soon to have none; there's no presumption that the interests of people as we have them count, or that people generally are to be respected.[2] He understood this to be a catastrophe-in-progress, and his label for it was—sometimes—*nihilism*.[3] So he devoted the most productive phase of his working life to laying out his remedy: a program having as its linchpin the invention of novel values.

Why Didn't Nietzsche Get His Act Together? Elijah Millgram, Oxford University Press. © Oxford University Press 2023.
DOI: 10.1093/oso/9780197669303.003.0003

32 WHY DIDN'T NIETZSCHE GET HIS ACT TOGETHER?

As we'll shortly see, this program faces what is on the face of it an insuperable obstacle; if I'm understanding Nietzsche's response to it correctly, it set much of the agenda for his mature writings. In *Zarathustra*, Nietzsche dramatizes rather than discusses the roadblock, with the aim of showing how standard techniques for managing evaluative innovations won't get us through it. This means that although philosophers in our tradition usually read past what they think of as the merely literary aspects of Nietzsche's writings, if we don't treat them as our entry point into *Thus Spoke Zarathustra*, we'll miss its point entirely. Since it will be necessary to interleave two very different treatments—that is, an explanation of that dramatization and a direct discussion of the philosophical issues—I'll have to ask the reader for more than the usual quota of patience, and you may want to treat section breaks as pause points.

Nietzsche's program for transforming a worthless humanity into something of value is a surprising attempt to abort and replace a familiar philosophical enterprise, that of spelling out and accounting for the value that humanity is assumed to have, already and across the board. Philosophers shouldn't take familiar enterprises for granted, and so Nietzsche's alternative deserves careful consideration. And whether or not we share Nietzsche's views about the need to redeem humanity as a whole, there's his idea, which is well worth thinking through, that values are to be invented rather than discovered, and that this is the proper business of philosophy.

3.1

Why do philosophers so frequently treat Nietzsche's most famous book as though it were a shameful family secret? The doctrines advanced in the book are—with an important qualification that we'll get to in due course—shared with Nietzsche's other mature writings; even the most analytic of Nietzsche scholars are comfortable reconstructing and discussing a great many of them. However, Kathleen Higgins memorably reports a young friend's description of *Zarathustra* as "kind of like a perverted Kahlil Gibran," and that characterization is spot on.[4] It's easy to assemble a long list of ways in which *Thus Spoke Zarathustra* reads badly: it's often pompous, and excessively flowery in ways that make straightforward points unnecessarily obscure; it's the sort of patchwork of pastiches that made postmodernism so very annoying; it's sentimental; it's preachy; it's writing that, by being

WHO WAS THE AUTHOR OF NIETZSCHE'S *ZARATHUSTRA*? 33

at once naively blasphemous and naively idealistic, appeals primarily to adolescents; it contains one of the most excruciatingly mixed metaphors—a vine with swelling udders (4:279/Z III.14)—that one is likely ever to run into; very often it's just plain kitsch. The philosophers' collective cringe is largely prompted by the book's stylistic excesses.[5]

There is, however, an important difference between Nietzsche and Gibran. The author of *The Prophet* was probably unaware of how awful his writing was, but Nietzsche was very self-aware indeed, and an acknowledged master of style; it's hard to believe that he didn't know exactly how it sounded. In *The Gay Science*, which acts as a runup to *Zarathustra*, we have confirmation that he did: evidently because he didn't trust his audience to realize what he was doing, he went out of his way to tell us that we shouldn't take the text of *Zarathustra* at face value, belatedly adding the following bit of instruction for his readers:

> "*Incipit tragoedia*" we read at the end of this awesomely aweless book.[6] Beware! Something downright wicked and malicious is announced here: *incipit parodia*, no doubt. (3:346/GS P.1)

If the book is stylistically hard for professional philosophers to swallow, that may well have to do with its being a parody; so we should approach *Zarathustra* by asking ourselves what it's parodying, and why.

The plan of action is as follows. I'll begin by identifying the genre being parodied. Then I'll supply a bit of historical context that today generally gets overlooked: the so-called Higher Criticism, and one of Nietzsche's several appropriations of it. That will allow me to identify the postulated author of *Thus Spoke Zarathustra*—that is, the character implicitly presented to us as the author of the text we're reading. Knowing what sort of author we're encountering will tell us how to read the doctrines we find there. That in turn will allow us to broach the question of why Nietzsche took the trouble to present us with this particular authorial perspective.

At that point, I'll move to the forefront a complaint that contemporary readings of Nietzsche's doctrines of the Eternal Return and of the Overman have had to face, and put on the table a famous and distinctive Nietzschean proposal which I mentioned a moment back: that we are to invent values, and that these values should be not only novel but idiosyncratic. To anticipate, the difficulty of firming up the content of a newly-introduced value, never a trivial exercise in any case, is exacerbated when the values are of the sort

34 WHY DIDN'T NIETZSCHE GET HIS ACT TOGETHER?

that Nietzsche is inviting us to fashion. The authorial perspective taken on in *Zarathustra* is, I will suggest, Nietzsche's attempt to bring us to appreciate just how difficult a problem it is.

Once Nietzsche's literary framing has been explained, I can turn to the question of what to make of the Overman and the Eternal Return. I'll consider how effective these ideals are going to be in imbuing humanity with value; as it turns out, they're much less important than Nietzsche's presentation makes them seem initially. Pretty much all the heavy lifting is done by his lower-key proposal, namely, that our lives are to be improved, and made capable of compelling respect, through the particular and idiosyncratic values that we invent.

3.2

The title of *Thus Spoke Zarathustra* is a heavy-handed allusion to an Old Testament marker of prophetic discourse ("thus saieth the Lord"), and it's reiterated frequently in the book, as a closing signature to one or another speech.[7] Like the later prophets of the Hebrew Bible, Zarathustra delivers impassioned speeches to uninterested crowds, demanding of them that they change their ways. Like the prophets, he often speaks in parables, and, like the prophets, he sometimes shifts into verse. Although there are of course differences—for instance, and this is a point to which we'll return, prophets are assigned their missions by God, but *Zarathustra*'s stage-setting tells us that God is dead (4:14/Z P.2)—*Zarathustra* presents itself as prophesy, and part of the holy scripture of a nonexistent religion.

A book parodying holy scripture is so far of a piece with Nietzsche's other later works; his mature writings, we're starting to see, typically reappropriate one or another literary genre, and the first question to ask when reading them normally is: which genre is it in (or riffing on)? The prose form is being adopted—or manhandled—in order to make one or more points, and typically Nietzsche's most immediate point turns on the sort of person who might write such a book. If that framing hypothesis is correct, then making sense of *Zarathustra* will involve first of all figuring out what Nietzsche wants to convey about the sort of person who writes books in its genre. *Zarathustra* is holy scripture. But what sort of person authors a bible, or part of one?

The mid-nineteenth century saw secular second thoughts about the origins of the Bible crystallize into a scholarly movement whose enormous intellectual impact we've almost forgotten. The Higher Criticism proposed to treat the Bible like any other historical document: thus, as a product of human rather than divine authorship. Higher Critics attempted to reconstruct the histories, processes and agendas that had shaped the texts we now have.[8] Although secular biblical scholarship is still with us, you should be aware that today's version of it differs a great deal from that of the mid-nineteenth century. Lacking much in the way of archeological background, the Higher Critics focused almost exclusively on internal textual evidence. And, as with many Enlightenment intellectual enterprises, the Higher Critics are likely to strike us now as overly invested in debunking the religion in which they were raised, and as having about them a good deal of the village atheist.

As a classics scholar, Nietzsche was bound to be familiar with the figures and ideas in this iconoclastic field, and in fact he owned a copy of Julius Wellhausen's influential *Prolegomena to the History of Israel*.[9] Wellhausen wasn't by any means the sole or most original member of his movement, but he synthesized the Higher Critics' ideas about the Old Testament into a scholarly narrative that captured the imaginations of his contemporaries, and I'm going to lean heavily on this work in particular.

Now, the date of the edition is the year in which Nietzsche began *Zarathustra*, so using this volume as our foil involves tradeoffs. On the one hand, we still have Nietzsche's own marked up copy, and while it's naturally hard to date Nietzsche's marginal markings, they're an extremely helpful (even if retrospective) guide to the aspects or elements of Wellhausen's book that Nietzsche found most salient. And the doctrines of Wellhausen's school are captured quite dramatically in what became their canonical rendering. On the other hand, we have to remain agnostic as to how directly the volume influenced Nietzsche's composition.[10] What matters here is that the ideas circulated widely at the time. A relevant example of this sort of reading of the New Testament is David Strauss's *Life of Jesus*, with which Nietzsche was also quite familiar, and Wellhausen's *Geschichte Israels*, a trial run for the *Prolegomena*, had been published in 1878.[11]

Against traditional views which imputed divine or inspired authorship to the Bible, or which took its historical books to constitute an authentic record contemporaneous with the ancient early Israelites, Wellhausen argued that a great deal of the Hebrew Bible was one or another much later forgery, manufactured by priestly elites in order to confer legitimacy on their institutional privileges and prerogatives. *Deuteronomy* and related texts were presented as

36 WHY DIDN'T NIETZSCHE GET HIS ACT TOGETHER?

dating to the period of religious centralization in the later Judean monarchy; what Wellhausen dubbed the "Priestly Code" was a product of the post-Exilic period. In each case, practices and evaluative perspectives of the later period were backdated, and anachronistically imposed on earlier stages of Israelite history. Such later forgeries often helped themselves to earlier documents, which they clumsily wove together into the texts we now have; the distinct sources, as well as later editorial alterations, were alleged to be distinguishable and datable on the basis of stylometric evidence.

Now, in his *Antichrist*, Nietzsche wrote:

> The concept of God falsified, the concept of morality falsified: the Jewish priesthood did not stop there. The whole of the *history* of Israel could not be used: away with it! These priests accomplished a miracle of falsification, and a good part of the Bible now lies before us as documentary proof. With matchless scorn for every tradition, for every historical reality, they translated the past of their own people into religious terms, that is, they turned it into a stupid salvation mechanism of guilt before Yahweh, and punishment; of piety before Yahweh, and reward.
>
> the priest ... measures peoples, ages, individuals, according to whether they profited or resisted the overlordship of the priests ... in the hands of the Jewish priests the great age in the history of Israel became an age of decay; the Exile, the long misfortune, was transformed into an eternal punishment for the great age—an age in which the priest was still a nobody.
>
> (6:194–195/AC 26)

This passage is visibly derived from Wellhausen, and could serve as a precis or abstract of his treatise; together with similar passages nearby in *The Antichrist*, it confirms what we know from his frequent and emphatic underlining, that Nietzsche perhaps treated Wellhausen as an authority, but in any case paid close and careful attention to his work.[12]

The common denominator of the Higher Critics' rereading of both the Old and New Testaments was that a religious canon is normally the product not of the time at which the religion originated, but is assembled at a much later date by functionaries of that religion. An institutionalized religion inevitably has a very different perspective, and in particular, a very different system of values from that of its founders—whether they were charismatic leaders of lower-class protest movements or the primitive nomadic predecessors of a subjugated state. Thus the writings those

WHO WAS THE AUTHOR OF NIETZSCHE'S ZARATHUSTRA? 37

institutions canonize will systematically misrepresent the early historical stages of the religion's development.[13]

Looking ahead, if *Thus Spoke Zarathustra* is modeled on holy scripture as Nietzsche understood it, we should expect its implicit author to be something on the order of a priest of a religion that claims Zarathustra as its founder, writing at a time much later than the events it depicts, from a perspective that cannot avoid systematically misrepresenting them. Thus we should further expect the book's ideas about humanity and its value, their familiarity from his other works notwithstanding, to turn out to be a perversion of Nietzsche's own view and proposals.[14] So let's consider whether the Higher Criticism's reading of the Bible is in fact guiding Nietzsche's composition of *Zarathustra*.

3.3

Indeed, Nietzsche seems to have quite self-consciously gone out of his way to mark *Thus Spoke Zarathustra* with the telltale features that the Higher Critics had so famously claimed were to be found in the Old Testament.

Taking after Ibn Ezra, the Higher Critics made a great deal of the presence in the Bible of turns of phrase such as, "And the Canaanite was then in the land" (Gen. 7:6), or "There arose not a prophet since in Israel like unto Moses" (Deut. 34:10), or "Joshua made the Gibeonites at that day hewers of wood and drawers of water . . . even unto this day" (Josh. 9:27).[15] Because such locutions inform you of the temporal displacement of the writer from the events he's recounting, they're incompatible with traditional views about the Bible's authorship, and motivate the project of determining who the real authors of the Bible were. Now, very early on in *Zarathustra*, we read:

> And here ended Zarathustra's first speech, which is also called "the Prologue" (4:20/Z P.5)

—implying a long (presumably religious) tradition in which the speech has been given a name. Or again, at the end of sec. 1 of "On Virtue that Makes Small," we get: "On that same day, however, he made his speech on virtue that makes small"; as before, the implication is that the speech about to be presented is already in circulation, and known by that name (4:212/Z.III.5.1). Or again, in "At Noon," a remark is identified as "Zarathustra's proverb"

38 WHY DIDN'T NIETZSCHE GET HIS ACT TOGETHER?

(4:342/Z IV.10); the "proverb" is repeated at 4:353/Z IV.12, and a further proverb is attributed to Zarathustra at 4:396/Z IV.19.1; evidently a number of sayings are already known as "Zarathustra's proverbs." Or again, an event is identified as "that long-drawn-out meal which the chronicles [better: the history books] call 'the last supper'" (4:355/Z IV:12). Briefly, *Zarathustra* presents itself as having been composed much later than the events it reports.

The Higher Critics had argued that when post-Exilic priests wrote historical works, they clumsily inserted features of the social organization of that much later date into the historical narrative. *Zarathustra* adopts the conceit that its author is doing the same. The setting is some sort of pastoral society long ago: Zarathustra walks; he doesn't take trains or even carriages, and no one else seems to, either. The forests have saints in them, and the villages have tightrope shows. Perhaps it's supposed to be the Middle Ages, perhaps not; in any case, it's a great deal earlier than the nineteenth century. But we find this older time peppered with all manner of anachronisms: newspapers, chairs (i.e., professorial chairs in a university),[16] the Kantian thing-in-itself (4:38/Z I.3), egalitarian ideologies (4:128–131/Z II.7), Kantian aesthetics (4:156–159/Z II.15),[17] military uniforms (4:58/Z I.10), complaints about the State (4:170/Z II.18; 4:61f/Z I.11), about the overspecialized academics and scholars whom Nietzsche describes as "inverse cripples" (4:178/Z II.20), about housing developments (4:211f/Z III.5.1), and about the emerging bourgeoisie (4:262f/Z III.12.21). At one point Zarathustra returns from the future, "to you, O men of today, and into the land of education" (4:153/Z II.14); his complaints identify the land of education as late nineteenth-century Europe.

Wellhausen and others had argued that internal textual evidence showed the Bible to have been assembled from many disparate sources. *Zarathustra* mimics this also. There are collections of speeches; we've already noticed two named speeches, and the title "Zarathustra's Speeches" (4:29) further marks them as a compilation of already available material. There's also some rhymed verse (4:285f/Z III.15.3), as well as "songs" of Zarathustra, meant to imitate psalms—notice the repeated "Selah" and "Amen"—all integrated somehow into the book.[18]

Nietzsche isn't just parodying the Bible: he's parodying the Bible as the Higher Criticism understood it. If he is, then the putative author of *Zarathustra* is someone cobbling together and rewriting older texts, and in the course of doing so imposing his own ideology on his materials. And if

WHO WAS THE AUTHOR OF NIETZSCHE'S *ZARATHUSTRA?* 39

that's right, *Zarathustra* differs strikingly in one respect from Nietzsche's other mature writings.

In his other late works, the authorial characters are directly or indirectly named, and, throughout, their name is "Nietzsche." At the outset of this chapter, I reiterated my agreement with Nehamas's suggestion that Nietzsche's books are best read by asking who their authors are. We've now reached another point at which we have to part ways with Nehamas's reading. Nehamas assumes that Nietzsche's books all share a single author. I'm in the course of making the case that each of the later books presents us with a distinct author, and that these authors are, and not by accident, quite different from one another. However, because most of them are *named* "Nietzsche," my disagreement with Nehamas is a relatively complicated one to resolve. The instance we have in front of us, however, is uncomplicated: the postulated author of *Thus Spoke Zarathustra* is something like a priest of some not-yet-founded religion, writing at some time in the distant future.[19]

One point is quite clear. The use which Nietzsche makes of the Higher Criticism tells us that he means *Zarathustra* to represent not his own ideas and—to use the relevant part of his vocabulary—values, but rather his ideas and values as they'll be perverted and corrupted by being institutionalized. If that's correct, we have on hand an important consequence for how the book is to be read. It is irresponsible simply to pull passages from *Zarathustra*, and treat them as assertions of Nietzsche's views—which is, almost without exception, what scholars who have helped themselves to *Zarathustra* have done.[20]

Why would Nietzsche (the once-living, breathing writer) have taken the trouble to present us with a literary construction of this form? Philosophers delivering injunctions not to misinterpret them in one or another way are common enough. But why would Nietzsche have written an entire book in which he presents possible misreadings? And moreover, why would he have regarded such a book as a philosophically central work, and been positively exuberant at his own achievement? If we're on the right track, it must be because the institutionalization of values amounts, in one or more ways, to a central problem in Nietzsche's philosophical enterprise, and because he thought that with *Zarathustra* he was addressing it. So it's time to turn to Nietzsche's philosophical agenda; I'll begin with some criticism of the way in which two famous doctrines are familiarly ascribed to *Thus Spoke Zarathustra*.

40 WHY DIDN'T NIETZSCHE GET HIS ACT TOGETHER?

3.4

Twenty-five or so years back, a New Age self-help book which disguised itself as a thriller made it to the bestseller lists. *The Celestine Prophecy* told the story of its protagonist's pursuit of an ancient document containing the very secrets of existence. In the course of a typical chapter, in which he might, say, narrowly escape death at the hands of soldiers intent on suppressing the document, a capital-letters Insight is revealed to him, such as: people try to win conversations, which is a bad thing; or, if you have a bad feeling about something, don't do it; or, don't cut down those beautiful old-growth forests. That is, the chase after the ancient document reveals "secrets" that are in fact no more than truisms, platitudes of which the book's readers are no doubt already convinced.[21]

Nietzsche can present us with a very similar problem. Heidegger correctly observes that Zarathustra is given the role of the teacher of the Eternal Return and then of the prophet of the Overman.[22] These doctrines have received a great deal of exegetical attention, and the results share in what we can call the *Celestine Prophecy Problem*. Take the Eternal Return: on the most mainstream family of interpretations, its point is, more or less, that you should ask yourself whether you're happy enough with the way your life is going to want to do it over again.[23] Whatever we ultimately think of the recommendation,[24] it's familiar and even trite; we don't need a prophet to descend from the mountains to tell us that we should live so as not to have regrets, and that a satisfactory life is one that we would be willing to relive.

Or again, the Overman, as he seems to be sketched in *Zarathustra*, comes off as a personality type that will synthesize the hypertrophied traits and capabilities of today's "higher men," the academic specialists, ascetics, clergy, Dostoyevskian nihilists, and so on cataloged in Part IV; these traits systematically deform people's characters and lives into what would be, other things equal, occasion for regret. However, once we understand the "higher men" as the historical preconditions of the Overman, we will no longer find their existence regrettable. (They'll have been "redeemed".) This bit of Nietzschean doctrine isn't trite and overfamiliar in the way that the Eternal Return is, but it nonetheless doesn't deserve its very own prophet. Even if it's heartening to think that all those human bonsais haven't gone to waste, we no more need a Zarathustra to preach it to us than we need a Celestine Prophecy to tell us not to try to win conversations or lie to children.[25]

3.5

Oversimplifying somewhat, as this family of interpretations of the Eternal Return has it, we're being advised to live so that we don't regret the past: neither our own decisions—nor, and this tends to get overlooked in the treatments at which we've just gestured—the variously sorry state of humanity until this point. The way to do this is to come to understand apparently regrettable aspects of ourselves and our world as necessary preconditions for, or part and parcel of, something that we wholeheartedly choose and affirm. Once one sees one's trials and tribulations as the *sine qua non* of one's success, one is in retrospect happy that one underwent them; likewise, once one sees our depressing history as the precondition for our glorious future, one will no longer be thinking: *if only*... The Eternal Return is meant as a test that this condition has been attained; if you'd be willing to have history as a whole, and your history as a part of it, repeat itself unaltered infinitely many times, then you must have managed to get past your regrets in pretty much this way.

The problem, now, is that there's too much to be redeemed: in Nietzsche's own case, the marginalized life of a near-invalid, someone who would be a street person if he didn't have a disability pension, living out a lonely and ignored existence in a succession of cheap Italian and Swiss hotels. Even more pressingly, affirming the Eternal Return is a matter of reaffirming not just one's own past, but *all* of the past—and the future, as well. That includes the entire history of Christianity, just for starters, and what is hardest to stomach, a world full of defective, deformed, and—he repeatedly tells us—nauseating humanity. Here's Nietzsche's character playing up that response:

> Naked I had once seen both, the greatest man and the smallest man: all-too-similar to each other, even the greatest all-too-human. All-too-small, the greatest!—that was my disgust with man. And the eternal recurrence even of the smallest—that was my disgust with existence.

Elsewhere he recounts a vision, deploying a related image that, we recall, has earlier been glossed for the readers:

> A young shepherd I saw, writhing, gagging, in spasms, his face distorted, and a heavy black snake hung out of his mouth. Had I ever seen so much nausea and pale dread on one face?

42 WHY DIDN'T NIETZSCHE GET HIS ACT TOGETHER?

> The bite on which I gagged the most...was...my question: What? does life *require* even the rabble?...my nausea gnawed hungrily at my life.

And in the book's Preface, in his attempt to shock an audience out of its complacency, Zarathustra indicts them:

> The earth has become small, and on it hops the last man, who makes everything small..."We have invented happiness," say the last men, and they blink.[26]

The description does not indeed move his listeners, but it is meant to be deeply disturbing.

Let's start to use Nietzsche's word, "values," to cover, among other things, the standards by which you assess the relative worth of one thing and another. What could be *so* valuable as to redeem *that* past? And what could be so valuable as to redeem *our* worthless humanity? By the lights of the values we deploy in real life, nothing fits the bill.[27] At first glance, *Zarathustra* is naturally read as proposing that the Overman will be so supremely valuable as to retrospectively justify his hard-to-swallow past. But not only does this sort of reading fail to explain why the Overman is *that* valuable, it loses track of Nietzsche's problem. That was, we saw a moment back, precisely that life requires the dishearteningly valueless version of humanity that we see around us. ("What? does life *require* even the rabble?") So insisting that humanity as it is and has been is required by the Overman shouldn't count as a solution to it. Once we remind ourselves that there's more to the Eternal Return than the trite injunction to be alright with your life, the doctrine, as Nietzsche's interpreters have been construing it, seems simply unbelievable.

But there are two very different ways to come to have something that's valuable; one is to take available standards as a fixed frame of reference, and to acquire something that is sufficiently valuable by their lights; the other is to alter the standards so that what you have, or perhaps could come to have, will count as more valuable. If we need to redeem the past and our fellow man, and if, given our current values, nothing could count as valuable enough to do so, then we must replace our current values with values that permit the past, and even *those* fellow men, to be redeemed. This train of thought appears as one of several motivations for a distinctively Nietzschean innovation in moral theory, the invention of new values.

In *Zarathustra*, Nietzsche repeatedly presses this agenda on his reader. For instance, "On the Three Metamorphoses" charts the path followed by promising personalities: they start out by taking on challenging obligations, precisely because they're challenging; then they challenge the values they inherited, which underwrote those challenging obligations; finally, they make up new values (4:29–31/Z I.1). In "On the Flies of the Market Place," we're told that what's really important is something that doesn't get a lot of attention, namely, the invention of new values: "Around the inventors of new values the world revolves: invisibly it revolves." Would-be inventors are warned that if they want to be in that line of work, they do well to stay away from distracting and unappreciative hypemeisters, who are dismissively compared to irritating insects (4:65–68/Z I.12). Similarly, "On Great Events" tells the reader not to pay attention to large political events; what really matters is the invention of values, which is the sort of quiet (and apolitical) business that scarcely gets noticed (4:166–171/Z II.18). And in a section on "Gift-Giving Virtue," we're reminded that we've inherited a great deal in the way of randomly and badly chosen values, and these have in some Lamarckian manner really become *part* of us; that we can still experiment with and create new values, and get it right; and finally, that if you just follow someone's instructions about creating values—even Nietzsche's, or Zarathustra's—you're doing it wrong (4:97–102/Z I.22).

If our account of the literary frame is correct, we need to be suspicious about whether these pronouncements convey Nietzsche's own views accurately as they are; in due course I'll get around to considering some of the more important ways he's misrepresenting himself. For the moment, let's just register that what is evidently the same agenda is prominently on display elsewhere: as we'll see in ch. 4, *Beyond Good and Evil* promotes "philosophers of the future," who are characterized as legislators of new values.

This gives us a different way to think about the Eternal Return: as an ideal to bring to bear in the assessment of, not in the first place decisions or self-interpretation, but values that we currently deploy or are considering adopting. If that's right, we should be construing the Eternal Return as something on the order of a proposed metavalue: a value whose function is the first place to regulate other values. And we also have in the offing an associated way of understanding the Overman, although to reintroduce this concept we need to invoke Nietzsche's proprietary notion of "self-overcoming."

44 WHY DIDN'T NIETZSCHE GET HIS ACT TOGETHER?

The life cycles of important practices, values, institutions, character traits, and so on, Nietzsche has it, typically have crude beginnings, but over time, the practices, etc., become ever more refined and purified versions of themselves.[28] That very process brings them to a point at which they're transformed into something deeply different from their earlier versions, and cut loose from their original functions and uses: they "overcome themselves." Being a gentleman might serve as an illustration, though it's not Nietzsche's own.[29] Originally, behaving like a gentleman was a matter of requiring others explicitly to acknowledge one's aristocratic social status; now we think of a true gentleman as someone who puts people at their ease, especially by never reminding them of differences in social status.

Now, in "On Old and New Tablets," Zarathustra explains: "There it was too that I picked up the word 'overman' by the way, and that man is something that must be overcome"; so we can take it that the Overman is what man will overcome himself into.[30] And in a section titled "On the Thousand and One Goals" (4:74–76/Z I.15), Nietzsche's character announces that " 'man' ... means: the esteemer"—that is, the creature that creates values. He explains that hitherto "peoples" have introduced systems of values that allowed them to meet pressing collective challenges, and these have accordingly varied with group environments. (That is, if you live on Dune, the planet that serves as the setting for Frank Herbert's well-known science-fiction novel, your tribe probably holds the supreme value to be water conservation.) So the Overman will exhibit a refined, purified version of value creation, presumably one that has pulled itself free of its original function: it will no longer primarily serve group self-preservation, and values will come to be selected in view of very different considerations. Once again, it looks like Nietzsche is sketching the formal outlines of a metavalue. The Overman, who is supposed to justify and redeem humanity and its past, to make life worth living, and to make humanity command respect, is a personification of an improved form of value creation: bringing to bear Nietzsche's view of those improvements elsewhere, what's being advertised to us is the supreme value of inventing values.

The Overman and the Eternal Return are sketched or gestured at, rather than concretely presented. This is a point we'll return to shortly, but for now, we can suppose the reason to be that the values that Nietzsche wants us to invent and adopt can't be exhibited, if they haven't yet been invented. Instead, Nietzsche turns his attention to the question of what is involved in inventing values, and to an apparently insuperable problem that such a program faces.

3.6

The notion of a value travels with a great deal of baggage: just as a reminder, values are today thought to be either something you discover, in which case they are, in J. L. Mackie's familiar description, "queer," that is, too unlike anything else in the world to be either comprehensible or believable; or they are, again per Mackie's characterization, mere projections of your emotions or other attitudes onto the world around you.[31] It *is* Nietzsche's term, but invoking it nowadays gets in the way of clear and productive discussion, and accordingly, I'll temporarily deploy a handful of partial substitutes to get us going. *Standards* are suitably innocuous and will serve us for part of the way—although there's more to a value than just the standards it imposes, for as the discussion of self-overcoming informs us, values also behave like the sort of ideals or aspirations whose nature it is to be progressively refined.

Standards can be big and hifalutin, as the Eternal Return seems to be, or small and low-key—as in sheepdog trials. Standards are used in assessments, but they can, importantly, themselves be assessed; which means we can use them to represent Nietzsche's interest in the "value of values" (5:253/GM P.6). Standards can be introduced and discarded, and so they track Nietzsche's insistence that values come and go.[32] Nietzsche's proposals quite reasonably set off alarm bells: if people *are* going to be inventing idiosyncratic values, well, who knows *what's* going to come of that? By thinking through the ways we have of introducing and assessing standards in ordinary life, we can somewhat reassure ourselves on that score; the invention of values doesn't have to mean that anything goes.[33]

Now, philosophers who are used to thinking of values as though they were Plato's Forms will ask how we are to assess novel standards or values more generally, and be likely to leap to this conclusion: by appeal to the *real* values, which consequently can't be themselves invented. If you have this impulse, let me ask you to resist it. Values are, *inter alia*, assessment tools. When you assess one thing or another—which may itself be a novel assessment method, for instance, a proposal for ranking philosophy departments—you deploy forms of assessment you already have available. (You might, in this case, consider the effect on your faculty of adopting a software package that measures "productivity"; or you might think about the pros and cons of relying on a widely used website that offers a ranking of philosophy departments; to do so, you might examine the effects of using these metrics on faculty research programs.[34]) But there's no standard set of assessment tools you always deploy, and at this point there are no methods of assessment that weren't once themselves, perhaps long ago, adopted in roughly the same manner. In Nietzsche's way of thinking, to be what we nowadays call a moral realist is to imagine that your standards are somehow *just there*; that is, it's to have *forgotten* that the components of our collective cognitive repertoire have histories, and are found there because, one by one, they were added to it.[35]

The design and implementation of standards is generally a nontrivial exercise. Legislatures are in the business of passing laws, that is, of introducing new standards of a certain sort, and none of us are surprised when a law turns out to have been badly drafted. Further, once the law is on the books, it's normal for a regulatory agency to be given the ongoing task of determining what it requires; it's normal for courts to have to determine what the law says about this or that case.[36] The need for these expedients makes it obvious that even competently drafting legislation isn't sufficient to determine its content; that's done gradually, through that body of incrementally built up regulation and precedent. We're also used to the idea that as the content of a body of law is firmed up in this manner, it can fail to unfold the law as intended, and we even have a word—"originalism"—for the program of keeping interpretation in line with the initial intent. Evidently laws can gradually be corrupted in the course of their interpretation, in practice replaced by very different laws, and even neatly inverted into their opposites. Moreover, all of that supposes that the regulating agencies and the accretion of precedent *do* work to determine a content; however, if precedent isn't treated as binding, if there are many inconsistent precedents or regulations, and if a citizen can pick and choose, then in the end, functionally there is no law at all. Now, legislation is a special case, but it's representative of the issues that have to be managed for the introduction of standards more generally.[37]

As Plato noticed, a philosophical problem which arises with respect to individuals can sometimes be seen, writ large, in political or social structures, and the converse is true as well: the problems that governments face when introducing novel standards are present, writ small, when we focus on the lone value innovator. Nietzsche returns to them repeatedly in *Zarathustra*, where they take an especially poignant form. For instance, in "On the Way of the Creator," the value innovator is advised that he's in for a rough time: it's not just that he'll have to surrender his former ambitions, which generally have been framed in terms of other people's values and standards, but that he'll have to enforce adherence to his novel standards on *himself*; this is difficult in particular because it's hard to stay on track in the face

WHO WAS THE AUTHOR OF NIETZSCHE'S *ZARATHUSTRA*? 47

of self-doubt. Elsewhere, and recall why it matters that we can identify a Nietzschean concern in his other writings, he tells us that "whoever attempts [independence] . . . without inner constraint . . . enters a labyrinth . . . [where] no one can see how and where he loses his way . . ."[38]

So suppose you take yourself to have invented a value, say, the Eternal Return, or the Overman. Suppose, for that matter, that you have a "eureka"-like epiphany. What is there to make all of that more than merely the illusion of comprehension and commitment, more than just empty patter? There's all the difference in the world between really having (or coming to have) a value, and simply saying that you have.[39] The job of "philosophers of the future," we're told, is to invent values, but this will require that the values be filled in with a determinate content.

If this is to happen, long-term consistency matters; the value must be, I will say, *stabilized*. For instance, "it is enough to create new names and estimations and likelihoods in order to create in the long run new 'things.'" New nomenclature has to be held onto until "it gradually grows to be part of the thing and turns into its very body"; if everyone adopts the posture of Humpty Dumpty—that words mean what *I* want them to mean—there won't be a stable vocabulary picking out stable objects. That is, insisting on "new names" and so on will be effective only if one succeeds in being persistent and consistent in how the assessments, etc., are applied.[40]

We can't expect this sort of consistency unless something has been done to make sure that many individuals, over a long period of time, exhibit it. A church that maintains and enforces a theological outlook, by suppressing heresies, might do the job. Universities that train up generation after generation of students into a Kuhnian "paradigm" might do so as well. I'm going to quickly generalize, and let these observations stand for the following claim: that, normally, new values are stabilized by institutionalizing them. Indeed, our discussion of what it takes to implement legislation has likewise suggested that the well-trodden path to stabilizing a value is institutionalizing it.

3.7

Now, Nietzsche has presented us with an elaborate warning against just this sort of institutionalization, or so I've been arguing. *Zarathustra* invokes the Higher Criticism to bring home the point that institutionalizing Nietzsche's own new values would invite the treatment that the dictum that all animals

48 WHY DIDN'T NIETZSCHE GET HIS ACT TOGETHER?

are equal received in George Orwell's *Animal Farm*. *Zarathustra* exhibits to us a future perspective, one which incorporates Nietzsche's values and views, and for which they are no longer revolutionary novelties, but a matter of course. This particular perspective, we saw, is modeled on Wellhausen's priestly forgers (or perhaps their analogs in Strauss's treatment), whose most important trait is that they systematically misrepresent the history, the mores, and indeed the values of the past they describe. We are, I concluded, being invited to see the postulated author of *Zarathustra* as bound to misrepresent Nietzsche's own ideas and values, and now would be a good time to give a Nietzschean example of the effect he's anticipating.

Since both the misrepresented past and the misrepresenting author are fictional, we should tread with caution when embarking on a catalog of the errors being made by the would-be author of *Zarathustra*—and this is in any case not the occasion for assembling the list. That said, at least one iconic misrepresentation is prominently on display. We noted that the title, and repeated refrain, is an allusion to an Old Testament prophetic signature. But that signature runs, Thus says the Lord—*not*, Thus says the prophet. Nietzsche's reason for the substitution is clear enough: God is dead, and so the prophet cannot be his emissary. However, that over-famous pronouncement is just a dramatic way of saying that there's no supernatural or metaphysical authority on which to foist responsibility for one's evaluations. Thus there is never really any authority for your assessments but your own, and when you evaluate one thing or another, you could, if you wanted to be up front about what you were doing, append: I'm speaking for myself here.

That's what Nietzsche's Zarathustra does. But in the soppy and worshipful perspective of the future religion of Nietzsche, it's inevitably treated as a sacred pronouncement, and as itself authoritative, and so the very low-key gloss on Zarathustra's assessments, "or anyway, that's what *I* say," becomes the prophetic "thus spoke Zarathustra." That is, the utterance has been recast, Wellhausen-style, into a form which gives it a significance almost exactly opposed to its original content.[41]

Nietzsche is pointing us to a trap. Values are not effective—they aren't socially or personally real—until they're embodied in an appropriate perspective. That evidently takes time, and so producing the perspectives that new values require normally presupposes more than a modicum of evaluative stability, which in turn normally requires institutionalizing those values. Institutionalizing a value requires perhaps reverence for it; or treating it as authoritative; or taking it absolutely seriously. But if you're a value

WHO WAS THE AUTHOR OF NIETZSCHE'S *ZARATHUSTRA*? 49

inventor (or, more carefully, if you're the self-aware inventor of values that Nietzsche hopes you'll become), you can't have too much reverence for any extant values, and if you're going to put yourself in a position to reassess favorably the parts of your world that you now find unbearably disgusting, you can't have too much reverence for the values that underwrite your present assessment. If the values which Nietzsche is recommending to us are betrayed precisely by being institutionalized, it's no wonder he has his character worry:

> my *teaching* is in danger; weeds pose as wheat. My enemies have grown powerful and have distorted my teaching till those dearest to me must be ashamed of the gifts I gave them.[42]

3.8

Just now we have three interrelated claims on the table: First, that we should take very seriously the enterprise of inventing new values. Second, that the Overman and the Eternal Return are best thought of as metavalues which Nietzsche's protagonist is prescribing, the one recommending the invention of values, and the other, a benchmark to use in assessing the values that we have and that get invented. And third, that we should be reading Nietzsche on the assumption that he's misrepresenting his own view. Where is the misrepresentation in those first two claims?

Let's return to "On the Thousand and One Goals," and give a more extended paraphrase of the prophetic-sounding speech. What today analytic philosophers call moral realism—that idea we mentioned a couple of turns back, roughly, that the values are already present and there to be discovered—is an error. Values are a human production, and are to be understood as, in the first place, an aspect of a survival technique. Until recently, systems of values have been specific to ethnic or cultural groups; they normally prioritize demanding activities and achievements that are critical for the collective survival of the group that adopts them. Different environments present different challenges, and it follows that different ethnic and cultural groups will typically have very different systems of values.

Individuals creating values are a novel phenomenon (as is the individual itself and, Nietzsche suggests, not coincidentally). When individuals create values for their ethnic or cultural group for self-interested reasons, things

50   WHY DIDN'T NIETZSCHE GET HIS ACT TOGETHER?

don't work out well for the collective; but there's room as well for value creation by individuals that isn't driven by self-interest ... and at that point there's a sudden swerve, to the suggestion that in place of the multiple "goals" of the many peoples, we might have a single goal for humanity—"one yoke for the thousand necks," a single system of values that will one day direct *everybody*. And although it's unstated here, we know from other passages that the single goal is to be the Overman.

For more than one reason, it's hard to believe that the complaint that "humanity still has no goal" represents Nietzsche's views correctly. First, in *The Gay Science*, he takes time out to criticize the notion that goals are a primary explainer of action—that they control what it is that people actually do—as a naivete and a misconception.[43] Second, the Overman as a *goal* won't make humanity valuable in anything but an instrumental sense.[44] Certainly we shouldn't assume that Nietzsche shares now-prevalent, that is, generally Kantian attitudes about what acknowledging the value of another person comes to; for instance, he seems to think that one way to respect someone is to treat him as your *enemy*. Nonetheless, to see someone as an instrumentally necessary precondition to something you care about won't underwrite anything on the order of respect for them.

Third, a large part of Nietzsche's diagnosis of the ills produced by our extant one-size-fits-all values is that they *are* one size fits all.[45] As we've registered, in *Beyond Good and Evil*, the inventors of values are called "philosophers of the future"; Nietzsche looks forward to their very finicky stance when it comes to foisting their opinions and values on others: " 'My judgment is *my* judgment': no one else is easily entitled to it—that is what such a philosopher of the future may perhaps say of himself" (5:60/BGE 43). Similarly, at one point Zarathustra tells us that "he has discovered himself who says, 'This is *my* good and evil' " (4:243/Z III.11.2). But if Nietzsche's doctrines were to be institutionalized, all this would have to change; a church cannot persist if it allows constant and idiosyncratic evaluative innovations on the part of its members, and it will have no alternative but to streamline the range of allowable options, probably down to one.

And finally, the book conveys the impression that the Overman is a dominating feature of the landscape of a far-off future: "you could well create the overman. Perhaps not you yourselves, my brothers. But into fathers and forefathers of the overman you could re-create yourselves: and let this be your best creation" (4:109/Z II.2). "In your children you shall make up for being the children of your fathers: thus shall you redeem

WHO WAS THE AUTHOR OF NIETZSCHE'S *ZARATHUSTRA*? 51

all that is past. This new tablet I place over you" (4:255/Z III.12.12). But the Overman, we've been supposing, is Nietzsche's icon for the metavalue of inventing values; if the invention of values is as pressing a matter as Nietzsche seems to think, why should it be deferred to some apparently indefinitely later time? In any case, we're given mixed signals as to whether it *is* being deferred: we've noticed Zarathustra offering advice to aspiring value inventors, quite definitely in the tone of voice one adopts when encouraging younger contemporaries.

The early Christians understood the kingdom of God to be just around the corner—or perhaps to be already present, Nietzsche suggests (6:206f/AC 34). This state of mind isn't compatible with a long-lasting, stable, continent-spanning ecclesiastical bureaucracy, one that is in the business of accumulating such assets as the Vatican art collection. In order for there to be a Catholic Church able to promulgate the values of Christianity, the kingdom of heaven has to be put off until much later. Rather similarly, an institution that was in the business of inculcating Nietzsche's dramatic metavalues would have to itself be stable: stable enough, *inter alia*, to administer the relevant standards consistently. Perhaps institutions don't do a bad job of it when the standards they're administering are the same for everyone. But what institution could survive a constant diet of idiosyncratic, personalized, newly invented standards, aspirations, and so on?[46] In very much the manner of inversions of value that the Higher Critics ascribed to the authors of both the Hebrew and the Christian Bibles, the holy scripture of the imaginary religion we're contemplating will have to have transformed the value of inventing values into something manageable, something bureaucratically safe, something that will go into effect only *one day.*

3.9

If those two very dramatic and larger-than-life metavalues are Nietzsche showing us what institutionalization would make of some very differently intended evaluative innovation, then our next question is what this way of stabilizing the original innovation must be getting wrong.

The Overman and the Eternal Return make humanity, or anyway its successor, out to be valuable in a manner that's peculiarly reminiscent of Kant: rather as human beings were held to be unconditionally valuable, in that they're the creatures that rationally set ends for themselves, so future humans will be valuable in that they invent values for themselves—and present humans will be valued as a necessary precondition to all of that. However, we've also been piecing together another picture, on which we had better not be preoccupied by one or two supreme values, which we construe as goals to be achieved in the distant future. The invention of novel values is important, alright, but what you need are values that are suited to *you*, and starting right now. If that latter view is Nietzsche's, the mythologized super-values get his ideas upside-down and backwards—just as the literary frame we've identified instructs us to anticipate.

Nietzsche's composition of the book, I've been suggesting, gives us reason to prefer the second of the two strikingly different views as that of the imaginary religion's founder. But can we advance philosophical reasons for taking Nietzsche to endorse it, over and above the textual considerations?

If, as we saw, novel values acquire determinate contents over time, that should be true of Nietzsche's evaluative proposals as well. And a little experimentation will confirm that conclusion. Even if we're right in thinking that the Overman is meant to represent the value of inventing values, we don't have a determinate conception of what doing so would amount to—not enough to see how it's going to make humanity and its past worthwhile. (Are we supposed to be inventing just *any* values? What if they're silly, or demeaning?) The point goes for the Eternal Return as well: there are many ways we could end up looking back at human history and affirming it, and not all of them can be what the Eternal Return ought to come to represent. For example, in *Zarathustra* itself, we are told that if your affirmation is merely indiscriminate, you're an ass:

> Verily, I also do not like those who consider everything good and this world the best. Such men I call omni-satisfied ... I honor the recalcitrant choosy tongues and stomachs, which have learned to say "I" and "yes" and "no". ... Always to bray Yea-Yuh ["I-a," that is, a phonetic rendering of "Yes" in German]—that only the ass has learned, and whoever is of his spirit.[47]

We need to discriminate among the ways we might affirm our past and accept our fellow human beings.

Without having the superlative metavalues clearly in focus, we aren't able to make sense of the personal investment we're supposed to come to have in them; if we know next to nothing about the Overman, how can we care enough about the prospect to will the Eternal Return? If we know next to nothing about the Eternal Return, how can we decide whether to sign on to the success concept we are apparently being offered?

3.10

The Celestine Prophecy Problem turns out not to have been easily avoidable; if we can only take seriously a value whose content has been sufficiently firmed up, and if the values that Nietzsche is trumpeting are only beginning that process, they will at the outset be very, very *thin*, and we shouldn't be surprised if they seem not to amount to much. One way or another, the evaluative novelties that Nietzsche has his character advance will have to themselves be articulated and stabilized, and we should be interested in what they can amount to when they are. Let's first turn to the strategy of institutionalization as it has been playing out in the real—as opposed to Nietzsche's fictional—world.

For academics such as myself, the obvious way to go about determining what Nietzsche's superlative metavalues come to would be to interpret his writings; exegesis is among the more delicate facets of the institutionalization of a value, but it's the one some of us are most at home with. How should we think of what that process comes to, when the text in question is *Thus Spoke Zarathustra*?

We can find Nietzsche orienting us in a passage from *The Gay Science*—which is, once again, the runup to *Zarathustra*—in which he's considering what it takes to make innovations stick.[48]

An innovator's disciple announces to his master:

> I believe in your cause and consider it so strong that I shall say everything, everything that I still have in my mind against it.

To which the innovator replies:

> This kind of discipleship ... is ... the most dangerous, and not every kind of doctrine can endure it.

In order for a new doctrine to become a full-fledged and worked out position, it must survive long enough to acquire followers with the sort of commitment

54 WHY DIDN'T NIETZSCHE GET HIS ACT TOGETHER?

and training that enables them first to fill in the details, and then to defend it. The innovator tells us that he wishes

> for the seedling to become a tree. For a doctrine to become a tree, it has to be believed for a good while; for it to be believed, it has to be considered irrefutable. The tree needs storms, doubts, worms and nastiness to reveal the nature and strength of the seedling; let it break if it is not strong enough. But a seedling can only be destroyed—not refuted.

If we take Nietzsche to be strategizing about the reception of his own innovations, we should conclude that he's looking for a way to make his doctrines and evaluative claims (or demands) temporarily irrefutable. And his innovator tells us how one might go about it:

> I am thirsting for a composer ... who would learn my ideas from me and transpose them into his language ...: who could refute a tone?[49]

Nietzsche did try his hand at composing a "Hymn to Life," not very successfully. He was much more adept at literary than at musical composition, but he apparently treated the former on the model of the latter.[50] Thus the tactic of deferring the straightforward presentation of a philosophical theory and of argumentation for it until the ideas themselves are relatively entrenched was implemented by presenting them as inspiring prophecy, and even as "songs" and rhymed verse. That is, it looks like *Zarathustra* is written the way it is in order to postpone the standard philosophical assessment of Nietzsche's proposals until such time as they have a following, and, more ambitiously, until such time as the values being advanced have been sufficiently articulated to withstand—and to *merit*—the assessment.

The apparent success of Nietzsche's manipulations is genuinely astonishing. Popular uptake of his writing, and especially of *Zarathustra*, has indirectly generated sustained interest in his work among a still small but ever-growing community of professional philosophers. These philosophers, some of whom have come to devote their lives to commentary on Nietzsche's writings, are progressively articulating ever more carefully debugged versions of his theoretical views. As objections are raised to one scholar's formulation of, again for instance, the Eternal Return, another scholar produces a more sophisticated reformulation that handles those objections;

WHO WAS THE AUTHOR OF NIETZSCHE'S *ZARATHUSTRA*? 55

and as objections are raised to the reformulation in turn, yet another and still more nuanced reformulation is produced. Nietzsche could not himself, in the short time he thought he had to live, and at the frenetic pace at which he consequently worked, have managed these elaborately crafted constructions; instead, he seems to have delegated, and successfully, much of the step by step fabrication of his intellectual position to his followers.

Again, the task of constructing theoretically refined versions of Nietzsche's view, and a practice of exegetical casuistry around them, is part (the part that is, for academics, closest to home) of the institutionalization (and thus the stabilization) of the evaluative stances which Nietzsche appears to recommend. However, although I've just made a show of being amazed at Nietzsche's success in recruiting today's Nietzsche specialists to fill in his ideas and values for him, recall that *Zarathustra* is warning us that their exegesis and casuistry is not, after all, going to count as *success*. The problem isn't just that Nietzsche's parable asks us to resist the posture historians of philosophy naturally assume, that they're telling you what's there on the page already. I began by pointing out that academic philosophers today respond to *Thus Spoke Zarathustra* with a collective cringe: *if only* Nietzsche hadn't written *that*. But although in this case the responses tend to be extreme, the initial reaction on the part of academics to just about all of Nietzsche's mature writing has been to balk at it, and understandably so. His views about morality, about social organization, and much else have struck his readers as outrageous; Nietzsche's criticism of the value of truth, and of the motivations and the social function of academics are hard to square with conducting an academic life within academic institutions.

And consequently, we've been positioned to witness the very phenomenon that Nietzsche represented and anticipated in *Zarathustra*: that of his own doctrines being turned upside down in the course of being assimilated and appropriated—albeit within universities, rather than by a newly founded church. Nietzsche scholarship has taken form as a succession of interpretations that have over time rendered Nietzsche's views ever more familiar and ever less shocking.[51]

As an aid to the reader, I can propose a litmus test for whether a commentator is treading this path. In one of his middle-period works, Nietzsche remarks:

It goes without saying that I do not deny—unless I am a fool—that many actions called immoral ought to be avoided and resisted, or that many

56 WHY DIDN'T NIETZSCHE GET HIS ACT TOGETHER?

called moral ought to be done and encouraged—but I think the one should be encouraged and the other avoided *for other reasons than hitherto.*

(3:91f/D 103)

Per Nietzsche's appropriation of Wellhausen *et alia*, perhaps we should expect academics' readings of Nietzsche to make him progressively more tame, and invoking this passage can be treated as an indication that an academic reader is trying to disarm Nietzsche's views in just the manner we're considering. Indeed, these lines are widely quoted, with one recent book reproducing the excerpt *twice.*

Here I am myself presenting an interpretation of the doctrines of *Zarathustra*, and I am myself an academic. So we need to take fully seriously the possibility that I too am succumbing to the temptation to make of Nietzsche's ideas something that will have a comfortable home in the academic institutional environment—a concern I'll take up in our second Interlude. But for now, we can say this much: Nietzsche's Wellhausian concerns about the reception of his work don't seem to have been misplaced.

3.11

Let's accordingly proceed to an alternative way of figuring out the content of the two metavalues. When we squinted at their larger-than-life, mythologized versions, we were unable to see why inventing values is valuable enough to redeem humanity and its past; further, we were unable to see what redeeming humanity and its past would amount to clearly enough to explain the stake Nietzsche seems to think we have in it. One might well expect that the pieces would only fall into place as we worked our way into coherent candidate understandings of the value of inventing values; surely we could not do that other than by accumulating experience with inventing one value after another.

Although the metavalue of inventing values is perhaps novel, values have been invented before, and they do change our assessments of people of the past. To the ancient Greeks, work was a humiliation, not a source of pride; today, it's normal for someone's self-esteem to be tied to their occupation. Our historically recent value—call it the *dignity of labor*—allows us a new-found retroactive respect for members of the Greek lower classes.[52] Perhaps as we make the metavalue of inventing values our own, that will change our assessment of former value innovators. The Impressionists formulated a system of standards and aspirations, enunciated an accompanying ideology, and cultivated a distinctive painterly sensibility—that is, they produced a novel, local and temporary value, one that governed the production of works of art over the lifespan of their movement. So perhaps in the future we'll come to admire them not just as painters but as, more importantly, evaluative innovators. Alfred Otto Wolfgang, who took "Wols" as his working name, turned his compulsive doodling into moderately ambitious art, thus making his own early doodles important in retrospect; because of his efforts, some of his viewers have come to see doodles differently in general; here, an artist's adoption of idiosyncratic values made something of a trivial activity.[53] Perhaps his viewers should be admiring his evaluative innovation as much as they admire his doodles.

At this point we can take up a concern that the reader has no doubt had for some time now. Early on, I started using the notion of a value, but without properly introducing it; I managed stretches of the argument with the help of more modest surrogates, such as 'standard' or 'ideal', and I suggested that, in Nietzsche, "value" labels a concept that folds together standards, priorities and the initially vaguely formulated, but incrementally refined aspirations that mobilize individual personalities and whole societies. And by now you're probably wondering what exactly values are, and how exactly they're supposed to work.

Nietzsche's style, all on its own, makes it unlikely that we'll find answers to those questions which meet the demand in that *exactly*. But backing away from such answers isn't merely a matter of interpretative responsibility to Nietzsche's intellectual and literary mannerisms. Values are inventions; as they cease to be inadvertent and become the self-conscious products of our efforts, we can expect that what it is to be a value will change, firm up, and quite possibly do so in more than one configuration of its components. Think of analogous questions: What is an automobile? What is a computer? What is a telephone? How exactly do each of those devices work? They've come to have more definite and much better understood answers after a century of experience with seeing them repeatedly reinvented. (At the outset, there was no useful answer to: what exactly are they, and how do they work?) And our sense of what an *invention* can be has similarly developed, especially over our last several hundred years of ever more rapidly paced and diversified experience with the phenomenon of the self-conscious inventor.

58 WHY DIDN'T NIETZSCHE GET HIS ACT TOGETHER?

In roughly the same manner, we can expect to be much clearer in due course about the ways in which the assessment dimension of a value is integrated with its motivational aspect, with its role as a progressively articulated ideal and so on—but only once we've accumulated experience with self-consciously fabricating values and putting them to use. We can also expect to arrive at a much better sense of the various purposes to which values can be put, in something like the way that we came to see what could be done with computers, cars, and telephones as we accumulated experience with *them*. In Nietzsche's writings we have already observed values serving in different roles: there were the older, shared values, which mobilized groups and coordinated their activities, and the values, tailored to individuals, that help them to accept what they can no longer change. I've found that philosophers tend to assume that what a value is *for* is, as it were, written into the value itself. But if tools generally have as many functions as you can find for them, that will also be true of assessment and navigation tools in particular.

Our appreciation of past episodes of evaluative innovation is what makes the importance of the invention of values intelligible. The more of these episodes we investigate, the stronger and more entrenched that attitude may come to be. If value invention is done well, rather than as it has gone in the past, people will both become valuable per the values they invent, and valuable in that they're inventors of values—and to the extent that Nietzsche's proposals get uptake, these will turn out to be much the same thing. As our appreciation of the value of inventing values grows, our respect for those who participate in it may well extend to those further portions of humanity that have been (usually undercover) inventors.

If this is the process by which we come to grasp the superlative metavalues that seem to be on offer, that grasp is acquired incrementally and is always incomplete. Moreover, the redemption of the past seems to be a piecemeal matter; we now respect laborers, but not everyone is a laborer, and we may one day come to admire value innovators, but not many people invent values. What Nietzsche finds, not to mince words, *revolting* about humanity is in large part how successful the Christian-inspired striving for a kind of generic littleness has been; undoing *that* can only be an arduous and step-by-step process, because each person has to come up with an individualized way to grow and flower. All of this suggests that, whether or not Nietzsche meant it this way himself, the Eternal Return is best thought of as something like a Kantian Idea of Reason—a limit concept, a pole star that we can orient ourselves toward but at which we should not expect ever to arrive.

WHO WAS THE AUTHOR OF NIETZSCHE'S *ZARATHUSTRA*? 59

But now, and breaking off our anticipations of how this version of the process of articulating these metavalues is going to pan out, it seems clear that we can't use the Eternal Return and the Overman to leapfrog over the piecemeal, much more mundane invention of much more ordinary values. The only agenda we have any real grip on is *that*.[54]

If I'm seeing it aright, then, the most important of the intentional misrepresentations in *Zarathustra* is the substitution, for an important, very demanding, even urgent call to arms, of a pair of utopian, impossibly hypervaluable metavalues, which have been displaced into a future distant enough so that we don't now have to live by them.

3.12

That suggestion invites a textual objection, and I want to raise and address it in order to bring into tighter focus the status of Nietzsche's insistence that values are to be invented rather than discovered.

First, the objection: the very large project on which Nietzsche claimed to be working before his collapse was the "*Umwertung aller Werte*," conventionally but clumsily translated as the "revaluation of all values."[55] Throwing out all of the values we now have, and replacing them with the Overman, the Eternal Return, will to power and so on *would* be upending our values; but could the piecemeal, step-by-step introduction of one idiosyncratic value after another really be the global "*Umwertung*"? And in that case, could this have been, as I've just claimed, the real agenda?

Today we (that is, we analytic philosophers) operate with a distinction between substantive moral theory and metaethics; while it's not part of Nietzsche's vocabulary, it's a useful shorthand. Upending our values could be merely a (substantive) matter of displacing them with other values, or it could in the first place be a matter of reconceiving what values are (metaethics). Under the latter heading, we might cease to understand values as, say, unchangeable Moorean properties, belonging to a world peculiarly above or behind the ordinary one, and instead take them to be devices which we can design, produce, deploy, and discard. The metaethical reimagining of value is no less dramatic a global reversal of our evaluative practice than the substitution of one set of values for another.

Anticipating how a priestly caste, as seen through the lens of the Higher Criticism, would be pressed to reconstrue this metaethical proposal, we can flag two aspects of the doctrine it would be likely to evolve. First, priests have a stake in making their supreme values out to be the way things simply are. (We noticed, in note 12, Nietzsche telling us that what they want is announced to be the will of God.) Thus one plausible perversion of Nietzsche's views would be to tone down his metaethical revolution, which has to do with what being a value *is*—there is no way values simply are; rather they're to be *made*—into no more than a change in the contents of the values.

But second, the priestly reflex is to further make values impressive by making them *impossibly large*. In the instance I was just alluding to, what the priests want is "the tastiest pieces of meat"—which is implausibly made out to be a matter of divine concern. The business of religious functionaries is making big deals out of little things; even today, we're all-too-familiar with the notion that deviating from locally standard procedures for human reproduction will get you sent to hell, to be *tormented forever*. That cast of mind is reflected in the impossibly large hyper-values that "Zarathustra" ends up preaching: the Eternal Return means that you'll do what you're doing, over and over, *forever*; and the Overman is likewise made out to sound larger than life, in rather the way gods have always been.

If that's the right way to read *Zarathustra*, the moral seems to be that the thoroughgoing revision of our evaluative practices shouldn't be confused with grandiose but superficial changes to those practices as we have them. Nietzsche's theoretical and practical innovations are meant to be deep and demanding, which isn't the same thing as ostentatiously gigantic.[56]

3.13

You might think at this stage that I'm claiming to have reconstructed what Nietzsche *really* thought—the *true* doctrines underlying the Overman and the Eternal Return—as opposed to the misrepresentations of the implicit author of *Zarathustra*. Previewing themes of the upcoming chapters, here's why I don't take myself to have done quite that. I've been suggesting that, in Nietzsche's later works, ideas, theories, arguments, ethical stances, and so on are inflected by the personalities of the implicit authors of the various books that Nietzsche wrote: by, to use his own term for it, the several perspectives that he puts on display in them. If that's right, it has three immediate consequences for how to read those books.

WHO WAS THE AUTHOR OF NIETZSCHE'S *ZARATHUSTRA*? 61

First, earlier on I concluded that it's illegitimate to treat Zarathustra's utterances as assertions of Nietzsche's views; but a rather similar, albeit less extreme warning is in place for Nietzsche's mature corpus in its entirety. Passages that have the Eternal Return and the Overman as their topic are distributed—albeit sparsely—throughout both Nietzsche's later published work and his *Nachlass*.[57] But they don't allow for the straightforward transcription of the views Nietzsche actually endorsed. As we're starting to see, for each pronouncement about, say, the Eternal Return, a reader has to ask: who is supposed to be speaking to me, and what does that tell me about how to take what I'm reading? That complicates the task of saying what Nietzsche thought about any particular topic considerably; you can't simply turn from *Zarathustra* to, say, *Beyond Good and Evil*, find a seemingly salient passage, and conclude that this is Nietzsche's *real* view. Rather, you have to develop a reading of, in this instance, *Beyond Good and Evil* that allows you to frame that passage first.

Second, and this is a philosophically more delicate point, I think we need to resist the temptation to try to look behind those differently inflected presentations of Nietzsche's ideas, to find out what he *really* thought. Nietzsche is exploring an alternative mode of philosophical deliberation, on which there are *just* the different perspectives, and the views taken on various questions within them; you can move from one to another, and develop a progressively clearer and richer understanding of the subject matters you're considering, but it's not as though there's an aperspectival way things really are, that Nietzsche, casting off his own wardrobe of personalities, is going to endorse.

Third, this means that we also need to resist the temptation to turn to Nietzsche's pronouncements about the Overman and the Eternal Return in his journals, as telling us what he really thought—or maybe, what he *tentatively* really thought. The notebooks contain a great deal of raw material, some of which was used for the published work. But it is, just by virtue of being unframed raw material, still waiting to be positioned within one perspective or another.

We're early on in the process of laying out the arguments for this set of Nietzschean reading instructions, and so the advice will go down more easily, Mary Poppins-style, with an illustration. *Beyond Good and Evil* contains what is clearly enough a discussion of the Eternal Return, and we can excerpt the parts that we need.

62 WHY DIDN'T NIETZSCHE GET HIS ACT TOGETHER?

> Whoever has endeavored... to think pessimism through to its depths...
> may just thereby, without really meaning to do so, have opened his eyes
> to the opposite ideal: the ideal of the most high-spirited, alive, and world-
> affirming human being who has not only come to terms and learned to get
> along with whatever was and is, but who wants to have *what was and is*
> repeated into all eternity, shouting insatiably *da capo*—not only to himself
> but to the whole play and spectacle, and not only to a spectacle but at bot-
> tom to him who needs precisely this spectacle—and who makes it necessary
> because again and again he needs himself—and makes himself necessary—
> What? And this wouldn't be—*circulus vitiosus deus?* (5:74f/BGE 56)

Here the Eternal Return is presented as a way of understanding the world
to revolve around *you*: you're so wrapped up in yourself that you accept the
world in its entirety as a sort of appendage. The problem with taking this
way of construing it for Nietzsche's is not just how unattractive this sort of
hypernarcissism is, and not just that, as we've already noticed, the thought
seems to be very differently motivated elsewhere, but that the early stretches
of the book in which it appears are devoted to criticism of the traditional,
robust conceptions of the self on which this sort of emotional investment in
one's own self would be supportable. The passage presents us with a puzzle—
how could the author of this book, at this point, be saying *this*?—and so can't
be used as is, as a shortcut to what Nietzsche himself really thought.

All this means that I now need to add a retrospective qualification to my
descriptions, both in the course of the argument to this point and below, of
positions, claims, assessments, and so on as *Nietzsche's*. Because Nietzsche is
taking issue precisely with our practices of (as philosophers of my tribe say
it) propositional-attitude ascription (if you're from a different tribe: of saying
that such and such is what so-and-so thinks), all of those attributions have
to be taken with a grain of salt: they're more complicated, and more hedged,
than they sound.

3.14

If I'm seeing it right, in *Zarathustra*, Nietzsche doesn't present a solution
to the problem he's pressing on us: that the normal method of stabilizing a
novel value, namely, institutionalizing it, will corrupt the very sorts of values
that Nietzsche is calling on us to invent. Identifying the problem, which is

WHO WAS THE AUTHOR OF NIETZSCHE'S *ZARATHUSTRA*? 63

what the book does, was headway enough. And while we've been exploring various paths through it, I don't believe that Nietzsche signed off on any of them. You'll have noticed that they shared an assumption, to wit, that making a value determinate enough to be put to use, whether by baking it into an institution, or by accumulating the sort of hands-on experience with it that I am myself inclined to recommend, takes a great deal of time. But if the values you invent are supposed to be tailored to your own personality and needs, they had better be available in time for *you* to use them.

I'm going to be presenting Nietzsche's subsequent efforts as focused on putting in place a method—and providing a demo of it, in his own work— that would allow the rapid prototyping and stabilization of novel values, and so avoid the trap laid out in *Thus Spoke Zarathustra*. We've just gestured at what I think that method was: surveying and articulating such a value from different perspectives, which here take the tangible form of differently oriented versions of Nietzsche's own personality.

For the moment, we still need to address a question about Nietzsche's motivations. The self-aware invention of quite possibly idiosyncratic values is a general-purpose capability that Nietzsche is adding, or so he hopes, to our practical and intellectual toolkit. But the concern that evidently drove his efforts was one highly specific application, namely, correcting the worthlessness (or near-worthlessness) of humanity as it now is. Sports fans have a good deal of latitude in deciding which team to root for; why does Nietzsche insist on rooting for humanity as a whole, rather than dismissing the parts of it that he finds unattractive, as belonging to some *other* team?

We reminded ourselves that, for Nietzsche, values shouldn't be one size fits all: that something counts as a deal breaker for you, when you're thinking about whether your life is worth living, may be, entirely legitimately, a fact about *you*, rather than a generally required commitment, to be supported by compelling arguments. And this is how Nietzsche's unusual efforts on behalf of the value of humanity strike me. If God is dead, we've lost the original warrant for the old monotheistic notion that, like coins minted bearing the face of the monarch, human beings are imbued with value by being made in the image of their Creator.[58] Rather in the manner of Enlightenment intellectuals, who had argued themselves into atheism and then experienced it as a devastating loss, to be made good through philosophy, Nietzsche seems impelled to make good the loss of the religious, but also—following on his treatments of morality—the metaphysical and moral versions of the value of humanity.

64 WHY DIDN'T NIETZSCHE GET HIS ACT TOGETHER?

We ourselves can ask whether, as its religious sources become ever more distant, the production of intellectually sanitized surrogates will continue to be a nonoptional philosophical activity. In perhaps the most famous passage in *The Gay Science*, Nietzsche's "madman" proclaims that, like light on the way from very distant stars, the news of the death of God has not yet arrived (3:480–482/GS 125). Today, most philosophers no longer regard themselves as having to take a stand on the existence of God, the historicity of miracles, and so on. The value of humanity was originally a theological view, and has recently become a dogma of moral metaphysics; historically inclined readers will recall how Auguste Comte thought he had discerned a pattern in the history of science, in which the metaphysical replacements for theological doctrines wash away, leaving behind purely "positive" theories. Over the long term, is the notion that human beings are ends in themselves likely to fare any differently?

In attempting to look beyond Nietzsche's own preoccupation with shoring up the value of humanity, I don't want to be heard as implicitly advocating a savage future of *Einsatzgruppen* and concentration camps. The practical analog of the shift to Comte's positive stage of a science is taking hands-on responsibility for the things that matter to us. To forestall those concentration camps, it won't suffice merely to incant phrases like "human rights"; if we want human beings to have (as philosophers say it nowadays) moral standing or moral status, we'll need to make those arrangements ourselves, and not pretend that there is somehow a metaphysical fact of the matter, already. That might be addressed via the Nietzschean expedient of value invention, or in some other manner.[59]

For now, however, allow me to second Nietzsche's view that fully acknowledging the problems involved in firming up the content of a novel value *is* philosophically important. One of his genuinely liberating innovations in moral philosophy is the thought that our values don't have to be the ones we've inherited, don't have to be taken as given, and don't have to be one-size-fits-all. We can *invent* values. As we've seen, it's quite possible to overstate the promise, both philosophical and practical, of this insight; but it has great promise, nonetheless.

The promise is only realizable, however, if the idiosyncratic values one invents are made full-bodied and effective—real, we might say, rather than merely prophesied. The normal and relatively well-understood path to the stabilization of value is institutionalization. Nietzsche reappropriated Higher Critics such as Wellhausen to produce, in *Also sprach Zarathustra*, a display of the ways in which institutionalization is likely to turn precisely the sort of values that Nietzsche most hoped we will come up with entirely inside-out and upside-down. Without alternative methods of solidifying our evaluative inventions, they will not be at all the liberating steps forward that Nietzsche had hoped for; and that's every bit as much our problem, today, as it was Nietzsche's in 1883.

The payoffs, even if less dramatic than those Nietzsche announced, may after all be in the neighborhood of the ones he anticipated. It's an unavoidable truth about philosophy that you don't get anything for free, but in moral and political philosophy it has for some time now been taken for granted that we get the value of humanity for free—and not just of "humanity" as an abstraction, but of each and every last human being. It's even an indicator of how *much* this has been taken for granted that it's never put in quite those words.

Thus I'm sympathetic to Nietzsche's insistence that if we are to respect our fellow man—and *ourselves*—that will have to be earned. The idea that a large part of earning both the right to such respect and the ability to muster it up can come of making the invention of novel values an ongoing activity seems to me an original and promising tack. It's one that I think we can take without adopting the over-the-top postures that Nietzsche has the implicit author of *Zarathustra* attribute to his prophet, and as perhaps the discussion to this point has convinced you, that's probably just as well.

First Interlude: What Was Nietzsche's Genealogy?

If we've correctly identified the concern that drove the composition of *Zarathustra*, we should be brought up short: supposing that Nietzsche expects the methods of interpretation that we academics take for granted to water down ideas, betray his evaluative innovations, and generally generate perverse results, we face two connected but not identical questions. First, what does Nietzsche think the right way to go about interpretation is? And second, what's the right way for us to read and make sense of the body of writing that Nietzsche left us?

We're going to have to develop a take on these issues in stages; in particular, if we allow that there's no interpretative methodology it's reasonable to apply across the board—if sensitive reading adjusts its procedures to the material it is working with—we can only expect the pieces to fall into place as we make our way through those texts. But we have enough on the table already to introduce a first Nietzschean account of interpretation, and along with it, a puzzle.

I'll do that by talking us through an ongoing debate as to whether Nietzsche introduced a distinctive genealogical method—a question no doubt prompted in part by Nietzsche's own choice of terminology. In German, as in English, only human beings have genealogies; even animals merely have pedigrees, and large-scale social phenomena normally only have histories. How could there have been a *genealogy* of morality?[1]

The question for us is not just how to proceed. It's a commonplace that Nietzsche was a perspectivist (and we'll take up just what that comes to in a later chapter of this book). It's a further commonplace that Nietzsche's perspectives are tightly tied to interpretations: they shape, constrain and are products of interpretation. So getting clearer about how Nietzsche thinks of interpretation should help us out in explaining perspectives. (In addition, to be sure, laying out the dispute will have the benefit of giving readers further traction on the book we selected as our entry point into Nietzsche's later work.) While I don't exactly want to take sides in that disagreement over the genealogical method, I mean also—borrowing now a turn of phrase from Nehamas—to make a suggestion about the genealogy of genealogy.[2]

On the one side of this back-and-forth, we have Raymond Geuss affirming that "Alexander Nehamas is doubtless right to claim that for Nietzsche 'genealogy' is not some particular kind of method or special approach, rather it 'simply *is* history, correctly practiced'" (1994, sec. 4). What makes it a "genealogy," on this view, is how it's selective about what it includes; in a Gilbert and Sullivan opera, *The Mikado*, there's a character, Pooh-Bah, who "can trace [his] ancestry back to a protoplasmal primordial atomic globule. Consequently," he continues, "my family pride is something inconceivable." Genealogies mention the ancestors who were famous, or aristocratic, and consign the disreputable or unimpressive relations to obscurity; Pooh-Bah is funny because he gets this so oddly wrong; a genealogy *prunes* a family tree. Nietzschean histories, like any history, highlight some aspects of the past at the expense of others, but Nietzsche's terminological choice shows him to be self-aware about it. Still on that side, we have Maudemarie Clark, who proposes that Nietzsche's history of morality is a genealogy because it's the history of couplings—just as literal genealogies are about who married whom, and who their children, with the presumably no-longer-separable

WHAT WAS NIETZSCHE'S GENEALOGY? 67

traits inherited from the parents, were. The *Genealogy's* three Essays, on this variation of the just-ordinary-history take on it, present three of the strands that were woven together into morality as we know it.[3]

On the other side of this debate, we have Michel Foucault and his epigones, who see genealogy as a technique whose theory and blueprint are outlined in two pivotal sections of the book. I'll take a moment to spell out how that technique is supposed to work.[4]

When one looks back into the history of, in the famous example Nietzsche sketches, punishment as practiced in premodern times,

> one must distinguish two aspects: on the one hand, that in it which is relatively *enduring*, the custom, the act, the "drama," a certain strict sequence of procedures; on the other, that in it which is *fluid*, the meaning, the purpose, the expectation associated with the performance of such procedures . . . the procedure itself will be something older, earlier than its employment as punishment . . . the latter is *projected* and interpreted *into* the procedure . . .
> (5:316/GM 2.13)

Updating his example, in our penal system over the past century and a half, we see new functions imposed one after another on already existing structures and patterns of activity. The "drama" is stable: people are confined in large buildings with solid walls but also exercise yards; they're closely supervised by guards; they wear uniforms . . . and all the rest of it. Early on in its present form, imprisonment was imposed as a regulated form of collectively mediated retribution, an orderly replacement for the lynch mob; its function was to inflict a measured dose of suffering on lawbreakers. At some point, although vengence still has its advocates,[5] that came to be considered a less-than-respectable reason for imprisonment. Instead, people were sent to prison, just as before, but for the deterrent effect; incarceration continued to inflict suffering, which was understood, however, to be in the service of a further and somewhat more generous goal. Then deterrence too became an unacceptable justification; castigated as ineffective, the standard anecdote in this connection was the way that pickpockets came to public hangings to work the crowd. And so criminals continued to be sent to prison, but now in the name of rehabilitation and reform. During the 1980s, America's penal system was reframed yet again; this time prisons were meant to be a sort of holding pen. Pretensions to rehabilitation were abandoned, the announced function of prisons being merely to keep undesirables off the

68   WHY DIDN'T NIETZSCHE GET HIS ACT TOGETHER?

streets. And for all I know, there is now some new reason given out for the facilities run by our Departments of Corrections.

Such a history of reappropriations underwrites a skeptical argument, which we can lay out in two passes. First, we see that relatively stable underlying structures—institutions, procedures, even devices and biological organs—are repeatedly taken over and repurposed by the successive loci of agency that manage to take control of them. (Nietzsche's own way of thinking about a locus of agency is marked by his phrase, "will to power"; let's bypass the issues that raises for the moment.) When a locus of agency seizes control of a structure, it provides an interpretation of and justification for the structure; while underlying structures remain more or less the same, the justifications for them come and go. However, if justifications for one and the same thing just come and go, they're obviously *post hoc* rationalizations, and consequently incredible. So you ought not to believe the justifications that accompany institutions, procedures, devices, and so on. The genealogical method, on this way of construing Nietzsche's intent, consists in producing such a history, with this skeptical point: in the illustration, whatever the powers that be tell us are the reasons we lock people up, we oughtn't take those reasons at face value.[6]

Notice that we're seeing what looks to be Nietzsche's conception of interpretation in action:

> the cause of the origin of a thing and its eventual utility, its actual employment and place in a system of purposes, lie worlds apart; whatever exists, having somehow come into being, is again and again reinterpreted [*ausgelegt*] to new ends, taken over, transformed, and redirected by some power superior to it . . .   (5:313/GM 2.12)

Most of Nietzsche's readers assume that interpretation is the sort of thing that *they're* used to doing: the explication of a text, meant to stay as faithful to it as possible, and so an activity that leaves the text it's interpreting intact. Thus interpretation amounts to adding a layer of explanation to a text that remains constant throughout. But here, interpretation isn't a matter of standing back and saying something to oneself or one's friends; in that it forces whatever is being interpreted to fit a function, it's not just hands-on, but *coercive*.

Turning now to the second phase of the skeptical argument, in each of these reinterpretations, as the coercive nature of the activity implies,

WHAT WAS NIETZSCHE'S GENEALOGY? 69

there will in fact be some change to the underlying structure. (At any rate, when the apparent repurposing is not merely rebranding.) Sometimes that amounts to light editing; for instance, when the point of a prison officially became rehabilitation, parole and vocational training were integrated into penal institutions, and the death penalty and flogging were deleted. While the "drama" remains *mostly* as it was, each new interpretation introduces changes at the margin. But the cumulative effect of these alterations is that eventually the structure isn't a good fit for any function at all. Sticking with our example, prisons were made very unpleasant places when they were understood as punishment and deterrence.[7] They continued to be unpleasant, even when they were supposed to be rehabilitation facilities. Reinterpretation as rehabilitation introduced parole, a feature of the institution that stayed with us, even when the announced objective came to be keeping criminals off the streets. But the aspects of a prison that make it effective as retribution and deterrence undercut its effectiveness as a therapeutic framework; paroling convicts is putting them on the streets, rather than keeping them off... and in the end, prisons suit none of these purposes particularly well. Moreover, even the presumably superseded interpretations are still in play; you can elicit most of them from an audience easily enough. The upshot, Nietzsche tells us, is that

> As for the other element in punishment, the fluid element, its "meaning," in a very late condition of culture (for example, in modern Europe) the concept "punishment" possesses in fact not *one* meaning but a whole synthesis of "meanings": the previous history of punishment in general, the history of its employment for the most various purposes, finally crystallizes into a kind of unity that is hard to disentangle, hard to analyze and, as must be emphasized especially, totally *indefinable*. (Today it is impossible to say for certain *why* people are really punished: all concepts in which an entire process is semiotically concentrated elude definition; only that which has no history is definable.)   (5:317/GM 2.13)

What goes for punishment in medieval and earlier times goes for prisons in our own day, and briefly, when you perform a genealogy, you'll find— provided the subject you're investigating has been around long enough for it to support the exercise—that it's undefinable. You'll realize that you can neither say what it is nor what it's for; it can no longer be reduced to the elements in its past.[8] This is how new meanings and new values come into

70 WHY DIDN'T NIETZSCHE GET HIS ACT TOGETHER?

being; although you can no longer define them, inspecting their history is the best way to understand them.[9] So far the Foucauldian version of the genealogical method.

Although the central or paradigmatic instances of interpretation as Nietzsche conceives it have subjugated populations or institutions as their objects, literary texts can also be interpreted in this way, and let me offer a frankly speculative suggestion as to where Nietzsche found his model for the activity, and how he came to think about it the way he did.

As we've now seen, Nietzsche was a close reader of Wellhausen, and Wellhausen both described and exhibited a dramatically different approach to interpretation than the one scholars are instructed is their task; it's in fact very much in the spirit of the reappropriation of institutions and reshaping of human raw material that takes center stage in the Foucauldian rendering of genealogy. We observed in the last chapter how, in Wellhausen's rereading of the Old Testament, the deuteronomists and later priests repeatedly and systematically reinterpreted the older documents and oral traditions available to them, by editing and rewriting them so as to foist their own incompatible views and evaluations on the earlier material.[10]

Moreover, Wellhausen didn't merely describe this sort of interpretation; he exemplified it. (As I indicated earlier, although academics today tend to think of him as having been in their line of work, in his frame of mind and his practice he was much closer to Enlightenment figures such as Voltaire.) Faced with a recalcitrant passage, for instance, Wellhausen had no scruples at all about insisting the text was corrupt, that the passage was a later interpolation, or came from a different source—or he might alter it, letter by letter, until it said what he wanted. Because Wellhausen's emendations often turn on Hebrew spelling, I'll substitute an English illustration of the procedure. Suppose you want to claim that the author of your text is thoroughly selfish, and suppose the recalcitrant passage reads, "In times of trouble, they can go to help." The Wellhausen approach would be to provide a citation to the chapter and verse, adding a remark such as, "reading of course 'l' for the final 'p.'" Textual interpretation, Wellhausen-style, is something you do with a pair of scissors and the sensibilities of a cowboy.[11]

Nietzsche, as we're starting to see, is very much given to flipping over values and turning them upside down. To a respectable academic, what Wellhausen does is irresponsible and simply unacceptable. But when Nietzsche, who was after all trained as a classicist and whom we see to be a very sensitive reader of texts, noticed what Wellhausen was doing, he responded—or this is my guess, but it's not something we can demonstrate—with enthusiasm, and it became his model for the exercise of will to power that the account of interpretation we find in the *Genealogy* amounts to.[12]

I don't have a stake in that debate over what Nietzsche meant by genealogy, but if a genealogy is an interpretation of history, and this is what interpretation consists in, then we should expect to see history violently rewritten, in order to impose upon the past a novel interpretation that serves the values of the genealogist. When the history seems to validate or underwrite those values, we should not be overly credulous; Nietzsche has gone out of his way to remind us that they are likely to have been egregiously forced on the materials at hand. And if all this does turn out to be right, then Nehamas and Geuss are mistaken: genealogy is, precisely, history *incorrectly* practiced.

4

Who Was Nietzsche's "Good European"?

(How to Read *Beyond Good and Evil*)

Three decades back, in what has remained an insufficiently discussed essay, Alexander Nehamas faced up to the unreadability of a central Nietzschean text, *Beyond Good and Evil*: "my own experience," he reported, is that it "seems to disappear from consciousness, and memory, as soon as it has been read—consumed but undigested." The problem arises, Nehamas decided, out of trying to read the book as though it were a philosophical treatise of the usual sort, that is, by trying to read simply for the content. The book makes sense only once you correctly identify the literary genre it's in—a monologue, in Nehamas's view—and only when you read it for its "postulated author," here, the character we are to understand to be delivering the monologue. That character, Nehamas argues, is being presented to us as a "philosopher of the future."[1]

As the previous chapters have made evident, I agree with Nehamas that when we read Nietzsche's mature works, we have to ask ourselves what genre they're placing themselves in (or parodying), and moreover that we have to read them for their implicit authors, if we're going to make out their philosophical agendas. But I mean to correct the substance of his reading in a number of regards. Nehamas has misidentified the literary genre of *Beyond Good and Evil*. He has misidentified its implicit author. He has accordingly failed to account for the very features of the book that make it unreadable when it's approached with the methods to which analytic historians of philosophy are accustomed, and he has overlooked the ways in which it resists his own theory of authorship. Finally, the implicit author of the book, I'll argue, cannot be one of Nietzsche's philosophers of the future. Nehamas has failed to register the book's *raison d'être*, or one of them: that of showing us what's getting in the way of the invention of novel values.

Why Didn't Nietzsche Get His Act Together? Elijah Millgram, Oxford University Press. © Oxford University Press 2023.
DOI: 10.1093/oso/9780197669303.003.0004

4.1

If we're going to be considering the character presented to us by *Beyond Good and Evil* as its author, we'd better give him a name. The default, which would be to go with what we find on the title page, would be in various ways misleading.

Nehamas's essay dates to a period in which one didn't want an accusation of the so-called intentional fallacy to stick, and he went out of his way to distinguish his postulated author from the "writer"—in this case, the flesh-and-blood human being, Friedrich Nietzsche, who produced the manuscript of *Beyond Good and Evil*, sent it to the publisher, and so on. (For first-timers, the fallacy takes two forms: the narrower and more plausible, that of conflating what an author meant to say with what he *did* say; and the broader—but this was how the concept was in practice applied—that of taking biographical information about an author to be relevant to the inter-pretation of his writings.[2]) I don't myself think that this distinction must, as a matter of interpretative principle, always be in place, but I agree that the character in question here is a highly artificial construction, one whose relation to the former Basel faculty member should at any rate start out as an open question.[3] Moreover, while Nehamas believes we should take all of Nietzsche's works to share a single implicit author, we're in the middle of testing the hypothesis that each of the later works presents us with a distinct author.[4] For both of these reasons, it would be confusing to use "Nietzsche" as the label we want.

I find it's generally very helpful to follow Nietzsche's own reading instruc-tions. (And I'll continue to signal, as I just have, that I take doctrines or positions or moves to belong to a theoretical common denominator of the later works with the tag "Nietzsche," as in "Nietzsche's reading instructions"; one of the objectives of this chapter is to make headway in thinking about the status of such attributions.) As we've seen, Nietzsche sometimes gives these instructions at the outset of his literary productions.[5] In particular, he generally goes out of his way to identify the author projected by one of his books. So we won't be surprised when we notice that he wraps up the Preface to *Beyond Good and Evil* by placing himself: "we who are neither Jesuits nor democrats, nor even German enough, we *good Europeans* and free, *very* free spirits." Since he's emphasized that penultimate phrase, let's call the character we'll be engaging Nietzsche's "Good European."[6]

74 WHY DIDN'T NIETZSCHE GET HIS ACT TOGETHER?

While we're paying attention to reading instructions, let's dispose of Nehamas's claim that the book is "a long, sustained, sometimes rambling and disorganized but ultimately coherent, monologue."[7] Its sections 197 and 198 respectively conclude with:

> This for the chapter "Morality as Timidity."
> This, too, for the chapter "Morality as Timidity."

The work is evidently presenting itself as notes for a book, and presumably is a somewhat redacted journal. We'll want to explain why the Good European's literary output should come to us in this form, and I'll suggest a reason in sec. 4.8.

What kind of person *is* this Good European? Nietzsche isn't going to make do with subtle or brief hints: we're first given a highly theoretical psychological frame, whose content would nowadays be classified as philosophy of mind and theory of agency; we're given a race-theoretic backstory which, within that frame, accounts for the workings of this particular mind; and finally, we're given elaborate and extended displays of the Good European's mind at work. That is, a great deal of effort is devoted to presenting, as the title of a recent commentary phrases it, "the soul of Nietzsche's *Beyond Good and Evil*."[8] Rehearsing the layers of this self-portrait will occupy us for the coming sections, after which I'll turn to the philosophical agenda of the literary exercise.

4.2

The first part of *Beyond Good and Evil* is largely devoted to displacing a mistaken metaphysics of mind (although this isn't its only objective). On the incorrect but widely shared view that it criticizes, mental states and activity are attributed to a grammatical subject that has been reified into a simple substance; Nietzsche's label for the error is "atomism."[9]

Atomism is by no means confined to theory of mind, and getting to the bottom of the philosophical and practical confusions it involves turns out to be a complicated matter. (Nietzsche takes it quite seriously, and in due course we'll put his ideas about it, as they're advanced in *Beyond Good and Evil*, side by side with the somewhat differently inflected run for their money they're given in *The Gay Science.*[10]) But the aspect of the mistake that he emphasizes in his discussion of "the prejudices of the philosophers" is treating the self as having no internal structure.

The techniques available to nonspecialists, but also to philosophers and social scientists, for describing psychological processes, states, and the human behavior they cause turn on identifying a person as the owner or subject or producer of a mental state or action, where the subject is, more or less as a matter of notation, treated as a structureless—"atomic"—unit. In line with recent philosophical usage, I'll say that we describe activity and cognition by attributing a mental state or action to an individual, and I'll call these techniques *attribution-based*. (For instance, when, a couple steps back, I described the thinking that eventuated in a distinction between "writer" and "author," I did so by ascribing *to Nehamas* a position with regard to the intentional fallacy, which purported to explain an ensuing action, *his* making the distinction; that is, as we analytic philosophers say it, propositional attitudes and an action were jointly attributed to an agent.)

The picture as we've come to have it requires pausing to sort out some pieces a little more explicitly than Nietzsche did. We can distinguish a weaker and a stronger form of attribution: we're not sure so-and-so *really* believes it, even though he did *say* it, and even think it. If you were to press him on it later, he might tell you, and convincingly, that it had just popped into his head, and that he blurted it out, but he hadn't really meant it. (However, if the thought was going to be ascribed to anyone, we know *whose* belief it would be, alright.) That's to say, we're allowing the weaker, but disallowing the stronger attribution.

Nowadays the stronger form of attribution gets a great deal of attention, while the weaker is undertheorized, both today and, unless I'm missing something, by Nietzsche himself. Since we need a way of keeping them straight, let's replace Nietzsche's word, "soul," with "self" and "mind": in the pictorial imagination that seems to guide or anyway be coordinated with our ascriptive practices, the former will be the structureless and extensionless anchor that is conjured up by strong attitude attribution, and the latter, a sort of container of mental states that you might or might not disavow.[11]

There's more content built into the descriptive practice than perhaps you think. On the one hand, both forms of attributability treat the attitudes and actions as though they were so much luggage that the mind or agent acquires and discards; on the other, while your airline will check one suitcase regardless of what you've packed into the others, your propositional attitudes and actions are required to exhibit a good deal of consistency, if we're to say that they really are yours. Thus, and for instance, against this conceptual background, when someone acknowledges that doing something would be a very bad idea, but decides to do it anyway; or decides not to do it, but then does it after all—that's a paradox (the puzzle of *akrasia*, or weakness of will). As we noticed in the Introduction, because attribution-based representational conventions keep the paradox perpetually in play, they become recurring occasions for philosophical theorizing.

Because there's no point-mass Cartesian ego on which to hang psychological-state attributions, when they *can* be pulled off successfully, that will be due to, first, the psychic parts of the person in question standing in the right sort of configuration, and second, to the operation of that person's psychological machinery being, so to speak, sufficiently well oiled. Nietzsche follows a long line of philosophers in analogizing the constitution of the self to that of the political state. In persons whose inner lives resemble absolutist monarchies, and in which the routinized and unquestioning execution of subsidiary tasks by their psychic components can simply be taken for granted, actions and attitudes are naturally attributed to the (not-further-examined) self. Louis XIV, the icon of absolutism, is given a nod; just as the monarch identified himself with the state he ruled, the governing element of this personality configuration takes itself for the person in its entirety.[12]

Nietzsche was probably mischaracterizing the view from Versailles; the Sun King in fact spent a great deal of attention and fiscal wherewithal on coopting and neutralizing his nobility, whereas if you were unpacking the point-mass coathook image into directly stated theses, foremost among them would be that the attribution-supporting structure, whatever it is (e.g., coathook or container), takes care of itself, and doesn't need to be maintained or sustained.[13] Be that as it may, the person who is so composed exhibits a distinctive phenomenon and experiences a distinctive phenomenology: "free will," a phrase that reflects a confused metaphysical interpretation of that smoothly functioning and fully integrated internal administrative apparatus.[14]

By contrast, personality configurations that don't manage this degree and mode of functional integration will fail to support the straightforward attribution of attitudes, intentions, and actions, and thus the turn that Nietzsche is taking isn't merely of historical interest. Mainstream analytic moral psychology for some time now has accepted the constraint that selfhood must consist in the configuration of one's psychological components, and starting around 1970 we've seen a series of attempts to account for the full-fledged attribution to a person of his mental states and actions.[15] It's been presumed throughout that such attributions *are* normally underwritten by some suitable psychological structure (though generally not the one that Nietzsche came up with); it's been taken for granted that our occasional lapses from whatever that configuration turns out to be count as defects: blameworthy, sanctionable, and to be repaired as expeditiously as possible.[16]

On Nietzsche's understanding of the workings of agency, the highly integrated agent is a very demanding accomplishment, and one that must accordingly be expected to materialize only infrequently. In due course we'll consider what's needed to bring it off, and why it's so difficult. That in turn will put on the table the question of whether we should treat this particular finish line as nonoptional—whether failure to attain it is failure *tout court.* However, before we take up those issues, we need to resolve an interpretative question that's been put squarely on our plate: is the Good European—again, the character being presented to us as the implicit author of *Beyond Good and Evil*—one of the entirely (or almost entirely) unified agents of contemporary moral psychology, a self whose opinions, other attitudes, intentions, decisions, and actions are unproblematically attributable to *him*? Or is he the human-sized analog of a failed (political) state, one whose putative beliefs are not much more than blurts, and whose apparent actions can legitimately be shrugged off as merely the activity of his subpersonal parts?

As the name we have adopted for him suggests, the Good European purports to be just that: in important respects, typically and characteristically a European. And he provides us with an account of how Europeans of his day are configured psychologically. So let's turn to that.

4.3

In the course of trying to diagnose skepticism and paralysis of the will, the narrator describes "our Europe of today" as "the arena of an absurdly sudden attempt at a radical mixture of classes, and *hence* races" (5:138/BGE 208). Due to what German revolutionary nationalists subsequently made both of Nietzsche and of the concept of race, remarks like that one haven't for the most part been faced up to and thought through. The reflex response, that Nietzsche is obviously a racist (*that* kind of racist), plays out either

78 WHY DIDN'T NIETZSCHE GET HIS ACT TOGETHER?

in violently condemning, charitably ignoring, or defensively excusing and denying that aspect of his writing. (Among academics, that is; Nietzsche's reception elsewhere has been a different matter.[17]) Nietzsche's misogynist remarks, which we'll get to soon enough, are treated similarly.

However, we shouldn't take it for granted that the notion of race Nietzsche is invoking is the one with which we're familiar; because the concept was being renegotiated over the latter half of the nineteenth century, it was indeed quite fluid as *Beyond Good and Evil* was underway. Rather, we need to let our narrator tell us what his races are, and how they're being mixed. I'll return to the question of whether Nietzsche was racist or sexist once we've equipped ourselves to address it; right now, we can begin with an announcement on the part of the Good European:

> One cannot erase from the soul of a human being what his ancestors liked most to do and did most constantly: whether they were, for example, assiduous savers and appurtenances of a desk and cash box, modest and bourgeouis in their desires, modest also in their virtues; or whether they lived accustomed to commanding from dawn to dusk, fond of rough amusements and also perhaps of even rougher duties and responsibilities; or whether, finally, at some point they sacrificed ancient prerogatives of birth and possessions in order to live entirely for their faith—their "god"— as men of an inexorable and delicate conscience which blushes at every compromise. It is simply not possible that a human being should *not* have the qualities and preferences of his parents and ancestors in his body, whatever appearances may suggest to the contrary. This is the problem of race.   (5:218f/BGE 264)

We need to register that this way of thinking is not confined to the Good European; in *The Gay Science*, for example, Nietzsche deploys it to launch an *ad hominem* criticism of Kant:

> In Europe, scholars grow out of all kinds of classes and social conditions . . . Once one has trained one's eyes to recognize in a scholarly treatise the scholar's intellectual *idiosyncrasy*—every scholar has one—and to catch it in the act, one will almost always behold behind this the scholar's "prehistory," his family, and especially their occupations and crafts.
>
> Where the feeling finds expression "Now this has been proved and I am done with it," it is generally the ancestor in the blood and instinct of the

scholar who approves from his point of view "the finished job"; the faith in a proof is merely a symptom of what in a hard-working family has for ages been considered "good workmanship." One example: When the sons of clerks and office workers of every kind, whose main task it has always been to bring order into diverse materials, to distribute it over different files, and in general to schematize things, become scholars, they manifest a tendency to consider a problem almost as solved when they have merely schematized it. There are philosophers who are fundamentally merely schematizers; for them the formal aspect of their fathers' occupation has become content. The talent for classifications, for tables of categories, betrays something; one pays a price for being the child of one's parents.   (3:583f/GS 348)

The conception of race we see here is likely to strike us as Lamarckian: if your father was an accountant, and his father was an accountant, and so on, you're a born accountant, in something like the way that border collies are born sheepdogs; if your parents, and grandparents, and great-grandparents were farmers, you have the soul of a farmer, and so on. And long-lasting ethnic or cultural groups may similarly generate personalities of a given type; I truncated that last passage before getting to Nietzsche's remarks about the intellectual habits of Jews. Members of such "races" will have personalities tightly organized around—to begin using a concept that we're going to discuss shortly—a dominant drive; in these examples, maybe the drive to balance the books, and be obsessively neat about it, or the drive to garden. As the ever-more-sharpened character trait is passed onto descendants occupying a hereditary social role, personalities are produced that thoroughly subserve the trait; we can imagine the typical personality within the accountants' guild to be one whose every aspect is inflected by that compulsion to actuarial neatness.

Europe used to be a region in which social roles were predominantly hereditary, and social mobility, next to unknown. Consequently, Europeans of the past were, almost all of them, personalities presumed to be structured in this sort of way. The Good European seems to construe this sort of psychology as reassuring: at least such a thoroughly organized personality knows who it is and what it wants.

As the barriers between hereditary social roles fall, and as such races are interbred, the people that result contain within them, as a disorganized medley, the drives and other personality traits of the former races; such personalities don't *have* a dominant drive. Continuing the toy illustration,

80 WHY DIDN'T NIETZSCHE GET HIS ACT TOGETHER?

if your ancestors on one side were accountants, and your ancestors on the other side were farmers, you no longer know who you are or what you want: you're a psychological mess. (The rose bushes and the spreadsheet are *both* calling out to me...what to *do*?!) But now, we're given to understand, Europeans (and Germans) are mixed, in just this sense, only much more so. Their personalities are, as Nietzsche puts it, "multiple and manifold." "The Europeans...become increasingly independent of any *determinate* milieu that would like to inscribe itself for centuries in soul and body with the same demands" (5:182/BGE 242), and Nietzsche's Good European invokes this ongoing process to explain how it is that "we modern men are determined...by *different* moralities," such that "our actions...are rarely univocal" (5:152/BGE 215).[18] The same etiology accounts for the development by the "hybrid European" of highly refined historical sensibilities (5:157/BGE 223f); for the ease with which it will be possible to enslave Europeans of the near future, as well their occasional knack for tyranny and despotism (5:183/BGE 242); and, as we've remarked, for their skepticism, which "always develops when races or classes that have long been separated are crossed suddenly and decisively" (5:138/BGE 208)—and which Nietzsche glosses as an inability to commit to one thing and follow through with it.

Will the typical European be a unified agent, as contemporary moral philosophy imagines such a person, and as Nietzsche characterizes the phenomenon? Not likely: recall the early section instructing us that unity of agency is a matter of the unquestioned subordination of the components of a psychological system to a controlling component (5:31–34/BGE 19). Thus what underwrites the attribution of attitudes and actions to the agent, all at once as it were, is the consequent ability, on the part of its controlling component, to treat its own stances as the stances of the whole—and on the part of other people, their having it pan out, when they treat as the stances of the whole what are in the first place the stances of the controlling component. The Lamarckian adjustment of the elements of a personality into this type of configuration is disrupted by "that enchanting and mad *semi-barbarism* into which Europe [has] been plunged by the democratic mingling of classes and races" (5:158/BGE 224). That mingling has been recent and rapid, and so insufficient time has since passed for anything like tight reintegration. It follows from the Good European's account of race and its recent history that Europeans will not normally be unified agents, which means that attribution-based psychological description will routinely produce paradoxes.

WHO WAS NIETZSCHE'S "GOOD EUROPEAN"? 81

4.4

However, perhaps the Good European is an exception to the overall trend; we're informed that Napoleon, Goethe, Beethoven, Stendhal, Heine, and Wagner all managed to anticipate a "new *synthesis* and...the European of the future," that is, to weave together the culturally variously sourced strands of their personalities (5:201f/BGE 256). In fact, a reconstruction of the process which would eventuate in such an outcome has been gradually emerging within the recent secondary literature, and here's a thumbnail of the state of play.[19] While drives aren't by any means the sole component of a Nietzschean psychology, they're evidently the primary architectural element.[20] One drive can assimilate another, as when my drive to shop and my drive to present well to others merge into a very familiar drive to be fashionable.[21] As ever-more-contoured drives recruit one another into still-more-elaborately-articulated drives, a core self emerges; at the limit of this process, when no freestanding drives remain to be assimilated, the psychological raw materials that constitute a person have been completely synthesized into a self whose stances and pronouncements are one's own: after all, there are no leftover and competing drives to gainsay its authority.[22]

If the shorthand helps, you should think of this as a psychologized appropriation of the first-*Critique* notion of synthesis of cognitions. (If not, you can skip this paragraph.) In Kant, the unity of apperception was transcendental, that is, a formal aspect of the architecture of the mind. That cognitions are assembled into more complex cognitions—e.g., subjects and predicates into judgments, or atomic judgments into logically complex judgments—is something you're aware of from the inside, and it's not an appropriate or even possible domain of empirical investigation. (Rather, it's presupposed by any empirical investigation.) Now Nietzsche is fully cognizant of the metaphysical difficulties that arise out of treating synthesis as an empirical phenomenon.[23] But if I'm reading him correctly, he's taking it on board nonetheless, and also taking on board what he regards as the practical upshots of the move. In particular, any real-world process can fail, and fail frequently. A real-world process of synthesis will operate on whatever the real psychological inventory is (drives, affects, and so on, rather than, Nietzsche thinks, the psychological correlates of the entries in a well-behaved table of forms of judgment, along with their components).[24] The limit of an empirical process of synthesis—that is, the fully unified mind, one that can

82 WHY DIDN'T NIETZSCHE GET HIS ACT TOGETHER?

pass, in most circumstances and to a casual observer, for that atomic self—is all-too-likely never to be reached.

The recap was quick and oversimplified, and there are various problems to resolve before signing onto the reconstruction. Nonetheless, my take on it is that these ideas are genuinely present in Nietzsche's writings. If they are, the question of the Good European's mode and level of internal organization is so far unresolved. Perhaps the Good European lives out the internal chaos we've been primed to expect from his interracial background, but perhaps he's reintegrated himself, in line with the template we've just sketched; perhaps the first-person plural in his off-the-cuff "we Europeans of the day after tomorrow" (5:151/BGE 214) is meant to place him alongside the likes of Goethe. However immodest the comparison may make the latter possibility seem, we have a dialectical reason to take it seriously: Nehamas's reading, which is one of our foils, has it that, as a matter of exegetical method, a postulated author must be a coherent character, one who forms and executes the elaborate intention to write the book we are interpreting.

So how are we to settle which of these competing alternatives is realized by the implicitly presented character?[25] Nietzsche (or his avatar) isn't going to leave us hanging: he *shows* us.

4.5

My experience with reading Nietzsche and watching others read him is that it's best not to postpone addressing those parts of his writing that make one personally uncomfortable. Since I'm Jewish, I'm going to start off with some opinions about Jews, volunteered by the Good European under the heading of "Peoples and Fatherlands":

> That Germany has amply *enough* Jews, that the German stomach, the German blood has trouble (and will still have trouble for a long time) digesting even this quantum of "Jew" . . . that is the clear testimony and language of a general instinct to which one must listen, in accordance with which one must act. "Admit no more new Jews! And especially close the doors to the east (also to Austria)!" thus commands the instinct of a people whose type is still weak and indefinite, so it could easily be blurred or extinguished by a stronger race. The Jews, however, are beyond any doubt the strongest, toughest, and purest race now living in Europe . . . they

WHO WAS NIETZSCHE'S "GOOD EUROPEAN"? 83

change, *when* they change, always only as the Russian Empire makes its conquests—being an empire that has time and is not of yesterday—namely, according to the principle, "as slowly as possible."

That the Jews, if they wanted it—or if they were forced into it, which seems to be what the anti-Semites want—*could* even now have preponderance, indeed quite literally mastery over Europe, that is certain . . .

(5:193f/BGE 251)

These are opinions of almost the sort that at the time you could have heard in pretty much any pub in Germany or Austria-Hungary.[26] That is, the opinions themselves are uninteresting, and what matters for us here is how they're bookended. Now, at the outset the narrator announces:

Forgive me, for during a brief daring sojourn in very infected territory [that is, of "nationalistic nerve fever and political ambition"] I, too, did not altogether escape this disease and began like everyone else to develop notions about matters that are none of my business: the first sign of the political infection. For example about the Jews: only listen!

(5:192f/BGE 251)

And then we're given the tirade I've just excerpted, concluding with:

But here it is proper to break off my cheerful Germanomania and holiday oratory; for I am beginning to touch on what is *serious* for me . . .

(5:195/BGE 251)

The Good European gives the same framing to other, related opinions: all of Part VIII, "People and Fatherlands," comes with a very similar pair of bookends. Its first section starts off with rambling remarks about how the *Meistersinger* is "something German in the best and worst senses of the word, something manifold, formless and inexhaustible in a German way; [it has] a certain German powerfulness and overfulness of the soul" and so on (5:179f/BGE 240). And then suddenly, at the beginning of the next section, we're told:

We "good Europeans"—we, too, know hours when we permit ourselves some hearty fatherlandishness, a plop and relapse into old loves and narrownesses—*I have just given a sample of that.* (5:180/BGE 241, my emph.)

84 WHY DIDN'T NIETZSCHE GET HIS ACT TOGETHER?

In rapid succession the reader encounters passages on the "German soul" (5:184/BGE 244), more on "German music" (5:187f, 200f/BGE 245, 255), talk about German books (5:189/BGE 246), German style (5:190f/BGE 247), more German opining about Jews (5:192/BGE 250), and some good old German hostility towards the English (5:195–198/BGE 252f). And then, finally, in the last section of the Part, we find the matching bookend:

> the more profound and comprehensive men of this century . . .: only in their foregrounds or in weaker hours, say in old age, did they belong to the "fatherlandish"—they were merely taking a rest from themselves when they became "patriots." (5:201f/BGE 256)

Evidently, the whole of Part VIII is Nietzsche's Good European taking a rest from himself; what are we to make of that? One thing is clear enough, that the framing undercuts the straightforward attribution of these opinions and attitudes to himself, or to his character; they have the status of extended blurts—"holiday oratory," "matters that are none of my business," "taking a break," a "relapse," and so on. Let's float this hypothesis: the owners of these opinions (if we're still going to try to attribute them) are subpersonal components of the Good European's psychology, the obvious candidates being various drives, in this case, the character's nationalistic and antisemitic drives.

4.6

The hypothesis is confirmed by a longer and more elaborate display of yet another drive, in this case, misogyny. Directly prior to the run of nationalistic and antisemitic ranting we've just surveyed, we're treated to a series of unfortunate comments about women-in-general. Just to give you a sense of their tone, here's a representative sampling:

> Stupidity in the kitchen; woman as cook: the gruesome thoughtlessness to which the feeding of the family and of the master of the house is abandoned! Woman does not understand what food *means*—and wants to be cook. (5:172/BGE 234)
>
> A man . . . who has depth . . . must conceive of woman as a possession, as property that can be locked, as something predestined for service and achieving her perfection in that. (5:175/BGE 238)

WHO WAS NIETZSCHE'S "GOOD EUROPEAN"? 85

> Almost everywhere one ruins her nerves with the most pathological and dangerous kind of music ... [which] makes her more hysterical by day and more incapable of her first and last profession—to give birth to strong children. (5:177/BGE 239)

As before, the views are familiar and not themselves interesting; but also as before, they come bookended:

> at the bottom of us, really "deep down," there is ... something unteachable, some granite of spiritual *fatum*, of predetermined decision and answer to predetermined selected questions.... there speaks an unchangeable "this is I"; about man and woman, for example, a thinker cannot relearn but only finish learning—only discover ultimately how this is "settled in him."
>
> "convictions" ... [are] signposts to the problem we *are*—rather, to the great stupidity we are, to our spiritual *fatum*, to what is *unteachable* very "deep down."
>
> After this abundant civility that I have just evidenced in relation to myself I shall perhaps be permitted more readily to state a few truths about "woman as such"—assuming that it is now known from the outset how very much these are after all only—*my* truths. (5:170/BGE 231)

(The closing bookend is simply the end of Part VII of the book.)

Belief is governed by Moore's Paradox: that is, saying that you believe something, but that it's not true, counts as on a par with a contradiction.[27] And to say that something you think is an unteachable stupidity counts as a variation on Moore's Paradox; when you do so, you're dissociating yourself from the claim, which can no longer be attributed to you as a belief, that is, as something you take to be *true*. Rather, it is at most one of *your* truths: "creations of value which have become dominant and are for a time called 'truths'" (5:144/BGE 211).

The failure of attribution is somewhat trickier than the cases we've already surveyed, in that the Good European informs us that they are how "an unchangeable 'this is I' ... is 'settled in him'" (5:170/BGE 231). I take it this is a way of registering that the misogynistic drive that's expressing itself is an important and inextricable part of the character's personality, one whose postures it would be dishonest to shrug off as mere lapses or slips of the tongue. Nonetheless, the opinions are treated as indicating something about what the character is like (as "signposts"), rather than as endorsed by an individual who is capable of univocal affirmations.[28]

The Good European is putting his lack of agential integration emphatically on display. The author of *Beyond Good and Evil* is not some tiny absolutist monarchy, whose activities exhibit "free will," and whose attitudes support attribution-based practices of psychological description. Just as his race-theoretic backstory seemed to promise, he is (borrowing a phrase from Michael Bratman) a psychic stew of unregimented drives.[29] When he seems to be speaking, the speaker is, anyway most of the time, actually just one or another drive.

4.7

A few years back, an essay by Paul Katsafanas moved the investigation of Nietzsche's ideas forward by reopening the question of how drives are to be understood in his work. A drive, he proposed, is distinguished by having two distinct objects, which Katsafanas dubbed (just a bit confusingly) its *aim* and its *object*. For example, if the drive is shopping, the aim is *having lots of stuff*, and maybe evolutionary psychologists will tell us that the aim can be functionally accounted for in terms of the need to build up a horde of supplies that will get me through the winter. The object of the drive, at the present moment, is this knickknack I've encountered at the craft fair. A drive pursues its aim by inducing the recurring pursuit of its objects; continuing the illustration, I keep spotting objects that look purchase-worthy, and wanting to buy them. Thus the aim of a drive is never satisfied: once I attain one of the drive's objects (I buy the knickknack and bring it home), I may be sated for a while; but then the drive will seek a new object.

On Katsafanas's rendering of the notion, drives control perceptual salience and concept application; for instance, my shopping drive makes me notice sales, or again, some people have a drive to clean, and it makes them notice messes and dirt. Drives are evaluative orientations: a drive tags something as its object by altering my perception of it, as when my shopping drive makes me perceive the 30%-off item as a real bargain.[30]

Although I'm usually aware of the objects of my drive-expressing behavior, I needn't be aware of its aims at all: I know that I'm buying the knickknack, but it escapes me that this is an expression of the drive to shop, whose aim is to fill up my home with *stuff*; I may well deny that I'm a shopaholic, a hoarder, or whatever. And this means that when I think I'm acting out of careful deliberation, I'm likely often to be the mere catspaw of a drive. While I tell myself that I'm buying it because I'm actually *saving* money, and I'm sure I'll have a use for it later, in fact it's going to join the pile of rubbish stacked up in my garage and basement, and that's obvious to everyone but me.

While Katsafanas's account of the drives is a significant advance over previous discussion, it's not all that tightly tied to Nietzsche's own writings, and now that we have two or three actually quite elaborate displays of drives in action, we can amend it.[31] Evidently the characteristic and primary mode of expression of a drive, as Nietzsche conceives of them, is *talking*. Indeed, very near the beginning of *Beyond Good and Evil*, he observes that any drive, given the chance, will philosophize (5:20/BGE 6); and what we observe his antisemitic, misogynistic, and German nationalist drives doing is *not* generating actions directed to changing the world around him—as my Katsafanas-style shopping drive does, by leading me to acquire ever further knickknacks—but rather, *verbal* behavior, in these cases, uncontrolled harangues.[32]

This indicates that drives cannot be individuated, as Katsafanas suggests, by their aims, objects, and evaluative orientations, although these are likely enough each an important aspect of what a drive comes to.[33] When Nietzsche announces in passing that "thinking is merely a relation of [our] drives to each other" (5:54/BGE 36), aims, objects, and evaluative dispositions don't explain why. However, if we press and extend the analogy between individual psyches and political states, it's natural to adopt political parties as our model for Nietzschean drives. A political party is recognized, first and foremost, by its rhetorical style, and only secondarily by its platform (its concrete policy objectives will normally change from time to time) and its aims (which also alter, although often more slowly, and which typically resist clean definition). Political parties have a characteristic manner of construing the world; these ideological frameworks are a decent first-cut approximation to the perspectives induced by Nietzsche's drives. And if you'll forgive me the cynicism, political parties start thinking—start producing novel reasons, consider whether and how to adjust their positions and so on—only when they're wrestling with competing parties; thus the comparison does give us a way to begin making sense of the puzzling remark which we just noticed. So think of your drives as the analogs, within the small-scale polity that is you, of political parties in the polity proper.[34]

We can finally state the needed correction to previous discussions of Nietzsche's racism, antisemitism, and sexism. We've established that in the Good European the process of synthesis isn't far enough along to support

88 WHY DIDN'T NIETZSCHE GET HIS ACT TOGETHER?

(strong) attribution-based description of his psychology.[35] But the way we're used to considering whether someone is racist or sexist invokes just those attribution-based descriptive practices: we ask, say, whether he holds (*really holds*) this racist view or has that sexist attitude. Faced with the Good European, we have to stop and rethink the question. When asking whether someone is, say, racist, are we asking what attitudes are to be full-fledgedly attributed to the individual? In that case, the Good European is not racist, etc., simply because he isn't enough of an agent for any attitudes to be properly *his*. Or does it suffice for racism, etc., that the inclination (moreover, the *irresistable*, even *unchangeable* inclination) to blurt out racist, sexist, and antisemitic remarks is there in the psychic stew? (Recall that we've been informed that his misogyny is "an unchangeable 'this is I'" [5:170/BGE 231].) In that case, the Good European—as Nietzsche himself[36]—is indeed racist and so on: we're being shown, repeatedly and even heavyhandedly, the respective drives to be present and active. But to the unexplicated and flatly posed questions—whether Nietzsche is a racist, is sexist, antisemitic, and so on—there are no straight answers, and for philosophically interesting reasons.

4.8

We've reached the point where we can articulate our second thoughts about Nehamas's line on *Beyond Good and Evil*, and Nietzsche's corpus more generally. "To interpret a text," Nehamas tells us, "is to construe it as someone's production, directed at certain purposes." We're now in a position to see daylight between the two clauses of that pronouncement. We have before us a character, who's represented as having produced the text, and so who can, if you like, be called its implicit or postulated author—the "character [is] a hypothesis which is accepted provisionally," on the way to the "ideal interpretation" that is the text's "regulative ideal." ("Authors," Nehamas tells us, "are formal causes"; "the author...is not a person; it is a character who is everything the text shows it to be.")[37] But this isn't production on the basis of purposes, because this character isn't competent to have purposes: at any rate, not purposes that are extended enough and elaborate enough for the production of a book to count as an intentional action on its part. It's no accident that the literary genre in which *Beyond Good and Evil* places itself is notes in a journal, fragmentary and preliminary materials for a volume that would be a lengthy and controlled composition, and which consequently remains unwritten. With a qualification I'll introduce momentarily, the present reading treats the text as the product of a coherent character, meaning that there's a character which *we* can describe coherently as giving rise to the book we have in front of us. But the character himself is systematically and pervasively incoherent, in a way that forestalls the full-fledged attribution of beliefs, intentions, or actions to him. (A coherent portrayal of an incoherent persona no more makes that persona coherent than a hundred-dollar bill's *really* being counterfeit makes it *real* currency.)

Philosophers have become accustomed to thinking of "agent" and "action" as two sides of a single coin, organized around the teleological structuring of what thereby turns out to be a fully attributable course of activity; it's precisely because we are trained to treat authorship as purposive in this sense, and because we read for authorial intention, that we analytic philosophers are, as we saw Nehamas observing at the outset, so prone to experience the book as simply unreadable. In fact, that presumption is so deeply entrenched that when moral philosophers need a model for unified agency, it's authorship to which they turn (as when Korsgaard, 2008, ch. 3, describes actions as "authored" by an agent). But we're not in a position to treat *this* author "as the agent whose actions account for the text's features," if we're giving those notions anything like the substantial sense they've come to take within recent moral philosophy and theory of action. In Elizabeth Anscombe's very influential way of construing actions, they're constructed as a series of steps, themselves subsidiary actions, proceeding to a termination point; the action's end has explanatory priority, which is to say that the steps are selected so as to arrive at the end.[38] But Nietzsche cautions us elsewhere against this way of thinking, by asking:

> Is the "goal," the "purpose" not often enough a beautifying pretext, a self-deception of vanity after the event that does not want to acknowledge that the ship is *following* the current into which it has entered accidentally? that it "wills" to go that way *because it—must*? that it has a direction, to be sure, but—no helmsman at all?   (3:607f/GS 360)

In the Good European, we have before us a failed agent, a very small-scale Lebanon or Pakistan, someone who does not manage to shape his activity into either Anscombean actions or Korsgaardian agency.

90 WHY DIDN'T NIETZSCHE GET HIS ACT TOGETHER?

Briefly, my alternative to Nehamas's reading agrees that we're being presented with a character: in fact, on a number of occasions, we observed, the character explicitly tells you that he's putting himself on display. We can accept that our interpretative "regulative end" (perhaps not "for each text," as Nehamas believes, but anyway for a text such as this one) "is to construct . . . a complete historically plausible author" for it.[39] But a coherent description of this author should not, in a case like this one, amount to seeing the text as his intentional action, motivated by his various propositional attitudes.

At this point an advocate for Nehamas is likely to object that I'm conflating two very different concepts: the Good European, according to him, is the speaker of the monologue of which the book consists, and on a par with the narrator of a novel; the postulated author is projected by Nietzsche's corpus as a whole. Even if the speaker—or as I have it, the dilettantish diarist— is incapable of supporting attribution-based psychological description, the postulated author, whose intention is to represent precisely *that*, is another matter entirely.

We can only examine Nietzsche's work a piece at a time, and that's a task we currently have underway. However, let me ask you not to assume that the agential lapses we are seeing in *Beyond Good and Evil* are merely local. They extend throughout the later writings, and collectively amount to the phenomenon we are examining scaling up to characterize the corpus as a whole.

And Nietzsche criticizes that widely shared Anscombean conception of action; it's not as though, normally, the stages of an action are selected in view of, or fitted to, its termination point. That end, the alleged goal or objective, doesn't have the explanatory priority we tend to ascribe to it; rather, as we just noticed, a course of activity has an inertia of its own, which is likely to largely determine its progress and direction. The non-Anscombean theoretical views are a common denominator of the mature writings as well. So insisting that the Nietzschean corpus is a very ambitious Anscombean action, whose agent must be seen projected behind it, is an extremely uncooperative approach to the text. Imagine someone whose theory of interpretation requires you to determine what demon or spirit animates a text, and imagine him applying that approach to a seventeenth-century Spinozist tract, one arguing that there are no demons or spirits. Not that this sort of thing didn't happen often enough during the seventeenth century, but looking for the postulated author of a group of texts that seem to be in the business of arguing that postulated authors are a philosophical

mistake is to stubbornly go against the grain of this book, and of Nietzsche's corpus as a whole, in pretty much that manner. After all, we're told
(admittedly in a different connection, but still), "if somebody asked, 'but to a
fiction there surely belongs an author?'—couldn't one answer simply: *why?*"
(5:54/BGE 34)

And now that promised qualification. Our attribution-based methods of
psychological description *do* presuppose coherence of a very particular sort
within a character. If Nietzsche is right, our notation—our *only* notation for
describing what people are and have been thinking, doing, and so on—has
misrepresentation built into it. Thus the agential lapses of a would-be self will
bleed out into descriptive failures and incoherence when we try to present
and make sense of it. This means that we have to be extremely cautious as
we proceed. Gottlob Frege famously had to ask for a pinch of salt from his
readers, and if we are to avoid overly distracting circumlocution, I'll need
to do the same: when I use markers like "as the Good European holds"
or "as Nietzsche believes," or "if Nietzsche is right," or mention "his non-
Anscombean views," please keep in mind how much less there is to such
attributions than meets the eye.[40]

4.9

We've reached the point where we can also entertain second thoughts about
the complex of ideas we were considering earlier, on which the unified self
is attained gradually, through the successive syntheses of drives—until, at
the endpoint of the process, we find a self that is largely identical with a
single, highly structured, very contoured, and very subtly oriented drive.[41]
The autonomous agent that emerges at this limit is envisaged as something
to which we should aspire, and I marked it as an open question whether
Nietzsche was purporting to have managed it.

But let's rethink the proposal, now that we've seen what drives the Good
European—and if I'm reading it right, Nietzsche—found within himself and
put on display. The antisemitism, the nationalism, and the misogyny are
each of them *ugly*; the literary mode is close to that of Henry Miller's *Aller
Retour New York*, an epistolary novel meant as the unvarnished depiction
of a character with no redeeming features. What would a unified drive,
synthesized out of *these* drives, look like—perhaps an especially thuggish
candidate for the *Sturmabteilung*'s goon squads?

92 WHY DIDN'T NIETZSCHE GET HIS ACT TOGETHER?

To be sure, the objection-in-progress to the synthesize-it-all-up view would be tricky to bring home if Nietzsche didn't regard those drives as unsavory. If he were proud of his misogyny and so on, why wouldn't he be even more proud of a drive that wove together the misogyny, antisemitism, and so on? And he certainly has had the reputation of indulging himself in that sort of pride.

We'll examine Nietzsche's take on antisemitism more closely in ch. 7. Apropos his patriotic enthusiasms, in his notebooks he recommends, as part of "the education of the philosopher," "to be desensitised to nationalism through early travels" (7:780/WEN 32[73], emph. deleted). For the moment, we can invoke a bit of biography to test how far he accommodated his misogyny. During the period in which the later works were composed, Nietzsche spent his summers at resort towns in Switzerland, where he got to know other tourists. The women whose acquaintance he made, with whom he conversed on lengthy walks and the like, subsequently remembered him as a kindly and gracious gentleman: not someone who made offensive remarks, or disrespected them, or was in any way a ranting, sexist boor. Evidently the relation between Nietzsche's personality, seen as a whole from the outside, and the drives within was anyway mediated and indirect. The misogyny may have been unchangeably there on the inside, but its expression was pretty clearly thwarted in the presence of its most obvious prompts.

Nietzsche, when he looks, finds himself to be ugly inside, and he clearly doesn't think he's by any means unique in that regard. The synthesis of ugly drives can be expected to produce an unattractive unified self (although we'll shortly be contemplating a more palatable illustration of a partial such synthesis).[42] So it's hard to believe that Nietzsche is recommending that, appropriating his famous phrasing, we become who we are by synthesizing ourselves up into a sort of super-drive. And the problem is not merely that the product would not look good; a unified self of that kind would *own* all those awful opinions and attitudes. The disunified self is able to hold parts of its psyche at arm's length, and in cases like this one (but, don't pretend: aren't we *all* like this one?) there's much to be said for that.

4.10

You're likely to remember Nietzsche insisting, especially in the *Genealogy* but elsewhere also, that morality as we have it is one-size-fits-all (it's *leveling*, as

WHO WAS NIETZSCHE'S "GOOD EUROPEAN"? 93

people used to say, and inevitably it's leveling downwards, towards the lowest common denominator). Since people don't come all in one size or shape, there has been far too much in the way of procrustean fitting of people to a system of moral values that aren't well suited to them: as he puts it in the book we're now examining, moralities "address themselves to 'all'... they generalize where one must not generalize" (5:118/BGE 198). Moreover, even the people for whom it's shaped are getting a catastrophically bad product: we're given to understand that moral values are palliative medication, an expedient for managing the incurably sick. The therapy actually makes their illness worse, even as it distracts them from the pain and discomfort. And here being sicker means, to a first approximation: crazier. The patients to whom these values are administered—this being what priestcraft, to use the Enlightenment term, consists in—start out bitterly and resentfully eating their hearts out, and they end up bizarrely masochistic and living inside self-induced delusions.

There's a further criticism of older systems of value: that to a great extent they came about by accident. Social processes produced them; there were charismatic, influential people to whom they just *occurred*. But nobody thoughtfully invented and chose values that would work well for their clients; the knowledge you'd need to do it well—just for starters: of how cultures operate, of how individuals work "physiologically"—all of that simply wasn't available. So *of course* all the value systems turned out to be wastefully destructive (and self-destructive) at worst, and homeopathic at best.

The solution that Nietzsche proposes—and this is one part of his philosophical output that seems to me genuinely inspiring, whether or not you buy into all of his critique[43]—is to invent replacements for the defective values with which we have been living.

> Where, then, must *we* reach with our hopes?
> Toward *new philosophers*; there is no choice; toward spirits strong and original enough to provide the stimuli for opposite valuations and to revalue and invert "eternal values"; toward forerunners, toward men of the future who in the present tie the knot and constraint that forces the will of millennia upon *new* tracks. (5:126/BGE 203)

These values will be thoughtfully, intelligently chosen; and although they will not necessarily be one-use-only (on the contrary: as we have just been told, some of them are expected to have very long half-lives),

94 WHY DIDN'T NIETZSCHE GET HIS ACT TOGETHER?

they'll be *idiosyncratic*: tailored, when necessary, to the unique needs of their clients.[44]

> Are these coming philosophers new friends of "truth"? That is probable enough, for all philosophers so far have loved their truths. But they will certainly not be dogmatists. It must offend their pride, also their taste, if their truth is supposed to be a truth for everyman—which has so far been the secret wish and hidden meaning of all dogmatic aspirations. "My judgment is *my* judgment": no one else is easily entitled to it—that is what such a philosopher of the future may perhaps say to himself. (5:60/BGE 43)

Recall that "positings of values . . . which have become dominant . . . are for a time called 'truths'" (5:144/BGE 211, emphasis deleted); we shouldn't be thinking of their values and these judgments as distinct. Consequently, our working definition of a philosopher of the future is going to be: someone who invents values in an intelligent but idiosyncratic manner. That allowed, the question of whether the implicit author of *Beyond Good and Evil* is, as Nehamas has claimed, a philosopher of the future comes down to whether he's able to occupy this role, that of an inventor of values.

4.11

When you ask a class, or anyway this is my experience, to try out the Nietzschean exercise of inventing values, their initial and almost uniform response is to switch around the evaluative labels on one or another familiar description. ("Freedom is bad," they might propose. "Mullets are good.") But this is not what Nietzsche has in mind, and it will be helpful to work through concrete instances of value invention that are, unlike the new values Nietzsche seems to have had foremost in mind, the very opposite of grandiose.

Consider for a moment what it would be for me to invent a low-key value I might put to my own personal use: say, a distinctive writing voice, intended to serve as my signature style. The writing voice is to be a standard, one to which I am held by myself and others, even though it is one that I have made up for myself. Past a certain point it will not be possible to specify its demands explicitly, but if I'm doing it right, not because those demands are indeterminate; rather, the value (*inter alia*, the novel standard, a new aspiration or ideal, an accompanying sensibility) I'm introducing isn't reducible to the values I have already available—even the ones that justify developing and adopting this new value—and one mark or symptom of that fact is my not having the vocabulary I would need to fully articulate it. Nonetheless, if the style does come to govern my prose consistently enough and for long enough, an attentive reader will be in a position to determine whether I'm adhering to it; think of how you notice stylistic lapses in the works of novelists, poets, and so on.

However, suppose that I'm *unable* to stick to my would-be writing voice, and the problem isn't confined to outliers. Perhaps, again and again, I fail to resist the temptation to mimic other authors; I easily fall under the stylistic influence of the last thing I happen to have read. Perhaps I get swept away by a sense of outrage, and shift from written to spoken register without meaning to; perhaps I can't stop myself from putting the silly puns that occur to me down on the page . . . if this *keeps* happening to me, then I *don't* have a signature style, and I've failed even to produce the stylistic standard at all. The standard is, after all, firmed up in the course of rigorously conforming to it; it's not as though it is there, beforehand, the moment I announce it. (Remember that I couldn't *say* what it was, even to myself.) If from the outset I fail to live up to it badly enough, there never *was* any standard.

That failure, in the low-key illustration, is produced by an inner life that might well be experienced as a field of jostling drives. The punning drive, the urge to savage parody, the inner pressure to imitate . . . each in its turn elbows the others out of the way and for a short while takes control of my pen. Each of these drives has its own distinctive register, and so it ensues that *I* fail to have any single and uniform writing style of my own; that is, I prove to be unable to create the personal and idiosyncratic value to which I aspire.

To invent a value is in the first place to lay down the law for oneself and to have it stick; if you don't get as far as that, being able to "tie the knot and constraint that forces the will of millennia upon new tracks" isn't even in the offing (emph. deleted). Philosophers (as distinguished from "philosophical laborers") "*create values*":

> *Genuine philosophers . . . are commanders and legislators*: they say, "*thus* it shall be!" . . . Their "knowing" is *creating*, their creating is a legislation, their will to truth is—*will to power*. (5:145/BGE 211)

But this sort of legislation is possible only when the would-be philosopher of the future is capable of shutting down a pending deviation from that legislation, in the first place within himself.

It looks offhand like this is possible only when one is a unified agent: perhaps in the mode of an absolutist polity, perhaps as a personality that has reached (or almost reached) the limit of cognitive synthesis, and now is (or almost is) a single hyperarticulated drive; in any case, when one is not the Good European, as we've seen him in *Beyond Good and Evil*, the character whose unintegrated drives are constantly going off on jags and tangents. Nehamas notices that "the genuine philosopher's concept of greatness includes 'precisely strength of will, hardness, and the capacity for long-range decisions,'" and concludes that "*Beyond Good and Evil* itself *is* a philosophy of the future; its narrator (and its author as well) is a genuine philosopher."[45] That is a mistake: what's being exhibited to us is someone who is incapable of strength of will, of long-range decisions (or even short-range ones), and who therefore cannot be a legislator of values, that is, a philosopher of the future—and, yes, that is the *point*.

4.12

What's being elaborately and theatrically displayed for us is a minefield we can now see to lie between us and the realization of the new metavalue toward which we're being pointed: the value of inventing values. The Good European can't invent values, but—to put one of my cards on the table—*Nietzsche* can, and this is one of them. Since Nietzsche is, in my view, in a different way a disunified agent, his solution will involve taking back that offhand assessment of a moment back, that only unified agents can invent values.[46] I'll begin with a version of the problem that will become a more pressing issue down the road, and which is interesting in the context of those recent reconstructions of his views I gestured at in sec. 4.4. Then I'll proceed to the Good European's own way of rendering the Catch-22.

Suppose the invention of values to be the prerogative of the unified personality. The unified personality is the gradual product of the synthesis of, in the first place, drives. But the merger of disparate drives into a new drive with a more articulated aim is normally mediated by values; and in the case of the sort of personality that will be prepared to invent new values, mediated by values that aren't already available.

Let's sketch an almost-realistic illustration of the process we're imagining. If I were to look back at my own childhood through the lenses of Nietzschean theory (the version I was recapitulating in sec. 4.7, and towards the end of sec. 4.4), I would see my earlier psyche containing a drive to read—one expressing itself in the indiscriminate consumption of books. Probably I would also identify a drive to have *views*, expressing itself in all manner of (usually loud) opinions about things; a drive to write (again, indiscriminately); a drive to figure things out (but only certain sorts of thing) and so on. These drives, I would notice, were prone to get in each other's way; the child I was would have finished the unputdownable book, and suddenly realize that it was too late to start in on his writing assignment. All these drives (and of course others) competed with one another for scarce resources, for my time and energy—or maybe the scarce resource was *me*.

At some point, these drives were exposed to a *value*, one that was new to them, namely, *philosophy*. The new value served as something on the order of a catalyst for the drives: they folded together, and now this merged drive expresses itself in my trying to figure out specifically philosophical problems, in my articulating specifically philosophical ideas, in writing them out—and the reading, no longer indiscriminate, is in service of all that. Once the drives have been synthesized, the regulation of competing drives that formerly was such a problem pretty much takes care of itself.[47] Here we want to notice two things: that what effected the merger was a value, one that was already culturally available, and came with a great deal of articulated content; and that this particular value was able to do its job because it was equipped to give uptake to the actually quite generic drives already present in my younger self's personality.

The best candidates to be inventors of novel, idiosyncratic values will be those whose freestanding drives are *not* generic; whose drives will only fold together into some *non*standard configuration; who are *un*responsive to the culturally available values. In order to become the unified personalities who could be philosophers of the future, they need to avail themselves of the values only they can create, and which they can only create once they've become philosophers of the future. After all, the values capable of mediating synthesis of their drives are nonstandard; who but they could be positioned to shape the idiosyncratic values that they need?

Once again, I don't think that Nietzsche noticed or described quite this version of the problem we're now considering. And I don't want to claim that it's insurmountable. (Just for instance, you might wonder whether

98 WHY DIDN'T NIETZSCHE GET HIS ACT TOGETHER?

values could be explored imaginatively by a disunified agent, someone whose personality would coalesce simultaneously with the adoption of a new value, in something with the feel of a gestalt shift.) But it does suggest that we should see the path to becoming a philosopher of the future as much less straightforward than we might have anticipated or hoped.

Notice that we've stumbled on a further reason for rejecting the fully synthesized agent as an ideal and aspiration. Suppose we put to one side for a moment the problem of the unpalatable motivations that Nietzsche found within himself; after all, we've just given an illustration of a handful of much more acceptable drives being integrated into a drive toward philosophy— and what's wrong with *that*? What if someone was lucky enough not to have the sort of seedy underside that Nietzsche was portraying for us; wouldn't it be reasonable to aim for unity of agency in that case?

That doesn't seem to me to be the lesson of the example, however. Let's suppose that there's nothing wrong with a drive for social status *per se*; let's allow that there's nothing wrong with a desire for affirmation: to have what one is doing acknowledged and approved of, and to get what, in the 1960s, Eric Berne called "stroking." We can recognize these as entirely legitimate human needs, which—unlike misogyny and our other earlier examples—are nothing to be ashamed of. But we know what it looks like when these drives are integrated with a philosophy drive: you get careerist, compromised, pandering, and corrupt philosophy. In general, the integration of one's motivations has to be carefully circumscribed.[48]

4.13

At this point you might be wondering whether there's a workaround, one that wouldn't have occurred to someone living in a nineteenth-century economy, but which ought to seem live to us now. Formerly, garments were tailored to the person who was going to wear them; at some point the market grew enough to allow mass-produced clothes, purchased off the rack, in a vast range of sizes and fashion options. If there is a large enough buffet or smorgasbord of culturally available niche-marketed values, perhaps hardly anyone will need to invent values for themselves—in which case, the barriers to doing so will no longer be a pressing concern.

WHO WAS NIETZSCHE'S "GOOD EUROPEAN"? 99

Here I'm going to adduce my own experience, living in what is perhaps the most consumer-oriented economy in the world, as anecdotal evidence that we can't count on being well served this way. (If I come off as precious, my apologies.) I hike and, as a vegetarian, avoid leather footwear; over the course of my adult life, I've only sporadically been able to buy acceptable boots, which is to say that even when one's preferences are shared by a good many people, the invisible hand still can't be bothered. I live in a house that doesn't fit what I do over the course of the day; I can't afford a custom-built house, but for those who can, the normal remedy is having an architect design a home around their needs and preferences. I cook regularly, in good part because it's hard to find food I want to eat served in restaurants. And I could go on in this vein indefinitely; my life as a consumer consists for the most part in putting up with standardized niche products that don't fit me or my life very well. Why expect niche-marketed values to do any better?

Keep in mind that not everyone, in Nietzsche's view, needs to be in the business of inventing new values; different people have different needs. As I mentioned a few moments back, my younger self seems to have done perfectly well with an off-the-shelf value—although in ch. 11 we'll be able to reconsider just how much of a readymade it ended up being. There are a great many people who are happy with what they're served in chain restaurants, who are fully content with the clothing they find at the mall, who don't drift out the front door of the furniture store wondering why they don't see anything they'd want to take home. If you're one of them— if you're happy with the selection of more tangible commodities on offer— you may be likewise expect to be satisfied with an analogous market of prefabricated values. And maybe you will be . . . but then again, maybe you won't. Sometimes some of us *will* need those genuinely original values, and then the Nietzschean worry—that those of us who do are not equipped to produce the values we need—is live.[49]

4.14

You can't do a good job of inventing values the way Nietzsche wants you to—that is, not, as in the past, *blindly*, and also, not out of mere malice—unless you're widely informed and well informed. You have to

100 WHY DIDN'T NIETZSCHE GET HIS ACT TOGETHER?

be scholarly—*wissenschaftlich*—which involves being objective; you have to appreciate the lessons of history, especially regarding the effects that different systems of values have had on the populations that adopted them; you also must pay close attention to the physiological effects of various aspects of the management of day-to-day life; and there is much else besides.

To get all of this right—in particular, to harvest the lessons of history, and I'll confine my attention to that for now—you have to be very good at what subsequently came to be called *Verstehen*: the sensitivity that permits you to understand past and foreign ways of thinking and feeling *from the inside*. Because the lessons of history will come from *many* bygone cultures, it won't suffice to immerse yourself in *one* ancient civilization, in the way that the classicist whom Nietzsche started out being had done. You must be able to put on and take off the mindsets of other cultures rather as though they were items in your wardrobe, and we have become unprecedentedly well suited for it: "we are the first age that has truly studied 'costumes'—I mean those of moralities, articles of faith, tastes in the arts, and religions... this historical sense to which we Europeans lay claim as our speciality... only the nineteenth century knows this sense, as its sixth sense."[50]

The ability to doff and don *Weltanschauungen* has as a matter of fact, Nietzsche thinks, become almost normal in his day and age. (Looking back at the historiography of the era, we may think otherwise; but that's neither here nor there.) Now, if you *are* capable of this sort of emotional and intellectual shape-shifting, you don't have a strong or stable personality. But strong and stable personalities are what is needed for the creation of new values. Thus the two primary requirements on philosophers of the future—they aren't, like previous founders, simply ignorant of everything they would need to do the job right; they have the firm, unswerving, unbending, uncompromising consistency needed to institute new standards—are incompatible. Anyway on the face of it, to have the one is to lack the other: "*der wissenschaftliche Mensch*"—the scientific or scholarly person—is "a type that does not dominate and is neither authoritative nor self-sufficient" (5:133/BGE 206), but self-sufficient authority is just what is needed to legislate values: do not confuse the "objective spirit," we are warned, "with the *philosopher*" (5:134, 136/BGE 207).

I agree with Nietzsche in taking the problem to be solvable. After all, I gave a low-key example of value invention a turn or two back, and it's easy to supplement it with others. The founders of new cuisines (think Alice Waters

WHO WAS NIETZSCHE'S "GOOD EUROPEAN"? 101

and Deborah Madison) institute new standards that suit their own taste, and which aren't for everyone. (They institute new *tastes*, which aren't reducible even to the previous tastes of the innovating chefs.) In the previous chapter, we emphasized the work it takes to make a value socially and personally real, and here we can underscore that point, using this easygoing example. As the founding chef of Greens, in San Francisco, Madison put the contours of her new standards and aspirations on display, and not just for a day; the restaurant turned out meals in her style of cooking, consistently, year in and year out. She wrote cookbooks, giving instructions reliably enabling home cooks to prepare her cuisine for themselves, and so to experience it first-hand. In these ways and others, she educated a clientele to appreciate the food. She developed suppliers; the restaurant has its own farm, Green Gulch in Marin, I expect because only by being very hands-on about ingredients was it possible to maintain the standards she was creating. Briefly, on the one hand, creating a new value is not merely a matter of pronouncing its existence; on the other, when the work *is* done, Madison's version of New California Cuisine witnesses that it is doable. What's more, although I don't know her personally, I don't see any evidence of disunified agency in her work; the issue Nietzsche frets about seems not to arise.

Likewise, corporate branding done right can be tantamount to Nietzschean value invention.[51] And more ambitiously, we might look back, in our own disciplinary history, to the founders of philosophical traditions. Each tradition introduces standards for what counts as philosophy done right, and although at the outset the uptake is normally a little bumpy—we analytic philosophers tend to shake our heads when we read writing from the 1930s and 1940s—a few generations in, the aspirations and directives have become a kind of academic second nature. Since the thing *is* done, frequently enough, evidently it *can* be.

4.15

Two of the solutions Nietzsche floats—that scholars will serve the legislators, and that a legislator of values will have scholarship in his personal history—seem to me to be red herrings, but they have a close structural resemblance to a proposal Nietzsche makes in the book we're going to take up next.[52] Since we've been thinking about what it takes to introduce new values, let's look ahead to this one, as orientation for the upcoming chapter.

102 WHY DIDN'T NIETZSCHE GET HIS ACT TOGETHER?

In a section of *Thus Spoke Zarathustra* (a work that we've argued needs to be used very carefully, however), we're informed that those who learn too much cultural history have so many modes of comporting themselves available from their study of the past that they no longer know who they really are—and in fact, there's *nobody* who they really are (4:153–155/Z II.14). Elsewhere, Nietzsche worried that having to learn everything a value inventor needs to know is likely in various ways to ruin you for the task (11:518f/WLN 35[24]).

For what it's worth, this concern does seem realistic to me. At Ivy League universities, seniors tend to apply for the wide range of available year-abroad fellowships on offer. By and large, each application requires the student to invent a different story about who they are and why they're a good fit for that Marshall or Rhodes or whatever it is. And again and again one sees the successful graduate spending their year at Oxford or on the Pacific Rim or wherever it worked out to be having an identity crisis; having remade themselves into one person after another in rapid succession, they emerge from the final spate of interviews confused about who they are and what they want to do with themselves.

But in both the Preface and the penultimate section of *The Gay Science*, Nietzsche seems to be recommending an even more violent version of this sort of preparation. To be knowledgeable in the ways that would position you to be an inventor of the sorts of values he has in mind, you need to have

> know[n] from the adventures of [your] own most authentic experience how a discoverer and conqueror of the ideal feels, and also an artist, a saint, a legislator, a sage, a scholar, a pious man, a soothsayer, and one who stands divinely apart in the old style (3:636/GS 382)

—moreover, you need to have been *sick* repeatedly and with many different illnesses, because

> A philosopher who has traversed many kinds of health, and keeps traversing them, has passed through an equal number of philosophies; he simply *cannot* keep from transposing his states every time into the most spiritual form and distance: this art of transfiguration *is* philosophy.
>
> (3:349/GS P.3)

What we now recognize as the philosophers of the future require "a new means," the ability "to have experienced the whole range of values and desiderata to date" (3:635f/GS 382). And that, we can see, is a problematic demand: how can someone who is this internally unstable be in the business of inventing values?

Nietzsche's response is to announce a new value, which he calls "the *great health*," and which seems to be meant as a sort of meta-health: the ability to live through one after another physiological state (including many uncontroversial illnesses), in a way that allows you to learn from the experience of sickness, yet without undermining your potential as a legislator of values. And now we see all of the problems and challenges we have been surveying rearise at this next level: that you don't create a value merely by announcing it; that the contents of values have to be filled in and made substantial, and that in the meantime, we have no idea what this one would look like, or how it could work.[53]

Nietzsche's interpreters have been trained to treat announcements of this sort as certifying an accomplishment; if we are told of "a new health," it must be already a worked-out conception, and no doubt to be attributed to Nietzsche, or anyhow to his authors. But we're learning to take Nietzsche at his word in a different manner: until the new value is stabilized and imbued with determinate content, we can't know whether it will even have turned out to be possible. If it isn't, and Nietzschean value invention is contingent on realizing it, it will be like getting told that an elevator to low-earth orbit can be built just as soon as we can lay our hands on a large supply of unobtainium.

Looking ahead, we've been primed to search for answers in the self-presentations of the authors of Nietzsche's books. Since the author of *The Gay Science* is about to tell us that he has "become well again" (3:347/GS P.2), and since the criterion he's invoking is that new value, we'll want to see whether it's been convincingly filled out, and whether to the extent that it has taken shape, it speaks to the problem of those *prima facie* jointly unsatisfiable demands.

4.16

I suggested a few moments back that when we look to low-key and real-life cases, the invention of values seems difficult but quite doable, the objections we have just considered notwithstanding. What then was Nietzsche's contribution on this front, if his demand is already being met? We can think of it as having three prongs.

104 WHY DIDN'T NIETZSCHE GET HIS ACT TOGETHER?

First of all, he's bringing to our attention that there is something that we do, but which we can do more of, and do differently. Shifting back from the metavalue to first-order values, that we already *do* do something, but that there are standards yet to be produced for doing it, that it has yet to be noticed, is yet to be valued, and done in a manner that reflects its value— these are compatible.

> What is originality? *To see* something that has no name as yet and hence cannot be mentioned although it stares us all in the face. The way men usually are, it takes a name to make something visible for them.
>
> (3:517/GS 261)

People on occasion ate brightly prepared vegetarian food well before Edward Espe Brown, Deborah Madison, and Annie Somerville. Nevertheless, it makes a great deal of difference to have the style marked out by exemplary restaurants, well-authored cookbooks, and so on. And after the cuisine had been established, people, a good many of them, ate their vegetarian food *differently*.

Returning to the metavalue, although we have in the past improvised novel values, we somehow haven't *noticed* that we do this, and we don't value it as we should. And so we don't seek out occasions to invent values; we don't prepare ourselves to invent them. Probably part of the reason is that we've been handicapped by a professional philosophers' metaethical ideology (itself a reflection of popular metaethical ideology), which presumes values to be either facts, which you might discover, but more likely take yourself to already know; or a more or less fancy *whim*, a projection of a feeling or attitude you happen to have, and so, not something you could deliberately choose to fabricate. These options have posed a dilemma that has prevented us from grasping what it would be to invent a value, and also what values, the sort that we might invent, would be like; Nietzsche is offering us a path between the horns of that dilemma.[54] The awareness Nietzsche is trying to get us to have, that this sort of thing can be done on a much grander scale than, as in my first illustration, the adoption of a distinctive prose style, and that this is an aspiration worthy of our deepest ambition—that will be his (but not the Good European's) invention of a value, one that he hopes will mobilize us in ways we have not seen for a while, or perhaps ever.

Second, Nietzsche is posing a problem in *Beyond Good and Evil*: that it's something of a mystery that we *can* arrive at what lies "beyond good and evil"—beyond the corrosive, damaging straitjacket of the values we have inherited—or rather, that *we* could possibly legislate the sort of values that Nietzsche is determined to have us invent. Again, on the one hand, we have cultural (or perhaps it would be better to say, spiritual) resources that put us in an unprecedentedly good position to take that step: historical awareness, a painfully trained sense of truthfulness, and the self-overcoming of that sense of truthfulness (meaning, we are now too truthful to take the value of truth at face value). But on the other hand, our characters are not those of legislators of value, and not coincidentally.

Third and finally, Nietzsche is mandating this sort of legislation of value (or perhaps, inviting us to give ourselves such a mandate): the invention of novel values *is to become* a guiding priority.

Let's pause to collect the observations we've culled from the book—and also to consider what our own philosophical uptake of Nietzsche's moves should be. We've had the shortcomings of the templates we use for describing our own and others' psychologies brought to our attention, by having a character exhibited to us who doesn't fit those templates well at all. So however we proceed with our interpretation of Nietzsche, a first agenda item for us philosophers generally, and one on which we haven't made much progress in the intervening hundred and thirty years, is to develop alternatives to techniques of psychological description that build what Nietzsche called atomism into the notation.

Although I'm not ready to sign on to much of what Nietzsche thinks about the history and the real functions of the values we now live by, it does seem plausible that our action-guiding standards are formulated for agents who are at least pretty good approximations to those atomistic selves. Values (and moralities) should have actually existing clients. And so the investigation and development of values that are substantially different than those to which we've become accustomed seems to me well motivated.

We've resisted Nehamas's reading of *Beyond Good and Evil* on a number of points, but on our way to making the book readable we've further confirmed the correctness of his approach to this body of texts: the way to read *Nietzsche's* later writings (but I'm not making any claims about textual exegesis in general) is to ask who their author is supposed to be. But in doing

106 WHY DIDN'T NIETZSCHE GET HIS ACT TOGETHER?

so, and in view of Nietzsche's objections to atomism, we have to be very careful indeed about what assumptions we import from the theory of agency and action theory.

Finally, since the improvement on prior practice that Nietzsche is demanding is that novel values be introduced thoughtfully, deliberately, and in a way that's appropriate to their clients, we need to assess this very value—the metavalue of inventing values—in precisely this manner. Once we've thought through what it takes to invent such values, perhaps using case studies like those mentioned in passing, each of us will be in a position to form a judgment—not necessarily, as we noted, a judgment that will suit anyone else—as to whether to proceed, and act on the basis of Nietzsche's novel metavalue.

Appendix: Unpacking BGE §15

One of the entries early on in *Beyond Good and Evil* has occasioned a certain degree of puzzlement in Nietzsche's readers. I quote the section in its entirety:

> To study physiology with a clear conscience, once must insist that the sense organs are *not* phenomena in the sense of idealistic philosophy; as such they could not be causes! Sensualism, therefore, at least as a regulative hypothesis, if not as a heuristic principle.
>
> What? And others even say that the external world is the work of our organs? But then our body, as part of this external world, would be the work of our organs! But then our organs themselves would be—the work of our organs! It seems to me that this is a complete *reductio ad absurdum*, assuming that the concept of a *causa sui* is something fundamentally absurd. Consequently, the external world is *not* the work of our organs—?
>
> (5:29/BGE 15)

The objection he ponders is that on this neo-Kantian view, the material bodies are artefacts of our cognitive processing, which happens in our sensory organs and our brains. Now, mere artefacts aren't real: so they can't *do* things (and more generally, can't figure into genuine causal explanations). So the material bodies aren't real and can't figure into genuine causal explanations. But our sensory organs and our brains are material bodies. So on such a view, our sensory organs and our brains aren't real and can't figure into genuine

WHO WAS NIETZSCHE'S "GOOD EUROPEAN"? 107

causal explanations. The neo-Kantian version of synthesis is (supposed to be) a genuine causal explanation; it seems to follow that the neo-Kantian view is self-refuting.

Anderson, 2002, provides a careful and instructive reading of the passage.[55] He points to an extant version of the problematic view, which can be found at some length in a chapter titled "The Physiology of the Sense-Organs and the World as Representation," in Lange, 1950:[56]

> The physiology of the sense-organs is developed or corrected Kantianism, and Kant's system may, as it were, be regarded as a programme for modern discoveries in this field. (pp. 202f)

and Lange informs us of his conclusions:

1. The sense-world is a product of our organisation.
2. Our visible (bodily) organs are, like all other parts of the phenomenal world, only pictures of an unknown object.
3. The transcendental basis of our organisation remains therefore just as unknown to us as the things which act upon it. We have always before us merely the product of both. (p. 219)

> The eye, with which we believe we see, is itself only a product of our ideas; and when we find that our visual images are produced by the structure of the eye, we must never forget that the eye too with its arrangements, the optic nerve with the brain and all the structures which we may yet discover there as causes of thought, are only ideas, which indeed form a self-coherent world... (vol. iii, p. 224)

On the one hand, we're told that "the physiology of the sense-organs, has...produced decisive grounds for the refutation of Materialism" (vol. iii, p. 84); on the other, earlier on, in vol. ii, at Book II, p. 195n, that: "We must not...talk of the organisation of the *mind*, for this is transcendental, and therefore co-ordinated with other transcendental assumptions. We must rather understand by...physico-psychical organisation, what to our external sense appears to be that part of the physical organisation which stands in the most immediate causal relation with the psychical functions"; earlier in the note Lange remarks that the phrase "physico-psychical organisation" "is an attempt to indicate the idea that the physical organisation, as *phenomenon*, is at the same time the psychical one."

108 WHY DIDN'T NIETZSCHE GET HIS ACT TOGETHER?

However, I'm inclined to read the section we are considering as an argument for Schopenhauer's resolution of the tension. Schopenhauer also seems to have maintained both that our experiences are a product of our empirically discernable cognitive processing, taking place largely in the brain, and that one's brain, along with everything else, is merely part of the phenomenal world, which floats, as it were, atop the unstructured, roiling world of noumenal will.[57]

He managed to square these apparently incompatible views by adapting and extending a doctrine of Kant's, found in his *Religion within the Limits of Reason Alone* (1998): that the causally structured and deterministic world supervenes on noumenal free choices of character. (In Kant, standing back from the phenomenal world as it were, you choose the kind of person you are, and then your character plays out in the law-governed events in which you take part; in Schopenhauer's even more extreme version, your body expresses your underlying noumenal will: everyone, animals included, gets the body they deserve.) When Nietzsche points out the incoherence in Lange-like views, and concludes with the question that commentators have found so puzzling, I rather expect that he is reminding us of Schopenhauer's solution, which at the time would have been widely known. That solution does seem to prefigure certain aspects of the will-to-power metaphysics so often attributed to Nietzsche, and so the gesture may be intended as softening up for his own ideas.

Second Interlude: Was Nietzsche a Nazi?

In its literal sense, of course the question posed in this title is to be answered in the negative; the term is anachronistic, in that Germany's National Socialist party was founded a good while after Nietzsche died. Nonetheless, it flags an issue to which we have to face up. It has seemed to a good many onlookers—Albert Camus being perhaps one of the more thoughtful—that what Hitler and his followers did counted as taking Nietzsche's ideas to their logical conclusion, as in this take on the Eternal Return:

> To say yes to everything supposes that one says yes to murder . . . If the master says yes to everything, he consents to slavery and the suffering of others; and the result is the tyrant and the glorification of murder.[1]

The Nazis seemed to have adopted Nietzsche as *their* philosopher: as Crane Brinton put it, writing during World War II, "the works of Nietzsche are one of the principal divisions of the National Socialists' holy writings." And he further remarked on the unnerving "similarity in the general emotional tone (as distinct from specific ideas) of Nietzsche's writings and that of the utterances of the Nazi leaders." At the very beginning of our discussion, we had occasion to mention Hitler's staged photo op at the then-Nietzsche Archive; German soldiers were sent to the front with excerpts from Nietzsche's writings in their duffel bags; it was perhaps no accident that Heidegger, who thoroughly accommodated himself to the regime, gave his lectures on Nietzsche during that time.[2]

After the war, making Nietzsche palatable both within academia and to the general public required explaining away the apparently intimate connection between his philosophical output and the ensuing catastrophe, and the enterprise of reclaiming Nietzsche proceeded on two fronts.

First, it was pointed out that the Nazis were not the only ones to look up to Nietzsche; there was the socialist left, the *fin de siècle* youth movement, Christian theologians, Thomas Mann, trade fair promoters, you name it. If intellectuals and movements of almost any stripe could find him to be an inspiration, the fact that one particularly disreputable movement did so does not, it was argued, show there to be any special affinity between the work and the horrific deeds. Moreover, the case was made that members of the professoriat who did not flee Germany generally adjusted themselves to their political environment; those who stayed, and who took a professional interest in Nietzsche, would in any case present Nietzsche as congenial to the mandated ideology.[3]

But second, and for our purposes more importantly, it was argued that Nietzsche's doctrines were misappropriated and misrepresented by the German far right. Walter Kaufmann, whose translations I've been using, was perhaps the most important figure in this attempt to sanitize Nietzsche and render him intellectually respectable. Both in his influential book and his footnote commentary to those translations, Kaufmann made the case that the Nazis had misread passage after passage, had overlooked inconvenient stretches of text, and had been aided and abetted by the misrepresentations of Nietzsche's sister. Elizabeth Förster-Nietzsche had married a political antisemite, had actually moved to Paraguay with him to found a racially pure Aryan colony, and had later on presented *The Will to Power*, her selection of

110 WHY DIDN'T NIETZSCHE GET HIS ACT TOGETHER?

Nietzsche's journal entries, and thus a selection which reflected her temperament and sensibilities, as Nietzsche's own not-quite-finished *magnum opus*.[4]

Although his own personal sensitivities show through, and although one frequently has the sense of someone trying too hard, Kaufmann's case is persuasive; I won't rehearse it here.[5] Over and above the long and well-documented list of mistaken constructions put on Nietzsche's texts, it is quite clear that Nietzsche, had he lived long enough to encounter them in person, would have regarded the Nazis with disdain, as crude vulgarians and, intellectually, a lost cause. And, borrowing once more Brinton's pithy way of putting things, "it would be possible to list numerous specific passages from Nietzsche's work which, if written in Germany today"—again, this was penned while the Nazi regime was a going concern—"would probably send the author straight to a concentration camp" (1940, p. 140). In short, I agree with Kaufmann that the uses to which German revolutionary nationalism put Nietzsche would have sent him spinning in his grave.[6]

The question, however, is whether that disqualifies their interpretation. Let me say straight out that for my own part I endorse a practice of interpretation on which it does; the interpretation is to be held responsible to—and adjusted to fit—the text, and not the other way around.[7] But we have seen at any rate one of Nietzsche's ways of thinking about interpretation, on which it imposes a new purpose or function on older materials—and those materials themselves are: just raw material. The notion that interpretation is *faithful* to those materials doesn't belong to that way of thinking and, reminding you of the drift of the previous Interlude, a decent icon for this version of the concept can be found in the town where Nietzsche ended his life. The Nazis had meant to build regional administrative centers, to include, besides offices, space for mass rallies and other party activities; come the end of the war, the structure in Weimar was almost finished. The Communist East German government repurposed it, using the rally area as a parking lot, some of the office space for daycare, and so on; that involved a certain amount of remodeling. With the fall of the Communist government, the facility was in due course repurposed once again, this time as a mall. *That's* interpretation, according to the *Genealogy*.

The Nazis imposed an interpretation on the writings that Nietzsche left behind which cherry-picked, distorted, and abused those texts, and to reiterate, Kaufmann and others have done a thorough job of documenting that. But if the Nazis were after all just doing what Nietzsche himself thought interpretation *was*, how could he have had grounds for complaint? And is it obvious that Kaufmann—or anyone else—has standing to complain on his behalf?

If that was Nietzsche's conception of interpretation, why is it an objection to someone's appropriation of Nietzsche's texts when the reading proves unfaithful? And now we can lay out what looks like a problem for the way I am proceeding myself. On the face of it, it's only grounds for complaint if you think that Nietzsche's views of interpretation are just *wrong*; but if his views are wrong, why is it you also think he's philosophically interesting? To overstate the dilemma just slightly, either Nietzsche isn't worth anyone's time, or we don't get to complain about what the Nazis did with him.

We've begun making the case that Nietzsche's later books present us with authorial personae—in the case of the *Genealogy*, that of an intellectual or academic, someone who turns out to be deeply bitter, and who is unable to keep track of his own views long enough to avoid contradicting himself, often from page to page. We shouldn't be too hasty to attribute the Genealogist's theory of interpretation to Nietzsche across the board: anticipating our discussion in ch. 9, maybe this is how interpretation looks within the Genealogist's perspective; perspectives, as we'll see, provide very one-sided views of whatever comes within their ambits.

As we'll also be seeing, Nietzsche hopes to bypass the problem he's identified in *Zarathustra*, by providing a fast-forward alternative to the lengthy process of developing an institutionally sanctioned and maintained reading of a text. But because he saw the problem he was trying to avoid as that of being *misread*, we cannot presume him to have a view of interpretation on which nothing could count as a misreading—or on which a misreading is no fault. And because to take an interest in Nietzsche is not simply to adopt his views, the question of how to read him correctly, while not simply dismissing his ideas, is a problem for *us*.

I'm going to postpone speaking directly to the question of what method of interpretation I'm bringing to bear on Nietzsche's writings, and how far it's reasonable for me to do so, to our third and final Interlude. For now, keep in mind that once the question of Nietzsche's responsibility for Nazism comes up, it's harder to get him off the hook than you might think: he is not by any means a safe or innocuous philosopher.

5

Who Was Nietzsche's Convalescent?

(How to Read *The Gay Science*)

Let's begin with a literary question (we'll get to the philosophy in a moment). *The Gay Science* is generally felt to be a turning point in Friedrich Nietzsche's writing; together with *Thus Spoke Zarathustra*, it marks off the little-read middle-period works from his mature output. But in my experience, readers find it harder than expected to say just what the change of direction was; the book superficially resembles both previous and later work (especially *Daybreak* and *Beyond Good and Evil*, respectively). Can we give a clean description both of what falls on the two sides of the dividing line, and of why Nietzsche found it necessary to step over it?

In the previous chapters, I've suggested that the books dating to Nietzsche's late period are meant to present us with distinct characters, namely, their implicit or "postulated" authors. We're used to the idea that readers are to identify and keep track of the narrator of a poem or novel; the exercise we're being invited to perform is similar but, as it were, taking one further step backwards. Each of them, I've been arguing, is put before us in order to make a philosophical point.

The Gay Science went through two editions, the latter supplementing the original four Books with a new Preface and a fifth and final Book.[1] (There's also some bad verse, which in the interests of charity we'll ignore.) If I'm seeing it right, the first edition predates that series of persona-construction exercises, and is to be read as a further advance along Nietzsche's earlier philosophical trajectory; the second edition converts the book into that much less straightforward, much more self-aware enterprise: what is in the first place a portrait of the very person who had written those earlier works. That reframing ought to allow us to inspect and assess Nietzsche's reasons for committing himself to the literary device that gave its shape to the later compositions for which he's so well known. And as we do so, a number of the ideas in play in the book can be expected to come into sharper focus.

Why Didn't Nietzsche Get His Act Together? Elijah Millgram, Oxford University Press. © Oxford University Press 2023.
DOI: 10.1093/oso/9780197669303.003.0005

The jigsaw puzzle we're about to reassemble has a great many pieces, among them, Nietzsche's appropriation of the aphoristic tradition of French philosophy, his account of realism, his interest in Stendhal and in the troubadours, his largely unnoticed contribution to post-Kantian metaphysics and epistemology—and I'll also have occasion to register in passing his uptake of Ralph Waldo Emerson. (However, in this chapter I'll be able to bypass the two most-discussed doctrines of *The Gay Science*, namely, the death of God and the Eternal Return.) What with all those moving parts, the usual preview of the order of proceedings would be unhelpful, and I'll have to ask you for another helping of patience. But I can tell you up front that the picture printed on the puzzle will turn out to be of the self-overcoming of nihilism. The opening section of the book, as it was originally published, is titled "The teachers of the purpose of existence" (3:369/GS 1); by the time he finished its second edition, Nietzsche, or anyway the character he's giving us, had found a distinctive way into that line of work.

If the book does present us with a character, what should we name him? In his Preface, the author refers to himself as "Mr Nietzsche" (3:347/GS P.2), but one of the items that we have on our to-do list is the question of whether the character on display and the real human being doing the writing are one and the same. In any case, I'm in the course of arguing that Nietzsche's later works are meant to exhibit *different* characters. So we will want to select a way of referring to this particular character that leaves both those questions open. Naturally, the title of the work suggests calling him "the gay scientist," but that phrase comes with too many misleading connotations.

However, we're told at the outset that Mr Nietzsche is recovering from a long illness, and is feeling "the gratitude of a convalescent." Accordingly, let's dub the authorial protagonist *Nietzsche's Convalescent*; as our argument proceeds, it will I hope show the decision to be not unreasonable. With *that* label, our next question has to be what he's recovering from, and we shouldn't assume that we have to choose between a literal recovery from a medical issue or a metaphorical recovery from a philosophical one. Later on in the book, we have it explained to us that "philosophical idealism"—taking abstractions as one's philosophical preoccupation, as in Plato; Kant is alluded to also—is either a way of managing the sensual side of one's personality or simply a *disease*. Thus a philosophical stance, Nietzsche has it, need not be distinct from plain and simple bodily illness or decrepitude.[2] Getting a little bit ahead of our story, our protagonist's illness purports to be *realism*, and let's start in by explaining what, in Nietzsche's view, it amounts to.

5.1

In our academic culture, "realism" has come to mean two apparently very different things. To metaphysicians, it's the notion that there's a way things really are, which might well be different from how we think them to be—in an older philosophical vocabulary, different from the appearances.[3] In political science, however, realism denotes a cluster of ideas, emotional postures, and policy positions that echo the sound of "*Realpolitik*": for instance, that whatever they may *say*, political actors are pursuing their interests; that toughminded, straight-shooting, hard-bitten participants in the political arena acknowledge this without regrets; and that the political actors with which one identifies (one's nation-state, usually) had better do the same.

Now, in the way of seeing things that we find in *The Gay Science* (but not only there), these are just differently accented expressions of a *single* attitude. A term that entered Italian political vocabulary around the 1970s, *dietrologia*, captures the common element nicely. *Behindology*, to put it into English, is the insistence that the right question about almost anything is (and now try to hear the paranoia in the voice), "What's really behind that?" A metaphysical realist thinks that behind the appearances, shaped as they are by our sensory equipment, our cognitive processing, our cultural baggage, and even our mere location are the things in themselves, which the Kantians held to be so alien as to be literally inconceivable. A political realist thinks that behind the pleasant, humane appearances—altruistic concern for the welfare of others, for human rights, etc.—is the raw and often underhanded pursuit of self-interest. When a behindologist starts looking into things, he's usually already halfway to a conspiracy theory.

Nietzsche takes an interest in two contrasting aims of behindology (where this contrast is orthogonal to that other contrast we've just introduced). One of them caters to human beings' very peculiar need for life to have a purpose; the traditional way of providing it has been "invent[ing] a second, different existence [which] unhinges by means of [t]his new mechanics the old, ordinary existence" (3:371/GS 1)—cosmologies containing a heaven, a hell, a purgatory, and so on being the nearest-to-hand and most straightforward example. The other spirit in which a realist strategy is put to work is that of unmasking and undercutting the naive beliefs that have allowed people to feel comfortably at home in a meaningful world: you came to get help from the Great and Powerful Oz, but behind the curtain, it's really just a con man; adolescents think that they're being uplifted and transfigured by love, but actually it's just hormones. Nowadays, we would call this "cynicism"; although Nietzsche, who started out as a classicist and knew very well what the ancient cynics had been about, would have raised his eyebrows at this abuse of the term, I'll be helping myself to the contemporary idiomatic sense; I'll also use "behindology" and "realism," along with their paronyms, as equivalents.

5.2

Robert Pippin's recent discussion of *The Gay Science* was originally published in French under the very suggestive title, "Nietzsche, moraliste français"; although, as I'm about to argue, that characterization is only sometimes correct, it's both insightful and a large step in the right direction. What *is* a "French moralist"? More importantly, for our purposes: what did *Nietzsche* think a French moralist was?[4]

As the cliche had it, the Holy Roman Empire was neither holy, nor Roman, nor an empire; likewise, French moralists have not been particularly moralistic, nor have they always been French. Perhaps La Rochefoucauld and Chamfort are the quintessential instances, and while they were indeed French, they're known mostly for their cynicism about moral behavior.[5] Paul Rée, who worked alongside Nietzsche while he was ruminating over material that was to end up as *The Gay Science*, was attempting to make a French moralist of himself, and he was German.[6] If Pippin is right, Nietzsche was a French moralist—if I am right, Nietzsche at one stage of his life was a French moralist—and he was German as well.

The tradition comes with a stylistic default, works consisting of "maxims" or aphorisms: to a first approximation, these are polished, pithy, philosophical or more generally wise remarks that to our eyes today look to have been formulated for publication in a fortune cookie or on a teabag.[7] Here are a few typical instances, from that iconic French moralist, La Rochefoucauld:

Vanity, shame, and above all disposition, often make men brave and women chaste.

Gratitude is as the good faith of merchants: it holds commerce together; and we do not pay because it is just to pay debts, but because we shall thereby more easily find people who will lend.

116   WHY DIDN'T NIETZSCHE GET HIS ACT TOGETHER?

> The fidelity of most men is merely an invention of self-love to win
> confidence; a method to place us above others and to render us depositaries
> of the most important matters.
>
> Humility is often a feigned submission which we employ to supplant
> others. It is one of the devices of Pride to lower us to raise us; and truly pride
> transforms itself in a thousand ways, and is never so well disguised and
> more able to deceive than when it hides itself under the form of humility.[8]

Pippin emphasizes, correctly, that Nietzsche takes the French moralists
to be first and foremost "psychologists"; however, we shouldn't assume we
know what that means. (Among the people he most admires under that
heading are Stendhal and Dostoyevsky, and their work does not look like the
contents of any psychology journal today.[9]) Better to catch the drift of those
pronouncements: that if we're clear-sighted, behind the apparently generous,
admirable, other-regarding sentiments and actions we find self-interested
motives, laziness, and so on.[10] Human beings are fallible and—as the British
say it—dodgy creatures; the advice on offer in La Rochefoucauld is not to be
fooled or misled. That is, along with the stylistic markers, we recognize the
tradition of French moralism by what we can now describe as its realism—its
behindological view of humanity.

Daybreak and *Human, All Too Human* are the works in which Nietzsche
really does live up to Pippin's description—that is, in which he is modeling
himself on, especially, La Rochefoucauld.[11] But even here, as we should
expect of someone as philosophically ambitious and creative as Nietzsche,
when he inserted himself into that tradition, he did not merely aim to
produce derivative work—yet another imitation of what had come before.
Rather, he moved to advance it. The French moralists were in the business of
being, as we sloppily say, cynical, but, and here we have Nietzsche's attempt
to deepen their position, his predecessors weren't nearly cynical *enough*.

The criticism was deployed on several fronts. Right now, I'll sketch just one
such theme, so that you have the flavor of it. To the knowing insistence that
self-interest lies behind all those apparently high-minded acts of generosity,
etc., Nietzsche replies that we are giving people far too much credit when we
presume that they're organized and intelligent enough to act on their own
self-interest.

In the first place, the sheer mindlessness of custom explains more than
we would like of what we do. Piecing together an argument from some of

the moves in the first Part of *Daybreak*, in order to sharpen up the point somewhat: it's clear that everything that now has the status of custom was once an innovation. And in "those tremendous eras of 'morality of custom' which precede 'world history' as the actual and decisive eras of history which determined the character of mankind," to be moral *was* to be customary; there was nothing more to the moral sense than the imperative to do it the way it has always been done (3:32/D 18f, emph. deleted). Thus innovations would have been experienced as *ipso facto* immoral, which raises the question of how they could have ever been successfully introduced.

Nietzsche proposes that because people of those prehistoric eras took madness to be the voice of the divine, the only way, most of the time, to get a hearing for an innovation, and then to have it carry the day, was to seem, not to mince words here, crazy (3:26ff/D 14). And the most convincing way to seem deranged is to *be* deranged. Likewise, given the sensibility that identified what was moral with what was customary, the best way to have the self-confidence needed to propose a modification to the body of custom was to be mad. And so, for both of these reasons, and for a very long time, almost all innovations were introduced by, again to be blunt about it, madmen.

This means that even now, our morality, our religions, and our folk metaphysics are preponderantly the gradually accumulated residue of innovations laid down by insane would-be prophets. Nietzsche's very first example is grammatical sex—the bizarre practice, which English speakers encounter in their foreign language classes, of ascribing a sex to *everything* (3:19/D 3). Because the inventions of the deranged are almost certainly deranged themselves, our inherited morality, religion, and for that matter almost any other part of our intellectual apparatus is addled from the bottom up.[12]

The French moralists' trademark posture was realism: look *behind* the respectable front that people try to put up, and you'll see a mix of self-interested rationality and vanity. During his own French moralist stage, Nietzsche asked us to look *behind* the apparently self-interested calculation (and the apparent vanity) to see, among other things, the mindless obedience to custom—custom that has been deposited by processes which guarantee that acting on its basis will be the very opposite of calculating, self-interested rationality. When Nietzsche did take on the mantle of a French moralist, he was in the business of outdoing the realists at their own game.[13]

118 WHY DIDN'T NIETZSCHE GET HIS ACT TOGETHER?

5.3

That's all very well, but how could it be reasonable for Nietzsche to have thought of realism, that is, the *metaphysical* position, as one and the same with this sort of social and psychological wet-blanketism? Realism, whether in metaphysics, philosophy of language or philosophy of science, is a take on how the *world* is; isn't what's meant that it has a structure all on its own, without your help? It has nothing to do, and here is the objection taking shape, with the disappointing motivations that actuate human personalities.

And as you'd expect, Nietzsche's interpreters have largely gone looking in his writings for familiar responses to realism, which have usually turned out to be criticisms that twentieth-century philosophers later on fielded: roughly, arguments that the world's structure is not independent of how we construe it. But Nietzsche's own two-pass criticism of realism seems to have gone missing, and getting us in a position to present it will take first some warmup, and then what will look like a lengthy detour through medieval and nineteenth-century French cultural history.

First, the warmup. A while back, I found myself watching *The Incredible Hulk* (don't ask). For those who aren't familiar with the franchise, this is the embodiment of a childish fantasy, that when irritated or provoked you will turn into a large, green, raging, humanoid monster, and smash things. The comic books from which the film had been adapted were of course written for children, but now that those children have grown up into adults who can pay the price of a movie ticket, Hollywood is convinced, ticket sales say correctly, that a sizable number of them are holding onto the fantasy. And sure enough, adult-themed trappings, such as gestures at psychological depth, were being clumsily tacked on to the immature central theme.

Now, and this is a way to sloganize Bernard Williams on Nietzsche's mode of critique, a great deal of our philosophical subject matter is much more like *The Incredible Hulk* than we tend to suppose: again and again, when we see a bit of metaphysics for what it is, we recognize it as this sort of childish fantasy sustained into adulthood. Williams used Nietzsche's treatment of free will to show how that went, and I'll walk through that now; while it doesn't seem off-base to me, you'll want to recall from earlier chapters that Nietzsche has had other things to say about free will as well.

Here's how I end up thinking that the will is free. Someone has done something terrible to me, and I at any rate want to imagine that he didn't, even though there was plenty of explanation for why he did. So I imagine a little detached part of him that made him do it—something that was both *him choosing to do it*, and detached enough so that it might not have. And once I'm indulging myself in that picture of his inner workings, I don't merely have the satisfactions of allowing myself to daydream that things had gone differently than they did; I can then go on to blame him for what he did, in the peculiar way that the morality system blames: only for what one could have done otherwise. That is, "the needs, demands and invitations of the morality system"—this phrase is a term in Williams's own Nietzsche-influenced terminology—"are enough to explain the peculiar psychology of the will." "Nietzsche's approach," Williams sums up, is "to identify an excess of moral content in psychology by appealing first to . . . an interpreter . . . said to be—using an unashamedly evaluative expression—'realistic'"; "we . . . ask where [this notion of the will] comes from and what it does. It is not itself manifestly tied to morality, offering rather a picture of voluntary action in general, but there is a moral phenomenon, a certain conception of blame, which it directly fits." And that is the critique, or rather, its first pass: you have identified free will as a *fantasy*, one that has the mode or guise of metaphysics.[14]

I think that's right as far as it goes, which I'll suggest is about halfway. As we'll see in the next chapter, in his *Twilight of the Idols*, Nietzsche provides a "first example" of his "revaluation of values": instead of looking forward, to promised consequences, when we generate our evaluations, we are to look backwards, to the person performing the actions. It's not just that *The Incredible Hulk* is a fantasy; it is, after all, sold that way. It's that the people who indulge themselves in it are *childish*. We don't stop when we've observed that the function of someone's metaphysical construction, in his personality, is that of daydream or fantasy; we ask, and this is the critical second pass: What kind of person *would* need such a fantasy? (When it's free will, someone who is helpless and resentful, but right now we don't need to pause on this familiar bit of Nietzschean territory.) And our evaluation of the putative metaphysics anchors itself there, in our evaluation of the person who has it.

Right now, that complaint about the will is only an illustration, and you may be wondering how plausibly the two-pass criticism generalizes to the traditional subject matter of metaphysical realism: the physicalist's picture of the cosmos, or in more traditional philosophical discussion, substances, causation, and the like. We'll return to that question shortly, when we take up Nietzsche's contributions to post-Kantian metaphysics, but now for that detour.

120 WHY DIDN'T NIETZSCHE GET HIS ACT TOGETHER?

5.4

On the title page of *The Gay Science*, Nietzsche included a parenthetical "*la gaya scienza*" as a sort of subtitle, to make sure that his readers wouldn't miss his gesture at the troubadours. So we need to explain just what that gesture was, and the story I'm going tell you will be a mashup of a handful of ideas about the troubadours that circulated in the nineteenth century and somewhat thereafter, with some more recent descriptions of the medieval social background thrown in to make the picture cohere. You should take it with a large grain of salt. First of all, although some of his picture is clearly enough mediated by Stendhal, it's hard to tell which version of the rest of it Nietzsche would have assimilated. What will matter here is that he seems to have had something on the order of this image of the troubadours, even if we aren't in a position to make it more precise. And second, what passed for history a hundred-plus years back is now considered at best dubiously historical, and at worst, as entirely discredited. So when I talk you through it, keep in mind that for our purposes we don't need to decide what the truth about the troubadours was, and who amongst the historians has gotten it right.[15] What matters is that we're laying out something that is, *very* roughly, the version of the history that Nietzsche would have picked up—but that said, I'm selecting the abbreviated but most dramatic rendering.

If you're about my age, I expect you used to encounter village Freudians— the analog, I mean, in the world of psychoanalysis, of village atheists. And one thing you would hear from them, regularly enough, was that religion is just sublimated sex. Denis de Rougemont insisted that the explanatory gesture was almost exactly backwards: if you know your history, sex is, he corrected his readers, sublimated religion.[16]

Once upon a time, during the high feudal period, to be a knight was to occupy a hereditary position which combined the functions of an estate manager and an on-call human tank. At some point, a shortage of land to distribute to new nobility triggered unemployment in the human-tank sector of the economy, and because the economic and social function *was* hereditary, an out-of-work knight would be unqualified for any other job. Thus it came to pass that some of these luckless low-level aristocrats kept body and soul together by becoming permanent houseguests at the homes—the castles, that is—of their more fortunate landed colleagues. For such displaced petty nobility, it would be very important for a permanent houseguest to stay on the good side of lady of the castle, and flatter the mistress of the establishment; like the knights, such women had a real economic function, namely, the day-to-day management of a complex and multifaceted domestic production unit.

This social position became the default point of view of the troubadours, that is, of the most memorable singer-songwriters of the day, in something like the way that the default point of view of the sort of music that made Nashville, Tennessee, into a center of the industry is that of someone who is impoverished, lovelorn, on the run from the law, and so on. However, we need to keep in mind that, just as the successful country and western performer might well be leading a comfortable suburban life, troubadours came from many different backgrounds, and weren't themselves necessarily landless aristocrats; the social position of the narrator in a given genre isn't to be confused with that of the artist who works in it.[17]

At around the same time, a heresy briefly flourished in which one's union with God was described in sexual terms. (In the repulsive material world created by a second, evil god, "the marriage...of man and woman...is prostitution; there is no matrimony except that of the soul with God.") Since one is united with God when one dies, death was pictured as the transcendentally ecstatic consummation of a marriage. The Cathars were ruthlessly suppressed in the course of the Albigensian crusade, but out of the heresy grew a new way of talking—and singing—about romantic love.[18]

Thus in the troubadour's lyrical tradition, women were depicted as hyper-idealized, unearthly objects of aspiration.[19] In the narratives implicit in the *cansos*—the love songs that were evidently the most popular genre of troubadour output—rather than marrying the lady, the pining knight would purport to be a sort of romantic vassal of his beloved. The posture likely in part reflected the difficulties of a social position in which the objects of one's affection were doubly unattainable: not only would a lady be already married, during a period in which divorce was simply not an option; a widow of property would not remarry to someone who, because he has no land of his own, has to beg for his living. But in important part the literary conventions reflected the role in that heretical theology into which female protagonists were being substituted: originally, it had been God—or perhaps the Cathar Church personified—in that role.[20] If you were that sort of knight, you were going to be united with your beloved only in death; romance thus took what should still be, its cultural availability notwithstanding, a deeply unsettling turn, one that made, for instance, a mutual suicide into an emotionally satisfying ending to a love story.

122 WHY DIDN'T NIETZSCHE GET HIS ACT TOGETHER?

The lyrical compositions of the troubadours—*gai saber*, that is, as Nietzsche rendered it, "*die fröhliche Wissenschaft*," or "gay science"—account for much of what Stendhal found, when he produced his treatise on romantic love.[21] On Stendhal's account, you cannot love someone you see as they actually are; instead, you idealize them, obscuring your view of them with a constantly proliferating veil of fantasies and illusions about their perfections, and what serves as the object of your love is the glittering misrepresentation. Stendahl calls "the pattern of exquisite illusion . . . crystallization," where the term invokes his famous image of a branch tossed into the salt mines at Salzburg: left for long enough, the salt crystallizes around the wood, presenting you with a "bough studded with diamonds"; "when you are in love," he tells us, "you are always adding new perfections to your idea of your mistress."[22] Romantic love—its mores, its literary self-conception, and its ideology more generally—had been inherited from the troubadours, who introduced the practice of reconceiving the object of one's erotic affections as though she were a deity; since no one can actually live up to the billing, that means substituting a fantasy for the person. Stendhal, a clear-eyed observer of the mores of his time, described what he saw those around him doing, which was, to an eye-opening extent, that.

Now would be a good time to remind you that Nietzsche admired Stendhal as one of the "psychologists" that he was most fortunate to encounter, and we can see the uptake of his treatment quite directly in the work we are just now trying to piece together. For instance, in a section titled "Women and their action at a distance," Nietzsche describes how,

> as if born out of nothing, there appears . . . a large sailboat, gliding along as silently as a ghost. Oh, what ghostly beauty! How magically it touches me! . . . the boat with its white sails moves like an immense butterfly over the dark sea. Yes! To move *over* existence! That's it! That would be something!
>
> When a man stands in the midst of his own noise, in the midst of his own surf of plans and projects, then he is apt also to see quiet, magical beings gliding past him and to long for their happiness and seclusion: *women*. He almost thinks that his better self dwells there among the women, and that in these quiet regions even the loudest surf turns into deathly quiet, and life itself into a dream about life. Yet! Yet! Noble enthusiast, even on the most beautiful sailboat there is a lot of noise, and unfortunately much small and petty noise. The magic and the most powerful effect of women is, in philosophical terms, action at a distance, *actio in distans*; but this requires first of all and above all—*distance*.[23]

In his adaptation of Stendhal's model, men are prone to work up fantasies of what Goethe called the "Eternal-Feminine"; they're able to sustain those fantasies only provided they don't look too closely, because, as Nietzsche is reminding you, women are actually people, just like anyone else, and the fantasy dissolves when you see a flesh-and-blood person from close up.

In the immediately preceding sections, Nietzsche makes it clear that he intends the Stendhalian treatment of romantic love as a pattern for his own much more general discussion. He starts off the second Book of his work by addressing himself "To the realists," where the realism he intends is the kind that "subtract[s] the phantasm and every human contribution" from natural phenomena such as mountains and clouds—that is, metaphysical realism.[24] And almost immediately thereafter, he compares Stendhalian attitudes about women (rendered much more viscerally than in Stendhal, and we'll get back to that in a moment) to the scientific revolution:

> When we love a woman, we easily conceive a hatred for nature on account of all the repulsive natural functions to which every woman is subject... "The human being under the skin" is for all lovers a horror and unthinkable, a blasphemy against God and love.
>
> Well, as lovers still feel about nature and natural functions, every worshipper of God...formerly felt [about] everything said about nature by astronomers, geologists, physiologists, or physicians...
>
> (3:422f/GS 59; cf. 5:95/BGE 127)

Recapping, and belatedly explaining the title of Nietzsche's book: the original "gay science," that is, Provençal (or "Occitan") troubadour poetry and music, took some of the human animals that we all are, and clothed them in a layer of what in retrospect we can describe as Stendhalian crystallization. Nietzsche's "gay science" was going to be doing *something* like that, but not just to your crush: the fantasy was slated to envelope everything—and in the first place, *yourself.*

5.5

If all you knew about Stendhal was what I've told you until this point, you would expect *De l'Amour* to be a bitterly disillusioned attempt to persuade you to turn your back on romance, once and for all. After all, if you're realistic, you see what lies behind love: the elaboration of a fantasy that covers over what you love with an ideal, one that allows you to imagine that your emotions are appropriate to their object. As we might say it now, it drops out of his conceptual analysis of love, as one of its formal features, that when you are in love, you are *always* mistaken: "deluded lover" is a redundant turn of phrase.[25]

But that is not at all how Stendhal's book proceeds. On the contrary, a very substantial part of it consists in practical advice for lovers: cautions about how crystallization can be aborted or dissolved ("excessive familiarity can destroy crystallization"; "to destroy passionate love...prevent all crystallization by making love easy"), and of how to induce it (don't "imitate others"; be "the most unorthodox"; for the "very sensitive," having "a woman be easy of access" is necessary).[26] True, if you're realistic about love, you see that "to understand this passion...you must speak of it as a disease." But if you're *fully* realistic about the disease—about the process of crystallization—you can assess both its costs and its benefits. The benefits include a transformation in your perception not just of the object of your love, but of the world as a whole: the "new aim in life...changes the appearance of everything...[which becomes] new, alive, and pulsating with the most passionate interest"; "your beloved communicates more charm to her surroundings than she herself possesses." Stendhal also advertises the way that crystallization can make romantic interest sustainable. As a matter of fact, people are mostly pretty much like other people—they come in just a few patterns—and if you see people as they are, it's easy to become bored with a single individual over time, or for that matter with a sequence of love affairs. However, the fantasies you project onto your beloved can be endlessly varied; " 'imagination can escape once and for all from satiety.' "[27]

In a brief report of an exchange, we're told that "love...provides a sensitive soul, for whom *what is imagined really exists*, with...sublime visions of happiness and beauty...[and] provided that our admiration of the beloved is infinite, is the greatest happiness of all" (251f). Which would you rather have: the "leafless wintry bough" lying around near those salt mines, or the branch "covered with a shining deposit of crystals...[and] studded with a galaxy of scintillating diamonds" (45)?

What kind of grinch would you have to be, to insist on the "real" branch? Apparently, you might be an American. In the United States, he tells us, "there is such a *habit of reason*...that the crystallization of love there has become impossible"; but "their kind of happiness...is the happiness of beings of a different and inferior species" (164f).

5.6

The focus of Stendhal's treatment is his analysis of romantic love, which either consists in or is explained by crystallization. But the psychological process is more general than the phenomenon Stendhal is explaining; for instance, it accounts, he suggests, for the tendency of prisoners to die shortly before their release (247). And noticing that crystallization can be anchored by objects other than persons allows us to speak to the textual surface of *De l'Amour*.

Even by the lights of the time, Stendhal's treatise is oddly composed. For instance, it has footnotes, but here is the note attached to "You see a pretty woman galloping in the park": "Montagnola, 13th April 1819" (1975, p. 112). While it starts out focused on its announced topic, the analysis of love, much of the center of the book is taken up with observations about and comparisons between the mores and national characters of the French, the Italians, the Germans, the English, and so on. The penultimate stretch of the book is a lengthy collection of fragments: Rochefoucauld-like maxims, lists of books, excerpts copied out from novels and memoirs, bits of correspondence, and the like; the slim volume wraps up with a couple of short stories. And those descriptions of the Italians, of twelfth-century Provence, and so on frequently lapse into the gauzily incredible, in a way that reminds one of Margaret Mead's misrepresentations of Samoan customs and folkways.[28] As we know from his novels, Stendhal was capable of very tight writing; why does this literary production have the shape it does?

In crystallization, not only is the object of one's interest obscured by fantasies of perfection; as we noted, whatever turns out to be associated with that object becomes symbolically and emotionally freighted; we expect the crystallizing mind to wander from one thing to another. If, for Stendhal, the idea *of romantic love* was undergoing crystallization, the book as Stendhal gave it to us would represent his state of mind rather neatly. It's safe to conclude that this is the intent of the work: Stendhal's writing exhibits the process of crystallization toward an abstraction—romantic love itself.[29] Nietzsche's "gay science," which generalizes Stendhal's treatment of crushes and infatuations into a generic, across-the-board strategy for life, was a straightforward next step, because Stendhal had already exhibited as an object of crystallization something that was not a human being but a psychological and sociological phenomenon. As with the people one loves, when crystallization wraps the phenomenon or concept, of love in this case,

126 WHY DIDN'T NIETZSCHE GET HIS ACT TOGETHER?

in a cloud of pleasing illusions, we are shown it to be a poor life choice to insist on quickly turning the climate control to "defog."

5.7

Earlier on, I promised some plausibility for Nietzsche's thought that metaphysical realism and political realism are, once you get past the packaging, the very same thing. It would have been premature at that point to document that it *was* what he thought. But we can now turn back to unfinished business.[30]

The Prefaces both of *The Gay Science* and *Beyond Good and Evil* concern themselves with the guises of realism that we've been considering. "Supposing truth is a woman," Nietzsche famously begins the latter—"what then?" To be a "dogmatist," that is, "denying *perspective*," is "standing truth on her head"—and here we have to pause to unpack that metaphor. Remember that the social world of Germany, in the second half of the nineteenth century, was not too far removed from the sensibilities of Victorian England. When you turn a woman clothed in the garb of the time upside down, her skirts fall over her face, exposing parts of her body that were considered shameful and humiliating. In the *Genealogy*, when Nietzsche mentions "stand[ing] not only philosophy but truth itself on its head," that is, he continues, "the grossest violation of decency possible in relation to two such venerable females"; the image is meant to be juvenile, vulgar, and shocking (5:400/GM 3.24, emphasis deleted).

That intent is confirmed by the matching Preface to *The Gay Science*:

one will hardly find us again on the paths of those Egyptian youths who . . . want by all means to unveil, uncover, and put into a bright light whatever is kept concealed for good reasons. No, this bad taste, this will to truth, to "truth at any price," this youthful madness in the love of truth, have lost their charm for us: for that we are too experienced, too serious, too merry, too burned, too *profound*. We no longer believe that truth remains truth when the veils are withdrawn; we have lived too much to believe this. Today we consider it a matter of decency not to wish to see everything naked, or to be present at everything, or to understand and "know" everything.

"Is it true that God is present everywhere?" a little girl asked her mother; "I think that's indecent"—a hint for philosophers! One should have more respect for the bashfulness with which nature has hidden behind riddles and iridescent uncertainties. Perhaps truth is a woman who has reasons for not letting us see her reasons? Perhaps her name is—to speak Greek—*Baubo*? (3:351f/GS P.4)

Some recent readers of Nietzsche have been inclined to the view that the final gesture in that passage, at (as Kaufmann's elucidation puts it) "a personification of the female genitals," invokes a cheerful Astarte-like fertility goddess.[31] Bearing in mind that we've already seen Nietzsche mention the "hatred for nature on account of all the repulsive natural functions to which every woman is subject" (3:422f/GS 59), bearing in mind the sensibilities of the time and place—"a naked human being is generally a shameful sight" (3:588/GS 352)—and bearing in mind the indignation of that child in this very passage, at God watching her get dressed and use the bathroom, that take on it is evidently anachronistic. Rather, we're being given a version of Stendhal's point, framed using a sexualized metaphor that's been chosen for its shock value: when you look behind the attractive surface, what you find is not just grittier and mundane, but repulsive, disturbing, and even horrifying. That *is* what you find, precisely because we human beings are in the business of making up those attractive surfaces—the fantasies produced by crystallizations—to cover over mundane objects of interest, in order to sustain our interest in them. We can be aware that we're not seeing things as they "really are," and quite reasonably decide that that's *fine*. In the metaphor, women can look beautiful clothed, but when the clothes come off, what you'll see is a naked body and female genitalia: better to leave the clothes on. As another of Nietzsche's characters says it, "I want, once and for all, *not* to know many things. Wisdom sets limits to knowledge too."[32]

5.8

Retrieving that earlier synopsis of Williams's Nietzschean complaint about free will as our model, let's sort out the two-pass criticism of realism. First, we can remind ourselves of some of the many varieties of realism and their psychological functions. Under the heading of metaphysical realism, there was a version of it that you find downstream from Kant, and which Nietzsche seems to think is its most sophisticated and only stable form. (We'll pencil in more of that conception in chs. 9 and 10.) Whenever you represent the world in a way that allows you to reason about it, you're *mis*representing

128   WHY DIDN'T NIETZSCHE GET HIS ACT TOGETHER?

it, and you'll find that deeply unsettling. It's not just that you are, as in the Kantian picture, adding your own representational conventions to the sensory inputs, in something like the way that mapmakers adopt a preferred projection for their displays. As it sinks in that you manage to see the world at all only by not seeing most of what's in front of you, and by rendering it, in the most direct sense, falsely, you'll come to experience the world itself, more and more, as brutely intractable, as alienating, and as flat-out unthinkable. Sophisticated realism—looking behind the apparent metaphysics of the world—puts you face to face with a state of things that Nietzsche expects you to experience as hateful.

Then there's the version of metaphysical realism that was most popular in Nietzsche's day, and remains so in our own: materialism, or physicalism, as we'd say it. Here the Kantian thought that we can't know what things are really like is put to one side, in favor of the confident idea that we do pretty much know what they're like, and there's a uniform mode of quasi-mechanical explanation that accounts for literally everything. Nietzsche thinks it of as a clumsier and less self-aware form of metaphysical realism, one which has the effect, not of making the world unknowable and horrifying, but very well known, in a way, however, which makes it—and here's Nietzsche's very direct word for it—"*stupidest.*" "An interpretation that permits counting, calculating, weighing, seeing, and touching, and nothing more . . . would be one of the poorest in meaning . . . an essentially mechanical world would be an essentially *meaningless* world" (3:626/GS 373).

Now shifting to that other main category of realism: A political realist takes himself to be looking past the idealized sugarcoating with which the political players mislead the naive, to see the entirely interested—that is to say, in the sense that word has in expressions like "national interests"—drivers of ruthless decisions. This isn't necessarily a matter of seeing what *is* there: political realism often enough slides into conspiracy-theory fantasy, even when conspiracy theorists insist that they are simply refusing to be taken in.

We mentioned in passing yet another form that metaphysical realism takes, which I suppose we can call *supernatural* (or *theological*) *realism*. In Nietzsche's view, by loading all the value onto another imaginary world, one devalues real life: pictures of a world behind the world, with a God, and a heaven, and a hell, and so forth arose out of "the Christian resolve to find the world ugly and bad."[33]

And last under this heading, a short way of characterizing French moralism might be: it's the view of *Realpolitik*—of political realism—only scaled down from states to individuals. The organizing theme of Rochefoucauldian cynicism just *is* being disillusioned, primarily in its dismaying view of human beings and what moves them.

There are evidently many forms that behindology can take, but they seem to have a common denominator.[34] To provide a nonsexual variation on Nietzsche's framing metaphor, one meant, however, to preserve its visceral quality, it's the attitude of someone who gives himself muttered reminders that what is *really* there, behind the face of whomever he is talking to, are layers of muscle, fat, and tendons, stretched over a skull—and he gives himself these sorts of reminders about *everything*.

We're going to pursue the characteristically Nietzschean mode of evaluation. Namely, what do we make of the realistic stance, and of the people who have it—of the realists themselves? What kind of person *would* be a realist? But notice that we have two distinct but related issues on our plate. There is the question of what realism *does* for you: is it a fantasy, or perhaps just an obsession, on a par with free will? And there's the question of *who* you are, such that you're thus invested in your realism. Neither issue is the same as a question of metaphysical fact—are there appearance-independent things behind the appearances?—even if identifying the cognitive role of an apparently descriptive claim as daydream or fantasy creates a fairly strong presumption on one side of that question. In the metaphor that Nietzsche is lifting from Emerson, the problem with wanting to stare at what's under someone's clothes is not that there will turn out to be nothing there. Sometimes, no doubt, realism is a fantasy, in the sense that there's nothing there; but either way, and this is Nietzsche's point, realism is a *personal failing*.[35]

5.9

We were asking ourselves how Nietzsche can find it reasonable to give a single treatment to both metaphysical and political realism. Let's look a little more closely at the state of play in metaphysics, as Nietzsche apprehended it, and at the move he proceeded to make.

In Immanuel Kant's first *Critique*, "things in themselves," or "noumena"—that is, the real items behind the appearances—were held to be in principle unknowable, but nonetheless there. That unpalatable doctrine presented philosophers of the time with an uncomfortable choice. The Idealists—whom we analytic philosophers remember as the tradition against which our own founding fathers rebelled—decided that if you couldn't know anything about them, the noumena were superfluous, and could be excised from one's metaphysics. (That is, they gave up on that "nonetheless there.") But there's another option: to identify the things as they really are with the material world investigated by science. (That is, you can give up on that "in principle unknowable," and in Nietzsche's day and age, in Germany, the live version of metaphysical realism was materialism.) And of course you can also try to split the difference: to allow that there are things in themselves which you can never see as they are, while insisting that there's a materialist account of how it is the appearances of those things look to us the way they do.[36]

Kant's game-changing move had been to explain the necessities that structure the world in which we live—most memorably, the Euclidean space we move around in, the mesh of causation into which everything seems to be embedded, and the physical objects located in that space—as side-effects of the way we "synthesize" everything we perceive, that is, assemble our sensory inputs into a systematized and unified representation. In Kant, the requirements of synthesis were analyzed formally: it was argued that any representation that had *these* features thereby had *those*; the actual noumenal goings-on behind the scenes were, recall, in-principle-unknowable; thus, synthesis wasn't something you could investigate empirically.[37] But when a philosopher comes to understand the things behind the appearances as the physical world investigated by the sciences, or splits the difference in the way we just indicated, he will accordingly take the process of synthesis to be an empirical process: when you represent the world, you do it with your brain, on the basis of inputs from your eyes, ears, and so on. To investigate the inevitable structural features of a person's representation of the world is thus to be engaged in—as we would think of it—cognitive science.[38]

Kant and his followers had supposed that what they were explaining were necessary *truths* (the "synthetic" ones, that is): why it is that space *is* (really is) Euclidean, why everything has a cause (it really *does*), why the world is populated by substances, and so on. Nietzsche's not properly recognized contribution to the neo-Kantian tradition was to argue that these sorts of cognitive artefact are not likely to amount to correct representations. Because over the past several decades we've finally caught up to Nietzsche's insight, we can reconstruct his train of thought in the vocabulary of bounded rationality. I'll introduce that conceptual frame more fully in ch. 9, but for now, here's a sneak preview.

The limited cognitive resources to be marshaled by the human brain, the urgent demands of hostile environments for timely responses, and the overwhelming complexity of most environments force tradeoffs, in particular, the sacrifice of accuracy in a representation for fast availability and usability. Borrowing an example from a discussion by Robert Nozick, if you look at both philosophical and ordinary linguistic practice, what underwrites modal intuitions that something or other is necessary is that we can't imagine alternatives to it. What accounts for that lack of imagination is that we're optimized by natural selection to solve problems efficiently and quickly: for many, many millions of years, it was faster for our human and pre-human ancestors to treat a predator as moving in a Euclidean straight line than to consider whether it was moving in a Euclidean straight line, or a Riemannian straight line. Ancestors that entertained non-Euclidean geometries in the wild were not long for this world, and so Euclidean geometry was burned into the silicon, as we now say it. That would have happened regardless of whether other options were possible (as we now think), or even if they were actual (as we also now think).[39] We're boundedly rational agents, and boundedly rational agents produced by natural selection can be expected to operate on the basis of systematically simplified misrepresentations of their environment.

The illustration shows us how bounded-rationality optimizations of our systems of representation are likely to amount to systematic *mis*representation. As we'll see in a more-worked-out manner later on, these misrepresentations present us with a hyperschematized and consequently deeply misleading version of the world we move around in, and are nonetheless absolutely unavoidable, if we're going to navigate it at all. But Nietzsche's version of this view presses past what Kant took to be synthetic apriori knowledge, all the way to what he and his followers were confident was analytic. Systems of representation are coordinated with the techniques that utilize them, and since Nietzsche thinks the most central of these are inferential, he is introducing—to the best of my knowledge, for the very first time—a bounded-rationality conception of logic itself.

If logic amounts to a way of regimenting misrepresentations, and if logic delineates what can be thought, it seems to follow that the way things actually are, which we're obscuring with our cognitive shortcuts, is literally unthinkable. Now, it's not an accident that we use that last word to express horror. Nietzsche is convinced that as you try to wrap your mind around the realization that, whenever you represent the world in a way that allows you to reason about it, you're *mis*representing it, you'll find yourself deeply unsettled. Conversely, individuals, causation, geometrical and arithmetical

132 WHY DIDN'T NIETZSCHE GET HIS ACT TOGETHER?

apriori truths, even logic—the very thinkability of your world—turn out to serve in a role strikingly similar to that of Stendhalian crystallizations. If we're obscuring the world with fantasized metaphysical perfections that make it livable and even pleasant, as with the imagined perfections we bestow upon our beloveds, Nietzsche can ask, rhetorically: what's so bad about *that*?

5.10

When cats are about to die, they look for a quiet place they can retreat into—maybe the back of a closet—while their life winds down. (As Nietzsche puts it, characterizing it as "prudence": "they go off by themselves, become still, choose solitude, hide in caves.") The engine of the realism from which Nietzsche's Convalescent claims to be recovering is a motivation that's variously characterized in his later works, but we can help ourselves to the label he eventually comes to use for this "disease of the will": *nihilism*.[40] Nihilism is waiting for and wanting one's death, finding reasons for detaching oneself from the world around one, and turning one's back on it. Realism, behindology that sees the ugliness behind whatever is attractive in the world, is nihilism at work. It's a convenient fantasy that serves the surrender, out of weakness, of one's dwindling life.

Here's a thumbnail of the account which the Convalescent is providing of his own alleged recovery—"alleged," to anticipate a question we'll broach soon enough. When Nietzsche, or rather, his authorial character, becomes cynical *enough*, his cynicism turns on itself. That is, once it's become clear to him that everything he sees involves systematic misrepresentation, the question of why that should be an objection to it becomes unavoidable. That brings him face to face with the possibility that the realistic insistence on truth is either a bit of vestigial moralistic piety or (and now we have one of Nietzsche's glosses on the slippery concept we introduced a few lines back) "a concealed will to death."[41]

Clicking on the thumbnail, to get a larger and more detailed image: I suggested earlier that the first edition of *The Gay Science* should be read as another exercise in French moralism, but one that could be expected to push the approach further than it had been, in the course of which it would criticize its predecessors. And that is indeed a good deal of what we see. For instance, and these pronouncements are very much in the spirit of Rochefoucauld, love is made out to be a form of possessiveness

WHO WAS NIETZSCHE'S CONVALESCENT? 133

(3:386f/GS 14), and Nietzsche explains to us that for the most part our sense that there's a great deal of good in the world is a matter of our inability to discern what motives are really at work (3:416/GS 53). Some passages straightforwardly extend the Rochefoucauldian approach: motives that earlier members of the tradition had overlooked, such as the feeling of power, are identified (3:384ff/GS 13), and we're told that in various ways we're far too unsophisticated about pain (3:550, 413/GS 318, 48). Standing on high principle—insisting on a "categorical imperative"—is often just a way of making submission and servitude palatable to yourself and to others (3:377f/GS 5). And there's much more along these lines.

So far, perhaps so familiar; but then the observations are turned on the presuppositions of French moralism itself. Earlier moralists' insistence on rational clarity, and on understanding what really lies behind the everyday human world, comes in for a new sort of criticism. What we think of as rationality is for the most part simply a strictly enforced discipline that produces convergence in judgments, without particular concern for the *truth* of those judgments. "Understanding" is how we misunderstand some of the interactions of our various drives. Consciousness, that is, our apparent first-person access to our own mental states, is limited to a shared vocabulary that serves social rather than individual needs: what we're normally able to describe of our inner lives is not much at all of what's actually there.[42]

We've seen that in other writings, Nietzsche observes that institutions, motivations, virtues, and many other things can be pressed to a point where they undergo a dramatic qualitative shift, and are typically redirected towards new aims. When we reach such philosophically rock-bottom topics as rationality, consciousness, and understanding, the realistic enterprise, possibly inevitably, overcomes itself. As we unmask misinterpretation after misinterpretation, the bounded-rationality deepening of those post-Kantian views makes it evident that misinterpretations are nonoptional: we come to "the realization of general untruth and mendaciousness... [:] that delusion and error are conditions of human knowledge and sensation" (3:464/GS 107). At this point, cynicism and realism succumb to metacynicism and metarealism: the stance towards the insistence on truth over interpretation becomes diagnostic.

Nietzsche's Convalescent waxes exuberant over the benefits of embracing the interpretations for what they are, and the reader ought to be reminded of Stendhal's over-enthusiasm for crystallization: "the world has become 'infinite' for us all over again... *it may include infinite interpretations*"

134 WHY DIDN'T NIETZSCHE GET HIS ACT TOGETHER?

(3:627/GS 374); "the sea, *our* sea, lies open again; perhaps there has never yet been such an 'open sea' " (3:574/GS 343). Now, if you're not yourself in love with the person that the Stendhalian lover is describing, you'll find his praises to be highly exaggerated, and this is why I've been leaving the Eternal Return out of this lap of the story we are telling. You'll recall its over-the-top demands, that one's interpretation transfigure absolutely everything, and remake the world into one you want to repeat, over and over and over again. At this point, all of that can strike you as quite possibly one of those fantasies typical of crystallization, and so, likely to obscure what right now we want to take as the focus of our attention.

Our interpretations are not only of the world around us, but of ourselves: Nietzsche famously announces that "we want to become those we are" (3:563/GS 335, emph. deleted). In the post-cynical stance that emerges from the self-overcoming of realism, you're perfectly well aware that your interpretations are the products of your own activity, and in that frame of mind, you can take on the task of configuring your own self-interpretation. With artists, the development of Stendhalian overlays for the world "usually comes to an end where art ends and life begins; but we want to be the poets of our life," and Nietzsche tells us what that involves:

> How can we make things beautiful, attractive, and desirable for us when they are not? And I rather think that in themselves [and here comes his nod to realism] they never are ... Moving away from things until there is a good deal that one no longer sees and there is much that our eye has to add if we are still to see them at all; or seeing things around a corner and as cut out and framed; or to place them so that they partially conceal each other and grant us only glimpses of architectural perspectives; or looking at them through tinted glass or in the light of the sunset; or giving them a surface and skin that is not fully transparent—all this we should learn from artists ...[43]

That is, in constructing your interpretation of your own self—in turning yourself into a work of art—you are to avail yourself of the repertoire of artistic manipulations, in which accurate representation is compromised in the service of an aesthetically compelling composition. And he provides further guidelines for the task of self-creation; for instance, if you can manage it, stylistic consistency is highly recommended.[44] Now it's clear why Nietzsche has made the turn from offering a reader a pile of perceptive but

5.11

In his subsequent work, a great deal more artifice was devoted to dramatization; in the second-edition revamp of *The Gay Science*, the character is more described than enacted. Much of the description is marked by section titles in the belatedly added Book V, many of which are in the first-person plural: "The meaning of our cheerfulness"; "How we, too, are still pious"; "Our question mark"; "The hermit speaks"; "The hermit speaks once more"; "The cynic speaks"; "We incomprehensible ones"; "Why we are no idealists"; "Our new infinite"; "Why we look like Epicureans"; "Our slow periods"; "We who are homeless."[45] When Nietzsche's character tells you about "us," he's telling you who he is and what he's like.

We've been recapitulating what Nietzsche sees as the intellectual trajectory of realism. But in doing so, we've also been recapitulating the personal progress of an intellect—of someone who starts out as a behindologist, very likely out of nihilism.[46] Recall that lengthy passage, early on in the volume, in which distance turns women into ethereal beings gliding past on magical sailboats; the disparaging tone is characteristically realist. (Closer up, behind the dramatic staging, you'll find bickering and pettiness.) By the time we've reached Nietzsche's injunction, from which I also quoted extensively, as to "what one should learn from artists"—the section title of GS 299—the very same techniques are invoked, and in particular, "moving away from things until there is a good deal that one no longer sees." But the disparagement is gone: Nietzsche's Convalescent has gotten to the point where he can encourage us "to be the poets of our life—first of all in the smallest, most everyday matters." The self-undermining of a sufficiently thoroughgoing realism is exhibited to us as also being the liberation of that intellect from his behindology: to his "new infinite," and especially to the prospect of the Stendhalian crystallization of his own self. *The Gay Science* began as the *ne plus ultra* of French moralism, and ends up as an exercise in narrative portraiture.

The narrative is uplifting. The Preface, in which "Mr Nietzsche" announces that he's convalescing, looks forward to a concluding description of his "great health": this consists in having as one's ideal what Nietzsche subsequently came to call the "revaluation of values," and in particular in a lack of respectful worshipfulness for inherited modes of valuing (3:635ff/GS 382). In retrospect, the *Gay Science*—not just its fifth Book, but from beginning to end—has exhibited this sort of not-particularly-respectful upending of values; so it evidences that the character is as announced, healthy again (albeit displaying a highly distinctive version of health—as we've earlier on been instructed to expect).[47]

Or does it? As I've just presented the Convalescent's progress, there is a natural path it follows, that of the self-overcoming of realism. To be sure, not every realist will proceed down that path—think of all the conspiracy theorists who never get around to seeing through their own behindologies— but as the Convalescent's strength returns, and the attraction of having it all finally be over fades, he's able to adopt the Stendhalian embrace of fantasy and illusion.

But that fantastic portrayal is in the first place a portrayal of *himself*: why should we believe that what the Convalescent is telling us is how things really are with him? Wouldn't someone who finds himself unable to get out of bed and get the day underway, someone who feels himself ebbing away, someone who is growing aware that he is terminally ill, but who in his diminished state desperately needs to evade that awareness, permit himself just *this* fantasy? Allowing yourself to slide into a daydream, a daydream in which daydreaming itself is a form of muscular self-creation: wouldn't you expect that from someone who is no longer able to do anything *but* daydream? If someone's cynicism has been developing out of his nihilism, so that the weaker he becomes, and the more he welcomes death, the deeper his cynicism gets, should we assume that it's the effect of a sudden return of strength when the cyncism becomes *so* deep that it turns into cynicism about itself? The apparent recovery from nihilism—"Mr Nietzsche's" announced convalescence— is, for all we know, merely the next stage of the progression of the illness.

If you reread *The Gay Science* keeping both of these possibilities in mind, and perking up your ears, so to speak, you'll find—or anyway, this has been my experience—that the text as written keeps both of them live. If I'm reading it right, one of the reasons that fifth Book was added in the repackaging was to intensify that particular ambivalence. Pointing you to the sort of moves I have in mind, we're given brutal behindological diagnoses of, among other phenomena, scientific realism, faith, scholarship, and morality— that last evoking the keep-those-clothes-on imagery of the Preface—along with a return to and overemphasis on the benefits of crystallization.[48] The behindology is announced as liberating—the "open sea" shown us by the death of God (3:573f/GS 343). But before he turns to the "ideal [which] runs ahead of us" (3:636/GS 382), he supplies heavy-handed indications that perhaps we should think twice about what we're hearing: a moment after characterizing himself as among the "children of the future," he says, of "the sirens who in the market place sing of the future":

> What we find in them is merely an expression—and a masquerade—of a profound weakening, of weariness, of old age, of declining energies. What can it matter to us what tinsel the sick may use to cover up their weakness?
> (3:629/GS 377)

He frames his target here as what in today's political discourse are called "liberals," but it's hard to not to hear the warning as applying as well to the prophetic-sounding pronouncements he is right then in the course of serving up. Sandwiched in between, we have pointedly personal responses to one subject or another—for instance, he doesn't respond well to Wagner *physically*; he's the kind of person who thinks on walks—that seem meant as a reminder to pay attention not just to the content but to the person.[49]

In the previous chapter I floated what might serve as an explanation: until the conception of a new value—of a new ideal of health—has been sufficiently solidified to be brought to bear, we aren't in a position to have a definitive view about whether someone is living up to it—or is just pretending that there *is* a conception of health under which he could count as healthy. Whether the character is healthy or in a state of terminal collapse has to in part be a matter of whether, in due course, a suitable conception of health—along with the conception of underlying strength it invokes—can be invented and made socially and personally real.[50] And so I won't try to resolve the issue, but instead will construe it as a warning. The release from realism can either be what it is for your life to be going very, very well—or a desperate last gasp, when your life is going badly indeed. Treat your own inclination to take that step with due caution.

5.12

Nietzsche began the book as it was first published by observing that one sort of behindology regularly ministers to the need for life to be meaningful, that the job is done by one round after another of implausible inventions, and that each round, sooner or later, succumbs to ridicule. The sort of thing he had in

138 WHY DIDN'T NIETZSCHE GET HIS ACT TOGETHER?

mind: human life was once of great interest to the gods, who are observing from behind the scenes; but as the sophistication of the public grew, the mythologies came to seem not just unconvincing, but silly. And in order for a behindology to confer a purpose on existence successfully, it has to be "something at which it is absolutely forbidden ... to laugh" (3:372/GS 1).

Nietzsche concluded the section with one of his many invitations to finish a half-articulated thought:

> Consequently—. Consequently. Consequently. O, do you understand me, my brothers? Do you understand this new law of ebb and flood? There is a time for us, too!

If I'm understanding Nietzsche's repackaging of his writing correctly, the intended completion shifted dramatically between editions.

When Nietzsche, still a French moralist, originally penned that passage, its point was that Christian cosmology and metaphysics—most prominently, but not by any means only that—would be dissolved by mocking realism: one sort of behindology would dispose of another. We live in one of those periods in which older ways of making life meaningful are headed for the trash heap; we are finally able to laugh at them again.

But with the self-overcoming of realism, the sense of the gesture changes. Because we understand perfectly well that our Stendhalian illusions *are* illusions, and because we can take the generous, tolerant attitude that Stendhal took towards his deluded lovers, pointing out that they are illusions doesn't have to dissolve them. And so we can make our lives meaningful without the behindology. In particular, our lives and selves will seem compelling and engaging, and the world itself seem meaningful, if we *compose* them that way; we know better than to tear away the layers upon layers of metaphorical gift wrap with which we make ourselves attractive to the world around us, and indeed to ourselves. In taking this step, Nietzsche has become one of the "teachers of the purpose of existence," but he's broaching a new way to fulfill what is now, he thinks, a basic human need. Realism had been the presupposition, but also the bane, of previous attempts to satisfy it; we can have the meaningful lives we crave, if we're finally realistic enough to let go of our realism.

6

Who Was Nietzsche's Psychologist?

(How to Read *Twilight of the Idols*)

We've seen Nietzsche intriguingly propose an agenda for philosophers of the future: inventing values. But while this part of his program strikes me as of both great theoretical and practical interest, it's less than obvious what the proposal comes to. What does inventing a value look like? And what would be accomplished by doing so?[1]

Now if we're reading Nietzsche correctly, there's no single, short answer to either question; inventions can serve many purposes, and indeed, the values which Nietzsche himself works at crafting are put to different uses in different places. But piecemeal answers count as headway—maybe the only sort of headway it's reasonable to try to make—and so now it's time to take up one of his last works, *Twilight of the Idols*, where he puts on display one purpose that the invention of a value can serve, and along with it, a surprise or two about the content of the value for which he's perhaps most famous.

I'll begin by drawing our attention to a handful of remarks about the "revaluation of values"—as it's conventionally translated—and using them to frame Nietzsche's attack on the most straightforward form of what it's now usual to call moral realism.[2] Then I'll introduce the novel value contrast—to foreshadow, between decadence and will to power—with which Nietzsche proposes to displace the older values he is attacking. And before proceeding further, I'll remind you of the way we're reading Nietzsche's later works not just for their doctrines, but for their implicit authors, on my way into taking up the question of who the author of *Twilight of the Idols* is supposed to be, and what we're being shown about him.

In due course, we'll be in a position to ask what the new value is for, and I'll return to what's probably the best-remembered part of the book, its discussion of Socrates. And here's where we're going: what rationality was for Socrates, his novel value construct is for the protagonist of *Twilight*.

Finally, I'll ask *why* we're being shown the author we'll have found, and I'll suggest that one thing he's meant to do is make a case for Nietzsche's willingness to deploy *ad hominem* arguments.

Why Didn't Nietzsche Get His Act Together? Elijah Millgram, Oxford University Press. © Oxford University Press 2023.
DOI: 10.1093/oso/9780197669303.003.0006

140 WHY DIDN'T NIETZSCHE GET HIS ACT TOGETHER?

6.1

At the outset of *Twilight*, we're informed that a "revaluation of all values" is in progress. A pause for vocabulary: "Revaluation"—"*Umwertung*"—is Nietzsche's neologism, and Walter Kaufmann, his best English translator, is trying to capture the sound of it with his own improvisation. However, to my mind his rendering sacrifices the flipping-over-tables sound of the German, and accordingly, I'll alternate between his "revaluation" and the "upending" of values.[3] Now, I've found that casual readers assume that Nietzsche means simply to substitute new standards or ideals for traditional evaluations, and while that's not exactly wrong, let's notice that there's more to it than that way of putting it would suggest.[4] What we're provided as a "first example" of such an upending involves an inversion of the order of acceptable explanation, and so a rewriting of what count as legitimate patterns of argumentation.[5]

Those traditional evaluations, we're told, are presented as dicta of the form, " 'Do this and that, refrain from this and that—then you will be happy. Otherwise...' " That is, the actions being mandated or prohibited are advertised as, respectively, causes of the outcomes one desires or hopes to avoid. On the contrary, we're now instructed, the actions are to be understood as *symptoms*. Changing out Nietzsche's list of examples for a case recently in the news, consider a prominent airline manufacturer's widely reported series of missteps: the decision to avoid an expensive certification process by building an aircraft that wasn't intrinsically aerodynamically stable, and to fix the problem in software; the implementation of a software fix vulnerable to a single point of failure; the decision to downplay the need for rapid and decisive pilot intervention in the case of software failure, both in manuals and training. Where stock analysts worry about the effects of these decisions on the share price, Nietzsche's "*recovered* reason" and "*higher* politics" tell us to ask what corporate culture makes choices like these; these mistakes show that "it has lost its sureness of instinct"—a company that finds itself performing actions like these is already doomed (6:89f/TI 6.2). That is, the first "revaluation" is the insistence that we look behind what someone does or thinks to the state of the person, or the kind of person, who *would* do or think that.[6]

We can see this inversion put to work in what looks like a round of preliminary metaethical and metaphysical groundclearing. There's a long philosophical tradition of producing theories in which a real world stands behind the world of appearances, and relatedly, of exclusive focus on a handful of very thin "highest values"—"the good, the true, the perfect." Rather than consider the arguments for and against, say, the Kantian version of these doctrines, or the Christian, we are to ask ourselves *what kind of person* would feel the need to juxtapose a real world, and such values, to the lived world of experience and the mesh of thick ethical concepts we deploy within it.[7] And we're given the answer right off:

> To invent fables about a world "other" than this one has no meaning at all, unless an instinct of slander, detraction, and suspicion against life has gained the upper hand in us: in that case, we avenge ourselves against life with a phantasmagoria of "another," a "better" life.
>
> ... Any distinction between a "true" and an "apparent" world ... is only a suggestion of decadence, a symptom of the *decline of life*.[8]

Very early on in the philosophy curriculum, we explain to our students that to dismiss a metaphysical or moral view on the basis of the personal traits of the person who holds it is an argument *ad hominem*, that is, an egregious fallacy.[9] So now that we've unpacked that very "*first* example of [the] 'revaluation of all values'" (TI 6.2/6:89, restoring Nietzsche's emphasis), we find it to involve, in its personalization of what seem to be impersonal questions, a dramatic revision of the legitimate modes of argumentation. The upending of values is not simply a quick reshuffling of the labels "good" and "bad," and it's not too soon to wonder how Nietzsche's diatribes are meant to persuade his readers. After all, unless you *already* accept his "revaluation," you won't find the arguments he gives against older ethical, metaethical, and metaphysical positions cogent.[10]

6.2

A moment back, we encountered in passing the new value concept that *Twilight* seems to be promoting. Elsewhere, decadence is introduced as what we would now call disunity of agency:

> What is the sign of every *literary decadence*? That life no longer dwells in the whole. The word becomes sovereign and leaps out of the sentence, the sentence reaches out and obscures the meaning of the page, and the page gains life at the expense of the whole—the whole is no longer a whole. But

142 WHY DIDN'T NIETZSCHE GET HIS ACT TOGETHER?

> this is the simile of every style of *decadence*: every time, the anarchy of atoms, disgregation of the will . . . [11]

And that way of thinking is confirmed in the book we are now examining:

> weakness of the will—or, to speak more definitely, the inability *not* to respond to a stimulus—is itself merely another form of degeneration.
>
> (6:83/TI 5.2)
>
> the essential feature [of "a strong will"] is precisely *not* to "will"—to *be able* to suspend decision. All un-spirituality, all vulgar commonness, depend on the inability to resist a stimulus: one *must* react, one follows every impulse. In many cases, such a compulsion is already pathology, decline, a symptom of exhaustion . . . (6:109/TI 8.6)

That is, decadence is being contrasted with self-control, and with coordinating one's activities in the service of an overall conception of what one is doing.[12] There are complications—for instance, altruistic inclinations are also announced to be "virtually the formula of decadence" and equated with "disgregation of the instincts"—but for now, let's register that the notion is wielded throughout as a primary value concept: to characterize a disposition or strategy or a way of thinking as decadent is thereby, in *Twilight of the Idols*, to condemn it.[13]

In the *Genealogy of Morals*, in what is probably his most famous discussion of a previous upending of a system of values, value concepts are treated in pairs; readers already familiar with it will recall how the good/bad contrast of early aristocratic ethics was dislodged by the good/evil contrast of so-called slave morality (that is, our own deeply entrenched moral frame). And his readers will also remember that Nietzsche puts a great deal of emphasis on the different priority relations within each pair; nobles formulate their positive value concept as a representation of what they admire in themselves, and the contrasting 'bad' comes later, as something of an afterthought; slaves, eaten from within by *ressentiment*, and preoccupied by the injuries and humiliations inflicted on them by their masters, arrive at 'evil' as the primary and negative evaluation—for the slaves, 'good' is the afterthought.

In *Twilight*, decadence must be one pole of a similar pair of evaluations, and we can adopt a phrase that Nietzsche introduces to label the contrasting positive assessment: *will to power*.[14] Although we've seen "strong wills" being mentioned approvingly, *Twilight* devotes almost no attention to unified agency successfully making its way through the world, and that central Nietzschean concept is scarcely invoked directly.[15] Thus the new value concept, decadence, quite surprisingly displays the priority ordering of slave morality's values: the negative pole of the concept pair figures as the emotionally compelling preoccupation, and the contrasting positive assessment looks to be scarcely an afterthought.

6.3

Nietzsche's later works—that is, from *Thus Spoke Zarathustra* on—become readable, or that's the case I've been making, when one asks who the (always carefully imagined) author of such a book is supposed to be. Once again, here I'm agreeing with Nehamas, who takes Nietzsche's writing to make sense once one sees it as projecting a "postulated author"—a character rather like the narrator of a book, but perhaps a further step back. With a recommendation like this one, the proof of the pudding is very much in the eating, but as in earlier chapters, we need to provide our author with a name and a thumbnail description, one that allows us to leave open the question of whether such an author is merely a literary artifact, as Nehamas insists, or rather, a brief biographical stage of the once living, breathing, former University of Basel faculty member. Giving our author a name will also enable us to hold open the related question of whether, as Nehamas has it, the various works that make up the corpus induce a single "postulated author" (which he's happy to call "Nietzsche"), or whether, as I'm attempting to make out, each of the later works is meant to display a *different* implicit author.

The book's title was originally supposed to be a phrase from its Preface, "The Idleness of a Psychologist."[16] And recall from ch. 5 that a "psychologist," in Nietzsche's vocabulary, is neither a mental health professional nor an academic researcher; rather, the term is used in the first place for literary figures in the French moralist tradition such as Rochefoucauld and Chamfort (as well as for novelists like Stendhal and Dostoyevsky).[17] The archetypal literary product of that tradition is the stylistically distinctive collection of "maxims"; lo and behold, the first part of *Twilight* is titled "Maxims and Arrows," and consists of the sort of epigrammatic, worldly pronouncements we would expect to find in, say, Rochefoucauld. So we do seem to be in the neighborhood of the label we need, and I'll refer to the putative author of *Twilight of the Idols* as "Nietzsche's Psychologist."

144 WHY DIDN'T NIETZSCHE GET HIS ACT TOGETHER?

With both the character available for inspection, and a primary value concept on hand, we're practically being invited to ask whether the one falls under the other: is Nietzsche's Psychologist himself a decadent? Recall that we've been equipped with a characterization that should allow us to answer that question: the hallmark of the decadent personality is the inability to restrain himself in the face of a stimulus or prompt. And indeed, as is standard in the later works we've been examining, we're shown the answer, heavy-handedly and at length.

6.4

Immediately prior to a very lengthy series of "Skirmishes of an Untimely Man," Nietzsche, or his character, announces to his reader that his "style ... is *affirmative* and deals with contradiction and criticism only as a means, only involuntarily."[18] And so those "skirmishes," especially the initial rounds of throwaway insults—just for instance, "*John Stuart Mill*: or insulting clarity"; "*George Sand* ... the milk cow with 'a beautiful style' "—are likely to strike that reader as a sudden swerve: whatever this is, it isn't affirmative, and the criticisms aren't calibrated toward any end, but rather seem to burst uncontrollably from the author's pen.[19]

Or again, the inability to control one's impulses will presumably exhibit itself in literary composition, among other ways in the inability to stick with stylistic constraints. And Nietzsche's Psychologist apparently endorses the entailment, telling us that "Plato, it seems to me, throws all stylistic forms together and is thus a *first-rate* decadent in style" (6:155/TI 10.2, restoring Nietzsche's emphasis). Surely the pot is making a point of calling the kettle black: as we've already noted, the book starts off with a collection of maxims in the style of Rochefoucauld; it then turns to a discussion of Socrates, which we will shortly take up, and which is stylistically continuous with the prose of the *Genealogy of Morals*; then we find an inventory of metaphysical errors, which we'll also shortly discuss, that recalls the writing in *The Gay Science*; and then it slides into that series of nasty rants, which we saw were dignified with the title, "Skirmishes," about people he doesn't like. The book works at being a stylistic hodgepodge, and indeed is much more so than Plato's productions, which most of us remember as anyway pretty consistently taking the form of Socratic dialogues.[20]

There's much more of this sort of thing scattered throughout the book, but let's turn to a sustained and more complicated display.[21] What strikes

WHO WAS NIETZSCHE'S PSYCHOLOGIST? 145

philosophers as the centerpiece of the book is a discussion of "The Four Great Errors," and let's quickly enumerate them. The first is "the error of confusing cause and effect"; we take causes for effects, and effects for causes. For instance, a popular diet book tells you to follow such and such a diet, in order to have the author's long, healthy life, where in fact it is the (particular type of) long, healthy life that makes the author able to stick to the diet (6:88–90/TI 6.1–2).

Second, we have "the error of a false causality"; causation is a projection of our ego-will model of action onto the world. Nietzsche was familiar with Auguste Comte, who had popularized the notion that our causal interpretation of the world around us is dessicated superstition; to treat *things* as *causes* was originally to treat them as minor divinities performing intentional actions, and those wood sprites and so on in turn were modeled on our understanding-from-the-inside of the actions we perform ourselves. And Nietzsche provides a brief Comtean argument, which he then presses into a deeper and more characteristically Nietzschean complaint. Metaphysical categories, like 'thing' and 'cause', are projections of our psychological categories, especially 'self' or 'I' and 'will'; but it's a crude mistake—pantheism, roughly—to assume that such a projection is appropriate. So identifying causes, so far the Comtean version of the argument, is always a mistake.[22] However, readers of Nietzsche's other works will recall that, in his view, we don't *have* selves or wills, and he reiterates those claims here: "The 'inner world' is full of phantoms and will-o'-the-wisps: the will is one of them...And as for the *ego*! That has become a fable, a fiction, a play on words..."[23] These are elements of a mistaken model of the mind, one probably derived from a grammatical convention. Talk about willing—what we would call intentional action on the part of an agent—is a superficial misreading of a much more complicated process. So our central metaphysical categories (esp. 'thing' and 'cause') are projections of *nothing*. So there are no causes, and no things; and in particular and especially, identifying causes is always a mistake.

Third, we have "the error of imaginary causes": we rapidly confabulate causes for our feelings, and such a fabricated "causal interpretation...inhibits any investigation into the real cause."[24]

Fourth and finally, there is "the error of free will": in order to be able to blame people, we insist that their actions aren't really caused (6:95–97/TI 6.7–8).

The incoherences in this catalog of metaphysical errors are hard to miss. If the very notion of a cause is a mistake, we are not in a position to complain

146 WHY DIDN'T NIETZSCHE GET HIS ACT TOGETHER?

that we tend to get the causes *wrong*, as the first and third errors charge. And if there are no causes, insisting that people's actions are uncaused is just getting things partially right, and not committing a further error. Worse, the accounts of the alleged errors are incoherent by the lights of this very stretch of text; most blatantly, the Comtean treatment that shows causation to be, roughly, mythological is itself a causal explanation, as are the explanations which Nietzsche's Psychologist supplies for the rest of the "errors."

We philosophers are trained to read away contradictions and incoherences in the historical texts we peruse, and the practice has been elevated into a methodological requirement, the Principle of Charity. But we've already seen, in our discussion of the *Genealogy*, that adherence to the Principle can be misplaced when the work at hand means to make the philosophical points it is after by exhibiting its putative author, and that author is being displayed as decadent, that is, weak willed, that is, unable not to respond to a stimulus. When such an author launches into metaphysics, and is reminded of various ideas—causation, free will, the self—in the subject area, he will burst out with one after another response, without being able to first vet them for internal or for mutual consistency. Consistency requires a strong will—in our vocabulary, unity of agency; in Nietzsche's vocabulary, will to power—and a decadent would produce a tirade of just the sort we have seen. If we are right in our general approach to Nietzsche's texts, to attempt to interpret these passages so as to eliminate these inconsistencies, that is, to treat the Principle of Charity as a nonoptional constraint on the interpretation, would be inept.[25]

6.5

The first extended discussion presented by the author of *Twilight* takes up "The Problem of Socrates," and let's remind ourselves where it ends up. Socrates was a decadent, beset by "the admitted wantonness and anarchy of his instincts," "all the bad vices and appetites" (6:69/TI 2.3–4). To manage his own disintegrating personality, he found "it necessary to turn *reason* into a tyrant"; "the hypertrophy of the logical faculty" became "his personal artifice of self-preservation" (6:72, 69, 71/TI 2.10, 4, 9). Socratic rationalism was widely imitated precisely because Socrates' difficulties were widespread; in Periclean Athens, "no one was any longer master over himself[;] the instincts turned *against* one another" (6:71/TI 2.9).

A healthy individual can trust his inclinations, which jointly project unified and internally coordinated agency. Once that's no longer possible,

WHO WAS NIETZSCHE'S PSYCHOLOGIST? 147

the Socratic innovation—to a first approximation, substituting argument for inclinations—postpones the collapse of a disintegrating personality. But Nietzsche is quite insistent that it does no more than mask and temporarily arrest the process:

> It is a self-deception on the part of philosophers and moralists if they believe that they are extricating themselves from decadence when they merely wage war against it. Extrication lies beyond their strength: what they choose as a means, as salvation, is itself but another expression of decadence; they change its expression, but they do not get rid of decadence itself. (6:72/TI 2.11)

Hyperrationality is a personality management technique; a prosthesis, but not a cure for the underlying illness.[26]

Recall the explanatory inversion which we identified as part of Nietzsche's upending of values. Plato's Socrates presented rationality as the path to a life of virtue and happiness; today, we might find ourselves involved in a discussion of whether rationality pays.[27] Nietzsche tells us instead to ask what sort of person needs to give rationality the sort of priority on which Socrates and his successors insisted (and still insist now): only someone who felt himself to be falling apart would find himself compelled to adopt this posture, and that tells us all we need to know. This sort of emotional stake in rationality shows one to be a decadent, which is, for Nietzsche's Psychologist, a definitive condemnation.

Socrates' insistence on hyperrationalism was itself the adoption and promulgation of a value, as Nietzsche understood the concept. In the proposed upending of values, we assess actions, and much else, by looking behind them, treating them as symptoms of the underlying personality that is the primary object of assessment; we assess that personality in the first place along the dimension of unity and disunity of its agency. So when Nietzsche's Psychologist condemns Socrates as decadent, we are being shown how a new value is used to evaluate and dismiss older values.[28]

6.6

We began by asking what purposes inventing a value can serve, and we're finally in a position to say what the introduction of the will-to-power/decadence contrast is for, in one particular case.

148 WHY DIDN'T NIETZSCHE GET HIS ACT TOGETHER?

Nietzsche's Psychologist, that is, the implicit author of *Twilight of the Idols*, is decadent: unable to suppress or even to tamp down his responses to whatever provokes them, unable to restrain his urges to lash out in the crudest schoolyard manner at one or another literary figure, unable to impose consistency on the views he articulates—and presumably, although we don't see it acted out, the chaos extends elsewhere in this character's life, to matters of practical and personal, rather than merely intellectual, import.

But disunified agents are unable to turn around the ongoing fragmentation of their personalities, much less repair the already-present damage. The best they can hope for is a prosthesis, a device that will help them manage their activities amidst the irreversible collapse of their selves. Socrates' prosthesis, the absolute prioritization of a particular conception of rationality, is pretty clearly unworkable for Nietzsche's Psychologist; Socratic rationality requires, in the first place, elaborately maintained consistency, and in the discussion of the "Four Great Errors," we've been shown that, for this character, consistency is a bridge too far. What more suitable psychological prosthesis is available?

Quite apparently, the vitriolic condemnation of decadence itself: the value that Nietzsche's Psychologist is promoting, with its slave-morality-like fixation on what it rejects, serves to keep this particular agent on point—or rather, as on point as he can be. The decadent agent is unable not to respond to a stimulus, and this value serves to direct his attention, and provoke his responses, to one stimulus after another.

Because, time after time, he responds in more or less the same way whenever his decadence button is pushed—that is, with a harangue in which Nietzsche's Psychologist explains some of his ideas, in the course of lambasting the decadence of whomever was brought to mind—the author of *Twilight of the Idols* was brought to write one after another section of what turned out to be the last book that Nietzsche published before his collapse. The device seems to have been, in this particular case, just what the doctor ordered.

In the case of Nietzsche's Psychologist, or maybe even Nietzsche himself, the will to power/decadence value construct as it's advanced in *Twilight* is there to keep that very decadent personality on track, by repeatedly providing it with one after another stimulus—stimuli to which the disintegrating person cannot but respond.[29] No doubt this is not the only use to which invented values can be put. But it's worth registering Nietzsche's deployment of it, inasmuch as in today's discussions of value theory and metaethics, this function of values is likely to be overlooked.

6.7

The upending of values that we're considering instructs us to look backwards, from the opinion or evaluation or position or attitude to the person who has it. Perhaps because philosophers try to assimilate new ideas to familiar ones, there's been a spate of recent publication announcing that Nietzsche is a virtue ethicist, and because one might think that this is the point of that instruction, it's a good occasion to consider how plausible the take is.[30]

To be sure, what we say about that will depend on what we see virtue ethics to be about, so let's separate out three characteristic elements of such positions. First, one might reasonably think that what motivates the different styles of moral theory in the mainstream is the question one starts out with. Consequentialists are first and foremost asking, How do we want things to *turn out*? Deontological theorists are motivated by the second of Kant's famous three questions: What should I *do*? Particularists of Iris Murdoch's stripe are wondering, How am I to *see* the situation I'm in? And virtue ethicists are primarily wanting to know, What sort of person should I *be*?[31]

Second, the treatments that generally get classified as virtue ethics presuppose that there *is*, anyway usually, a way a person is like: a coherent character, one that exhibits stable personality traits. When Nietzsche is read as a virtue ethicist, he's supposed to be distinguished by a nontraditional account of the character recommendation, as for instance when we're told that

> there is a core set of character traits—the pervasive virtues—whose cultivation is the means to the end of health and which, once cultivated, are that in which health consists. Among them are separation and love of solitude, spiritual independence, discipline, disdain for equality of humans, and courage.   (Welshon, 1992, p. 82)

And third, mainstream virtue ethics presupposes that there's a coherent, stable standard to be applied to such characters. To be sure, that standard can be hard to articulate; sometimes we're told that it's only the fully virtuous person who knows it when he sees it.

150 WHY DIDN'T NIETZSCHE GET HIS ACT TOGETHER?

Sticking to these three elements, what have we seen, making our way through Nietzsche's later works? On the one hand, he does seem to be very invested in asking what people are like, and he does seem to care deeply about the question, What kind of a person should I be? But on the other, as we've now seen at length, Nietzsche can't really expect most people to manage coherently constituted selves, and he can't expect them to exhibit stable personality traits; he certainly doesn't present *himself* that way.[32] Sometimes a self is a welter of unregimented drives, as we saw when we looked into his Good European. Sometimes people can't resist responding to whatever stimulus impinges on them; that's what we've just seen portrayed by *Twilight of the Idols.*

Moreover, we can't expect the evaluations prompted by the people that Nietzsche's various authorial personae consider to *add up* to a standard for assessing what are people like. After all, and leaving aside the shifts in perspective that we'll be discussing in due course, often enough they're uncontrolled expressions of Nietzsche's psychic components—in *Beyond Good and Evil*, for instance, blurts produced by misogynistic or racist or nationalist drives within him.

Evidently, to take Nietzsche for a virtue ethicist is to miss the deeper moves he is making against the too-neat methods we have of schematizing a person. To think of him that way will get in the way of learning both from his insightful theorizing, and from his writerly exercises in self-presentation.

6.8

I've been suggesting that the way into Nietzsche's later writings, this one among them, is to ask who the author is (and relatedly, what the genre of the book is supposed to be, or to be a parody of). Doing so usually leads you fairly directly to the first major point that the work is trying to convey. But at this stage of our discussion, you might be wondering whether *Twilight of the Idols* is presenting its readers with an unorthodox variation on the Liar Paradox—and what could be the point of *that*?

After all, we're instructed to conduct our assessments by looking back, from the view or value, to the person who has it.[33] When we look back, from *Twilight* to its author, the "Psychologist," we find a decadent. This decadent is making decadence out to be the final condemnation, and a more-than-satisfactory reason to dismiss the decadent's pronouncements. And

WHO WAS NIETZSCHE'S PSYCHOLOGIST? 151

one of those pronouncements was that instruction about how to conduct assessments.

If I'm following the train of thought, Nietzsche is addressing an issue that's been visible for some time now, though here I have to acknowledge that my take on what's going on is more speculative than it's been up to this point. I remarked earlier on that the Psychologist's methodological innovation—turning back for our evaluation to the person behind a view—seems to be endorsing what looks very much like *ad hominem* argument. We were all taught, early on, that *ad hominem* arguments are fallacies: "You're ugly and your mother dresses you funny" is not a way of debunking someone's opinions, or for that matter, his evaluative judgments. Even allowing that Nietzsche claims to be upending values, and that his recommendations are not supposed to be *already* thought legitimate, why should we accept this frankly outrageous proposal? Just because he's announced it?

Since Nietzsche is promoting the invention of values, here's a broader observation about inventions: they only work out if they're *motivated*. (I mean the term in the use found in questions like: "So, what motivates your theoretical position?") The iPod—recently discontinued as of the time of writing—was a portable music player, the consumer-owned hardware in a locked down IT ecosystem; content had to be downloaded from Apple, which charged a standard price for every track. The device, and the enterprise it was embedded in, was an invention with a point, namely, to solve the problem of how to sell music in a digital world, that is, once music was just files that anyone could download without paying. The solution was temporarily successful (it was displaced by the iPhone, Spotify, and Pandora), and in that respect resembled values as Nietzsche thought of them: also to be used *for a time*.

If values are invented, the inventor of a value should be as able as any other inventor to motivate his innovation. It's not a matter of simply saying, however loudly, that, say, *ad hominem* arguments henceforth count as valid. And if I'm right about this, Nietzsche is presenting his authorial character as a way of motivating that methodological-evaluative innovation.

Recall the pairs of opposing values we encountered earlier: the aristocratic good/bad contrast, the good/evil polarity of slave morality, and the opposing evaluations of decadence and will to power invoked by the authorial character. And recall that, in the manner of slave morality, all of the Psychologist's emotional investment seems, disturbingly, to be concentrated on the negative evaluation: he attacks what he sees as decadence, ferociously,

152 WHY DIDN'T NIETZSCHE GET HIS ACT TOGETHER?

but has scarcely anything to say *for*, or about, unified and expanding agency. He is, as Nietzsche sometimes puts it disparagingly, merely *reactive*.

The point is not that the decadence vs. will to power value scale is to be dismissed as the expression of a decadent personality. Elsewhere, Nietzsche seems much more interested in the other side of the coin; it's not just that he has more to say about will to power, but that when he invokes expanding agency as a positive evaluation, he manages to sound, for instance, *expansive*. It's rather that *this* development and *this* exercise of the new value is permeated throughout and made into what it is by the decadent personality whose expression it is; as in the "Skirmishes," it often descends into schoolyard insults and snide insinuations. A different character adopting and articulating this value could have it come out very differently, and you might end up assessing it much more positively. It's suddenly very plausible that we can't tell, merely from the label for this value polarity, whether it's reactive, in the way that the value system adopted by the *Genealogy's* slave class is, or rather the self-affirming expression of someone who is confident, happy with what he's doing, and pleased with how he's running his life.

If a more familiar case of this kind helps the suggestion make sense, consider egoism.[34] Sometimes it's plausibly lucid and thoughtful attention to self-interest; when someone like that explains, in a way you can respect, that he has to take responsibility for his own life, and that he has a kind of fiduciary duty to himself, that stance is one thing; but most of the time, as when you listen someone's not-well-thought-out insistence on an egoism that proves to be mostly confused enthusiasm for Ayn Rand, it's another. What egoism amounts to, and how well you're able to think of it, seems to be to a surprising extent a matter of whose egoism it is.[35]

Returning to the case at hand, to decide what you think of the value (the evaluative innovation which is probably most closely associated with Nietzsche in the public mind), you have to look back to the person whose value it is—in this case, Nietzsche's Psychologist. And if you then do condemn it, that's not yet to condemn the will-to-power/decadence contrast across the board; coming from a different character, you might well assess it differently. But if this *is* plausible, then Nietzsche has gone a long way toward motivating that turn to *ad hominem* argumentation, and I'm suggesting that this was part of what he was hoping to accomplish by displaying the character we've been calling his "Psychologist." Of course we do need to qualify that last remark. If this is what makes such arguments seem reasonable, not every *ad hominem* argument, and in particular, not the crude fallacies we were shown in our introductory philosophy classes, will pass muster.

Before we pause, we can make use of the interpretative proposal to weigh in on a view about Nietzsche that we mentioned in passing. Recall that Pippin characterizes Nietzsche as a French moralist, which certainly suggests that he takes Nietzsche to endorse, adopt, and approve of French moralism. But we should by now expect that a Nietzschean assessment of French moralism will proceed person by person: you assess *someone's* French moralism. The stance of Rochefoucauld is that of someone who is sober, canny, level-headed, and sees through the facades to what's really there behind them. The putative author of *The Gay Science*—also a French moralist of a sort—was very different: world-weary, and putting a brave face on his nihilism. (At any rate, if we found his insistence on his own "great health" unbelievable.) And *this* character—the author of *Twilight of the Idols*—is erratic and out of control: we might think poorly of *his* French moralism, even if we admire it elsewhere.

But even if we do think poorly of it, that very fact allows us to learn from him, in particular, that there's something to be said for the insistence that we give *ad hominem* argumentation a rethink.

Third Interlude: Are We Interpreting Nietzsche the Right Way?

A philosopher should in any case be self-aware about his own interpretive practice, and in two previous Interludes addressing this issue, I've been emphasizing that how to go about it is an especially complicated question when one is approaching Nietzsche's writings. The time has come to acknowledge the choice of method, in addressing oneself to this body of work, and consider how to make it.

At this point, the reader has seen the approach I'm taking exhibited at length, so for now here's a brief reminder, rather than a full-on account or manifesto.

Investigative tools have to be tailored to their objects, and techniques need to be adapted to materials. Just as there's no such thing as a tool that's the right one for *every* application, there's no exegetical method that suitable for any and every text whatsoever. (If anyone tells you otherwise, it's false advertising.) And so I don't mean to suggest that the approach I've been

154 WHY DIDN'T NIETZSCHE GET HIS ACT TOGETHER?

taking is generally usable; rather, I've been trying to work up a way in which to read *Nietzsche*.

Tools also have to be selected on the basis of what you're trying to accomplish. Now, in the case of interpretative tools, that's in part a matter of what questions you're trying to answer, and I own up to coming to the texts with my own philosophical interests. Just by way of illustration, the Eternal Return has come up now and again in the course of our discussion, and Kaufmann observes that the doctrine is meant as a rebuttal to Goethe: wanting to hold onto the moment is what will doom Faust, and the Eternal Return is precisely wanting to hold onto the moment forever and ever.[1] A reader with different interests could make that disagreement the starting point of an investigation, but here it's been left to one side—although I will circle back to the Eternal Return in sec. 11.5. In the course of pursuing my own philosophical concerns, I do want to equip my reader to read Nietzsche for himself; I don't take it to be my job to paraphrase all of him.

But in larger and more significant part, as a philosopher, my interest is in ideas, moves, and so on that might be brought to bear in ongoing philosophical work. Nietzsche might have gotten these right, and of course they also might just be mistakes; but if you share my philosophical interest, that means we should proceed in a way that allows that some of what Nietzsche thought might be right, or anyway have some truth to it—since that's an important way those thoughts could become candidates for being rethought and reused for oneself.

As a rule of thumb, once a philosopher has been dead for about a hundred years, if you actually have the thoughts he did, you are, strictly speaking, insane: what was an intellectual option in one century becomes literally unreasonable in the next. So history of philosophy done as what the New Age community calls "channeling"—preparing yourself in such a way that when you open your mouth, the voice of the departed emerges from it—is not making history usable. My own model is the sort of engagement exemplified by Peter Strawson's recovery of Kant: although I take very seriously getting historical context right, if the point of recovering the thinking of a figure in the history of philosophy is to serve one's own thinking, then one needs to rethink the thoughts of the philosopher in an intellectual idiom that is live, so that they are thoughts that one could have oneself.

I've complained on and off about the indiscriminate application of the Principle of Charity, so here is perhaps a local replacement for it. Keeping the point concretely tied to the body of work we're wrestling with, Nietzsche was a perspectivist, and so we want to approach it in a way that doesn't clumsily presuppose that he got it all wrong, and that there's nothing to be learned, after all, from recasting his thoughts into the sort of contemporary idiom I was asking for a moment back. Here, respecting the text—which is not the same thing as kowtowing to it—would mean holding off the assumption that there is a theory it presents, which it's our job to reconstruct. As we've also seen, Nietzsche is pushing back against the assumption that people are orderly enough to support our practices of ascribing beliefs and other attitudes to them. And of course, if you're trying to respect the text in front of you, you'll pay attention to the reading instructions.

And so we've been following those reading instructions. We've been trying to enter into one perspective after another, and to allow the way each book is written to tell us some of what Nietzsche thought we needed to know about the perspective it presents. We will, come ch. 9, make a point of being self-conscious about other perspectives that we'll invoke on our own account. Because we want to allow that it's worth thinking through Nietzsche's ideas about collapsing or just not-very-tightly-wired agency—after all, we want to be able to seriously consider whether perhaps he is substantively correct—we've done our best, in our own practice, to accommodate an author who, by his own lights, cannot support the full-fledged ownership of the views he presents. Or again, we're brought up on the conviction that *ad hominem* arguments are an intellectual embarrassment; we're in the course of seeing to what extent his very different views about that can be underwritten by his moral psychology (specifically, as we'll see in the next chapter, by his theory of drives), and we've been trying to avoid, in the *ad hoc* methodology we've taken on, brutely assuming that he must just be wrong about this.

All that, once again, was just by way of a reminder; the real presentation of the interpretative toolkit is the deployment that you have in front of you. Nietzsche's literary productions were in various respects not just original but very unusual, and so we had to work up an interpretative approach suitable to *him*. But now, how are we to assess what we've come up with?

We can discriminate three ways of approaching a text that we've run into so far. There's the self-effacing mode of reading into which analytic historians of philosophy are trained: channeling, as I put it a moment back. There are the brutal and egregious misreadings that I earlier introduced as the *Genealogy*'s apparent understanding of interpretation. And there's the style of reading which I was just sketching, which we can distinguish from both those options, in which one is not oblivious to one's location within a

156 WHY DIDN'T NIETZSCHE GET HIS ACT TOGETHER?

perspective, but is nonetheless both responsible and responsive to the texts with which one is working. If we can recognize these three options, and I hope you'll allow that we can, how are we to choose between them?

We've just now been wrestling with a distinctively Nietzschean mode of assessment: ask what one mode of interpretation or another betrays about *you*. Nietzsche tells us that his "eye grew ever sharper for that most difficult and captious... backward inference from the work to the maker... from the ideal to those who *need* it" (3:621/GS 370). Let's consider what we find when we apply it to the short menu of interpretative methods we just nodded at.

When we took time out to respond to the question of whether Nazism could be pinned on Nietzsche, we found ourselves resisting the easy excuses: the National Socialists sliced and diced Nietzsche's texts and ideas into something they could put to use, but weren't they conforming to the account of interpretation that served as the basis for the Foucauldian theory of genealogy? But now, it's worth remembering who constituted the core of that movement in the 1920s; Hitler and his inner circle were embittered and marginalized social failures. They were emotionally invested in getting back at a society that disrespected them, and they managed to recruit a great many Germans who felt the same way. That is to say, Nazism was a reactive and *ressentiment*-driven movement, and a good way to describe their policies might actually be: a modernized and extra-violent version of what, in the *Genealogy*, Nietzsche presents as the business of a priestly class. Faced with the cultural and psychological disarray of the Weimar Republic, the Nazis treated it symptomatically, by inducing extreme affects that (as Nietzsche reminds us) couldn't cure the illness, but rather made it worse. There were the mass rallies, at which people got carried away in a way we can scarcely imagine now. There was the way Jews as a group were made into a scapegoat, and other citizens were encouraged to indulge their most vicious urges, by smashing their stores, burning their synagogues, looting their homes, beating them up on the street—and ultimately, methodically killing the six million or so Jews they were able to lay their hands on.

Interpretation as the Nazis practiced it—blind, indifferent to what was to be found in the books Nietzsche wrote, what he had meant by it, and how he would have protested—was an expression of the response to being looked at as unhinged, lunatic riffraff and, in one of Nietzsche's favorite words, *canaille*. The uptake that turned out to be, among other things, a mega-pogrom was a variation on priestly therapeutic, and that is a very Nietzschean reason to disparage and avoid that mode of interpretation oneself. Recall that the

Genealogist, as a scholar and intellectual, is presented as a sort of secularized descendent of priests, and a current incarnation of the ascetic ideal.

At the other extreme, Nietzsche himself is decidedly unenthusiastic about the scholars who suppress their own personalities and interests in the name of accurately reflecting what is in front of them:

> The objective man is indeed a mirror: he is accustomed to submit before whatever wants to be known . . . Whatever still remains in him of a "person" strikes him as accidental, often arbitrary, still more often disturbing . . . he recollects "himself" only with an effort and often mistakenly; he easily confuses himself with others, he errs about his own needs and is in this respect alone unsubtle and slovenly . . . If love and hatred are wanted from him—I mean love and hatred as God, woman, and animal understand them—he will do what he can and give what he can. But one should not be surprised if it is not much . . . His mirror soul, eternally smoothing itself out, no longer knows how to affirm or negate . . . (5:135f/BGE 207)

I'll leave it to the reader to determine how far he's willing to follow Nietzsche here: to what extent he recognizes in these descriptions the practice and personalities we train for professionally, and how far he accepts the assessment.

But what are we to say about the version of interpretation that I've been building out, chapter by chapter? It's meant to be neither a heedless reappropriation that makes of Nietzsche's writings no more than a pile of raw materials, nor the pretense of a mere repetition of what's in front of us, in easier-to-follow language, by someone purporting to be entirely uninvolved. I'm up front about coming to the books I'm reading with my own philosophical concerns, but I want to learn from what I read, rather than to force it to say something I'd like to hear.

The Nietzschean mode of assessment we're considering makes that an awkwardly personal question, but one on which I'll ask the reader to suspend judgment until the final chapter, when I'll have been able to put all my cards on the table.

7

Who Was Nietzsche's Antichrist?

When Nietzsche signed the Preface to his *Twilight of the Idols*, he announced the date as "the day when the first book of the *Revaluation of All Values* was completed"—the reference being, not to the *Twilight*, but rather, *The Antichrist* (6:58/TI P). As I mentioned in the last chapter, that locution, "revaluation," is the now-conventional way of mimicking Nietzsche's own neologism, "*Umwertung*," in English. (An earlier rendering: "transvaluation.") But there's always something that goes missing in translation, and to keep the flipping-things-around sound of the German in play, I'll continue to alternate between that rendering, and "upending."

Having taught my way through this short volume a good many times, I'm aware of how the book strikes most of its readers: a village atheist's rant from beginning to end, mainly directed against Christians and Christianity, and finished so very close to Nietzsche's collapse and institutionalization that it's to be classified as of psychiatric, that is, biographical, rather than philosophical interest. That said, the writings for which Nietzsche is deservedly most famous have all, at one point or another, been dismissed as symptoms of his impending disintegration, and in case after case, closer and more careful reading has shown them to be remarkably crafted compositions, with philosophical agendas that have come to seem ever more compelling over the century and a half that have since elapsed. It's worth seeing what will come to light in *The Antichrist*, given equally generous treatment, and so I want to ask: how could *this* book possibly have been meant as the opening round of an upending of values—and not just of Christian, but of, as announced, *all* values?

7.1

If this is the question I propose to take on here, it sets a packed agenda; once again, I'm going to have to ask for more than the usual amount of forbearance on the part of my reader. Telegraphically: I will make the case that the

---

Why Didn't Nietzsche Get His Act Together? Elijah Millgram, Oxford University Press. © Oxford University Press 2023.
DOI: 10.1093/oso/9780197669303.003.0007

upending of values is in the first place *metaethical*. That will position us to ask how we are to approach the work as a literary artifact, which will in turn lead into another round of our discussion of how Nietzsche conceived of drives. And all of that will let us explain what is on the face of it an insurmountable problem that faces people like ourselves—a problem I take Nietzsche to be putting on the table in this book—when we attempt a revaluation of values.

Because the agenda has so many action items on it, a full-on road map would be distracting rather than a help; instead, let me foreshadow a few of the moves from its middle stretch. We've been proceeding under the working assumption that the right way into most of Nietzsche's later books is to ask and answer two questions: first, of what literary genre is it an instance or parody, and second, who is being portrayed as the author of such a book? We've been seeing that the philosophical points which Nietzsche means his books to make can fall into place as the answers to these questions are secured, and so we can hope to make Nietzsche's *Antichrist* readable by supplying them. To anticipate, *The Antichrist* is a riff on what's now a marginalized prose form, but in Nietzsche's day was part of the cultural mainstream: the antisemitic political tract. The German "Antichrist," as Walter Kaufmann and others have noted, can be rendered into English both as "Antichrist" and as "antichristian"; the punning title is telling us that the character who figures as the book's implicit author is someone who hates Christians in almost exactly the way that antisemites hate Jews.[1]

Nietzsche thought of antisemitism and of this antichristian variation on it as drives, and he took drives to be the architecturally weight-bearing components of psychologies. That latter point has been widely noticed, and in sec. 4.7 we nodded to a recent discussion of Nietzsche's moral psychology, in which drives are made out to be coherently focused on an intelligible aim or object—or rather, as we saw, on *both* an aim and a series of objects. We registered second thoughts, and we can now revisit and correct that view: antisemitism, we're about to see Nietzsche reminding us, is not only intellectually but motivationally incoherent; thus in *The Antichrist*, we have a book-length representation of a drive that violates our expectations of internal coherence.

The upending or revaluation of all values is urgently needed, Nietzsche insisted, as a response to decadence—to a first approximation, what we analytic philosophers call disunified agency. Moral philosophers today tend to think of unified agency as a matter of constancy in the pursuit of a prioritized system of goals, and so we imagine a disunified agent as pursuing his goals chaotically, letting one get under the others' feet, and neither systematically sticking to his announced priorities nor thoughtfully renegotiating them. When Nietzsche's readers today imagine a disunified agent on his behalf, they similarly default to the picture of a welter of poorly regimented drives. Little attention has been paid to the possibility of agency in which incoherence is internal to the goals or drives themselves, and Nietzsche's attempt to think this possibility through may help to make it much more live for us.

If values, all of them, are to be upended, someone is going to have to do the upending. But what if that someone is decadent, and that decadence is precisely what makes the task so very urgent? What if his decadence takes the extreme form of disunity *within* the drive that dominates his character: how can a personality built around an incoherent drive carry it off? The drift of the ensuing discussion, then, will be that *The Antichrist* was supposed to bring us to appreciate the difficulty that this problem poses for Nietzsche's metaethically revolutionary program.

7.2

What would it be to turn values—*all* values—upside down? There have been evaluative inversions in the past, and the *Genealogy of Morals* purports to tell us about one of them: in the clunky version of it we tend to convey in our classrooms, what was good by the lights of the ancient Greek and Roman aristocracy was relabeled "evil" by their slaves, while the enforced meekness, servility, and so on of the slaves were rebranded as virtues; we find a terse gesture at that story in *The Antichrist* as well.[2] *Twilight of the Idols*, which we saw dates to very near the composition of *The Antichrist*, is marked by a violent insistence on assessing everything and everyone for decadence, and occasionally endorsing the contrasting pole of the new value scale, will to power: here will to power vs. decadence is being proposed as the replacement for good vs. evil. And in *The Antichrist* itself, we are told not only that theologians stand value judgments on their heads, reversing the correct application of the concepts of truth and falsity, but that the Renaissance was "the revaluation of Christian values," in which, one takes it, humbleness and the like were demoted in favor of "bring[ing] the *counter*-values, the *noble* values to victory."[3] Is a revaluation of values primarily this sort of retagging, and if it is, is the revaluation that *The Antichrist* is advancing a straightforward rejection of Christian values in favor of some others?

That expectation treats the revision as much more superficial than it is. There is, to be sure, a rejection of a range of extant values. But Nietzsche's *Antichrist* tells us: "*we ourselves, we free spirits, are nothing less than a 'revaluation of all values'*" (6:179/AC 13). Or again, when another of Nietzsche's authorial personae announces that there are payoffs to be had even from the moralism he rejects, and rhetorically asks what those payoffs would be, he replies on his own behalf: "we ourselves, we immoralists, are the answer" (6:87/TI 5:6). The *Umwertung* is not value-theoretic musical chairs; rather, it shifts the locus of authority from the *values* to *someone*, or rather, perhaps a number of someones. Nietzsche's revaluation is one of *all* values, and not merely of the Christian values he happens to have in his sights at the moment, because it is—to use a term that Nietzsche did not have at his disposal—*metaethical*. To make out his innovation, or rather, this aspect of it, let's sketch the large-scale map of the analytic metaethics of the twentieth century.[4]

Metaethics has addressed the question of what values, metaphysically, *are*: that is, it comported itself as the metaphysics of value, and left to the ethicists and other moral theorists the question of which evaluations or standards for assessment were the right ones.[5] And for most of the last hundred years, there were two main camps a professional philosopher could join. One could affiliate oneself with cognitivism and moral realism, and in one way or another, agree that the values were *out there*, hovering over the valuable or worthless items in the world; alternatively, one could take on one of the many variants on noncognitivism, the spirit of which was that the values come from *in here*—that they're projections or expressions of emotions, commitments, or other attitudes, rather than descriptions held responsible to the evaluative facts. The unnoticed common denominator of both wings was an abdication of control and responsibility. If the values are out there, your job is to recognize and defer to them: they make demands of you, and you have no say in what those demands are. And if the values are in here, a matter of your emotions and so on, it was assumed throughout that the attitudes that determine your evaluative stance are not up to you: you can't help what you feel, and so your commitments were taken to be brute, something in the face of which you are passive. Our metaethics, from Moore on, was not in fact ethically neutral, but rather a way of mythologizing a systematic abdication of responsibility.[6]

The metaethical upending of all values, then, is in the first place a resumption of responsibility: instead of thinking of the values either as out there

162   WHY DIDN'T NIETZSCHE GET HIS ACT TOGETHER?

or as in here, that is, as mysterious or less-mysterious objects of which you might give a metaphysical or psychological account, the revaluation of all values makes of them something that *you* determine, rather than something in whose face you're helpless. (More carefully, since Nietzsche is quite aware that many people do and cannot but defer to others, directly or indirectly: that you can and ought to determine, if you are up to it.) The philosophy of value, which has hitherto largely been attempts to rationalize and make excuses for that helplessness, must become a very different sort of enterprise.

Thinking through the roughly contemporaneous *Twilight of the Idols*, we noticed Nietzsche, or his authorial character, giving a "first example of my 'revaluation of values' " which turns out to be a methodological requirement: when the time comes to assess a view or a person or a practice, ask yourself what kind of person *would* have that view, or be that kind of person, and so on (6:89/TI 6:2). We laid out a placeholder in ch. 2, and so we can postpone until later on the question of why Nietzsche thinks this is a reasonable demand, rather than an invitation to outrageous fallacy. Right now, it's straightforward enough to provide the backstory he seems to be asking for, I mean, to the posture that makes the subfield of metaethics possible, and even inevitable. We academics are one of the very late cultural products of what he calls slave morality. Slaves are used to accepting orders from above, as *just given*: what you have to do comes from above, is implacable, can't be questioned, and is simply *there*: to a slave, what he must do is a fact. When social changes free slaves of their human masters, that does not much alter their psychological structure and those mental habits in particular: as Nietzsche's Antichrist remarks, although not apropos academics in particular, "compulsion, *slavery* in a higher sense, is the sole and ultimate condition under which the more weak-willed human being... can prosper" (6:237/AC 54). The primary adjustment is where the orders come from; at the outset, it's no longer a human superior, but an imaginary person, God. Once God is also no longer on the scene, *values*, construed as facts that you simply have to accept and obey—Moorean nonnatural properties, the categorical imperative, and so on—occupy the role of commander. Alternatively, when in the absence of that master, it becomes your emotions that tell you what to do, you are, as Hume famously put it, a slave of the passions, and in the *Genealogy*, Nietzsche condemns such people as unable to give their word and unable to enforce their will on themselves over time; they are blown about not merely by outside events but by the flickering of their inner affective states (5:293f/GM 2.2). Expressivism may not be a defensible metaethical theory, but Nietzsche, were he to join our present debates, would likely take it to provide the correct account of metaethics itself: metaethics as we have had it over the course of the twentieth century has been the expression, intellectual to be sure, of an inner lack of autonomy, found in slaves who have lost their masters.[7]

Of course the frame of mind wouldn't be found solely among metaethicists.[8] As of the time of writing, the James Bond franchise is a lucrative concern that has been running for over half a century. The books and movies offer up wish-fulfillment fantasy, and *what* is that fantasy? Its protagonist is a secret agent who bears a "license to kill," and does so on behalf of his government. That is, the audiences are imagining indulging in violent, aggressive mayhem—on condition that it has been approved of and even ordered by the authorities. That, Nietzsche might have decided, is a fantasy which betrays the personality structure of a slave.

Looking ahead, we can entertain a preliminary explanation for the literary strategy of the text before us. Why is it not an argument for the revaluation, with its premises neatly laid out, and its evaluative conclusions drawn out for us, step by step? Perhaps because you can't argue someone out of slavishness: a slavish person will follow such an argument slavishly. When he accepts the conclusions as "following with logical necessity," thus, when he treats his being supposed to accept them as a *fact*, one that comes from above and outside, and when one of those conclusions is that he shouldn't be slavish, he's exhibiting a pragmatic contradiction. (And how would he resist the conclusion? We might expect it to be in the manner that slaves and bureaucrats resist orders they don't like: by complying slowly, lazily, badly, and grudgingly.) But if straightforward argument is not the way to go, what are the available expedients for initiating a revaluation of values, for those who need it most?

7.3

We will in due course return to the question of what's involved in assuming responsibility for one's evaluative judgments, but now it's time for a shift in key. What *is* that literary strategy; what are we to make of the very peculiar text we have in front of us?

Reminding you very quickly of our methodological frame, Nietzsche's later works—that is, from *Zarathustra* on—exhibit, over and above the views

164 WHY DIDN'T NIETZSCHE GET HIS ACT TOGETHER?

and claims they advance, an authorial character; if you're used to keeping an eye out for the narrator of the novels you read, you're almost there, and just need to take one more step back. Nietzsche, we've seen, isn't subtle about this; he typically tells you, quite early on, who that author is. Here, we observed, it's announced in the book's title, and that's part of a pattern: recall how, opening up the *Genealogy*, we're told in its very first line that the author is an intellectual; or again, *Beyond Good and Evil* is said, in its preface, to be the product of a "good European," and much of the work is taken up with explaining just what that amounts to. Moreover, we saw how the later works take a particular literary genre or form as their foil: as we observed, the *Genealogy* announces itself, in its subtitle, as a "*Streitschift*," that is, an intervention in a public controversy; *Zarathustra* is obviously a parody of Holy Scripture; *The Gay Science* takes over, with modifications, the aphorism-oriented form of Rochefoucauld, Chamfort, Rée, and so on. So the entry point into those works is to identify both author and genre, at which point it becomes possible to ask why Nietzsche has chosen both the one and the other.

As I indicated at the outset of the chapter, the "Antichrist" in the title does mean "antichrist," but it also can be rendered as "antichristian," where that is a parallel construction to "antisemite." Because antisemitism in Germany and Austria in the late nineteenth century was somewhat different than today's version, some orienting remarks are in place.[9] Whereas today to be antisemitic is understood as a matter of attitude—comparable to being racist towards other ethnic minorities, but directed against Jews—and not all that respectable, at the time, antisemitism was a political movement, and occasionally became the platform of successful political parties. Importantly for our purposes, there was a literary style that went with the movement. While much antisemitic writing took the form of pamphlets, a great deal of the German professoriat was proudly antisemitic, and thus there were well-regarded academics who wrote books arguing for and promoting their antisemitism. For instance, in the *Genealogy*, Nietzsche mentions Eugen Dühring more than once; a prominent philosopher, he was also the author of a screed titled *Die Judenfrage* ("The Jewish Question"). Paul de Lagarde, who was professionally a New Testament scholar, became known to the public for German nationalist and antisemitic essays.[10] Unlike today's antisemites, who either feel obliged to deny their antisemitism or are shunned by the mainstream, these were not marginalized figures; on the contrary. Nietzsche had begun his career as a professor and was quite familiar with this academic culture, as well as with antisemitism in the society more broadly. His sister had married an antisemite—again, not just someone with an anti-Jewish attitude, but a political activist, who wrote books promoting the platform.[11] Bruno Bauer, who stayed on Nietzsche's radar throughout his working life, followed his own *Judenfrage* with hostile encyclopedia entries.[12] Before they fell out, Nietzsche spent time with the Wagners, who were culture heros and antisemitic activists; a well-known essay of Richard Wagner's, "Judaism in Music" (1973), is typical of writing in this genre, available in English, and useful in providing a sense of the *sound* of the prose that *The Antichrist* is invoking.

Because most of us are no longer exposed to this sort of writing, Nietzsche's readers, at any rate in the United States, have largely not been in a position to recognize the genre that the *Antichrist* is appropriating: namely, some mix of the antisemitic pamphlet and the antisemitic academic or quasi-academic book.[13] With the literary background in place, the tone and register of the writing is instantly recognizable; I will document a bit of that below. And once we know what genre is being invoked, the pun in the title informs us who the authorial character is: we are being addressed by someone who is *just like* an antisemite—only instead of hating Jews, he hates Christians.

7.4

Let's pause to verify that this is what's taking place in the text, and also to start in on the features of such a personality, as Nietzsche is exhibiting them.

First of all, the antichristian posture doesn't merely imitate antisemitic views; it invokes them. One of the character's persistent complaints about Christians is that, deep down, they're really *Jews*. "The Christian," he tells us, "is merely a Jew of 'more liberal' persuasion." Or again: "The Christian... is the Jew once more—even *three* times more." Christians are "little superlative Jews" (6:221, 219, 220/A 44). The identification is not meant as a compliment; having compared God to the Wandering Jew, Nietzsche continues, "the god of 'the great numbers'... remained a Jew, he remained a god of nooks, the god of all the dark corners and places, of all the unhealthy quarters the world over!" (6:184/A 17). And he describes Paul, presented as the founder of institutionalized Christianity, as having "that rabbinical impudence which distinguishes him in all things..." (6:215/A 41); he had

166   WHY DIDN'T NIETZSCHE GET HIS ACT TOGETHER?

"the logician's cynicism of a rabbi" (6:218/A 44); he was "Paul...the Jew, the *eternal* Wandering Jew *par excellence*" (6:246/A 58: literally, the "eternal Jew"). The triumph of Christianity over Rome is "the whole *ghetto-world* of the soul *on top* all at once" (6:248/A 59, restoring Nietzsche's emphasis); although in our contemporary English, "ghetto" is used in connection with urban blight, recall that a ghetto was the locked-down part of a city designated for Jews. All in all, "even today the Christian can feel anti-Jewish without realizing that he himself is *the ultimate Jewish consequence*" (6:192/A 24). There are many further such passages.

It's important to *hear* the register. The distinctive tone of voice in which nineteenth-century antisemitic denunciations of Jews were expressed echoes throughout the book: "A *parasite's* [assassination] attempt! A vampirism of pale subterranean bloodsuckers!" (6:228/A 49) "The Christian and the anar-chist: both decadents...poisoning, withering, *bloodsucking*...This stealthy vermin which sneaked up...in the night, in fog and ambiguity, and sucked out of each single one the seriousness for *true* things..." (6:245f/A 58, restoring Nietzsche's emphasis). "We would no more choose 'first Christians' to associate with than Polish Jews...they both do not smell good" (6:223/A 46). And again, he remarks on "an ill-smelling Jewish acidity of rabbinism and superstition" (6:240/A 56; "Judain" also suggests an addictive, perhaps poisonous ingredient). To reiterate, this is the proprietary sound of the antisemitism of Nietzsche's contemporaries, much of which survived into the National Socialist period; Jews were talked about this way, and no one else; there are many further such passages; so the author of *The Antichrist* is going out of his way to make himself *recognizably* antisemitic.

The tone and vocabulary are complemented by traditional antisemitic themes. One of these is the Jewish conspiracy, and here is Nietzsche, or his author, striking that chord: The Jews "*have known how* to place themselves at the head of all movements of decadence (as the Christianity of Paul)" (6:192f/A 24; the emphasis is mine: "gewusst" makes it something they do intentionally). Of course, the Antichristian hates Christians, rather than, in the first place, Jews; so the complaint being aimed at Christianity is that it's all a Jewish conspiracy. And sure enough, we're eventually told straight out that "the cross [is] the mark of recognition for the most subterranean conspiracy that ever existed" (6:253/AC 62).

Was Nietzsche himself antisemitic? This isn't the place to consider all of the assumptions that are built into that question.[14] But here's one of them: generally, one takes up that question pretty confident that one knows what

WHO WAS NIETZSCHE'S ANTICHRIST? 167

it *is* to be antisemitic. Before we try to answer it, we ought to consider what Nietzsche thinks antisemitism is. And before we do that, we need to return to Nietzsche's understanding of drives.

7.5

Let's remind ourselves quickly of what by now is the received view of the distinctive features and workings of drives, filling it out a little further and folding together, I hope not too unfairly, aspects of the concept discussed by different authors. Because the point is to move past it, I won't aim for more precision than we need.

Drives can be contrasted in the first place with desires. A desire, as philosophers today tend to think of them, has an object, the thing you want to bring about; consequently, as far as their cognitive function goes, desires come with finish lines, and most of them come temporally prepared to get used up: once you've attained the object of your desire, you're done with it.[15] Drives, on the other hand, have not one object, but two, confusingly labeled, in this discussion, as a drive's *aim* and its *object*. As I type this, Nina is sitting in front of me, pulling on her claws with her teeth; in due course, she'll be done; but after a while, she'll start to feel the need, perhaps to redo her claws, but maybe I'll encounter her licking her back. She'll finish with her back, but later in the day, I'll see her scrubbing her face, and so on. Although the episodes have their respective objects—getting the claws done one way, the face done another, and so on—they're generated by a drive, which is characterized by its aim, namely, grooming. What the drive works toward need not be transparent to the creature it is moving; perhaps in this case it's about keeping a cat healthy and disease-free, but what does Nina know about any of that? The grooming drive, like drives generally, is inexhaustible; drives generate object after object, normally representable via desires; as desires are attained (or not) and crossed off the to-do list, the drive replenishes the list, generating ever further objects to be attained.

In human beings, as perhaps also in cats, drives operate by altering a subject's perception of potential objects and of circumstances more generally. Perhaps sociability is, in some people, a drive; its aim is, as we might say it, company; at a given time, its object might be a visit with family. As before, once the object is attained, the drive will shortly generate a new object: now it will be, maybe, a date, which would also serve as company.

168 WHY DIDN'T NIETZSCHE GET HIS ACT TOGETHER?

Someone motivated by sociability easily comes to see situations in which he isn't socializing as lonely, venues like bars, bowling alleys, and so on as warm, full of life, and inviting, and Christmas celebrations with family or dates as, perhaps, much more rewarding in prospect than they turn out to be in actuality.[16] We might say that the drive induces a justifying picture of the world around one—that is, a picture that provides justifications for all those objectives which the drive sets.

Stepping back for a moment to see how drives have their place in a descendant of Kantian synthesis, let's sketch that notion very quickly, for those readers to whom it is a new concept. (We did encounter it in sec. 4.4, but I suggested readers skip the explanation if they were going to find it unhelpful.) Kant observed that every part of your mind is part of *one* mind. For instance, if you're conscious of A, and also conscious of B, you can be co-conscious of A and B; that's a decent first approximation to what he labeled "transcendental unity of apperception." This sort of unity is attained by synthesizing smaller cognitive units into larger ones. You synthesize sensory perceptions into a spatially and temporally integrated unified field of consciousness; you also synthesize subsentential components of judgment (recognition of an object, recognition of a property) into judgments; you synthesize atomic judgments into logically compound judgments (conjunctions, and for that matter, arguments). And the limit of synthesis is *your mind*: your mind is transcendentally unified, in that what it is to be a part of your mind is to be synthesized, along with other cognitive components, into the unified mental structure.

However, in Kant, synthesis isn't an empirical process. We can't know anything about what goes on behind the scenes—about "noumena"—and, in any case, "process" is a temporal and causal description, and time, causation, etc., are, in Kant's view, themselves artefacts of synthesis. Rather, this talk of "synthesis" amounts to a formal description of the structure of the self, given from the inside; you can think of "transcendental" as meaning, roughly, that whatever is so described has to do with the necessary architecture of such a structure.

In the picture of drives that we see emerging in scholarly treatments of Nietzsche, he's appropriating and revising Kant's notion of synthesis.[17] Synthesis is now a cognitive process, which can be investigated empirically; it has a (temporally prior) starting point, the initially unsynthesized elements of the self, and, potentially, an endpoint, the fully synthesized self. The psychological elements being synthesized are, in the first place, drives and

WHO WAS NIETZSCHE'S ANTICHRIST? 169

affects, rather than, as in Kant, bits of sensory experience or judgments, or the components of judgments. And synthesis proceeds by one drive or affect "recruiting" others; when one drive recruits another, the former becomes intertwined with, but also imposes a new function on the latter. For instance, my drive to socialize recruits my hunger—my drive to eat—and the result is a more complex drive to social eating.[18]

7.6

Allow that Nietzsche takes healthy personalities to be organized around a dominant drive.[19] And allow that we're seeing a personality at work in the book. Then if we don't see evidence of *warring* drives, we should enter the work expecting a dominant drive at the center of the personality we're encountering, one that's speaking to us, inflecting the author's views, and accounting for its urges and aspirations. So let's see how much of the sketch we have just given of drives is borne out in *The Antichrist*.

The book doesn't seem to have a tightly organized argument, with a thesis that accounts for its beginning, middle, and end; rather, its author evidently has the urge to produce one denunciation of Christianity, and then another, and then another...: so far, this looks like the characteristic pattern of activity generated by drives as the now-standard rendering has them; the character is moved by what we can denominate his antichristian drive. (The drive's aim would be something on the order of: disparaging Christians.) Already, however, we can begin to worry about the fit between the rendering of Nietzschean drives that we have just seen and what we have in front of us. After all, the successive waves of activity look like expressive as opposed to goal-directed action.[20] The model drives we were considering set local objectives that then can be attained, as when hunger makes a particular dish seem enticing; as I eat it, I am fed, and duly sated, even if in short order I will get hungry again. But what are the diatribes that Nietzsche's Antichrist produces plausibly supposed to achieve?

We also see the recruitment of one drive by another on display, in more than one version. Quite likely the hybrid antichristian drive is a product of this sort of synthesis, plausibly between an antisemitic drive and the author's deep aversion to Christianity. But let's focus on the recruitment, by the antichristian drive, of another drive given a very prominent role in the *Genealogy of Morals*. For right now, we'll put aside what the inner workings

170 WHY DIDN'T NIETZSCHE GET HIS ACT TOGETHER?

of the will to truth turned out to be, once we looked behind the curtain. The will to truth demands honesty, intellectual fastidiousness, logical and pragmatic consistency, responsibility to evidence, and so on.

Now, notice a juxtaposition we are provided fairly late on in *The Antichrist*:

> "This is *our* conviction..." I have heard that sort of thing even out of the mouths of anti-Semites. On the contrary, gentlemen! An anti-Semite certainly is not any more decent because he lies as a matter of principle.
>
> (6:238/A 55)

This does sound like an expression of the will to truth. (To be sure, we're told this in the course of the authorial character's presenting you with *his* convictions, and I'll return momentarily to Nietzsche's elaborate display of his authorial character's pragmatic contradictions.) In the evaluative framing provided by this drive, lying is reprehensible, shoddy, low, and so on, all on its own: that you lie because the end can justify the means merely shows you to be dishonest. But having told you that the antisemite lies on principle, and that this doesn't make him any more decent, the very next section commences by instructing the reader that "—Ultimately it is a matter of the *end* to which one lies."[21]

Proceeding to fastidiousness in the use of evidence, the will to truth perceives cherrypicking one's evidence as cheating; taking truth seriously requires responsibility to *all* the evidence. With that in mind, here is a further condemnation of Christianity:

> The body is despised, hygiene repudiated as sensuality; the church even opposes cleanliness (the first Christian measure after the expulsion of the Moors was the closing of the public baths, of which there were two hundred and seventy in Cordova alone). (6:188/A 21)

Nietzsche may have gotten right the fact—or factoid—about the baths, but he's not being intellectually responsible in the use he makes of it. Over the history of Christianity—a 2,100-year-old religion that has spread out across much of the world—one can find *many* different attitudes toward cleanliness, from those of the feudal Spanish frontier to the scrub-and-buff Protestantism of Nietzsche's own Germany. Our authorial protagonist is being intolerably sloppy.

WHO WAS NIETZSCHE'S ANTICHRIST? 171

Similarly, Nietzsche's Antichrist complains that Christianity was a religion formulated for barbarians: "To the barbarian...suffering as such is not respectable...Here the word 'devil' was a blessing...man need not be ashamed of suffering at the hands of such an enemy" (6:189f/A 23). "Christianity needed *barbaric* concepts and values to become master over barbarians; for example, the sacrifice of the first-born, the drinking of blood in the Lord's Supper, the contempt for the spirit and for culture..." (6:189/A 22); as before, even if it's right, that's just one bit of the long and very varied history of Christianity. Why pick this stretch and forget the rest?

When someone's hunger is assimilated into and subordinated to his drive to socialize, you expect it not to just alter what and how he eats, but even how much: as tempting as it would be to order *all* of the desserts on the menu, as the table wraps up the meal, that just would not do; when everybody else turns out just to be having coffee, that's what you have, too. In something like that manner, but evidently in a more extreme version of it, the antichristian's scholarly disposition is being subordinated to his hatred of Christianity. When the ruling drive has a use for it, it kicks in, locally; and when the polemic is advanced by being less fastidious, the fastidiousness drops away.

7.7

If one thing contradicts another, they can't both be true, and so part and parcel of the aspiration to truth is the insistence on consistency. As Nietzsche displays it for us, an aspect of the subordination of the will to truth to the antichristian drive is sacrificing that demand. The ongoing discussion of Nietzsche's drives expects that the process of synthesis—the recruitment of one drive by another—will produce consistency in belief, preferences, and decisions: the synthesis of drives reverses the progress of decadence, or, as we would now say it, of disunity of agency.

Nietzsche's author pointedly puts on display a series of inconsistencies produced by a single drive; many of them are pragmatic contradictions, and I'll just indicate a few of the highlights.

To start off with a small reversal, the Antichrist complains about the deceptive impression the fanatics make on the masses, and accounts for it by dismissively remarking: "mankind prefers to see gestures rather than to hear *reasons*" (6:237/AC 54). But he insists that he is not deceived by the New Testament, "precisely because *I* do not read words *without* seeing

172 WHY DIDN'T NIETZSCHE GET HIS ACT TOGETHER?

gestures" (6:219/AC 44). He's not particularly interested in reasons: "I cannot stand a certain manner they"—the Christian Bible's characters or perhaps its authors—"have of turning up their eyes."

Proceeding to a larger instance, here is a methodological pronouncement:

> The biographies of saints are the most ambiguous kind of literature there is: to apply scientific methods to them, *in the absence of any other documents*, strikes me as doomed to failure from the start—mere scholarly idleness.
>
> (6:199/A 28)

It's plausible enough, but notice that it's laid down just before he starts interpreting the Gospels for his readers. The author lauds "the great, the incomparable art of reading well ... the *sense for facts* ... the cautious hand, patience and seriousness in the smallest matters, the whole *integrity* in knowledge" (6:247f/AC 59), and complains that the institutional founder of Christianity has made up his own history:

> the priestly instinct of the Jew committed the same great crime against history—[Paul] simply crossed out the yesterday of Christianity and its day before yesterday; he *invented his own history of earliest Christianity*. Still further: he falsified the history of Israel once more so that it might appear as the prehistory of *his* deed: all the prophets spoke of *his* "Redeemer." Later the church even falsified the history of mankind into the prehistory of Christianity. (6:216/AC 42)

But the author gives us a rendering both of Jesus as a childlike character, someone who has entirely surrendered his own will, and of his successors' misrepresentation of his person and teachings, all without any textual evidence, any careful reading—rather, he's fabricating his own history of early Christianity, thus, committing the very same sin of which he's accusing Paul and the later church. This is a very pointed, dramatically highlighted inconsistency:

> Another sign of the theologian is his *incapacity for philology*. What is meant by philology is, in a very broad sense, the art of reading well—of reading facts *without* falsifying them by interpretation, *without* losing caution, patience, delicacy, in the desire to understand. (6:233/A 52, restoring Nietzsche's emphases)

WHO WAS NIETZSCHE'S ANTICHRIST?   173

Of course, by this stage, the attentive reader will have been wondering for some time where Nietzsche's caution, patience, and delicacy have gotten to.

Such displays of inconsistency do not, however, prevent Nietzsche's Antichrist from demanding consistency, if he can use the demand to attack Christianity. The Antichristian's drive for consistency is inconsistently expressed: when it serves his political and emotional agenda, but not otherwise. For instance:

> there is a gaping contradiction between the sermonizer on the mount...
> whose appearance seems like that of a Buddha on soil that is not at all
> Indian, and that fanatic of aggression...[whose] wholly unevangelical
> concepts...[the Christian community] cannot do without: "the return,"
> the "Last Judgment," every kind of temporal expectation and promise.
>
> (6:202f/A 31)

That is, Christianity is held to the standards of consistency, when you can score a point against it that way: "*In fact*," he declaims, in a very Kierkegaardian cry of outrage, "*there have been no Christians at all*" (6:212/A 39). The complaint is odd coming from Nietzsche, given that he is portraying his Christ-character as another Prince Myshkin; while some of us admire Dostoyevsky's character, Nietzsche makes sure you remember the title of the novel—*The Idiot*—and explicitly labels Jesus a decadent, indeed, "this most interesting of all decadents" (6:202/AC 31). This acme of passivity is not, one would think, an object of admiration for the inventor of the notion of will to power, and failing to follow his lead shouldn't amount to grounds for an accusation.

There are far too many of these moments throughout this short book for us to review all of them. We can remind ourselves that one section of *The Antichrist* consists of a series of New Testament quotes, all of them scoring this sort of consistency point (6:221–223/A 45). And we can wrap up our selection from that very large smorgasbord with one last such evaluative reversal, where we hear that "even the Pharisees and scribes derive an advantage from such opposition: they must have been worth something to be hated in so indecent a manner" (6:224/A 46). Recall that Christianity is denigrated as being Jewish at bottom—but here, in a fit of rage at the Christians, the Antichrist concludes that the Jews must have been better than one had thought, since, after all, the Christians hated them. Once again,

174   WHY DIDN'T NIETZSCHE GET HIS ACT TOGETHER?

inconsistency is overlooked, and seems to be a side effect of, or even invited by, the authorial character's dominant drive.

The default explanation of his tolerating, and not just tolerating inconsistencies of this sort, would invoke a remark in his notebooks:

> *By which means does a virtue come to power?*—By exactly the same means as a political party: the slandering, inculpation, undermining of virtues that oppose it and are already in power, by rebaptizing them, by systematic persecution and mockery. *Therefore: through sheer "immorality."*
> (12:421/WP 311, restoring Nietzsche's emphasis)

Just as the Christians slandered their opponents, coopted their barbaric fears and values, and so on, Nietzsche is going to slander his own opponents, coopt their barbaric—antisemitic—fears and values, and the rest. And in doing so, he will not be consistent: since when was politics ever about consistency? But, I'm about to suggest, there's more to it than that.

7.8

The Antichrist's inconsistencies—and meta-inconsistency, that is, his being willing to demand consistency of his opponents with which he cannot be bothered himself—are not merely a tactical choice. I don't know that we want to accept Nietzsche's theory of drives as a viable moral psychology, but in some ways it's quite perceptive about antisemitism in particular. Like all drives, as Nietzsche conceives them, antisemitism seems to replenish itself: after a paroxysm of verbal or actual violence has exhausted it, its demands build themselves back up again, often enough taking on a somewhat different form, but remaining nonetheless recognizably the very same thing as before. Indeed, although the term dates to the 1870s, the phenomenon has been with us at least since the days of Xerxes: it is literally older than Western philosophy.[22] And over what is a very long period of time, one of the hallmarks of antisemitism has been the systematic incoherence both of the opinions that express it, and the courses of action it prompts.

As I write, the almost inevitable signature of one wing of a resurgent antisemitic extremism is Holocaust denial—produced back-to-back with a promise to finish the job next time through.[23] During World War II, the Nazi party's weekly poster magazine, the *Parole der Woche*, condensed its

WHO WAS NIETZSCHE'S ANTICHRIST? 175

messaging to fit on a placard, and the structure of the following thought is typical of those it conveyed: the Jews are so powerful that they run the world, and so we are going to do to them something you *could* do only to people who had no power at all.[24] Late on in the nineteenth century, Wilhelm Marr almost in the same breath declared that the war against the Germans was over, Judaism had won, and resistance was futile—and that he was founding a "League of Anti-Semites" to prosecute that war. Sartre (1995, p. 50) remarks on the characteristic posture of "a criminal *pure of heart*," a "sanctified evildoer" who "does Evil *for the sake of Good*." Over the nineteenth century, Jews were accused simultaneously of the sin of egotism or individualism, that is, the lack of concern for any sort of larger community, and also of acting only in the interests of their community. During the Enlightenment, Judaism was at the same time accused of being the source and hardest-to-extirpate reservoir of the superstitious evils the Enlightenment meant to dispel, and also "the source and most horrific example of . . . hyperrationality, self-interest, atheism, and stubborn materialism." Still earlier, during the Spanish Inquisition, the allegedly undercover Jews were accused of torturing the host; but of course, someone who retains his Jewish views does not think of it as the body of Christ, but rather as a baked good, something it would make no sense at all to torture.[25]

Nietzsche seems to be working to mimic and extend something of this pattern of incoherence in *The Antichrist*. In addition to the pragmatic contradictions we have been cataloging, we find a number of theoretical positions that are unstable in very much this manner; I'll just sketch one of them now.

Recall the book's description of the Christian personality: "The Christian and the anarchist: both decadents, both incapable of having any effect other than disintegrating, poisoning, withering, *bloodsucking* . . ." (6:245/AC 58). A decadent, recall, is falling apart as an agent; Christians have the upside-down values they do as a way of managing their impending disintegration.

But now, those very Christians toppled the Roman empire, whose strength and permanence Nietzsche emphasizes (6:245/AC 58); moreover, they completely reorganized society around their upside-down values: "And until now the priest has *ruled*" (6:179/AC 12). How, we might ask, do people who are falling apart manage to take over and run the world? Not until fairly late on was Christianity promulgated at sword point; for a very long time, its main resource was unrelenting self-control on the part of its adherents, that is, the very opposite of decadence. In the *Genealogy*, Nietzsche tells us that what has made the Jews victorious has been an "awe-inspiring consistency"

176 WHY DIDN'T NIETZSCHE GET HIS ACT TOGETHER?

in the inversion of values they advanced; they succeeded by "hang[ing] onto this inversion with their teeth" (5:267f/GM 1.7). Perhaps underlining the contradiction, Nietzsche devotes a significant stretch of the text to explaining that extreme decadents have no alternative but to cope by adopting an I-don't-fight-anything attitude.

The willingness to tolerate this sort of inconsistency strikes me as of a piece with willed suspension of disbelief. I've been told various times, sometimes at first hand but sometimes at second hand, what it was like to be a German living through the end of the war. As the Allied armies advanced, you knew that when they finally arrived, the Americans would butcher the civilians, rape the women, and so on and so forth. When the American forces finally did arrive, and of course did not do any of that, it was not that what you had thought you knew was disconfirmed by empirical evidence; rather, the show was over, and it was time to wake up, and go back to what you had known about the world all along. When antisemitism was the primary preoccupation of the political leadership of a totalitarian state, the state of mind of the participants was what is now sometimes called lucid dreaming. We should not be surprised to recognize in the conceptual structure of a drive that is postulated to account for the phenomenon of antisemitism the logic of a dream.[26]

As philosophers would expect, the conceptual incoherence characteristically plays out as incoherence in courses of action. When the Final Solution came into competition with military needs, the trains to the camps took precedence over trains to the front, apparently because Hitler thought that if he could just kill enough Jews, Germany would win the war.[27] (After all, Jews, the helpless people he was sending to the gas chambers, run the world.) During the nineteenth century, the complaint that Jews kept to themselves, rather than becoming fully integrated within the larger society, supported calls for excluding Jews from various professions, rolling back their civil rights, and the like.[28] And once again, we see something on this model playing itself out in *The Antichrist*. What is its author trying to accomplish? This first book of *The Revaluation of Values* concludes by proposing that we reset the calendar; instead of counting the years *anno domini*, shouldn't we count them "after [Christianity's] last day? After today" (6:253/AC 62, removing the emphasis)? Thus Nietzsche's Antichrist is adopting the posture that what the book not only was for, but accomplished, was finishing off Christianity, right then and there. If measureless self-control was what it took to overthrow the Roman Empire, impose new values on the wreckage, and all the rest of it, is a book consisting of a series of hostile, uncontrolled rants plausibly a way of doing *that* job? The antichristian drive doesn't have a strategy for destroying Christianity that makes sense, given what it has told you about Christianity.

On the received model of Nietzschean drives, we interpret activity as produced by a drive when we can see the drive exerting itself in inducing one relevant goal after another; but we can interpret activity as goal-directed only when it is rational enough both in its presuppositions about what's a way of achieving what, and in the internally consistent delineation of its objectives. Let's pause to spell out the main steps underpinning that point.

On that conception, a drive's aim is identified through the repeated occasions on which it generates goals for the agent. For instance, hunger is a drive with an aim, more or less, of eating food; your hunger generates, say, first a desire for a *croque madame*, after which you're sated for a while; but then it generates a new desire, this time for some of the turducken; and so on. But now, to be a goal is to be in-principle pursuable; one can envision intelligibly taken steps towards it. (When one cannot, Aristotle thought, we call putative desires mere wishes, but even a wish has to be intelligibly satisfiable.) If steps count as intelligible when there's a coherent story to be told about how they might attain the goal, then aims have to (repeatedly, of course) generate coherent plans of action; though this is not to say that one necessarily adopts them, and neither does it involve a guarantee that the plans one comes up with will actually work. Whereas in *The Antichrist* and elsewhere, Nietzsche exhibits drives without showing us anything like coherent plans of action, or even recognizable finish lines that candidate plans of action would be attempting to reach.[29]

When a drive induces an incoherent perspective, the omission is not simply laziness. A coherent plan of action can only be generated against the backdrop of a (largely, relevantly) coherent sketch of how things stand, and so—you can think of this as a Davidsonian point—if you don't have a more or less coherent background of belief, you'll find that you can't attribute goals to an agent.[30] But an incoherent perspective prevents one from producing largely coherent sketches of how things stand. Thus some of the drives Nietzsche exhibits, and the antichristian drive in particular, *couldn't* repeatedly generate coherent plans of action. Consequently, some of the drives Nietzsche puts on display don't have individuating aims, which means that it would be a bad idea to insist on thinking of drives, as they figure in Nietzsche's intellectual world, as individuated by their aims.

178 WHY DIDN'T NIETZSCHE GET HIS ACT TOGETHER?

When the drive runs on the logic of a dream, it cannot be identified through its goals or, consequently, its aims. Although perhaps some of the drives we discern in Nietzsche's texts—along with the drives that we analytic philosophers keep coming back to, that is, hunger and thirst and sex—conform to what was roughly Schopenhauer's template for them, the received model presupposes much more psychological coherence than Nietzsche allows is generally there.[31] In that case, how are we to think of drives, as Nietzsche understands them?

Nietzsche's Antichrist doesn't particularly engage in goal-directed action: we don't see him signing petitions, or engaging in political fundraising, or running for public office. Rather, we've observed, the primary mode of expression of the drive—and this is what we see on display elsewhere in Nietzsche's writings as well, when other drives are being given center stage—is *expression*, that is, speech. We recognize the drive, here as elsewhere, by its distinctive tone of voice, vocabulary, and more broadly, its register. At one point in *Beyond Good and Evil*, we saw Nietzsche looking to social and political structures as a model for the internal structures of individual agency (5:31–34/BGE 19), in a manner reminiscent, for just a moment, of Plato's *Republic*. And we took this to suggest that perhaps a good large-scale model for a Nietzschean drive would be the political party: the platforms of political parties are typically one or another hodgepodge of positions, not necessarily consistent, and those positions remarkably frequently reverse themselves over time. (Just for instance, it's often observed that in the US, the Republicans champion both enforcement of family-values social norms, and the noninterference of the government in private affairs; similarly, that the Democrats demand of overseas policy both that it promote human rights, but abstain from imposing Western values on other cultures; the Tories are now the party of the free market and capitalism, but in the nineteenth century they were the party that tried to protect large landowners from the free market and capitalism, which were at that time championed by the Whigs.) You don't pick out a political party by what it's trying to *achieve*. But a party typically *is* marked, sometimes over the course of centuries, by its distinctive manner of talking about the issues in which it takes an interest, and the way it construes the political scene more generally.[32]

Parties try to govern, that is, to take over their government, in something like the way that Nietzschean drives attempt to run the self, and to do this they try to recruit other parties. Sometimes those other parties are merely allies, whether of convenience or principle, but sometimes parties merge, as often in European parliamentary systems. The suggestion that drives can recruit one another, which does seem to me to be faithful to Nietzsche, is preserved in the analogy. So briefly, we can think of a drive as one of your inner parties.

In which case, we can also think of the correctly conceived logical object of a Nietzschean drive as, usually, a value. (Once again, a value as conceived by Nietzsche; we are only gradually, stage by stage, getting his complicated and nonstandard version of the notion into focus.) The antichristian drive does not exhibit itself in coherently designed and executed courses of action, but as you listen to it, it is clear what it is *about*, or what it is *directed towards*: it is, as the title of the book intimates, a mode of evaluation on which Christianity is all wrong, and everything that is wrong with the world—where Christianity is *what it is* to be wrong.[33]

7.9

Let's return to the pattern of argument we saw Nietzsche introduce, in ch. 6, as an upending of values: hitherto, what we've called *ad hominem* arguments we have condemned as *bad* arguments—as fallacies—but henceforth at any rate some of them are to be deemed *good* arguments. ("Some of them," because we shouldn't assume that the examples that students in all those community college critical thinking classes are given would count, for Nietzsche, as successful instances, rather than mere caricatures.) We were asking ourselves how to assess, and decide whether to adopt, this evaluative innovation, and we're now in a position to register a contributing consideration.

Innovations, and I'll return to this point in ch. 9, are intelligently adopted while taking into account features of the circumstances they'll be introduced into; a blind act of will executed in a vaccum is unintelligent. We used iPods as an illustration earlier on, so let's revert to them: as a locked-down hardware platform for distributing music, they made it possible once again to sell a product that had been unsustainably pirated; they offered the consumer ease of use, portability, and the ergonomic elegance for which the firm that made them had made its name; they'd become technically feasible at a marketable price point. And in just this way, innovations need to be motivated when the proposed innovation is evaluative, or a standard of assessment, and *a fortiori*, in the special case where what is to be assessed and evaluated is argumentation. On the working assumption that Nietzsche is inviting us to assess his upending of the standards of argumentation, what would have stood out to him as features that made *ad hominem* arguments worthy of a thumbs up?

We've been seeing an elaborately worked out example of a drive that expresses itself by generating claims, positions, and arguments adduced in its support. But as the antiquity of the antisemitic phenomenon indicates, reasons for the actions a drive prompts aren't to be taken at face value. If the first recorded attempt at a Holocaust, as described in the dark comedy of *Esther*, antedates Christianity, we shouldn't put too much stock in the reasons Christians gave for their pogroms. And not only were the very same pogroms to be found in the Muslim world, the patterns of persecution reappeared under modern secular regimes—of course, with differently couched justifications. The reasons adduced for the actions produced by a drive are themselves expressions of that drive; they do not explain the actions, but rather are to be regarded diagnostically, as some of the drive's symptoms. The various misdeeds for which Nietzsche's Antichristian castigates Christianity—like the conspiracies for which antisemites castigate Jews—are part of the motivating picture induced by the drive; they are explained by it, and do not explain it.[34]

Going back to a drive discussed in a earlier chapter, when a misogynist husband, on his way into yet another round of wife beating, begins to berate his victim, as his voice turns louder and sharper, and he starts enumerating reasons she is in the wrong, it's not as though the dismal episode is composed of an initial theoretical phase, where it makes sense to treat the accusations and alleged evidence for them as the justifying basis for the inevitable second stage, in which he will pummel her silly. Rather, the verbal abuse is the very same phenomenon as the pummeling, an expression of a drive, that escalates gradually from a less to a more physically violent mode. There's no point in either the victim or third parties engaging the *content* of the outbursts, and judiciously weighing the evidence for and against. And likewise, the antisemitic accusations that erupt into pogrom are not something different from the pogrom itself; it is not as though there was a preliminary phase in which hypotheses are being floated that, if accepted, would justify the pogrom. For this reason, the notion that the verbal expression of antisemitism is protected freedom of speech, while of course its violent sequels are to be prohibited and condemned, rests on a confusion.[35]

In cases like these, directing one's efforts to the contents of the utterances, and to determining whether they have the balance of evidence in their favor,

WHO WAS NIETZSCHE'S ANTICHRIST? 181

shows—when it isn't willful self-deception—remarkable naivete. (At most they are utterances produced, as Nietzsche remarks in a related connection, "in order that what happens necessarily and always, spontaneously and without any purpose, may henceforth appear to be done for some purpose" [3:371/GS 1].) Normally, the only puzzles it's worth figuring out have to do with the person who is producing them: in Nietzsche's understanding of how people are put together, those would be, first, understanding the drive expressing itself in those utterances, and second, determining its structural role in the personality it inhabits. That is to say, in cases like these, an endorsement of what we've been calling *ad hominem* argumentation—that one is to turn back from the claims, positions, and assessments to the person whose positions and so on they are—is an entirely plausible guideline.

We haven't by any means shown that all opinions, arguments, theories, and so on are in anything like as bad a state as in our illustrations. We may be warranted in tuning out when the talk-show pundits come on, but even Nietzsche concedes that there are intellectual products that are not simply the blurts of a drive.[36] Perhaps there are less dismissive assessments to be given of intellectual and evaluative products of drives, and as we'll see in ch. 9, drives can correct one another, and when they wrestle with each other, the result is, sometimes we should presume, "thinking" (5:54f/BGE 36). Nonetheless, Nietzsche evidently has the view that the low-quality pattern is a good deal more widespread than the particularly egregious cases we find it easy to acknowledge; for instance, we traced out his extended display of the riccocheting thought processes of unselfaware intellectuals in ch. 2. And the farther the extent of the pattern, the farther the plausible reach of *ad hominem* argument.[37]

7.10

For Nietzsche, decadence was a fraught concept, and as he returned to it, adopting one after another perspective on it, he gave it a number of overlapping but not obviously equivalent characterizations. Nonetheless, one passage which we have already noted is a relatively clean entry point, and let's repeat it, so that we have it before us:

> What is the sign of every *literary decadence*? That life no longer dwells in the whole. The word becomes sovereign and leaps out of the sentence, the

> sentence reaches out and obscures the meaning of the page, and the page
> gains life at the expense of the whole—the whole is no longer a whole. But
> this is the simile of every style of *decadence*: every time, the anarchy of
> atoms, disgregation of the will...[38]

Decadence is, or at any rate has as its primary manifestation, the inability of an agent to produce a coherent and sustained course of action, of one form or another.

An agent configured around a dominant drive that projects a justifying picture of the circumstances surrounding him that is incoherent, or for that matter sufficiently out of joint with reality, will fail to manage coherent and sustained courses of action, or so we argued. (The inability to attribute an aim to the drive, we saw, was likely to be a symptom of this problem.) What will happen when such an agent tries to create a new value?

Pausing for a word of caution: values are inventions, Nietzsche thinks, inadvertent, for most of human history, but to be made to order from here on out. It's a consequence of that way of thinking about them that we're not in a position to provide anything like a conceptual analysis of values generally; the track record of our self-consciously inventive technological culture shows that one only understands what a given invention comes to after it's been around long enough to become stable and solid—or defunct. If Nietzsche has his way, values are going to be repeatedly reengineered, in ways we can't now anticipate. So in addressing our question, we'll have to proceed gingerly.

One of the functions that values serve, in Nietzsche's intellectual world, is to guide action; so think of the directives that parents give small children. Typically, parents announce standards and rules, and we've all encountered fathers and mothers who, having done so, are unable to enforce them consistently. When that happens, and especially in extreme cases, the problem isn't just that their children are not being provided structure, and that that's what children need to thrive; it's that, in such a household, there *are* no rules or standards for the children's conduct. The content of standards and so on, this being a point that holds generally and not just when childrearing is at issue, is underwritten by systematic and consistent enforcement.

Recall that Nietzsche's metaethical *Umwertung* is in the first place a matter of shifting responsibility for what one is doing from something external— a person or abstraction to which one defers—to oneself. So the sort of consistent enforcement that delineates the content of the standards built into your new value, and thus, the content of the value itself, has to come

WHO WAS NIETZSCHE'S ANTICHRIST? 183

from *you*. It looks like the novel values that Nietzsche has especially in mind (unheard of, and tailored to one's personal, individual needs) depend for their very existence on one's ability to mobilize oneself as a coherently unified agent.

Let's accept a point we saw being made in our treatment of *Zarathustra*: that to introduce a new value of one's own design, it's not enough to announce it, say, to give it a name. Values, in their role as guides to action, take shape through their consequences; if a value doesn't induce a coherent pattern of those consequences, its content is eroded (or perhaps fails to materialize in the first place). Then it seems to follow that if one is built around a drive that plays out in one's own behavior, vision of the world, and discourse as endlessly incoherent, one's attempts at a revaluation of values—both at producing particular new values, intended to replace the values one has inherited, and one's assumption of responsibility for one's values—are bound to fail.

7.11

Values, in Nietzsche's world, are complex and multifaceted items; they have a number of tasks, and let's remind ourselves of another of them. Drives, we saw, aren't generally well characterized by their aims; Nietzsche's conception of values allows us to think of them as, sometimes, the objects of drives.

So imagine a somewhat disunified agent, of the sort I suggested earlier we philosophers tend to bring to mind first: perhaps a teenager with independently active drives for glamour, specifically coming by way of activities and poses that gather followings on social media; for aesthetic experience, tied especially to sensory vividness; for intellectual stimulation, especially by literature and philosophy; for intense social interaction, with family, friends, romantic interests, and acquaintances generally... Our teenager's drives, we should suppose, get in the way of one another, as when sudden trips produce those vivid experiences on Mexican beaches, along with dramatically composed documentation on Instagram, but preempt homework and classroom time. Or again, when time and emotional energy drain away into the social media black hole, and notice that the glamour-oriented drive does not necessarily motivate her to do things that will *make* her more glamorous, as the received model of Nietzschean drives would suggest. Scrolling through social media, we can suppose—it is a typical enough response—mostly just makes her *depressed*.

184 WHY DIDN'T NIETZSCHE GET HIS ACT TOGETHER?

And now further imagine that an encounter with Alexander Nehamas's reading of Nietzsche, with Nietzsche's not-quite-romantic entanglement Lou Salome, and with Anaïs Nin introduces her to a new value: that of one's life as a work of art.[39] If that value takes hold in the right way, a large part of which is receiving uptake from those drives we've just sketched, they might be woven together into a new and more complex drive. Suddenly the strands come together: sensory experience is found to be enriched, through what these days is called "cognitive penetration," in the course of encounters with modernist stream-of-consciousness literature. Self-presentation on social media is now a form of artistic endeavor that metabolizes those experiences and social interactions. And at this point, while the conflicts between competing demands on her time haven't resolved themselves, the value makes them resolv*able*. Briefly, one of the very important functions of values is to catalyze or mediate the synthesis of potentially, and perhaps actually, conflicting drives into unified patterns of motivation. And so the invention of values thus appears as, among its other possible functions, therapy for decadence, and maybe even its cure.

Now Nietzsche's problem comes fully into view. A decadent personality, plagued by incoherence, perhaps of the very kind that we see exemplified in *The Antichrist*, apparently needs just that sort of therapy: a value that can be given uptake by its various drives, and which can merge them into a soul whose internal political structure supports what Nietzsche thinks of as greater will to power. An idiosyncratic value, one tailored to the configuration of the drives found within a particular agent, is best produced by the agent himself: won't he know himself better than anyone else? And who else is going to bother? But the invention of value requires the already present ability to muster up a consistent pattern of enforcement and compliance. And if you're decadent—and especially if your decadence has penetrated down into the very content of your dominant drive—you can't muster up that consistent pattern. So now it seems as though the therapy is unavailable precisely to those who need it most.

7.12

Those who need it most are probably not very different from us. We are, for the most part, not-all-that-unified agents, and when we experience inner chaos as burdensome, we no doubt find attractive the thought of a new value, one that's tailored to weave together our competing drives and other bases of motivation into an integrated whole. Perhaps antisemitism and our implicit author's antichristian drives exhibit egregious and over-the-top incoherence, but if drives are like political parties, inchoate drives should not be at all out of the ordinary. When parties merge, and their platforms and ideologies have to be somehow welded together, we expect a misshapen compromise between them; what guarantees that when you conjure up a value, to serve as the object of a drive you're synthesizing out of whatever psychic materials happen to be available, what comes out will make sense?

In my own view, surveys of even one's immediate neighborhood—that is, looking at one's acquaintances through this Nietzschean conceptual lens—confirm the expectation. People do seem to be interpretable as containing drives, often enough, but when those drives are mirrored by values that remain internally consistent under sustained inspection, it's sufficiently unusual to occasion remark. When we cast around for and formulate values to serve as bases for synthesis, we're placing demands for followthrough on ourselves that could be met only by someone who did not undergo much in the way of agential disruption in the first place.

There are likely many workarounds for the problem, and perhaps even ways to meet it head on. Maybe the values you need don't have to be homemade DIY projects; perhaps our argument to this point merely tells us that Nietzsche's "philosophers of the future"—those who are going to be inventing the values from here on out—had better not be afflicted by this particular disability. We expect new fields in mathematics to be explored by mathematically gifted individuals; why should the development of new horizons for agency not be the preserve of the agentially gifted—those who easily project well-coordinated plans of action, and whose progress is not disrupted by literally aimless drives? Insisting on bespoke values is unnecessary, if carefully curated values will do.

Perhaps bootstrapping can turn an apparent vicious circle into an effective solution: the only somewhat coherent value that renders a complex of motivations somewhat more coherent can then itself be adjusted and rearticulated, and as each of the value and the corresponding drive is more cleanly delineated, the other can then be still more clearly recast. We've given some attention to an important aspect of Nietzsche's conception of values: that they are progressively tightened up, in the normal case eventually undergoing the deep qualitative transformations that he calls "self-overcoming."

186 WHY DIDN'T NIETZSCHE GET HIS ACT TOGETHER?

Or perhaps reintegrating one's personality isn't always necessary. A prosthesis that provides external prompting and support might suffice. And indeed, *Twilight of the Idols* seemed to show us values being fabricated to serve precisely that purpose. Finally for now, in Nietzsche's world there are many other uses to which values can be put; personality management is not the be-all and end-all of the exercise of inventing them, and even if we can't solve this problem, investing in the ongoing reinvention of values is still an intelligent way to allocate our individual and collective resources.

Nonetheless, given his moral psychology, the application we've been considering must have seemed quite inviting, and a likely solution to many of the problems he was most concerned with. I've been suggesting that *The Antichrist* was—among its various agendas—facing up to the likely solution looking less likely. And it's hard to know how Nietzsche meant to proceed: he never did write the further volumes of his projected *magnum opus*, and it remained unfinished at his collapse. Instead, his last endeavor was devoted to another project, a short autobiography that emphasized his own thoroughgoing decadence, and which took a very different approach to addressing it.

8

Who Wrote Nietzsche's Autobiography?

It's time to take up one last book—in fact, Nietzsche's very last book—before proceeding to an overview, and to asking what we are to make of what we've seen. I want to bring a theme we've seen come up repeatedly to bear on contemporary discussions of practical reasoning and moral theory. That will position us to elicit a further Nietzschean angle on another topic we philosophers today discuss hardly at all, but which we'll finish up with in ch. 11, namely, the meaning of life.

In those contemporary ongoing discussions, unity of agency receives, at any rate within the analytic tradition, a surprising level of deference. Just to give you a sense of what it looks like, here's a sampling of the more prominent positions in which unified agency has figured recently. Whenever there's a choice to be made, a unified agent must be on hand, and so arguments about practical reasoning—about how to figure out what to do—can treat unity of agency as a starting point. Or again, a properly assembled agent is unified, and so unity is something that you can demand of an agent in something like the way you can demand of a house that it have no holes in the roof. Or yet again, freedom of the will gets analyzed as a form of practical unity; this makes agential unity an indispensible precondition for an indispensible good.[1]

At this point in our scrutiny of Nietzsche's writings, however, we're ready to identify a line of criticism that's strong enough to motivate rethinking this cluster of received views about the unified agent. To commence, I'll reconstruct a Nietzschean anthropic argument for his version of unity of agency. (And what's an anthropic argument? We'll get a tighter fix on the notion in due course, but for now, imagine someone asking why the Earth seems so amazingly hospitable to life: not too hot, not too cold, an atmosphere with plenty of oxygen, and so on. And imagine him getting the reply that if it weren't, he wouldn't be here asking the question, so he shouldn't act surprised.[2])

A moment ago, I said "Nietzschean"—as opposed to "Nietzsche's"—for more than one reason. Since we'll circle back to the deeper one only in due

---

Why Didn't Nietzsche Get His Act Together? Elijah Millgram, Oxford University Press. © Oxford University Press 2023.
DOI: 10.1093/oso/9780197669303.003.0008

188 WHY DIDN'T NIETZSCHE GET HIS ACT TOGETHER?

course, here's a stopgap: his writings present Nietzsche himself as a decisive objection to that anthropic argument. After presenting the problem for the argument that Nietzsche saw his own psychology to constitute, I'll consider what could serve a disunified agent as a surrogate for practical reasons. Since our next lap, in ch. 9, will be after a vantage point from which to look out over Nietzsche's perspectivism, I'll offer a preparatory suggestion: Nietzsche's surrogate reasons can be seen as an objection to the broadly shared preference for unified over disunified agency.

8.1

We need to get a clearer look at Nietzsche's portrait of agential unity and psychological health, and so it's time to talk through Nietzsche's expression, "will to power," and firm up two related senses that it takes. For now, let's think about will to power by way of *control*. (Why? It's a concept whose literal use doesn't require persons on either end of the relation. Because we'll be wanting to think about what a person is, in Nietzsche's way of seeing things, we want to avoid building presuppositions of personhood into our explanatory resources as much as we can.) Rather than trying to list necessary and sufficient conditions for applying the concept, we can point out a couple of its more obvious features.

First of all, control provides a basis for explaining what's being controlled; if I control the temperature of the room, you can explain the temperature by pointing to me. Control involves the ability to effect change, and entails that there are true contrary-to-fact conditionals about it: I *could* have turned up the thermostat, and then the room would have been warmer. Second, control implies monitoring, and monitoring, in all but the simplest feedback loops, requires memory. If you exercise control over someone by giving him orders, you have to be able to check on whether your orders have been carried out, and to do that, you have to remember what you told him to do.[3]

When you look around the world, you often see *patterns of control*. Take as an example the administrative structure of a university, because it's philosophically unmysterious, and is probably familiar to many readers. In a university, the office of the president exercises control over the different colleges and schools; the dean of a college exerts control over its departments, centers, and programs; a department's director of undergraduate studies partially controls what courses of study the undergraduate majors adopt.

Sometimes these patterns are relatively stable (as is often the case in an institution like a university), and sometimes they're not (as is also often the case with universities). When the pattern of control is reasonably extensive and relatively persistent, we can call it an *organization*.

Sometimes organizations are self-maintaining and self-perpetuating. A university maintains itself by pursuing and appropriating resources: soliciting money from donors and funding agencies, recruiting students, faculty, and so on. It also checks on whether its employees and subsidiary administrative units are executing the policies of the university, monitoring the performance of units within the university by conducting reviews. When an organization is in this way self-maintaining, we'll say it's *homeostatic*.

Sometimes such an organization doesn't merely maintain itself as it is, but rather grows; homeostatic and expanding organizations are a form taken by will to power that is of great interest to Nietzsche. The class of such centers of will to power would include, on his view, not just universities, states, companies, NGOs, and the like, but individual human beings and anyway some of their subpersonal parts, as well as other organisms.

Sometimes organizations are governed by priorities; that is, these priorities determine their choices. As we already know, the concept Nietzsche works with is "value," but because values are so multifaceted, we need to peel out some of the different roles they can play within a personality. So I want "priority" to be somewhat thinner than "value": a priority is exhausted by its role in determining choice. If we're picking out priorities by way of their functional role, as inputs to a decision-making process, the priorities of a dean's office might include controlling the budget by reducing the overall number of tenure lines. It's a priority because it could serve as input to a decision, say, to attrit the faculty by ten percent. Call such centers of will to power *priority-guided*.

Now suppose that *you're* a priority-guided organization, and you stop and ask what your priorities are. Just as this may be something we can't find out by asking you, it may be something you can't find out by asking yourself. So far there's no reason to suppose that you yourself know what your priorities really are: when we introduced the notion of a priority-guided center of will to power, we said that the priorities direct the choices, but we didn't say *how* they do that, and in particular we didn't say that awareness of the priorities is a necessary part of the pathway.

Let's start to use "will to power" in a second but related way, as the name of a priority, rather than for generic patterns of control: it will mean the importance of maintaining and extending the very priority-guided pattern of control of which it is a priority. Then the first conclusion of the argument we're assembling is that the will to power is your highest priority. That's a dramatic and surprising claim, because on the face of it, different people and more generally different organizations differ in what matters to them and what they pursue, and their own will to power isn't often advertised as the most important priority. University mission statements, to stick with our example, typically emphasize teaching, research, and service to the community, and while there's a good deal of variation, you'll have to look far and wide to find a university (or a competent university administrator) proclaiming its most important mission to be: getting bigger.

But now suppose that your top priority *isn't* your own will to power. Then some other priority is—or perhaps your priorities fluctuate in such a way that we would be disinclined to say that you have a top priority at all. A pattern of control complex enough to be guided by priorities is a very complicated and consequently easily disrupted thing, and its maintenence is highly demanding. Over the relatively lengthy period you've existed, situations almost inevitably will have arisen in which your priorities were in competition with one another, and in particular, in which the will-to-power priority dictated one decision, and your hypothetical alternative priority dictated another. But since what will to power dictates is just maintaining and extending the pattern of control that constitutes *yourself*, and since by hypothesis will to power isn't your highest priority, you must have been making decisions that disrupted and eroded that pattern of control.

The cumulative effect of such decisions must have been the disintegration of the pattern of control that constitutes yourself. But in that case, you cannot now be asking what your priorities are. If you're now well enough organized to ask yourself that question, it will turn out (your most sincere protests notwithstanding) that your top priority is in fact will to power. Nietzsche famously emphasizes anthropic bias as it appears in a special case of interest here: "*the value of life cannot be estimated.* Not by the living, for they are an interested party . . . not by the dead, for a different reason" (6:68/TI 2.2). But the point is more general, as becomes clear when we return to our example. Sometimes universities have to choose between opportunities for expansion and their official self-conception. America's Ivy Leagues, in the early part of the twentieth century, understood themselves roughly as finishing schools for the offspring of the WASP elite. During and after World War II, enrollment growth and federal funding gave these universities an opportunity to expand rapidly, and faced them with just such a choice. The Ivy League schools responded by changing their self-conceptions so as to allow them to exploit the new opportunities for growth, and, to make a long story short, you can be assured that if a university is here, healthy, and flourishing, then it has a well-entrenched corporate culture which makes such choices in only one way.

8.2

We'd better register a few points before proceeding further. Firstly, will to power, as a guiding priority, runs together the homeostatic and expansionist attitudes towards the organization that has it, and you might wonder whether the argument establishes that a priority-guided center of will to power must prioritize self-maintenance, but not that it must also be trying to expand. However, there are two things to be said in favor of keeping both aspects of will to power together. Organizations of this level of complexity don't come into being full-blown, like Athena from the head of Zeus, but rather bootstrap themselves from smaller and more modest kernels; if augmenting rather than merely maintaining the scope of the pattern of control weren't part of the organization's highest priority, it wouldn't have come into existence in the first place. Moreover, it's very unusual that merely attempting to maintain a steady state succeeds in doing even that; normally, trying to grow is necessary even to so much as stay as you are. Speculating as to why: perhaps, since downs are inevitable now and then, you need to be aiming for the ups that will even them out; perhaps the steady state is a much narrower target than growth, and so harder to hit. And perhaps control is sometimes a positional good: you're in an arms race with competitors. Nietzsche often complains about supposing that life aims at self-preservation rather than will to power.[4] Maybe we have part of an explanation for that.

Secondly, it's important not to confuse this argument with an appeal to natural selection. The argument operates at the level of the individual organization; Darwinian selection requires replicators. The argument doesn't invoke anything like populations that reproduce themselves, or the evolutionary history of organisms (or organizations) of a given kind, though of course it's compatible with explanations that turn on natural selection.[5] Not all selection is Darwinian selection, and in particular anthropic selection is not.

192 WHY DIDN'T NIETZSCHE GET HIS ACT TOGETHER?

Thirdly, in the case of a human being, we shouldn't assume that the pattern of control that constitutes it is coterminous with its body. An expanding human being, in this sense, is not the character in David Foster Wallace's *The Broom of the System*, who intends literally to incorporate the universe, by eating it. So it's sometimes possible for people to augment their will to power by sacrificing their lives.

Finally for now, you might think that priority-guided organizations are likely to persist because they have top priorities that are not will to power, but whose pursuit requires continued existence as a means. However, we can now see that if, realistically, one often achieves continued existence only by prioritizing will to power, and if will to power typically trades off at the margin with most other priorities, the apparent counterexamples will tend to be ineffective over the long run, and will tend not to endure. Aiming just at continued existence rather than at will to power is only too likely to put one in the position of being able to manage neither the continued existence, nor the further priority to which it was a means.

8.3

There's a way of seeing a university as really *just* being a self-perpetuating pattern of control of the kind we've been discussing, and Nietzsche experiments with the idea that you could see *everything* this way—even what we think of as inanimate physical objects. (This last is a suggestion that hasn't gotten much uptake, probably for good reason.[6]) As foreshadowed, we'll take up perspectivism in the next chapter, but let's jump the gun and think about how the argument we've just given can be pushed one step further, so as to solve a problem that has bothered Nietzsche's readers for a long while: that on the one hand Nietzsche seems to endorse a metaphysics of will to power, while on the other he presents himself as a thoroughgoing perspectivist. There are indefinitely many ways to parse the world, and a perspective that renders its contents as patterns of control is no more than one of them.[7]

Come the next chapter, I'll be explaining perspectives as (among other things) ways of simplifying what one takes the world to be like so as to make representation cognitively tractable. Assume that you'll be able to address your priorities more effectively if you see your world in terms of those priorities: someone who's trying to add to his butterfly collection will do better at it if the concept *butterfly* is part of his conceptual apparatus, if he's able to recognize butterflies, and if what he notices, when there are butterflies present, are the butterflies, rather than anything else. Then, given that your highest priority is will to power, you'll do better to have a will-to-power rendering of your world. Such a rendering might be a will-to-power *metaphysics*, as in: "*This world is will to power—and nothing besides!*" Or it might be somewhat less dramatic than that: a dean will do better at growing his piece of the university if he sees departments as repositories of lines, alumni as potential donors, changes in academic fashion as opportunities for starting up new programs...and all of these as features of or ways to change what I understand is now called the org chart.[8] To be sure, Nietzsche doesn't think that the assumption I just asked you for is always, or even nearly always, true. Christian ascetics, he holds, have will to power as their highest priority, but they can't afford to be aware of it, and they can't afford to see the world from the will-to-power perspective. But when it is true, the will-to-power perspective will generally be, while not more than a perspective, nonetheless the perspective of choice.[9]

To reiterate, I want to attribute the argument I've just outlined to Nietzsche in only the thinnest sense. It's assembled out of Nietzschean materials, and I'm fairly certain that the argument occurred to him. But I'm about to claim that he didn't endorse it, because he himself had to live through one of its biggest bugs.

8.4

The alert reader has probably had a complaint pending against the Nietzschean anthropic argument for some time now. Suppose it's true that you wouldn't have come to be the complex and delicate priority-guided organization that you are if (some variant of) will to power had not been your top priority. That doesn't show that will to power is still your top priority, because priorities shift. While the argument provides a reason—and let's just allow for now that it's a convincing reason—to think that a shift away from that priority will eventually prove your undoing, "eventually" can be a long way away. A while back, I'm told, there was a stretch during which Yale was making expensive decisions that put its version of intellectual integrity ahead of will to power. But while Yale also went through its share of financial difficulties, it stayed with us; it takes a while to burn through that much accumulated institutional capital. So the argument doesn't show that your top priority is will to power, because you could be someone who (or some organization which) has abandoned that priority, but hasn't yet fallen apart.

Now there are many ways to fail to have will to power as your top priority: you could have a different top priority; or you could have various priorities, none of which was ranked first; or you could fall short of having anything that amounted to *priorities* at all. Reminding ourselves of the label for the way Nietzsche understands himself not to have will to power as a dominant priority, let's rehearse a passage we've seen before:

> What is the sign of every *literary decadence*? That life no longer dwells in the whole. The word becomes sovereign and leaps out of the sentence, the sentence reaches out and obscures the meaning of the page, and the page gains life at the expense of the whole—the whole is no longer a whole. But this is the simile of every style of *decadence*: every time, the anarchy of atoms, disgregation of the will... (6:27/CW 7)

The notion of a priority was introduced in terms of its guiding function within the organization; priorities control the organization's choices, which entails control of the organization's constituent parts. The decadent is someone whose parts (which Nietzsche thinks of as, first and foremost, drives) are not effectively controlled; so the decadent is someone who has no priorities because the control structures that priorities presuppose are no longer in place.[10]

Since I mean to treat Nietzsche himself as the most important problem facing the Nietzschean anthropic argument, it's a suitable moment to turn to *Ecce Homo*. As its title suggests, it's another of Nietzsche's exercises in self-presentation, and his riff on the genre of autobiography; he offers it as a retrospective frame for his other published works.[11] As we by now also expect, *Ecce Homo* doesn't just tell you about Nietzsche—it puts him on display. That means that what it says can't simply be taken at face value; we'll have to look at what it's showing us as well.

Until this point, we've been leaving it an open question whether the authors of the books we've reconnoitered are literary artifacts, or whether we should identify the characters with the flesh-and-blood author, Friedrich Nietzsche, and treat the presentation as being about and of the once living, breathing individual. And to help keep that question before us, I've been giving the authorial characters their own names: the Genealogist, the Good European, Nietzsche's Convalescent, and so on. But the moment is approaching where we'll be in a position to resolve the issue, and since in any case *Ecce Homo* is presented as the autobiography of someone named "Nietzsche," that's what I'll call him. (However, until that moment I'll continue to develop the argument in a way that doesn't presuppose either outcome.)

Now Nietzsche doesn't do anything as straightforward as tell us that he's a decadent. On the contrary, we're given a flurry of pronouncements on the subject which include a number of direct and indirect denials. Let's make a start on a pretty characteristic declaration: "Apart from the fact that I am a decadent, I am also the opposite." (He glosses the remark almost immediately: "As *summa summarum*, I was healthy; as an angle, as a specialty, I was a decadent.")[12] We need to stop and think about how to take assertions of this sort. After all, Nietzsche could be giving us a clear-headed and nuanced assessment of his state; but we would also expect a personality descending into chaos to give us mixed signals which would sound very much like this.

Nietzsche follows this claim with a brief argument that he is the opposite of a decadent; one of his reasons is that he knows how to forget. Given his diagnosis of *ressentiment* as a type of sickness, that might mean merely that he doesn't hold a grudge. But it also might mean a good deal more than that: recall the second Essay of the *Genealogy* describing how proto-human animals became full-fledgedly human by coming to have a memory. So the question is what function forgetting has here, and conveniently enough, Nietzsche repeatedly shows us. I'm going to pick a couple of representative passages; I apologize in advance for their length, but a stretch of text that will allow its author to exhibit an ability to forget will have to be longer than the standard-size quote.

> At this point, a large reflection is necessary. One will ask me why on earth I've been relating all these small things which are generally considered matters of complete indifference: I only harm myself, the more so if I am destined to represent great tasks. Answer: these small things—nutrition, place, climate, recreation, the whole casuistry of selfishness—are inconceivably more important than everything one has taken to be important so far. Precisely here one must begin to *relearn*. What mankind has so far considered seriously have not even been realities but mere imaginings—more strictly speaking, *lies* prompted by the bad instincts of sick natures that were harmful in the most profound sense—all these concepts, "God," "soul," "virtue," "sin," "beyond," "truth," "eternal life."—But the greatness of

196 WHY DIDN'T NIETZSCHE GET HIS ACT TOGETHER?

human nature, its "divinity," was sought in them...All the problems of politics, of social organization, and of education have been falsified through and through because one mistook the most harmful men for great men—because one learned to despise "little" things, which means the basic concerns of life itself...Our present culture is ambiguous in the highest degree...The German emperor making a pact with the pope, as if the pope were not the representative of deadly hostility to life!...What is being built today will no longer stand in three years. — When I measure myself against my *ability*, not to speak of what will come after me, a collapse, a construction without equal, then I more than any other mortal have a claim to the epithet of greatness. When I compare myself with the men who have so far been honored as the *first*, the difference is palpable. I do not even count these so called "first" men among men in general, —for me they are the refuse of humanity, monsters of sickness and vengeful instincts: they are inhuman, disastrous, at bottom incurable, and revenge themselves on life...I want to be their opposite: it is my privilege to have the subtlest sensitivity for all signs of healthy instincts. There is no pathological trait in me; even in periods of severe sickness I never became pathological; in vain would one seek for a trait of fanaticism in my character. There is not a moment in my life to which one could point to convict me of a presumptuous and pathetic posture. (6:295f/EH 2:10)

Before considering the content, I recommend that the reader experiment with reading the passage aloud and with feeling. Keep in mind that I'm using Kaufmann's translation, but with a handful of emendations. Kaufmann leaves a sentence off the beginning, which I've restored. As per usual, he introduces paragraph breaks into the English, but in this case it's important to see that the flow of the passage is not broken up in this way; accordingly, I've removed them. Ellipses are Nietzsche's, and don't indicate that I'm abridging his text. Finally, a short passage originally deleted by his sister, and reproduced in a footnote, has been returned to the position it occupies in the original (and the currently standard German text).

To recap the progress of this stretch of Nietzsche's prose: He starts out in a low key, evenly modulated tone, explaining that his longish discussion of the little things in life has had a philosophical point; those little things are what matters, not the delusory ideas that we associate with religion, or with what Peter Viereck once called metapolitics (1965). Then, with the most minimal transition, we get a brief outburst of barstool metapolitics, in a register that's best described as fanatic raving. Then there's a moment of posturing—Nietzsche comparing himself to other "first men"—that's both presumptuous and a bit pathetic. And then he tells us, almost immediately, that he never exhibits fanaticism, presumptuousness, or a pathetic posture. No wonder Elizabeth Förster-Nietzsche felt that she had to excise the middle of this block of text.

Control, we pointed out, requires memory; here Nietzsche's capacity for forgetting is exercising itself moment-to-moment, and functioning to paper over blatant inconsistency, both at the level of opinion, and at the level of tone of voice and character. Let's look at just one more of the many passages that behave similarly, to preempt the worry that what we've just seen was somehow an exception. Keep in mind one of the puzzles posed by Nietzsche's writing, namely, that these theatrical presentations of loss of control are so rarely noticed: as in the *Genealogy*, he induces moment-to-moment lapses of memory in most of his readers:

> —That a *psychologist* without equal speaks from my writings, is perhaps the first insight reached by a good reader—a reader as I deserve him, who reads me the way good old philologists read their Horace. Those propositions on which all the world is really agreed, not to speak of the world's common run of philosophers, the moralists and other hollow pots, cabbage heads—appear in my books as naive blunders: for example, the belief that "unegoistic" and "egoistic" are opposites, while the ego itself is really only a "higher swindle," an "ideal" ... There are *neither* egoistic *nor* unegoistic acts: both concepts are psychological absurdities. Or the proposition: "man strives for happiness" ... Or the proposition: "happiness is the reward of virtue" ... Or the proposition: "pleasure and displeasure are opposites" ... The Circe of humanity, morality, has falsified all *psychologica* through and through—*moralizing* them—down to that gruesome nonsense that love is supposed to be something "unegoistic" ... one has to sit firmly upon *oneself*, one must stand bravely on one's own two legs, otherwise one is simply *incapable* of loving. Ultimately, women know that only too well: they don't give a damn about selfless, merely objective men ... May I venture here the surmise that I *know* women? That is part of my Dionysian dowry. Who knows? perhaps I am the first psychologist of the Eternally-Feminine. They all love me—an old story: not counting the *abortive* females, the "emancipated" who lack the stuff for children. —Fortunately, I am not willing to be torn to pieces: the perfect woman tears to pieces when she loves ... I know these

198 WHY DIDN'T NIETZSCHE GET HIS ACT TOGETHER?

charming maenads ... Ah, what a dangerous, creeping, subterranean little beast of prey she is! And yet so agreeable! ... A little woman who pursues her revenge would run over fate itself. — Woman is indescribably more evil than man; also cleverer: good nature is in a woman a form of *degeneration* ... In all so-called "beautiful souls" something is physiologically askew at bottom,—I don't say everything, else I should become medi-cynical. The fight for *equal* rights is actually a symptom of a disease: every physician knows that. —Woman, the more she is a woman, resists equal rights hand and foot: after all, the state of nature, the eternal *war* between the sexes, gives her by far the first rank. —Has my definition of love been heard? it is the only one worthy of a philosopher. Love—in its means, war; at bottom, the deadly hatred of the sexes. —Has my answer been heard to the question of how one *cures* a woman—"redeems" her? One gives her a child. Woman needs children, a man is for her always only a means: thus spoke Zarathustra. —"Emancipation of women"—that is the instinctive hatred of the *abortive* woman, who is incapable of giving birth, against the woman who has turned out well, —the fight against the "man" is always a mere means, pretext, tactic. By raising *themselves* higher, as "woman in herself," as "higher woman," as a female "idealist," they want to *lower* the level of the general rank of woman; and there is no surer means for that than high-school education, slacks, political voting-cattle rights. At bottom, the emancipated are *anarchists* in the world of the "eternally feminine," the underprivileged whose most fundamental instinct is revenge ... (6:305f/EH 3.5)

As with the previous passage, before considering the content, I recommend that the reader experiment with reading the passage aloud and with feeling.[13]

Once again Nietzsche is starting off with a series of claims that fall under "psychology" (which as we know, means what "French moralists" did), and they're worth taking seriously for what they are: that the cluster of concepts and views that have to do with self-interest and hedonistic psychology are deeply confused. As we've seen him do before, Nietzsche is positioning himself as highly critical of what the French moralists by and large took for granted.

But then, one of those assumptions, about love being altruistic, *reminds* him of women and what *they* think about love—presumably because "women" and "love" are associated in his mind, and one idea makes him think of the other. He begins a series of free associations, starting off with a diatribe about women. As he moves over the loose associations, the prose becomes choppier, and he's unable to finish a thought before being distracted by something else: antifeminist politics, resentful evaluations of the sort that one usually hears from men who have problems getting dates, and disturbing misogynistic fantasies come one after the other. And these are interleaved with a sudden complaint about "beautiful souls"—which doesn't have anything to do with women at all—and asides about democracy and voting rights.

It's tempting to charitably put these passages out of sight and out of mind; *Ecce Homo* was written very near to Nietzsche's collapse, and surely we can dismiss the erratic tone and so on as a symptom of his illness, thus, not necessarily philosophically important signposting. However, recall from ch. 2 that the *Genealogy of Morals* similarly develops an equally elaborate and obviously contrived display of its author's capacity to forget, and the *Genealogy* is widely, and in my view correctly, regarded as a masterpiece. If sudden swerves like these are a reason to dismiss *Ecce Homo*, they're a reason to dismiss the *Genealogy*, by this point one of the canonical texts of moral philosophy, as well; moreover, recall that it's not all that long since *all* of Nietzsche's work was dismissed as the product of dementia. So I don't recommend writing off *Ecce Homo* on these grounds.

And sure enough, when we look in the neighborhood of that second passage, we find—as per usual—its framing. Nietzsche begins the immediately preceding section with this pronouncement:

> This is also the point for a general remark about my *art of style*. To *communicate* a state, an inward tension of pathos, by means of signs, including the tempo of these signs—that is the meaning of every style; and considering that the multiplicity of inward states is exceptionally large in my case, I have many stylistic possibilities—the most multifarious art of style that has ever been at the disposal of one man. *Good* is any style that really communicates an inward state, that makes no mistakes about the signs, the tempo of the signs, the gestures—all the laws about long periods are concerned with the art of gestures. Here my instinct is infallible.
>
> The art of the *great* rhythm, the *great* style of long periods to express a tremendous up and down of sublime, of superhuman passion, was discovered only by me ... (6:304f/EH 3.4)

Surely the discombobulated swerves of that criticism of French moralism lurching into that misogynistic rant *would* be the style for communicating the inward state of decadence, and the juxtaposition with those remarks on style and rhythm is too pointed for it to be an accident. In these passages, Nietzsche is informing us that, yes, he is a decadent.

Why was inconsistency, in the first of those two passages, and the inability to keep one's train of thought on track more generally being papered over rather than rectified? By the time we come to it, Nietzsche has given us an answer: his discussion of climate, reading, and eating is organized by the thought that one has to husband a scarce resource: the energy one spends in coping with an unsuitable climate, heavy food, and so on. And there's a further type of activity that is just as much, or even more of a drain on the resource in such short supply:

> an instinct of self-defense...commands us...*to say No as rarely as possible*...The reason in this is that when defensive expenditures, be they ever so small, become the rule and habit, they entail an extraordinary and entirely superfluous impoverishment. Our *great* expenses are composed of the most frequent small ones. (6:291f/EH 2.8)

The exercise of control, the effort of maintaining a pattern of control involving consistency of character and of doctrine, is to a great extent the effort of saying *No* to elements that won't fit into a consistent pattern. And that effort is simply too great for Nietzsche (who has just finished telling us that he can handle only one cup of tea in the morning) to make.[14]

At the end of the section from which we extracted our first illustration of forgetfulness at work, Nietzsche tells us that his "formula for greatness in a human being is *amor fati* [love of fate or destiny]: that one wants nothing to be different" (6:297/EH 2.10). If we take it that this is what we've had explained and displayed to us, we can now see that we need to distinguish two very different evaluative foci of Nietzsche's thinking. The will to power, which we've already seen, is a *priority*, by which I mean to say that it guides action and choice, requiring an agent to take steps to maintain and extend the pattern of control that he is, by, in fact, exercising control: by forcing things to fit the pattern, which is to say, by not accepting them as they are. *Amor fati*, accepting things as they are, is a mode of acquiescence, and so is precisely *not* part of the exercise of control, which means that it's not in this sense a priority at all, and not compatible with the demands of will to power.

It's easy to allow the ambiguity present in the notion of interpretation to mask the tension between will to power and *amor fati*. But one way of doing interpretation—call it *active* interpretation—is an exercise of will to power; we saw the Foucauldian understanding of Nietzschean interpretation in our first Interlude, and recall Nietzsche's gesture at barbarian conquerers imposing social structure on a vanquished mass of humanity (5:325/GM 2:17). The other—call it *passive* interpretation—is precisely not such an exercise. Actual interpretations are inevitably mixtures of active and passive, but the difference between them is both real and practically important. When an administrator announces a "Faster, Cheaper, Better" initiative (the slogan adopted by a former NASA head), this could have the effect of changing what the departments, centers, and so on actually *do*—or it could merely mean that the bureaucrats start describing whatever they were doing already as "Faster, Cheaper, Better," while changing nothing. Decadence is the state in which the exercise of control over one's constitution is no longer possible, and *amor fati* is an evaluative attitude that belongs to decadence: "Accepting oneself as if fated, not wishing oneself 'different'—that is in such cases [of "Russian fatalism," the desperate exhaustion of a soldier who finally just lies down in the snow] *great reason* itself" (6:273/EH 1.6).

Nietzsche apparently *is* a decadent, and the confusing pronouncements are the way he papers over what as a decadent he's no longer able to render unconfused. The Nietzschean anthropic argument claims that if a priority-guided organization asks what its top priority is, it will turn out that the organization is guided by will to power. Nietzsche isn't exactly a counterexample to *that* claim (although we've seen in passing how to come up with what would be an exact counterexample). Rather, he illustrates a related objection: that you might turn out not to be *addressed* by the argument, because you could be asking the question even if you were not guided by priorities at all. Instead of priorities, Nietzsche has, and let's introduce a contrasting term at this point, a *meaning*—namely, *amor fati*. *Amor fati* is all spin doctoring, all aspect, all desirability characterization, and no guidance. His own concept, value, covers both, but once again, I want to be able to single out different aspects of his values, and the different roles they can play.

But now, since *amor fati* doesn't control behavior in the way that a priority does, what's it doing there? We evidently need to characterize the function of meanings in the decadent personality.[15]

8.5

Why go on? Why not commit suicide? Why not just *let go*, let your grip relax, and allow yourself to slide into a slacker's life?

202 WHY DIDN'T NIETZSCHE GET HIS ACT TOGETHER?

Questions like these haven't received a great deal of attention from philosophers in the analytic tradition, but a recent discussion exhibits the approach that comes to it most naturally. Christine Korsgaard has argued that action and agency are one's *plight*; you act because you *need* to pull yourself together and do one thing or another.[16] Normally I'm committed to ongoing courses of action in whose service I must mobilize myself, when the occasion arises: maybe I can't afford to slack off because I'm in the middle of rewriting the draft of a chapter, my cat has to be fed, the laundry has to get done, the exams graded, and vegan chicken soup brought over to a laid-up friend—although Korsgaard herself argues that one's commitment to one's ongoing agency doesn't depend merely on this sort of contingent commitment to particular objectives.[17] Unity of agency is consequently *re*unity of agency. In something like the way that an animal remains alive in virtue of activities like eating and sleeping, activities which reconstitute it, from day to day, as a living creature, synchronic unity of agency, that is to say, unity of agency in the moment, is a product of—is the advancing wavefront of—diachronic unity of agency, unity of agency over time. What we're seeing is how, when a representative and mainstream analytic philosopher tries to explain your stake in your unified agency, the answers she finds it most natural to offer to questions like "Why go on?" assume that you are *already* an agent.

Now, if you are an agent, the answer to this question will be a *reason*— a practical reason, since this is what agents consume in the course of making decisions, and so with content of a sort that you could express as a sentence. And whatever the merits of Korsgaard's insistence that your stake in your own agency is not contingent, if the Nietzschean anthropic argument is on the mark, someone who has his act together won't find the question particularly urgent. Remember, whatever the actual answer, your top priority already *is* going on.

For the decadent, however, "Why go on?" *is* an urgent question: he is, after all, in the process of falling apart. A useful answer to this question cannot be a traditional practical reason, that is, a reason for a decision addressed to the agent, for the decadent doesn't have a centralized command post, as it were, that makes effective decisions. The decadent doesn't exercise much by way of control over his parts, and so an effective answer to the question, one that will keep the components flying in more or less their former configuration, has to be addressed to the parts severally.

WHO WROTE NIETZSCHE'S AUTOBIOGRAPHY? 203

If the parts of a decadent are themselves person-like agents—as they would be, say, in a university bureaucracy—then the answer (or answers, because we shouldn't assume that the same answer will do for each component) might still take the form of a traditional practical reason. But when the parts aren't themselves agents, a suitable answer must take a form that appropriate parts can consume. Since Nietzsche thinks of himself as made up primarily of drives, the answer he seeks needn't be identified with a well-defined sentence-like content at all. Rather, it will be a *stimulus* to which the drives respond.

Nietzsche's interest and background in music are to be emphasized at this point. An amateur composer, he published several books on primarily musical subjects, and his other works contain much discussion of musical matters.[18] So it's not surprising that, time and again, we find Nietzsche thinking his way through some problem or other using musical analogies, and now that we've seen that what one offers to the drives by way of a response to the question, "Why go on?" might as well be *music*, we should ask what kind of music would do.

Early engagements with a philosophical problem can be telling precursors to more mature attempts on it, and so a good place to take this query would be Nietzsche's first book, where he argued that *tragedy* functioned as the ancient Greek answer to "Why go on?"[19] Accordingly, in thinking about available responses to this question, we should expect to find him using tragedy as a model, and in fact, towards the end of the book, Nietzsche considered how one would achieve, in music, the experience produced by tragedy, that "of having to see at the same time that [one] also long[s] to transcend all seeing":

> Quite generally, only music, placed beside the world, can give us an idea of what is meant by the justification of the world as an aesthetic phenomenon. The joy aroused by the tragic myth has the same origin as the joyous sensation of dissonance in music . . . we desire to hear and at the same time long to get beyond all hearing. (1:150, 152f/BT 24)

Nietzsche never abandoned this idea, and dissonance ended up being his way of thinking about one kind of stimulus that would effectively coax his drives forward, once they could no longer be coerced. Shortly after the comparison of tragedy to dissonance, *The Birth of Tragedy* entertains the notion

204 WHY DIDN'T NIETZSCHE GET HIS ACT TOGETHER?

that we could "imagine dissonance become man," and *Ecce Homo* unpacks the metaphor, doing its best to show how to do more than just imagine it. The drives—out of which the decadent personality is, to help myself to a nearby pun, composed—are lured onward by the very incoherence that, neatly enough, is the immediate effect of decadence.[20] The exercise of highlighting and contemplating these inconsistencies of tone, character, and doctrine—and of exaggerating them for artistic effect—is a self-conscious contribution that Nietzsche is able to make to his own continued psychological existence.

Identifying this strategy confirms our answer to the question of whether Nietzsche himself was really a decadent: it would make no sense to avail oneself of such devices if one were not. As a decadent, he is riddled through and through with inconsistencies of all sorts, inconsistencies which he's too depleted to eradicate. His interest in his own continued existence—if you like, his will to power—expresses itself in the construction and contemplation of a representation of that very decadence, which turns out, rather neatly, to be one of the very things that will keep his drives in some semblance of order.[21]

Here is the phrase I just quoted, with a bit more of its context:

> If we could imagine dissonance become man—and what else is man?—this dissonance, to be able to live, would need a splendid illusion that would cover dissonance with a veil of beauty.   (1:155/BT 25)

Amor fati shares with dissonance the function of meanings in the psychological economy of decadence—that is, to elicit a response from the drives.[22] (We can now explain the contrast between the two functional concepts we've been developing. Priorities *guide decisions*. Meanings are *personality glue*.) Dissonance needs to be cut with harmony if it's not just going to be out-and-out discord; the requisite effect, remember, is that one *both* desire to hear, and not to. *Amor fati* is the veil of beauty thrown over the dissonance, or anyway, the spoonful of sugar that helps the medicine go down.

8.6

The reader will by this point have another objection: doesn't the evidence I've adduced for this interpretation in fact undercut it? Allow that Nietzsche is displaying himself as a decadent. Still, his presentation of his own incoherent character is so artful, so masterful, and so controlled as to belie the overt content of the display. A decadent is someone who cannot control the parts that make him up, but Nietzsche's show of lack of control is so visibly intentional as to amount to precisely the presentation of a character that is in full control. And there's an additional objection that's best considered together with this one. We've been taking as one of our foils Nehamas's reading, on which the Nietzsche we're being presented with isn't the "writer," the lonely man desperately scribbling away in Swiss and Italian *pensions*, but the "postulated author": more or less, a character projected by the body of texts, on a par with the narrators of works of fiction. As a matter of method, to read a literary text is to reconstruct the text's postulated author, which means in turn to reconstruct that author's intention in producing such a text.[23] The exercise of reconstruction requires that the implicit author, Nietzsche in this case, be practically coherent and consistent; making the text out to be the product of a coherent intention is delineating a unified agent coordinate with that intention. So to take the Nietzsche presented by his texts to be a decadent, that is, a disunified agent, is on Nehamas's view a methodological blunder. And up to this point, although we pushed back a good deal, we've kept this a live possibility; it's time, finally, to discard it.

Nietzsche distinguishes the "driving force" of an action from its "directing force": as when, on a large ship, the engine and current propel the vessel forward, while the helmsman can make only small adjustments in direction (and sometimes, Nietzsche suggests, none at all; 3:607f/GS 360). On the Nietzschean model of the workings of the mind, a decadent's drives may express themselves in bursts of activity, whose occurence or even general shape the agent as a whole cannot control. The agent's purposes or goals, which Nietzsche analogizes to the helmsman, can however make minor adjustments to activities like these, and here it's worth remembering that writing, for Nietzsche, was often a two-pass activity: his published works are often enough lightly revised selections of raw material produced as journal entries.[24] If I'm reading this passage correctly, it tells us how writing produced by a decadent could come to exhibit the distinctive artifice that we find in Nietzsche's mature works (e.g., the sort of textual construction we saw in the lengthy excerpts from *Ecce Homo*). The appearance of control is managed by layering minor adjustments onto what amounts to an extended blurt, one emitted with hardly any control at all. Evidently, and overriding that first objection, one doesn't have to be master of oneself to write masterfully, and one doesn't have to be in control of oneself to write in a controlled style.[25]

206 WHY DIDN'T NIETZSCHE GET HIS ACT TOGETHER?

We want to be careful to avoid lapsing into a false dilemma. One horn of it is that Nietzsche is fully in control, betrayed by the moments of craftsmanship I've been pointing out; that's to say, he's merely mimicking an incoherent character. The other is that he is entirely out of control—more or less Rimbaud's *bateau ivre*—and unable to manage anything in the way of tactical or strategic maneuvering at all. The pull of that dilemma—the insistence that it *has* to be one or the other—shows how entrenched the theoretical picture under attack actually is, because if you look for even a moment, our lives are full of activities that slide between its horns. Indeed, this is where the *most* valuable things in our life land, and since we're engaged in philosophy, take philosophical writing: a book whose contents are simply written to spec—perhaps with a title like *[insert popular culture icon here] and Philosophy*—is almost certainly worthless; a book whose contents are fully involuntary *may* be fascinating, but don't expect it to come out philosophy. (I won't belabor the point for sexual or romantic love, where the unpalatable extremes are, respectively, partnerships that look like business arrangements, and obsessions; the love we value and hope for is neither exactly voluntary nor simply involuntary.) So it's not that I think *either* that Nietzsche couldn't help having it come out the way it did (because he was out of control of his own writing), *or* that it all proceeded according to plan. That the choice seems forced is, once again, a mark of how locked in we are to our interpretive practices.

Rather, Nietzsche was trying to make the best of a difficult situation, by reshaping, to the extent he could, writing that was scarcely supervised as his pen raced erratically along; the result is that it seems to be in some ways out of control, and in other ways to follow a large-scale plan-like trajectory. We're used to this sort of desperate maneuvering in other activities, as when downhill skiers navigate unfamiliar and challenging slopes; this was Nietzsche writing in more or less that manner, as he (to borrow a phrase from Tom Lehrer) slid down the razor blade of life. But since Nietzsche concludes the passage we introduced a half-step back with the pronouncement that "we still need a critique of the concept of 'purpose' "—and since in context, this amounts to a rejection of the widely shared and roughly Anscombian model of intentional action—let's pause for a little more sorting out.

We'll want to distinguish two strengths of the Anscombean rendering of action; call them *caffeinated* and *decaf*. As the caffeinated version has it, actions are constructed by selecting subsidiary or component actions on the basis of their suitability for effecting a designated end; this accounts for the "calculative" structure of an action. An action is constructed out of a series of steps (in an alternative rendering, it's built up out of nested subsidiary actions), and the person executing the action traverses those steps, one after the other, each one bringing him closer to the termination point of the series—the "end" of the action—at which point, he stops. Here the end has full-strength explanatory priority; the termination point at which he was trying to arrive can be adduced, in the course of the action itself, to justify the steps being taken, and Anscombe famously provided a template for the sort of interrogation that would elicit its structure: "Why are you opening the book?" "I'm checking a citation." "Why are you doing *that*?" "I'm cleaning up the draft of my paper." "Why are you cleaning it up?" "I'm sending it off to the editor."[26]

Decaf Anscombeanism weakens the explanatory priority of the end of an action; it consists in its being *as if* the stages of the action had been selected to arrive at their termination point. Perhaps you only realize, in retrospect, where you've arrived; nonetheless, you can describe how you got there *as though* there were a series of means taken to an end. This sort of after-the-fact explanation is possible as long as the action in question does come out "calculatively" structured, but doesn't impute an up-front intention to proceed as he did to the person executing it.

Nehamas's postulated author is the agent projected by understanding a text, or rather, a body of texts, as an Anscombian intentional action. In his earlier writing, he seemed to be thinking of it as a caffeinated action, projected however by a fictional author; aware of the comparison we just remarked, to what it's like to steer container ships, Nehamas has since adjusted the view: where you might well not have had an intention you could articulate, before embarking on what you did, the intention emerges as the action reaches its point of closure. That is, his current rendering of the postulated author makes its action out to be Anscombean, but decaffeinated.[27]

Either way, Nehamas's exegetical methodology takes for granted a theory of action that Nietzsche is criticizing. Should we really expect the activities that result from warring drives jockeying for control of one's body to eventuate in an action that can be given that sort of step-by-step, "calculative" description? Recall our earlier comparison of drives to political parties. Sometimes a government is run by a single party; sometimes a government is run by a coalition of parties that have agreed on a platform and an agenda, and that have procedures for developing coherent policy responses to events in real time. But often the parliamentary jockeying produces governance

208 WHY DIDN'T NIETZSCHE GET HIS ACT TOGETHER?

that can't reasonably be taken for end-directed, even after the fact. And analogously, when a person is put together in the manner we have been seeing (a field of quasi-independent drives, a full-on decadent), what it does, anyway over more ambitious time frames, will hardly ever come out as action directed toward an end—neither in prospect nor retroactively.[28] We've seen Nietzsche displaying this as his own predicament, and we've seen him attempting to make theoretical sense of it. If Nietzsche's philosophical views are interesting and important enough to justify the effort of interpreting him, we shouldn't proceed by interpreting him in a way that presupposes that those views can be dismissed.[29]

To be sure, the exercise of simulating an incoherent author is run-of-the-mill modernism; how do we know that's not what we're seeing here? The literary-artifact Nietzsche does not *need* the delicately drawn, self-undermining portrait of an incoherent personality; it's only in light of its living author's need for it that the elaborate construction makes sense.[30]

And there's a further, related point. A famous passage, titled "One thing is needful," starts off with the announcement: "To 'give style' to one's character—a great and rare art!" It proceeds to describe ways to shape oneself (or perhaps, we saw in ch. 5, misrepresent oneself) by imposing "the constraint of a single taste." I find, however, that almost all of Nietzsche's readers slide into misreading the text in front of them, by taking it that the one thing needful *is* giving that unified style to one's character.

In fact what we're told is required is "that a human being should attain satisfaction with himself," that is, "give pleasure to [himself]," and Nietzsche identifies two complementary strategies for doing so. If you're "strong," you can shape yourself to reflect that "single taste"; but if you're "weak," you're "well advised" to "shape and interpret [your] environment as *free* nature: wild, arbitrary, fantastic, disorderly, and surprising" (3:530f/GS 290, deleting some emphases). At this point, the evidence that, whatever his admiration for the former strategy, Nietzsche is pursuing the latter—it's overwhelming. Now, if in living out your life, you're adopting this mode of disorder as your own, how plausible is it that you'll be producing a large-scale, Anscombean, calculatively structured action, one which consists in elaborately rendering a coherent literary character that is something distinct from your flailing and thrashing?

Let's proceed, then, to take the Nietzsche we're discussing actually to be the living person that the portrait is *of*, rather than merely a literary artifact. Bear in mind, however, that we don't have to suppose that the representation

WHO WROTE NIETZSCHE'S AUTOBIOGRAPHY? 209

is faithful. Nietzsche was probably not someone whose mental health could be kept up by doses of dissonance for long; remember, in the end, the therapy didn't work. Although he's not best thought of as built up out of inadequately regimented drives, when he represents himself that way, he's representing *himself.*

8.7

Let's return to my earlier complaint about the use of the unified agent in contemporary philosophy. The new orthodoxy in moral philosophy is that if you're not a unified agent, then, from a practical point of view, you're not really *there*. (So there isn't really anything for an anthropic or transcendental or other action-directing argument to be applied *to*, when we're considering the decadent.[31]) Nietzsche's exercise in autobiography convincingly shows this rejoinder to be callous, practically irrelevant and unbelievable. It's callous in that people who are coming apart at the seams often end up on the street; when passersby step over street people as they enter the subway, they treat the street people as though they didn't exist; the rejoinder amounts to ideology that underwrites this kind of shoddy behavior: from the "practical point of view," the street people really *don't* exist.[32] But, second, it's no use to tell Nietzsche that since he isn't, properly speaking, an agent, he doesn't, from a practical point of view, exist. That won't make his very difficult, very immediate, and very personal problems any less pressing for him. Finally, the sheer sustained ingenuity of the Nietzsche corpus makes it impossible simply to dismiss its author in the way this rejoinder would like; if he's "not there," who wrote all those books?

Nietzsche, the patron saint and poster child of disunity, was not in a position to overlook the fact that disunified agency, disunified apperception, and disunified minds are, for some people, what it's like to be them. A great deal of philosophizing treats the unified self as a dialectical starting point: here you are, doing the philosophizing, so we can begin the argument with your transcendental unity of apperception, or with your unified agency, or whatever. But Nietzsche couldn't start with the assumption that he was a unified agent, because he just *wasn't*. One lesson to learn from our reconstruction of Nietzsche's predicament, and of his response to it, is that it's time to rethink the idea that the unity of the self is an Archimedean point in philosophy.

210 WHY DIDN'T NIETZSCHE GET HIS ACT TOGETHER?

Still, Nietzsche pined, loudly and frequently, for the unattainable attractions of unity.[33] Will to power successfully asserting itself struck him as *health*, and more than anyone else he glorified that rendition of agency, with the yearning of those who have never actually tasted the object of their desire, and so with a passion that has inspired his more callow readers ever since. And here he's still in line with the received attitudes; even when it's allowed that we can fall short of unity, it's taken for granted that this is a bad thing for the agent, that the agent is falling short of the standards to which he should be held, and that this is a defect to be remedied as expeditiously as possible.

But a second lesson to take away from our discussion is that unity of agency is overhyped. There's something it's like to occupy a perspective (in the sense that Nagel famously pointed out there's something it's like to be a bat), but during our brief encounter with the will-to-power perspective, we didn't pause to get a sense of what it *is* like.[34] To help remedy that, here is David Wiggins musing over a representation of the perspective in question:

> Two or three years ago, when I went to see some film at the Academy Cinema, the second feature of the evening was a documentary film about creatures fathoms down on the ocean-bottom. When it was over, I turned to my companion and asked, "What is it about these films that makes one feel so utterly desolate?" Her reply was: "apart from the fact that so much of the film was about sea monsters eating one another, the unnerving thing was that nothing down there ever seemed to *rest*." As for play, disinterested curiosity, or merely contemplating, she could have added, these seemed inconceivable.
>
> And the thought the film leads to is this. If we can project upon a form of life nothing but the pursuit of life itself, if we find there . . . no interest in the world considered as lasting longer than the animal in question will need the world to last in order to sustain the animal's own life; then the form of life must be to some considerable extent alien to us. (1991, p. 102)

The world as will to power is a disheartening and uninviting vision, and it is nihilistic: all priorities, and no meanings. It's not a coincidence that there is more to be said for and about the values that Nietzsche invented as psychological prostheses; just because they are meant to coax the drives onward, they're *attractive*.

8.8

At this point, we should be wondering whether a number of further famous Nietzschean notions—in particular, the Eternal Return and the Overman—when they're positioned as values, are to be understood as having been produced to occupy the cognitive role, not of priorities, but of meanings. On the supposition that the suggestion is correct, let's help ourselves to a B-movie from a little while back in order to draw one further conclusion for our exegetical practice.[35]

The protagonist of *Bubba Ho-tep* is a senior citizen who thinks that he's Elvis Presley. We see him marking time in his old age home, living an undignified, passive, and disintegrated life. When he comes to believe that he's the only thing standing between the other residents of the old age home and Bubba Ho-tep—the eponymous redneck mummy, returned from the dead to inflict on them a fate too tacky to mention in mixed company—he mobilizes himself. Or rather, he's mobilized by the emotional content of his value, and transformed from a disunified agent into an agent capable of making effective decisions, and of course he defeats the mummy and saves the old-age home.

The point I want to extract from my summary of this plot line is that, since what a meaning does is stimulate the drives, it's not always required to be intellectually respectable. The idea that a redneck Egyptian mummy has come back from the dead is just plain silly (indeed, it's there to provide the film with a comic dimension), but as long as it holds someone together as an agent, its suitability for that role isn't impugned by its silliness. Neither is it impugned by its untruth: the movie happens to suggest that the character may really be who he thinks he is, and in addition that the mummy is real, but none of this matters for whether defeating the mummy can operate as a meaning for the person we are being shown. Psychological effectiveness as a meaning is one thing; other intellectual merits are another.

Within Nietzsche scholarship, the Overman and the Eternal Return have been consistently treated as philosophical *doctrines*. Unsurprisingly, interpreters have worked to reconstruct them by producing one after another highly articulated theoretical rendering, each fine-tuned to meet objections raised to earlier treatments. However, a person's relatively simpler and relatively unintellectual psychic parts are more likely to be successfully addressed by values that are in soft focus. When values are deployed as meanings, they have to be, more or less, inspiring; when there's too much

212   WHY DIDN'T NIETZSCHE GET HIS ACT TOGETHER?

theoretical articulation, they stop being inspiring. If the cognitive function of meanings is to mobilize the elements of a personality, and if the Overman—or rather, bearing in mind our discussion in ch. 3, the novel value of inventing values—and the Eternal Return are meant to function as meanings, then the traditional exegetical approach to these Nietzschean ideas is no doubt a mistake.

We can see the will-to-power agent and the highly fragmented decadent as the two near-extremes of a spectrum.[36] Because we have a place in our lives both for priorities and for meanings, most of us probably fall somewhere in the middle of it, and I imagine that that is where most of us want to—or ought to want to—remain. Nonetheless, we shouldn't allow ourselves to be dismissive of personalities positioned towards the fragmented end of the spectrum. Recall that Nietzsche proposes that the right response to nihilism is to invent new values, and although this is sometimes a task he assigns to "philosophers of the future," I've just been suggesting that the Eternal Return, the invention of novel values, and *amor fati* are demos. While they were meant in the first place for Nietzsche's own consumption, they've proven inspiring to the psyches (and presumably to whatever is the actual counterpart of the Nietzschean drives) of generations of his readers as well. Nietzsche is showing you how it's done, and he doesn't do too badly at it. If his own example suggests that inspiring values are best invented by decadents, doesn't that count, all on its own, as a weighty recommendation for the disunified self?

8.9

At this point, I hope I've made the case that Nietzsche's later works are properly read as in the first place presenting authorial characters, that these are *different* authorial characters—and nonetheless, that with the exception of *Zarathustra*, they are all of them Nietzsche himself.

If you're not convinced, maybe it's because you're wondering how the authors could be different from one another, and yet also (except for one of them) all be one and the same real live human being. And if you allow the case has been made, you might be wondering whyever Nietzsche would have devoted so much of his life to this series of self-portraits. To address these questions, it's time to turn to Nietzsche's perspectivism.

9

What Was Nietzsche's Perspectivism?

Everyone knows that Nietzsche was a perspectivist. And while what "everyone knows" is often just not true, and we'll get to some of that in a moment, I don't necessarily disagree. However, practically all the philosophers who have that opinion also assume that they know what it *means*: to a first approximation, that perspectivism is a kind of relativism, and that a relativist theory is one according to which assertions or propositions aren't plain-and-simple true (or false), but rather, true (or false) relative to—*for* or *in*—something or other. For instance, if you're a cultural relativist, you think that claims are true-for-a-culture (or true for the people in a culture), rather than across the board, for just anybody. Likewise, on this way of taking perspectivism, if you're a perspectivist, you think that claims are true-in-a-perspective, or true for the people who have that perspective, rather than for just anybody. In this generic conception of relativism, truths anchored to disparate bases are strictly speaking incommensurable: depending on precisely how a philosopher construes it, such truths can't contradict one another; or, there's no principled way to designate one perspective as the *correct* perspective; or, no principled way to say of differently anchored truths that one of them has it right, and the other has it wrong. For Nietzsche's readers, the notion of a perspective is associated with that of interpretation, and so you also hear it said both that truths are interpretations, and that there are no truths, only interpretations.

Philosophers are very used to the idea that relativism is self-refuting, where the general shape of that thought is conveyed by a pair of questions: Is relativism *true*? Or is it just true-*for-you*?[1] Having those questions come up is a mark of the ready-to-hand way of construing perspectivism, and sure enough, discussion of whether Nietzsche's views are self-refuting in this manner is a recurring motif in the literature.[2]

However, Nietzsche's perspectivism has been misunderstood. His position doesn't fit the familiar relativist formula and, I'm about to argue, recovering it is the key to understanding the personal significance of the trajectory of

Why Didn't Nietzsche Get His Act Together? Elijah Millgram, Oxford University Press. © Oxford University Press 2023.
DOI: 10.1093/oso/9780197669303.003.0009

214 WHY DIDN'T NIETZSCHE GET HIS ACT TOGETHER?

his later writings. But to get there, we'll have to take the long way around, and I'll need to ask the reader, yet again, for an extra dose of patience.

I'll begin by assembling the raw materials that we need to introduce Nietzsche's conception of a perspective. That will allow me to explain how perspectives fall into place around values and drives, and why it is that the perspectives most of interest to us are human personalities. That in turn will put us in a position to look back on the books we've been discussing as Nietzsche's presentation of a series of perspectives (with one exception, they're all of them his own). To illustrate the workings of perspectives, I'll point out three exemplary perspective shifts, and draw our attention to the cross-corrections they allow us to make.

At that point, I can return to an issue we've had on our plate for some time now: Nietzsche's program of inventing values, and the challenges we've seen that it faces. Having several perspectives available to him allowed Nietzsche, or so he decided, to surmount those challenges; but traversing them went hand in hand with disunified agency—with decadence. That realization allowed Nietzsche to affirm his life, which involved accepting—and not *just* accepting—his ongoing and ultimately fatal disintegration. Thus it was his perspectivism that allowed him to live up to the demands of the Eternal Return.

9.1

I'm about to talk through Nietzsche's ideas about perspectives from the emerging perspective of bounded rationality. As we'll see, this is a research program which puts us in a position to recognize some of Nietzsche's innovations, but let me emphasize that the exercise will not be to classify Nietzsche as a bounded-rationality theorist (by way of concluding that he was making moves and adopting positions available to us elsewhere); in fact, Nietzsche's ideas push the envelope on work being done in that program, and so proceeding that way would suggest very much the wrong take. Rather, I mean to be explaining how Nietzsche understood perspectives, by recasting his views in a further perspective, with all the costs and benefits we'll see that to involve. To start out with, I'll tell you what you need to know about the bounded-rationality approach.

Even when the problem is set by the rules of chess, which are both simple and well defined, it may swamp human cognitive capacities; we can show that there's an in-principle-correct strategy, but our limitations (and also those of our electronic surrogates) haven't allowed us to find it, which is why we *play* chess—whereas adults don't play tic-tac-toe. And most of the world is much messier, and much more complicated, than a chess board. The problems we face are typically not nearly as well defined, and may well not set us up to find anything that would count as *the* correct solution. In both sorts of circumstance, cognitively limited agents have no alternative but to fall back on heuristics: shortcuts and rules of thumb that may not always get the right answer, but which aim to, often enough, get an answer that is good enough. Indeed, *satisficing*—setting a threshold for what counts as good enough, and selecting the first result of a search to come in over that threshold—was the first such technique to receive extended investigation and discussion.[3]

It's perhaps less widely recognized than it should be that our methods of representation are a very important aspect of our heuristic techniques. In a messy, complicated world, the first step toward addressing an overly demanding problem is usually to simplify one's description both of the circumstances and of the problem itself, and here's a real-life example that has recently come in for sometimes heated discussion. American undergraduates bound for law school face what is cognitively and emotionally a very demanding decision: deciding where to enroll is a large life choice, and law schools differ from one another along indefinitely many dimensions. Some are better places to study human rights law, others better if you're interested in intellectual property, others are better for corporate; some are intellectually more challenging, and some less; there's the quality and also interests of the faculty, which are largely a different matter; there's the campus aesthetic, the geographical location, and its political climate; there's the spouse's job and comfort level; there's whether the spirit of the law school is creative and theoretical; there's how welcoming and encouraging the faculty and staff can be expected to be; there's the culture of the university as a whole, how far it bends toward the sustainable and inclusive...[4] The prospective student might well not have settled how important each is, in comparison to the others. Moreover, reliable assessments of each of those aspects are likely to be hard to come by.

So, as many readers will know, a magazine, *US News and World Report*, has stepped up, and publishes a ranking of law schools. Applicants by and large now deploy this heuristic: attend the highest-ranked law school to accept them. The heuristic depends on the ranking—on the simplified representation—and just about all of the work is done *by* the

216 WHY DIDN'T NIETZSCHE GET HIS ACT TOGETHER?

representation. Getting ahead of ourselves just a bit, when the ranking was introduced, knowledgeable insiders complained bitterly that the ranking was a *mis*representation. Too many components of the assessment, evidently selected because they were easy to measure, were folded together not by lawyers or teachers, but journalists, that is, nonexperts who couldn't be expected to understand either the content of the studies or what teaching law involves. That one law school ranks higher or lower than another on this measure, the complaint continued, doesn't tell students what they need to know, when they're getting ready to make this sort of choice.[5]

In early work on bounded rationality, heuristics were contrasted with in-principle-correct methods: for instance, the *right* way to make choices (or anyway, this is still an oft-repeated view) is to maximize utility, but when that's too hard to figure out, you satisfice instead. And the gold standard for in-principle-correct methods was generally taken to be deductively valid argument (with Bayesian inference as a close runner up).[6] In Nietzsche's view, however—and this puts him out on the bleeding edge of work on bounded rationality today—even those gold-standard methods are themselves heuristics, and they depend on radically simplified representations, indeed, on representations that are *so* radically simplified as to be, one and all, *mis*representations.

Let's peel apart this characteristically compressed analysis into some of its layers. First of all, the representations that heuristics deploy normally commit sins of omission. In one of his lesser-known children's books, Lewis Carroll amusingly described "a map of the country, on the scale of a mile to the mile...: the farmers objected [that] it would cover the whole country and shut out the sunlight[,] so we now use the country itself, as its own map, and I assure you it does nearly as well."[7] Our representations have to be enormously thinned out, if they're to be usable at all.

Most dramatically in this vein, discussing the "origin of the logical," Nietzsche tells us that the "tendency... to treat as equal what is merely similar—an illogical tendency, for nothing is really equal—is what first created any basis for logic. In order that the concept of substance could originate—which is indispensible for logic although in the strictest sense nothing real corresponds to it—it was likewise necessary that for a long time one did not see nor perceive the changes in things."[8] Laying out this stretch of his train of thought a little more slowly, everything is in flux, and every state of affairs, when carefully examined, turns out to differ from any other in unimaginably many ways.

WHAT WAS NIETZSCHE'S PERSPECTIVISM? 217

Consequently, when you take yourself to be encountering the very same feature or property yet again, or when you take yourself to be reencountering a stable and persisting object, the simplification you're imposing is so drastically procrustean as to be no better, really, than those law school rankings we were discussing a moment back.[9] The methods of representation that support our most important heuristics, and we'll develop this side of Nietzsche's position momentarily, not only omit, but inevitably falsify.

Taking yourself to be encountering the same again is what underwrites repetition, and repetition is perhaps the most basic and certainly an absolutely indispensible logical operation. To construct a logically tight argument, you must repeat the names, predicates, and so on that figure into them; in this too-familiar syllogism,

1. All men are mortal
2. Socrates is a man
3. So, Socrates is mortal

"Socrates," "...is/are a man" and "...is/are mortal" each appear twice—and if they couldn't, you couldn't have an argument at all.[10] Using the same name or the same predicate more than once, Nietzsche thinks, is in turn to presuppose that an object or a property can be reidentified: roughly, that you can point to it once, and then point to it again. But when you try to point to the object again, it's not really there anymore: it's changed, and what you're pointing at is something *else*. (In the sense that Heraclitus meant it, you really *can't* step into the same river twice.) And so, Nietzsche infers, multiple uses of a name or predicate are a deep falsification; in *our* world, you can't ever reidentify anything. Logic was originally underwritten by our ancestors' sheer obliviousness to what they saw in front of them, and since then, we've become positively skilled at ignoring everything that we exclude from our predications and reidentifications; logic, he concludes, can't capture the world as it really is.[11]

Almost as dramatically, Nietzsche highlights the clumsiness of our causal inferences:

Cause and effect: such a duality probably never exists; in truth we are confronted by a continuum out of which we isolate a couple of pieces, just as we perceive motion only as isolated points and then infer it without ever actually seeing it. The suddenness with which many effects stand out

218 WHY DIDN'T NIETZSCHE GET HIS ACT TOGETHER?

misleads us; actually, it is sudden only for us. In this moment of suddenness there is an infinite number of processes that elude us. An intellect that could see cause and effect as a continuum and a flux and not, as we do, in terms of an arbitrary division and dismemberment, would repudiate the concept of cause and effect and deny all conditionality.   (3:473/GS 112)

We slice up continuous and bottomlessly filigreed processes into units, which we treat as self-contained and more or less static; in the language of comic-strip artists, we turn them into panels separated by gutters.[12] Then we try to correlate some of these units with others and, having suppressed almost all of the available explanatory resources, take one of the units for the explanation of the other. (What does this look like in real life? On a recent walk, my companion remarked: "It's three o'clock, no wonder I'm hungry.") Once again, the conceptual schema that underwrites an extraordinarily important class of inferences rests on a ruthless simplification, one that is tantamount to flat-out misrepresentation.[13]

Those procrustean simplifications are shaped both by natural and cultural selection:

> Innumerable beings who made inferences in a way different from ours perished; for all that, their ways might have been truer. Those, for example, who did not know how to find often enough what is "equal" as regards both nourishment and hostile animals—those, in other words, who subsumed things too slowly and cautiously—were favored with a lesser probability of survival than those who guessed immediately...
>
> The beings that did not see so precisely had an advantage over those that saw everything "in flux"...No living beings would have survived if the...tendency to affirm rather than suspend judgment, to err and *make up* things rather than wait, to assent rather than negate, to pass judgment rather than be just had not been bred to the point where it became extraordinarily strong.[14]

One side of these remarks is by now a familiar enough idea; for example, your visual processing is implemented around the assumption that things mostly stay the same size; so when something is getting bigger quickly in your visual field, you treat it as getting closer fast, and you duck, or flinch, or slam on the brakes, without stopping first to ponder whether perhaps it's *expanding*.[15]

WHAT WAS NIETZSCHE'S PERSPECTIVISM? 219

Thinking of logic as much the same kind of process is not familiar, and we'll need another lap to get enough of Nietzsche's picture of it on the table. Before we do, however, let's turn to what cultural selection has gone on to do with the hardwiring:

> Consciousness has developed only under the pressure of the need for communication ... particularly between those who commanded and those who obeyed ... As the most endangered animal, [man] *needed* help and protection ... he had to learn to express his distress and make himself understood; and for all of this he needed "consciousness" first of all, he needed to "know" himself what distressed him, he needed to "know" how he felt, he needed to "know" what he thought ... Consequently ... each of us will succeed in becoming conscious only of what is not individual but "average." Our thoughts themselves are ... translated back into the perspective of the herd. Fundamentally, all our actions are altogether incomparably personal, unique, and infinitely individual ... But as soon as we translate them into consciousness *they no longer seem to be.*
>
> (3:591–593/GS 354, deleting some emphases)

You can't communicate a need, command, piece of information, etc., unless you're aware of it, and we have in place a signaling system that allows us to communicate suitably generic needs, commands, pieces of information etc. So to use the signaling system, we have become aware of the generic needs, occasions for commands, information, and the like. Now, consciousness is expensive, and by and large we won't incur expenses that can't be accounted for by functionality. So, anyway for most of our history, we won't have developed consciousness any further than its function requires. It follows that we'll remain unconscious of contents that aren't part of the generic communication code. However, people's internal psychological economies are nuanced rather than generic, and much more complex than any socially usable code. So, and this conclusion would have been more surprising to Nietzsche's contemporaries than to us, we're inevitably unconscious of almost everything going on inside us—in our bodies or our "minds."

The shoreline is a fractal, but on the map it's drawn as a fairly smooth line, one which has a length—but the apparent length is dependent on the scale to which the map is drawn.[16] Getting simplifications and omissions tailored to the needs of our heuristics often enough requires a process very

220 WHY DIDN'T NIETZSCHE GET HIS ACT TOGETHER?

like that of converting a portrait into an anime character. One of these we've already seen: what Nietzsche calls "atomism," black-boxing the objects you think about and treating them as though they had no internal structure. We do this, he thinks, not only with the hypothetical atoms of the chemistry of the period, but with minds: when a personality is fully controlled by one of its elements, it can be a superficially successful emulator for a unitary mind, but many minds aren't organized this way, and even when one is, it succumbs to the illusion of "free will"—that when the governing element decides, the action *just* happens, with no intervening steps.[17]

Nietzsche takes himself to be debunking a myth widespread among philosophers, and taken for granted by laypersons: that the world consists of items that can be fairly treated in our reasoning as simple or cleanly organized repeatable units. What it takes to subsume individuals under a general description—and so to get logic off the ground—as Nietzsche sees it is conceptually very close to the conversion of a photorealistic image into a cartoon.[18] When we reason about even mundane objects, and *a fortiori* when such metaphysically exotic items as persons and their minds are in play, we routinely mistake the artefacts of a bounded-rationality strategy for the way the world is, on its own. Moreover, what we do to get logic itself off the ground is of a piece with Nietzsche's reinterpretation of the more traditional metaphysical preoccupations:

> We have arranged for ourselves a world in which we can live—by positing bodies, lines, planes, causes and effects, motion and rest, form and content; without these articles of faith nobody now could endure life. But that does not prove them. Life is no argument. The conditions of life might include error. (3:477f/GS 121)

Nietzsche here is correcting Kant, who thought he was explaining apriori *truths*. Through the lens of bounded rationality, the central subject matter of metaphysics has been ways in which representation is compromised. Our inevitable misrepresentations support the heuristics that creatures like ourselves rely on to expeditiously take a next step.

> This is the essence of phenomenalism and perspectivism as *I* understand them: Owing to the nature of *animal consciousness*, the world of which we can become conscious is only a surface- and sign-world, a world that is made common and meaner... thin, relatively stupid, general, sign, herd

signal; all becoming conscious involves a great and thorough corruption, falsification, reduction to superficialities, and generalization.[19]

We're not done with saying what makes up a perspective, and what it turns out to be. But already we can see that construing it as yet another form of relativism is mistaken. The centerpiece of a relativism, we said, was that truth is always truth-*for*; if perspectivism were a kind of relativism, Nietzsche would be telling us that truths are truths only within a perspective. What we're served up by our perspectives, however, are not truths, but *falsehoods*. The further mark of a relativism was incommensurability, which in this case would be the incommensurability of claims formulated within different perspectives.[20] We'll see in due course that, for Nietzsche, the most important payoff of having multiple perspectives at your fingertips is that what you can see in one of them allows you to register the limitations of, and correct, what you can in another. Perspectives are not incommensurable, and inside the bounded-rationality perspective, we shouldn't be at all surprised: approximations are an innocuous family of bounded-rationality representations, and who would be sophomoric enough to insist that one type of approximation can't be used to correct another, or that all approximations are on a par, with nothing to choose between them?

An alert reader is likely to be worrying that in preempting the prospect of a self-refuting relativism, we've merely sharpened up the worry that Nietzsche's position is self-refuting. If every claim is advanced within a perspective, and perspectives serve up not truths but falsehoods then, as Maudemarie Clark once put it, we have a "hopeless self-contradiction" due to "the problem of self-reference. If it is supposed to be true that there is no truth, then there is apparently a truth after all; and if it is not supposed to be true, it seems that we have no reason to take it seriously"; worse, we have no reason to take any of Nietzsche's other claims about what is wrong with our values seriously.[21] But we can now see that the reaction is a misstep, and one that is easily corrected within the bounded-rationality perspective.

I hope it is clear that in talking through Nietzsche's perspectivism from the bounded-rationality perspective I'm engaging in the very sort of simplification and caricature I've been describing on his behalf. I'm taking an intractably messy phenomenon, black-boxing a great deal of internal structure, setting aside processes that overlay and fuzz up the relatively clean functionality I'm invoking, and generally, I'm helping myself to devices that conceal complexity and are bound, sometimes, to lead us into errors.[22] My

222 WHY DIDN'T NIETZSCHE GET HIS ACT TOGETHER?

crude line drawing of a view presented in fragments and overlays, whose assertions and presuppositions are not nearly always mutually consistent, both misrepresents it, and is nonetheless being offered as the best way to think about it for present purposes.

Within this perspective, it's straightforward to acknowledge that we often do work with cartoons that are so extreme as to amount to, not partial truths, but caricatures. We even work with idealizations that contain internal incoherences, and are in principle unrealizable—thus, with what are by any reasonable lights genuine falsehoods and misrepresentations—which are, despite everything, the *right* way to think through one problem or another.[23] In the world of bounded rationality, certain kinds of falsehoods are, *pace* Clark, to be taken *fully* seriously, and the rendering I've been giving you is, I hope, a suitably realistic illustration. A highly schematized version of perspectives, maybe it's not the truth—and certainly not the final truth— about them, but it's useful precisely because it's conducted from, and subject to the limitations of, one perspective in particular.

We don't want to walk away with the impression that Nietzsche's view is less radical than it is. It is easy to agree that sometimes we reason with approximations; we're more likely to balk at the suggestion that it's all and only approximations, approximations all the way down. And the startle factor is even greater than that way of putting it suggests. Approximations, idealizations, and other ways of conveying how things stand that are only kind of true, sort of true, or true in a way count as partial truths, or so it seems to me. The much more extreme techniques which the notion of partial truth won't fit—the ones I've been shorthanding as cartooning and caricature—are plausibly sometimes necessary. But do they have to be the mainstay, even the exclusive medium, as Nietzsche had it, of our thought? Here what matters is that we can understand a view on which representation is all and only caricature—caricature all the way down—and see how, as philosophers, we should take it fully seriously, even as we wonder whether it's overstated.[24]

9.2

Over and above coming to see one's surroundings as containing persistent objects and repeatable properties—already making up an impossibly simplified cartoon of that environment—constructing a useable perspective requires thinning out the objects and properties that register on one's awareness. Naturally, in the name of cognitive efficiency Goodmanian predicates and Lewisian merelogical sums—the "object" consisting of a fish and the upper half of the Eiffel Tower, that sort of thing—must be rendered almost always invisible. But even perfectly recognizable items have for the most part to become merely part of the background. We have mass nouns like *grass* for good reason; one of the effects of certain psychedelics is to disable this sort of backgrounding, and their devotees will sometimes tell you about being able to see the blades of grass, all of them, in their distinctive individuality, one by one—but it's not a coincidence that, during those episodes, they're not competent to engage in a great many other activities. So not only are the things we see to one degree or another misrepresented; we can't afford to see most of what is around us at all.

In that case, what settles which representational elements are foregrounded, and which pressed into the background? In the bounded-rationality way of seeing things, there are always tradeoffs; per Nietzsche's own example, the quick-and-dirty regimentation of one's sensory inputs into *the same yet again* trades off a careful and complete appreciation of one's situation for speed and survival. But any tradeoff presupposes assessments, of how much and how the competing considerations in play matter. Assessments, as Nietzsche construes them, are governed by values. And so we should expect perspectives to fall into place around values.

Recall that, as Nietzsche deploys the concept, values are themselves multifaceted, complex, and have many functions: they operate as priorities and as standards; as ideals that overcome themselves; they can serve, we saw, as prosthetics for disunified agents. So saying that perspectives fall into place around values doesn't mean what it would, if someone were to say it today.[25] But since we're sketching Nietzsche's ideas within the bounded rationality perspective, here we'll treat values schematically, presenting them as they appear in that perspective: as the ingredient that does the job of enabling these tradeoffs.

Up to this point, we were focused on aspects of the implementation of perspectives that Nietzsche's prescient gestures at evolutionary psychology and meme selection tell us should be uniform across human cognition. But values vary from group to group, and in recent memory—this being a matter of keen interest to him—from individual to individual. So we should expect the perspectives of different groups and different individuals to differ. They will pick out different classes of objects (since we can expect these objects figure into inferences jointly, we can think of them as ontologies). And they'll

224 WHY DIDN'T NIETZSCHE GET HIS ACT TOGETHER?

be picked out not only by constraints on information processing but, and here Nietzsche is picking up a family of costs and benefits that haven't been part of the bounded-rationality conversation, their emotional consequences:

> it might be a basic characteristic of existence that those who would know it completely would perish, in which case the strength of a spirit should be measured according to how much of the "truth" one could still barely endure—or to put it more clearly, to what degree one would *require* it to be thinned down, shrouded, sweetened, blunted, falsified.   (5:56f/BGE 39)

Here the purely cognitive burden isn't distinguished from the question of what you can and can't *stand*.[26]

The perspectives we've been focused on are implemented in a psychology, and the primary structural components of a psychology, in Nietzsche's way of seeing it, are drives. We saw earlier on that, as Nietzsche understands drives, they are for the most part not adequately modeled as goal- or aim-directed; a drive is rather like a political party, and let's quickly remind ourselves of where that analogy went. Taking as my illustration not exactly a party, but a political organization, and opening up a copy of the Sierra Club's magazine, I find political advocacy focused on the environment. But as becomes apparent on perusing even this one issue, "the environment" isn't a single aim or objective: its pages include pieces on wilderness preservation, global warming, mercury poisoning, agricultural monocultures, teflon frypans, and more. Now although the Club isn't focused on anything like a single goal, someone reasonably fluent in our contemporary political culture can nevertheless tell you, without having himself been told, what the Sierra Club's position on each of these questions almost certainly is. (Moreover, one can do so not only without looking at the magazine article that advances such a position, but without seeing the reasons or the arguments adduced to support it.[27]) The Sierra Club is oriented, not towards a goal or aim, but towards a value—"environmentalism" might be a terse but adequate label for it—and recognizing the value allows one to anticipate the otherwise disparate aims and goals of the movement.

A drive, like a political party, can often (not always!) be seen as oriented toward a value, or values, in rather this manner. A drive and the value that acts as its pole star move in tandem, and so when perspectives fall into place around values—again, bearing in mind that the perspectives we're looking at have to be *effected* within a psychology, in real time—it will frequently

WHAT WAS NIETZSCHE'S PERSPECTIVISM? 225

enough be equally convenient to say that a perspective has fallen into place around a drive (or a configuration of drives).[28]

Let's break to start thinking about the extent to which a perspective is under one's voluntary control, and more particularly, whether one can adopt a different perspective at will. You might offhand take this for an easy question, but I've found that those who do are likely to give diametrically opposed answers. No: a perspective is in the first place constituted by what you can see, and what you can see is a matter of preprocessing; you don't see the preprocessing—precisely because it underwrites your awareness, you're not aware of it—and so it won't respond to your will.[29] Yes: surely I can decide to become, say, a classicist, and by immersing myself in Greek and Roman culture, come to see the world the way they did; Nietzsche's own education is a striking example of someone retrieving the perspective of the ancient world in this way. The answer we will have a use for is more complicated, and turns on the issue of what's required for voluntary control.

Sticking with Nietzsche for a moment—because taking up the distinction between what's voluntary and what isn't had better be left for its own occasion—we have a guide to what underwrites the notion in passages we've already encountered (5:31–34/BGE 19 and 5:293f/GM 2.2): a personality has to be very tightly organized, likely with one of its drives in full control of the rest, but in any case integrated in such a way as to render it *unswerving*, when it is buffetted, both externally and internally, by circumstance. These are demanding conditions, and it's clear that in Nietzsche's view there's a great deal less in the way of voluntary action than we normally suppose. We've seen the author of the *Genealogy* dramatize his own moment-to-moment unsteadiness, and so when he tells us that " 'objectivity' . . . [is] the ability *to control* one's Pro and Con and to dispose of them, so that one knows how to employ a *variety* of perspectives and affective interpretations in the service of knowledge" (5:364f/GM 3.12), we should be alert to the irony: this is not someone describing his own experience, and not someone who can manage objectivity himself.

With that in mind, consider a personality tightly enough organized for its actions to be fully voluntary, that is, to be the sort of intentional action we philosophers naively take for granted as the norm. If complete control by a single drive is what accounts for it, then whatever value the drive projects will dominate the tradeoffs that determine the perspective it primarily occupies. Given the hold of the primary perspective, we can expect the attempt to occupy a secondary perspective to be managed *through* the

226   WHY DIDN'T NIETZSCHE GET HIS ACT TOGETHER?

primary perspective, especially in attempts to reconstruct the conceptual and evaluative scheme of the former within the latter. When the new perspective has to be mastered by translating it into the already operative perspective, it's unlikely to make available much in the way of insight that's unavailable to the primary perspective—in something like the way that someone who understands a foreign language by translating back, sentence by sentence, into his native tongue won't have the benefits of hearing things the subtly and often deeply different way a native speaker of the foreign language does.

An attempt to induce another perspective directly, if it's controlled enough to count as fully voluntary, will thus provide only a *dependent* secondary perspective, one where it's possible to reduce the ontology, concepts, and other elements of the secondary perspective to elements of the primary perspective. Culturally available perspectives, which need not be thus dependent, can however be induced indirectly, for instance, as in Nietzsche's own case, by studying the languages, history, and literature of ancient Greece and Rome. For now, two observations on that front: Nietzsche may have exhibited, in *The Birth of Tragedy*, the from-the-inside understanding of the Greeks that we're considering as a target, but even diligent scholarship only rarely has it as an outcome.[30] Second, the time and effort involved in such an accomplishment means that one can't expect to add more than one—perhaps two or three—additional perspectives to one's repertoire over a lifetime.

Is that right? And here I'm anticipating a response you may be having: can't you immerse yourself in a new perspective just by, say, reading the right kind of novel? (Perhaps Kafka, or Nabokov's *Lolita*—both purported counterexamples I have had pressed on me.) Anyway, don't novelists sometimes generate new perspectives, which anyhow they occupy? How hard can the task we're considering really be?

Once again, let's remind ourselves just how unusual an achievement it is when a work of fiction induces a new perspective—recall, a new way of cognizing the world, of cutting out the pieces you see in a different manner, putting them crisply and exaggeratedly front and center, and forcing a great many other things into invisibility ... just to start in on what perspectives do. Now, contrast how costly it is, in terms of time and effort, merely to read such a novel, with what it takes to live with it until it changes the way you think, or to get to the place where you could write it. Shifting the illustration, since I know philosophy better than I do the world of literature, take those philosophers who do succeed in constructing and conveying new perspectives; usually, it's the work of a lifetime, and usually, those to whom the perspectives are conveyed manage to learn to think fluently in the terms provided by no more than one of them. That's how we came to have Quine, and the Quineans; Davidson, and the Davidsonians; Rawls, and the Rawlsians... and when Wittgenstein managed to construct two such perspectives over the course of a career, that was remarked upon, because remarkable.

(Thus as I ask you to see things for a stretch from the bounded-rationality perspective, and then in passing invoke the perspective of, say, comics and graphic novels, what I'm inviting you along on is intellectual tourism. For those gestures at cartoons to make their point, you don't need to have acquired the frame of mind in which you could successfully author a graphic novel. And more generally, following a train of thought laid out by someone inside a perspective you don't yourself inhabit is very different from mastering the mode of thought, in a way that allows you to spin out your own arguments within that perspective.)

Briefly, it looks like perspectives one can fully control will be dependent on one's primary perspective—or if independent, then costly to acquire. To be sure, there's a great deal more to say about perspectives; we've been talking through Nietzsche's perspectives from the bounded-rationality perspective. Thus, for instance, when we take up matters of style, in the next section, we'll want to switch perspectives briefly, and recall our observation that drives, like political parties, are best distinguished by their rhetorical styles. In a literary perspective on perspectives, we might be able to say, as does Kaufmann, that "experiences... are not fictions in the sense that they are made up of whole cloth. They are more like historical novels that take their point of departure from something that actually happened" (2017, p. 61). Each perspective gives you a one-sided view, and that's true when we take the bounded-rationality perspective on perspectives.

But for now, we're equipped to take this next step. In Nietzsche's view, human personalities are organized by the drives that structure them: by a single dominant drive, in what Nietzsche regards as a healthy individual, and perhaps by a handful of relatively independent drives, in somewhat more decadent characters. Let's allow that the considerations in play more than suggest that other animals and institutions—and even research programs and philosophical traditions—can be expected to generate and occupy perspectives; the bounded-rationality perspective, which we've been deploying, is an instance. Nonetheless, if perspectives fall into place around drives and

228 WHY DIDN'T NIETZSCHE GET HIS ACT TOGETHER?

the values they project, then for our own purposes we should treat a human personality as the paradigm and central case of a perspective.[31]

9.3

We've stepped our way through Nietzsche's later works, and have found each of them to present for our consideration a human personality, namely, the book's implicit author. Looking back with the conceptual equipment we've just put in place, we can see these as a series of perspectives. With the exception of *Thus Spoke Zarathustra*, whose authorial character we identified as a religious functionary from a science-fiction future, each of these authors is a version of Nietzsche himself, and so each of the perspectives we've had exhibited to us is one that Nietzsche at one point occupied. I think we can best make sense of these literary exercises by talking though Nietzsche's writing process; I need to acknowledge, before launching in, that here I have to take the greater liberties required by a biopic-style narrative reconstruction.

Nietzsche seems generally to have presumed, without much argument, and overriding the implications of some of his own observations, that psychological health would be in part a matter of having one's personality stably structured around a dominant drive.[32] However, he had found himself to be anything but psychologically stable. In the course of composing *Zarathustra*, it was brought home to him that building a book to display its author could be gotten to do philosophical heavy lifting. Although that author was a literary invention, the lesson learned was more general. And so Nietzsche turned to documenting his own internal rearrangements, in more or less real time; thus the later books show us, one after another, the successive perspectives that their hapless subject lived through.

Nietzsche wrote frantically, blurting his thoughts out onto the pages of his journals at an astonishing pace; he rapidly revised portions of the material he produced into one after another volume. (However, in a departure from the usual way of handling blurts, that is, embarrassedly moving on, he was to preserve them and treat them as raw material.) As we've seen, the author was kept constantly in the spotlight, positioned as the pivot of the argument, and used to carry the main point of each work. Nietzsche wrote to beat the clock: a manuscript had to be completed before the perspective it depicted collapsed, as his personality—his *self*—shifted into a new configuration.

WHAT WAS NIETZSCHE'S PERSPECTIVISM? 229

Sometimes the Nietzsche of these desperate exercises in self-display did have a dominant drive as its temporary center of gravity: there were the characters we named his Genealogist and his Antichrist, where however the organizing drives turned out to be not at all what they might have seemed. Sometimes the character was a constellation of relatively independently acting drives, and we recall the Good European of *Beyond Good and Evil* staging his misogyny, antisemitism, and German nationalism for us. Sometimes the character we were shown was the decay product of a more structured self: we remember the protagonist of *Twilight of the Idols*, spinning up a prosthetic value to forestall—or rather, postpone—his collapse, and also the author of Nietzsche's autobiography, in his state of almost complete disintegration.

To remind you of the flavor of those literary self-presentations, let me quickly gesture at one that I've opted not to give the full treatment: *The Case of Wagner*, which takes up subject matter that I don't feel myself to be sufficiently musical to properly disentangle.[33] As per usual, it identifies its genre for you: in this case, it's a "letter".[34] And you'll recall from ch. 8 that it provides our working definition of decadence as, now helping ourselves to a different passage, "the decline of the power to organize" (6:47/CW N2), and in particular, the inability to subordinate the parts to the whole. But then, notice that this alleged letter has *two* postscripts, and then an epilogue on top of that, for a total of about half the length of the body of the text. That is, the authorial persona of this very short book is being exhibited as someone who can't organize what he wants to say ahead of time, and who has to keep adding one after another lengthy "oh, and one more thing." The disorganization is in addition on display at the sentence level, where "excessive liveliness in the smallest parts" (*ibid.*) again and again aborts what in elementary school we were told was a complete thought ended by a period. And as per usual, we're given a disavowal belied by the performance in which it is wrapped:

> I am, no less than Wagner, a child of this time; that is, a *decadent*: but I comprehended this, I resisted it. The philosopher in me resisted.
>
> Nothing has preoccupied me more profoundly than the problem of decadence—I had reasons.   (6:11/CW P.1)

All that should sufficiently call to mind what we've been seeing in our treatments of Nietzsche's more substantial works.

At this point, it would be natural to begin cataloging the different ways that central Nietzschean concepts were reconstrued in one perspective after

230   WHY DIDN'T NIETZSCHE GET HIS ACT TOGETHER?

another, and to take up questions such as: how are we to reidentify an object of attention across different perspectives? can we integrate what we see in different perspectives into coherent and consistent theories? if not, what form should a philosophical engagement with them take on? But I want instead to turn to a more personal question: if I'm right about what Nietzsche was doing, and also correct in thinking that he understood perfectly well that he was devoting the brief remainder of his sentient and sane life to it, how could creating a record of these transient perspectives have been so important to him as to justify the choice?

Let's return to perspectives, considered as bounded-rationality devices. Any bounded-rationality technique is going to get things wrong sometimes, as the price of faster or less resource-intensive performance; a perspective accepts an extreme version of the inevitable tradeoff, systematically deleting most of your field of vision, and violently distorting what's left. When you occupy a perspective, you're going to miss a great deal, and be prone to mistaking artefacts of the preprocessing for the way the world is. Worse yet, while the history of evolutionary theory has been a slow struggle against panglossian and adaptationist accounts of its products, Nietzsche was aware, early on, that the intellectual widgets that arise out of actual historical processes are quite likely not to be well designed for the jobs to which they're put. The problem isn't exactly that we think with falsehoods; rather, it's that to get away with thinking with falsehoods, those falsehoods have to be well-chosen, high-quality, specially effective misrepresentations. But given what must be the history, what are the chances that the cartoons and caricatures we work with *are* up to scratch?[35]

9.4

Now it's time to notice how the failings of one perspective can be caught and corrected from within another; because the point is important, I'll give three illustrations.

Nietzsche has too often been read as having a peculiar metaphysics closely related to Schopenhauer's, on which the matter which makes up the world is will-to-power, conceived as a sort of raw, energetic striving for dominance. The view is usually imputed to him by leaning heavily on the notebooks, but it has a presence in the published writings as well; you can find the putative author of *Beyond Good and Evil*—our Good European—apparently willing to entertain it.

> Suppose nothing else were "given" as real except our world of desires and passions, and we could not get down, or up, to any other "reality" besides the reality of our drives—for thinking is merely a relation of these drives to each other: is it not permitted to make the experiment and to ask the question whether this "given" would not be *sufficient* for also understanding on the basis of this kind of thing the so-called mechanistic (or "material") world?
>
> In the end not only is it permitted to make this experiment; the conscience of *method* demands it. Not to assume several kinds of causality until the experiment of making do with a single one has been pushed to its utmost limit (to the point of nonsense, if I may say so)—that is a moral of method from which one may not shirk today... The question is in the end whether we really recognize the will as *efficient*, whether we believe in the causality of the will: if we do—and at bottom our faith in this is nothing less than our faith in causality itself—then we have to make the experiment of positing the causality of the will hypothetically as the only one.

If the "experiment" pans out,

> then one would have gained the right to determine *all* efficient force univocally as—*will to power*. The world viewed from inside, the world defined and determined according to its "intelligible character"—it would be "will to power" and nothing else.— (5:54f/BGE 36, with some abridgement)

First, let's register an aspect of the Good European's perspective that seems to be responsible for the way this train of thought proceeds. We saw that his own experience is that of warring drives within *himself*; that is no doubt why he can toss off that claim, that "thinking is merely a relation of these drives to each other," with such assurance. And so it's not surprising that the way he parses the world puts drives front and center, and not surprising that they figure into his perspective as a sort of template that it's natural to use to make sense of whatever else he encounters.

There are quite a few "supposes" in this highly compressed transcendental argument, and it's too infrequently noticed how unlikely it is that Nietzsche

232 WHY DIDN'T NIETZSCHE GET HIS ACT TOGETHER?

would be willing to allow them.[36] They mark the Good European's awareness that these are occasions for second thoughts. So let's focus on an element of the argument that isn't flagged as hypothetical: that requirement of parsimony in scientific explanation, wholeheartedly affirmed as a matter of conscience from which one may not shirk.

Not all that much later, Nietzsche's soul, as he might have put it, shifted to a different configuration—one inducing another perspective. We identified Nietzsche's Psychologist as adopting the literary pose of French moralism, in which one cynically looks behind intellectually and morally respectable postures, to the base motives that explain what people do. It's a matter of course for this character, occupying this perspective, to look behind high-minded appeals to scientific method, and to discern, behind those moralistic imperatives, a debunking explanation:

> To derive something unknown from something familiar relieves, comforts, and satisfies, besides giving a feeling of power. With the unknown, one is confronted with danger, discomfort, and care; the first instinct is to abolish these painful states. First principle: any explanation is better than none. Since at bottom it is merely a matter of wishing to be rid of oppressive representations, one is not too particular about the means of getting rid of them: the first representation that explains the unknown as familiar feels so good that one "considers it true."
>
> Thus one searches not only for some kind of explanation to serve as a cause, but for a particularly selected and preferred kind of explanation—that which has most quickly and most frequently abolished the feeling of the strange, new, and hitherto unexperienced: the *most habitual* explanations. Consequence: one kind of positing of causes predominates more and more, is concentrated into a system, and finally emerges as *dominant*, that is, as simply precluding other causes and explanations.[37]

What underlies that scientific conscience is the need to find comfort in the face of the unfamiliar; it's the same impulse that children assuage by calling their mothers to their bedsides, to read them the stories they've had repeated to them verbatim, night after night. The etiology and implicit criticism of explanatory monism undercuts the defense of a will-to-power metaphysics which we're considering. (To remind you: different perspectives needn't be incommensurable.) We are then not surprised that in the perspective of the

WHAT WAS NIETZSCHE'S PERSPECTIVISM? 233

Psychologist will to power is a value—the opposing pole to decadence—and not a metaphysical *stuff*.

Proceeding to a next illustration, this being one that exploits the perspective of a likely reader: you'll recall that I began the discussion of *Zarathustra* by drawing your attention to its many stylistic shortcomings. The controlling problem of the book, we argued, was how the stabilization of a value can go awry, and in ch. 3 we focused on external techniques for entrenching a value-under-development, in particular, institutionalization. But there are also internal aspects of the stabilization of a value—its internalization—which are discussed in Nietzsche's writings largely under the heading of acquiring tastes. We're now in a position to float a hypothesis as to what those many, many lapses of taste are doing in *Thus Spoke Zarathustra*.

The book's postulated author, we determined, was a priest, the product of a decadent priestly culture in which the religion of Zarathustra has reached the point of composing its analog of the Bible. And as the Higher Criticism reads it, the Bible is every bit as badly written as *Thus Spoke Zarathustra*.[38] The Wellhausian authors of the deuteronomic corpus and the Priestly Code are, on almost every dimension, abysmal writers.

But this is not how the Bible seems to us. In language after language, it stands as a paradigm of stately composition and forceful yet dignified prose: think of the King James Version in English, or Luther's translation of the Bible into German.[39] Earlier on, we considered how that can happen: just as there are two ways to make the Overman valuable enough to redeem his past, so there are two ways we could have made the Bible into beautiful prose. One would be to rewrite it once more, to conform to the improved stylistic standards of a later generation; for obvious reasons, this didn't happen. The other, which consequently must have happened, is to alter the retrospective assessment of the writing, in this case by altering the literary sensibilities and tastes of its readers. A holy text whose status ensures that it serves as an ideological reference point gradually becomes a stylistic reference point as well; if the Higher Critics' implicit assessment of the literary qualities of their object of study is correct, it follows that, eventually, even incompetently written schlock can be transformed into a classic of world literature.

Space activists like to respond to the question of whether there is life on Mars by saying, "No, but there will be." Is *Thus Spoke Zarathustra* well written? No, but if its reception goes down this path, it will be. Already Nietzsche's out-of-control prose no longer sounds nearly as over the top as

234 WHY DIDN'T NIETZSCHE GET HIS ACT TOGETHER?

it once did; to academics who work on Nietzsche's texts day in and day out, it is coming to sound *normal*, entirely by dint of the familiarity a canonical text acquires. Although the process is proceeding unevenly—the *Genealogy* is much better digested than *Zarathustra*—Nietzsche's works as a whole have been canonized: as is evident on the page in front of you, there is now a standard edition, and apparatus that allows exegetes to cite chapter and verse.

Thus its stylistic surface is an invitation to consider how, from a perspective downstream from its implicit author, *Zarathustra* looks like the King James Bible to English-speaking Christians, or, for that matter, the Old Testament, in the original Hebrew, to contemporary Hebrew novelists and poets—or the Koran, to today's consumers of Arabic literature. From the perspective of the present, notwithstanding our having lived through the beginnings of the process, the future perspective is deeply alien: how could we hope to reshape our literary tastes into *that*?

The remote tastes of both the postulated author's perspective and of his successors are a stand-in for the exotic values prescribed for overcoming our resentment of the "it was," and making it possible for the Overman to redeem our past. No doubt we're being shown a further dimension along which such values are liable to be corrupted, but an additional point is being made: when we understand what we're getting ourselves into, we ought to be wondering just what kind of decision this is supposed to be. It seems to me that *Thus Spoke Zarathustra* provides us with a deeply disturbing illustration of what it would be to embark on—and come out the other end of—the process of taking on the tastes that would accompany the institutionalization of Nietzsche's values.[40]

Zarathustra's subtitle announces it as a book for all and none, and any reading of the text as a whole owes a gloss on that description. Here, belatedly, is one candidate: it's meant to capture the attention of callow adolescents and unwashed Romantics now (the "all"), and it will, if things go as Nietzsche anticipates, one day be read by people who are, as far as we are concerned, aesthetic versions of logical aliens, by virtue of having been educated into tastes that make the book into great prose. (Since no one has these tastes yet, they are the "none").[41] But if this is what we're being offered, a reader will be brought up short only if he comes to the book from *another* perspective (his *present* perspective), one in which it's *not* already an elegant masterpiece. We find the saccharine worshipfulness objectionable, but if we didn't have that very gut-level response, would we have the worries we ought to?

WHAT WAS NIETZSCHE'S PERSPECTIVISM?   235

Turning to a third and last illustration of the payoffs of perspective shifting, recall that we saw Nietzsche's Psychologist telling us to look back to the person behind the action, to see if he is "well-turned-out" or whether he exhibits "laboriousness"—which itself "is an objection": Nietzsche's character, it seems, was insisting on assessment by *ad hominem* argument, by looking back to the person who has a particular position or view and assessing *him*, rather than conducting the assessment by looking forward to the position's consequences.[42] We also recall, from sec. 2.2, that Nietzsche's Genealogist identified "redoubling" or "reduplication" as a fallacy, highlighting the special case in which you look behind the actions to judge the distinct self or soul that produced them. Like the lightning, which is not two different things—the flash, and the bolt that caused it—so the person is not two different things, his actions, and the self that produces them. But unlike the redoubled lightning, redoubled persons were marked as likely to be a form of motivated self-deception. How are we to take this? Is it just an inconsistency, to be either acknowledged or explained away?

We're taught early on that the *ad hominem* argument is a fallacy. (Just as a reminder, and *very* roughly—because when Nietzsche deploys them, they are *sometimes* a good deal less crude than our paradigms—these arguments treat an evaluation of the person who has a view as an evaluation of the view.) Now to treat a form of argument as a fallacy—to say it is *no good* as an argument—must be the application of a value. That's why insisting that arguments of this kind are good arguments can be Nietzsche's ("first") example of his revaluation or upending of values.

Values, Nietzsche holds, are invented, so let's allow that this is him asking us to adopt a value of his own invention. This means that insisting that the arguments he provides are something other than *ad hominem* arguments, or alternatively, that we do accept *ad hominem* arguments as sometimes legitimate, is not acknowledging what is on the table.[43] Those responses are inadequate in that they appeal to what we currently allow to count as a good argument. But if Nietzsche is upending our values, the question isn't what we think of such arguments *already*, but rather, whether we're going to accept the proposal, and adopt the new value. How should we think about whether to do so?

In this chapter, I've been conducting the discussion for the most part by invoking the bounded-rationality perspective as a frame, but for the next point or two, I'm going to invoke a rather different perspective. There's *something* that Nietzsche's turning away from consequences is getting right. In an

236 WHY DIDN'T NIETZSCHE GET HIS ACT TOGETHER?

earlier chapter, we used the Impressionism as an example of a movement governed by a value that its members had invented. The consequences to which one could appeal to justify the adoption of the value are primarily the paintings which the Impressionists went on to produce; however, if you haven't already adopted their value, how is it that you'll agree that the paintings are valuable?[44]

In these sorts of cases, it's the job of critics—and even if they do it only very rarely, this is really the activity that justifies their professional existence—to put people who are encountering, in this case, art governed by a newly invented value in a position to appreciate something they aren't already equipped to appreciate. And if you look back on the occasions where the challenge is met successfully, you'll find that it's met not by pointing out consequences, but by pointing out, say, aspects of the new form of painting that are striking, but also that are problematic in one way or another.

The shift into the perspective of the Genealogist that I was prompting a moment ago is doing more or less that work. In earlier chapters, we reminded ourselves that the *Genealogy* is, very dramatically, in the business of *ad hominem* arguments. Like criticism of that kind, it shows us that these arguments let you do a lot with them. And it also shows us one of their problematic aspects: when you look back, from the position to the person who has it, there's a trap, the mistake of redoubling or reduplication. (It's not the only trap: remember behindology, which we discussed in ch. 5.) Maybe it can be avoided, by taking the trouble not to imagine, as it were, a second person underneath the pattern of activity that is all there actually is to him: that is, maybe with a little effort some *ad hominem* arguments can avoid lapsing into reduplication. Or maybe not. Either way, it's this sort of thing that we need to have visible, and to bear in mind, as we consider the Psychologist's startling recommendation for what to count as a good argument, and what as a bad one. Switching into a different perspective— here, the Genealogist's—provides that cautionary note, to accompany the recommendations of Nietzsche's Psychologist.

Returning to the formal point we're after about perspectives, and returning from the perspective of art criticism to that of bounded rationality, by now, every reader will be familiar with the way that navigation tools allow their users to switch between map layers. And generally, the most useful of these maps are the closest to Nietzsche's understanding of *all* representation. For instance, the contour lines you see on the topo layer are a deep misrepresentation of what you'll find as you hike, in just about the way that the smooth curve of the shoreline on another layer of the map misrepresents its fractal geometry. (It's not just that you don't see lines on the ground as you walk around, but that there are no continuous lines to trace at a given altitude, when you're on real dirt.) But the different layers allow you to compensate for and to correct their respective omissions and misrepresentations: the satellite imaging reminds you of the idealization built into the topo map; the topo map highlights aspects of the landscape that are almost impossible to make out on the shaded terrain map; the terrain map corrects the misimpression left by the road layer, that the trailheads are accessible in an ordinary street vehicle. Nietzsche famously writes:

> There is *only* a perspective seeing, *only* a perspective "knowing"; and the *more* affects we allow to speak about one thing, the *more* eyes, different eyes, we can use to observe one thing, the more complete will our "concept" of this thing, our "objectivity" be.   (5:365/GM 3.12)

We need to remember that this passage presupposes the perspective of an authorial character—once again, Nietzsche's Genealogist, who has his own investment in objectivity—and itself needs correction. Nevertheless, we can be confident that perspectivism is not a variety of generic relativism; as we see in our illustrations, perspectives are not incommensurable, and having different perspectives on hand is valuable first and foremost in that perspectives can correct one another.[45]

9.5

How valuable *is* that? Nietzsche laid down an enormously ambitious challenge to his readers and to himself: the invention of values that are not one-size-fits-all, but suited to the needs of—and the possibilities open to—their inventor. Although we can't say ahead of time what precisely these values will be, we know that Nietzsche is calling on us to reverse two thousand years of striving for sameness and for *littleness*. Living up to his own demand, Nietzsche invented a value to guide both his own activities, and the ongoing and difficult process of managing his personality: a metavalue, namely, the urgency and overwhelming importance of inventing values in the way we've started to describe.

238 WHY DIDN'T NIETZSCHE GET HIS ACT TOGETHER?

We saw Nietzsche exhibiting what seemed at the outset to be an insuperable obstacle. Newly created values have to be stabilized: as their content is filled in, and as they're applied in unforeseen circumstances, there have to be systematic, ongoing reality checks. The previously and even currently available technique for providing these has been institutionalization, as when the value is promulgated and further articulated by a church—or perhaps an academic tradition. But institutions are collectively operated enterprises, and then the value can't be tailored to the idiosyncratic needs of an individual. In any case, the institutional process of stabilizing a value is effective over time spans that guarantee it will be firmed up too late to be of use to its inventor. And finally for the moment, Nietzsche took himself to have learned a lesson from the Higher Criticism: that when it comes to mandating that people invent their own standards and aspirations, institutions will over time twist such a mandate into a mode of conformity that's compatible with institutional persistence. Conformity of this kind requires *un*inventiveness, and a posture of submission and acquiescence that amounts to perpetuating the very littleness Nietzsche hoped to displace. We saw how, in the perspective of a priest, even Nietzsche's metavalue would, over the long run, be corrupted and perverted into something on the order of the infamous Overman.

The obstacle, it turned out, can be, not exactly *overcome*, but sidestepped. When the inventor of a value adopts one after another perspective, those different perspectives are able to provide the reality checks that institutions can't. For these purposes, perspectives are configurations of a human personality, so the solution is available only to a would-be value inventor whose personality repeatedly reconfigures itself. In Nietzsche's case, the perspective shifts required for the type of cross-correction the inventor of values needs were not under anything close to his full control. Thus the solution we've started to consider was made available to him by the way his personality repeatedly and involuntarily reconfigured itself. Nietzsche's label for this sort of disunified agency was decadence; only a decadent could manage the invention of the sort of values Nietzsche is calling for. But by the lights of the metavalue that Nietzsche had invented and adopted for himself, bringing off the invention of values of this sort was supremely important. It followed that the form that disunified agency took in Nietzsche's own life was worth the price he had to pay for it: it would have been worth just about any price.

Let's remind ourselves of some of the costs. As he worked through the books we have discussed, Nietzsche quite likely was haunted by the thought

WHAT WAS NIETZSCHE'S PERSPECTIVISM? 239

that he was dying of syphilis. (We'll fill that suggestion in further come ch. 10.) Whether he did or not, he lived out the course of that illness, in which progressively more erratic cognition culminated in delusions of grandeur, incoherence, lengthy paralysis, and an early demise, and along the way he suffered near-constant migraines and episodes of vomiting. Since he couldn't hold down a job, he was consigned to a threadbare existence, the impoverished tourism that nowadays teenagers take for adventure, but made into his harrowing daily grind. Disunified agency isn't good at restraint and self-control; as Nietzsche lashed out at one after another of his ever-dwindling circle of friends and acquaintances, his life grew lonelier and lonelier. The fragmented, often violent writing he was able to produce was too unlike what the readership of the time was used to finding in the bookstores, and so his labors were almost entirely ignored until after his final collapse.

There are two very different things Nietzsche might have been thinking, and I can't be sure that he distinguished them himself. Spelling them out, first, even if there could be more controlled ways of repeatedly shifting perspectives, the lurch-by-lurch collapse of his psyche was how *he* managed to monitor and supply the needed reality check to the values he was inventing. A businessperson looking back might realize that there had been other and less difficult expedients for getting an enterprise off the ground, but be content in retrospect with how he had started up *his* company. And likewise, once Nietzsche's travails were understood as the steps through which his evaluative inventions were accomplished, they perhaps could be reaffirmed and belatedly endorsed as part of, or an aspect of, the accomplishing itself.

But second, Nietzsche might also have had the not unreasonable impression that his sort of decadence would be a precondition for *anyone's* invention of the personalized and deeply novel values he was demanding. We noticed, a couple of steps back, the plausible connection between a lack of voluntary control over the perspectives one adopts and the independence of subsequent from initial perspectives. That independence was, also plausibly, needed if the further perspectives were to serve as the reality check Nietzsche was after. Nietzsche made the historical sense—the ability to project oneself into the frame of mind of past times and other places—out to be the special talent of the nineteenth century. (He did emphasize the costs of developing it: after sufficiently many changes of intellectual costume, you no longer know who you really are.) But it wasn't as though all of that very refined history put those historians in a position to see what was wrong with what

240   WHY DIDN'T NIETZSCHE GET HIS ACT TOGETHER?

they were doing, and relatively early on in his career, Nietzsche found himself writing what is now a famous essay on "The Uses and Abuses of History" to point it out to them (1:243–334/UM 2). Closer to home: our own historians of philosophy are taught the methods of, specifically, analytic history of philosophy, and use them to reconstruct the perspectives of past philosophical traditions. How often do we see their command of those past perspectives allowing them the critical distance that would play out in the reassessment of their home tradition—either analytic philosophy as a whole or its historical wing? So Nietzsche may have been convinced that his sort of invention of values was something that only someone in his own predicament could pull off successfully.

I'm uncertain what the correct view here would be; I do routinely recommend to my students familiarity with a number of philosophical traditions, so as to have at their fingertips the means of correcting oversights in one or another of them, and don't expect the outcome to be critical faculties that are somehow stunted.[46] But either way, if this is what it took for Nietzsche to invent personalized values for himself, once we understand repeated perspective shifts as essential to his process of debugging and firming up the content of these bespoke values, the hardships he underwent were not external costs but *what it was* to be living up to the demands of his metavalue. And so Nietzsche had an interpretation of his own life, on which he accepted and even loved his fate, on which he could affirm the way his life had turned out, and on which he would willingly do it all over again, exactly as was. Having formulated the Eternal Return as the benchmark for a successful life, and having invented a value, along with the theoretical constructs that showed to his own satisfaction that he had met that benchmark, he managed the sort of narrative closure for himself that we see too often in novels, but rarely in our own normally haphazard lives.

However, our own treatment can't end here. If you're like me, the account of his own life that Nietzsche put in place strikes you, once all the pieces have been fit together, as overly *neat*, and I can't but think that it must have seemed that way to Nietzsche himself. Which would be a problem: his framing of his life could do its job only if were emotionally compelling, and it's hard to believe that any story as tidy—and apparently contrived—as this one could produce the requisite depth of conviction. At any rate, I don't believe that it sufficed, the evidence being the further steps Nietzsche took to arrive at his emotional stopping point; the next chapter turns to that next—and for him, very last—lap.

Appendix: Truth and Lie

We've already seen Nietzsche worrying about the low quality of our intellectual toolkit, and this is an occasion to remind the reader of his early unpublished essay, "On Truth and Lie in the Extra-Moral Sense" (1:873–890/WEN pp. 253–264). In the analytic wing of Nietzsche scholarship, it's become almost the accepted wisdom that Nietzsche abandoned the claims enunciated in it, and for good reason: the view—or rather, the hodgepodge of inconsistent views—of truth it presupposes is roughly Schopenhauer's bungled uptake of Kant.[47]

I see the piece rather differently, and although I want to allow that the ideas come out somewhat garbled, I take it seriously as an early attempt to articulate a thought that underwrote Nietzsche's later insistence that our truths are substantially falsehoods. (As we've been attempting to capture it: in something like the way that those law school rankings were alleged to be.) A number of different trains of thought aren't kept distinct, and their expression is indeed inflected by Kant read through Schopenhauer (which may be why we don't find the material repurposed in a subsequent book). However, the underlying insight, it seems to me, wasn't what the interpreters have taken it to be, and was never given up.

I'm going to take a shot at recasting one of these trains of thought more cleanly than Nietzsche did, so that we can see both how to give it the credit it deserves, and how to resist it. That will mean departing from his own rendering, filling in both the steps that he noticed, but didn't bother spelling out, and the missing steps that we would notice, and he would not have. So this will be a departure from our standard approach to the explication of a text.

Nietzsche seems to have taken over from Emerson the idea that literal language is fossilized metaphor:

> The poet made all the words, and therefore language is the archives of history, and, if we must say it, a sort of tomb of the muses. For, though the origin of most of our words is forgotten, each word was at first a stroke of genius, and obtained currency, because for the moment it symbolized the world to the first speaker and to the hearer. The etymologist finds the deadest word to have been once a brilliant picture. Language is fossil poetry. As the limestone of the continent consists of infinite masses of the shells of animalcules, so language is made up of images, or tropes, which

242 WHY DIDN'T NIETZSCHE GET HIS ACT TOGETHER?

now, in their secondary use, have long ceased to remind us of their poetic origin. (Emerson, 1971–2013, III:13, "The Poet")

But let's ask ourselves what's involved in this process.

As we could now say it, metaphors are indefinitely productive: when an occasion arises to provide a paraphrase, there's always more content to be cashed out.[48] Taking as our illustration a metaphor we've already encountered, that man is made in the image of God was to say that we are His coinage, stamped with the face of the monarch, and when we start unpacking it, that means that humans are specially valuable through the authority of their creator, in something like the way that coins are legal tender by the authority of a government. It means that damaging or destroying a person is disrespecting God, rather as defacing or forging currency used to be considered lèse-majesté. It means that, like those coins, everyone is worth exactly the same... and it's clear that you could go on indefinitely in this way. Were you to do so, you'd face the tricky task of distinguishing between intended and unintended but legitimate continuations: could we complain that our fellow men have been debased by an admixture of the wrong metals? Do we see counterfeiting and coin clipping amongst our fellow men? And then of course there would be apparent consequences we would disallow; currency is fungible, but we saw that the rabbis took exception to making that out as part of the metaphor's content; or again, that God *looks* like a human being was certainly not what the monotheist text had in mind.

Now, we tend to think of literal senses as having definite, exhaustively characterizable contents; that's why it's reasonable for dictionaries to try to define words.[49] So to literalize a metaphor is to discard most of its indefinitely extensive content, and that is how, on Nietzsche's early view, most or even all concepts are produced. An example that is perhaps more apt than the one Nietzsche gave in the essay might be "Caesar"; originally someone's name, it came to be a title, designating the holder of an office. If the decision as to what to keep and what to throw away is made intelligently—in view both of the inferential and other uses we mean to put the term to, and the features or patterns in the world we want it to track—we'll have a useful intellectual tool.

But how often do we actually stop and ask ourselves which elements of a metaphor are inferentially important and need to be kept, and which can be discarded? The occasions on which the literalization of our metaphors is done thoughtfully are evidently very, very rare. The intellectual usefulness

WHAT WAS NIETZSCHE'S PERSPECTIVISM? 243

of a concept produced by *randomly* deleting aspects of some metaphor or other isn't likely to be high on average. So most of our concepts aren't likely to be intellectually useful. And that's why when we apply our concepts—or the other literal elements of our linguistic repertoire—we're almost bound to be producing untruths, and not just untruths: in the title of his essay, Nietzsche calls them "lies," and to be a lie takes more than just not being true. (You *know* better.) The suggestion must be that, deep down, we're aware of how horribly shoddy our thinking is.

Long ago, looking up at the stars, some of our ancestors metaphorically characterized a group of them as a water bearer. Although the adjacency of the stars in a constellation is an illusion, and although the membership of stars many light years away in this sort of arbitrarily designated set has no significant effects on anything on *our* planet, many of us even today speak of constellations as though they were *things*, read horoscopes, imagine that astrological signs determine who might be personally compatible as a mate, and much else along the same lines. It is in some very thin sense true that a particular star belongs in a designated constellation, in something like the way that it's true that, in those law school rankings, this institution ranks higher than that one. But when you talk astrologically, everything you say is substantively false, and because you so absolutely ought to know better, we might well count it all as lying—in, as Nietzsche put it, an extra-moral sense. Nietzsche is asking us to face up with open eyes to the possibility (which despite that view shared by some prominent interpreters, has nothing to do with a Kantian doctrine of the unknowable world of things in themselves) that all of our intellectual equipment is in as bad a shape as this.

And the situation is worse than even that makes it sound, because the process is not a one-off. After whatever counted as the first round of literalization, lost somewhere in a prehistoric past, we took these crooked skeletons of metaphors, and used them to generate further metaphors. Some of these were in turn skeletized, in the very same way: our ancestors threw out some content, pretty much at random, and kept a little bit of content, also at random. We've had this process running ever since, making trash out of junk out of garbage, and Nietzsche later gave us an especially important example of what a lap or two around this track looks like. Causation is either a metaphor-like projection of willing onto the outside world, or perhaps even a metaphor proper. Substances are similarly a projection of the *I*— the inner self. But there is nothing inside that matches our phenomenology of the *I*, or of willing. The physicists' atoms, the theologians' God, and the philosophers' thing-in-itself are in turn metaphor-like projections of substances and causation. Whyever think that, at the point at which we've arrived, what we have is decent intellectual equipment? Wouldn't inferential reliability be an incredible coincidence?[50]

I don't think we need to accept the dismaying suggestion just like that; there's more than one way to push back.[51] But we also don't want simply to dismiss the possibility, without seeing it for what it is.

10

What Was Nietzsche's Tragedy?

We've been examining what are usually classified as Nietzsche's later or mature works, and—a good deal of messiness notwithstanding—have seen how they're segments of a single intellectual and philosophical trajectory, one whose innovations ought still to be of great interest. But every philosophy is "necessarily the philosophy of the person who has it," and so now I want to turn to that person, and to Nietzsche's first book, in which he announced that "it is only as an *aesthetic phenomenon* that existence and the world are eternally *justified*."[1] It does seem to me that it ultimately provided the template for his attempt to justify his own existence to himself. And so *The Birth of Tragedy* accounts, in a very different way than we have so far considered, for that trajectory. At any rate, that's the case I will now try to make.

If I'm purporting to frame Nietzsche's later philosophical work so as to explain its personal importance to him, in the mode of, as we might say it now, existential-crisis management, why, you may be wondering, is the story I'm about to tell of philosophical rather than merely biographical interest? That is, why is it more than the addition of a touching human interest story, or a superfluous literary flourish, to the properly theoretical exposition that is by this point complete? If this is what you *are* wondering, your question is probably posed rhetorically, but recall that part of Nietzsche's own revaluation of values was the insistence on assessments that proceed by looking behind metaphysical views and evaluative stances to the person who does, or would, have them. (Recall also that what the turn to this mode of assessment amounted to was much more complicated, and much harder to simply dismiss, than what we were all taught was the fallacy of the *ad hominem* argument.) If we think that Nietzsche's ideas and arguments earn the attention we've devoted to him so far, we ought to proceed one step more, and see what we would find were we to turn his own preferred mode of assessment on *him*. If we were confident that we could without further ado shrug off this component of his upending of all values, why would we have devoted so much time and thought to unraveling the perspectivism, the invention of values, and all the rest of it?

Why Didn't Nietzsche Get His Act Together? Elijah Millgram, Oxford University Press. © Oxford University Press 2023.
DOI: 10.1093/oso/9780197669303.003.0010

246 WHY DIDN'T NIETZSCHE GET HIS ACT TOGETHER?

Here's a different way to defuse that first rhetorical question. If, like me, you're an analytic philosopher by academic birth and upbringing, you're trained to treat philosophical work *impersonally*. But Nietzsche is quite critical of that very training; here he is in the *Genealogy*:

> training for "impersonality," for self-forgetfulness, for "*incuria sui*"—: how thoroughly, how subtly the ascetic priest has known how to employ them in the struggle against pain!
>
> Oh, what does science not conceal today! how much, at any rate, it is *meant* to conceal! The proficiency of our finest scholars, their heedless industry, their heads smoking day and night, their very craftsmanship—how often the real meaning of all this lies in the desire to keep something hidden from oneself! Science as a means of self-narcosis: *do you have experience of that?*
>
> [Scholars are] *sufferers* who refuse to admit to themselves what they are . . . [:] drugged and heedless men who fear only one thing: *regaining consciousness.*[2]

When you find yourself inclined to put the question of the personal import of Nietzsche's work to one side, remember that one of the strands of that work was diagnosing that very inclination. Indulging it too freely is thus begging the question against him. But we can return to this issue once we have the materials to reassemble Nietzsche's earlier-on diagnosis, and to put it to use.

We'll proceed as follows. To start with, I'll provide a two-pass synopsis of the theory advanced in *The Birth of Tragedy*, highlighting first the picture it provides of Attic dramatic art, and then Nietzsche's recycling of Schopenhauer's metaphysics. As questions of historical, artistic, and metaphysical plausibility will not matter for the treatment I'm developing, I won't attempt to defend either of them on Nietzsche's behalf. In particular, Schopenhauer was that peculiar combination, a gripping but weak philosopher, and as Nietzsche noticed one misstep after another, he eventually achieved a good deal of critical distance from the doctrines in *The World as Will and Representation*; there wouldn't be much point for us in shoring up views that Nietzsche himself dropped. Rather, the focus will be on what it takes for tragedy to reconcile one to the awfulness of a human life.

Then I'll lay out the way in which both the intellectual construction we've seen and Nietzsche's extensive portrait of his own personality, which we've

WHAT WAS NIETZSCHE'S TRAGEDY? 247

also seen, match the blueprint his younger self had laid out. After briefly reminding you how the theoretical moves fit together, we'll turn to the sheer misery of Nietzsche's own life, take up how the theory overlaid the ghastliness, and consider what emotional work we can suppose that fact to have been doing for him.

10.1

When you look at the world straight on, and don't allow it to be obscured by your own emotional convenience, what you'll be facing, Iris Murdoch pronounced, is "intolerably chancy and incomplete"—and that, Nietzsche proposes, is how it seemed to the ancient Greeks; he more than suggests that in this regard they saw matters aright.[3] What you accordingly have to cope with is not simply the inevitability of one after another unfortunate and even gruesome turn of events, but the world in its entirety being pervasively, deeply, and systematically chaotic. In *Genesis*, before God separates the sky from the ocean from the land, the Hebrew description of the proto-world, *tohu va-vohu*, is traditionally rendered as "without form and void"; when you look past the evanescent illusion of orderliness, that's what the world you live in is *now*. Chaos is inhospitable to human life; in a world like ours, your best bet is not to be born in the first place. But here you are; that best-for-you outcome is no longer attainable; as you stare into the reality around you, surely suicidal ideation is a normal and entirely understandable response.

However, it's not the only one. An alternative way of facing up to that horrific vision of brutal turmoil is to try to lose yourself in it and identify with it. Activities supporting this coping strategy include, especially, drunken, orgiastic festivals, in which one loses all sense of constraint or—and we'll return to this aspect of it momentarily—even of being a individual distinct from the universe around one and from the other people in it. Perhaps the Dionysian rites were less culturally alien than that makes it sound; since about the 1960s, more or less this way of talking has accompanied the consumption of psychedelics, although wine is now considered a genteel and sedate narcotic, and not a drug that might once have served in place of LSD.

But enthusiastic immersion—literally enthusiastic, since the word comes from Greek, to the effect that a god is within you—in an enactment of the vision of underlying chaos is not a viable response in the medium to long

248 WHY DIDN'T NIETZSCHE GET HIS ACT TOGETHER?

term. A Rio-style Mardi Gras or a Burning Man has to come to an end soon enough, at which point its participants return to lives that they perceive as pointless and miserable. Moreover, as Nietzsche remarks, "the Dionysian state with its annihilation of the ordinary bounds and limits of existence contains, while it lasts, a *lethargic* element"; after it's over, you have "*gained knowledge*, and nausea inhibits action" (1:56f/BT 7). Filling out that thought, the posture of enthusiastic identification is self-deceiving. If the world is really seething, roiling chaos, to insist on trying to act as part of the chaos yourself, with the implication that, very crudely, you're on the same side as the chaos, which is to say, the winning side—that's pure pretense. After all, you know very well, even if while reveling, you manage not to think about it, that it's not possible to lead a coherent human life in a deeply inchoate world; as Nietzsche remarked in one of his journal entries, "It must be possible to *live*; therefore pure Dionysianism is impossible."[4] Identifying with the inchoate world is not really a coping strategy; it's metaphysical Stockholm Syndrome.

An alternative response is to bring into sharp focus an illusory ideal order, and let the fact that things just happen slip out of view. The arts, especially in very artificial and controlled genres, can support this posture, with the cozy standing out as something of an icon of the class: these detective stories conclude with their Hercules Poirot summoning everyone to the drawing room for a complicated but tight argument, one whose premises—"clues"— have been made available to the reader, that so-and-so must be the murderer. Cozies are read for the reassurance that in the end there always is an answer and an explanation for it, and if you think hard enough, you can figure out what they are.[5] Not only disposable genre fiction but genuinely great art can be put to this end, and not just art: what Nietzsche called "Alexandrianism," and what we would probably call the scientific spirit, is first and foremost an attempt to prompt a specifically aesthetic response to our world, by making it seem intellectually tractable and transparent to reason; this is

a profound *illusion* that first saw the light of the world in the person of Socrates: the unshakable faith that thought, using the thread of causality, can penetrate the deepest abysses of being, and that thought is capable not only of knowing being but even of *correcting* it. This sublime metaphysical illusion accompanies science as an instinct and leads science again and again to its limits at which it must turn into *art—which is really the aim of this mechanism.*

WHAT WAS NIETZSCHE'S TRAGEDY? 249

> [T]he image of the *dying Socrates*, as the human being whom knowledge and reasons have liberated from the fear of death, is the emblem that, above the entrance gate of science, reminds all of its mission—namely, to make existence appear comprehensible and thus justified; and if reasons do not suffice, *myth* has to come to their aid in the end—myth which I have just called the necessary consequence, indeed the purpose, of science.
>
> Anyone who has ever experienced the pleasure of Socratic insight and felt how, spreading in ever-widening circles, it seeks to embrace the whole world of appearances, will never again find any stimulus toward existence more violent than the craving to complete this conquest and to weave the net impenetrably tight.   (1:99, 101/BT 15)

We've gotten used to contrasting science, scholarship, and philosophy with art, but Alexandrianism is an art project, that of trying to make the world *appear knowable*, by covering it with a net of logic and argument. Nietzsche complains that it's an *aesthetic* failure, first because, as Kant brought us to see, once we manage enough in the way of careful, self-aware reasoning, we're forced to the conclusion that there are limits to reason, and that we *can't* know the world completely; at this point the project breaks down, and it all seems once again mysterious and dark.[6] Second, scientific aestheticizing doesn't, Nietzsche elsewhere observes, produce the *right* aesthetic effect; when science identifies itself with the production of mechanistic explanation, the impression it's all too likely to produce is one of meaninglessness. As Nietzsche bluntly words it, the world comes to look *stupid*, and thus Alexandrianism—Enlightenment rationality, in its current incarnation as science, but considered as primarily an aesthetic enterprise—is a failure by its own implicit lights.[7]

Returning momentarily to the scholarly and scientific posture of impersonality, when it's not simply an evasive manuever, we can now see it as putting oneself in the proper frame of mind to appreciate Alexandrian artworks, rather in the way one would empty one's mind and accustom one's eyes to the half-light, when contemplating a Rothko. Here, impersonality is a stance whose point is the aesthetic response it enables. To insist on impersonality in philosophy *might* be to accept that view, but then one would be taking that stance to be essential to philosophy, without considering whether there are other equally rewarding postures one could adopt. Or, and more likely, it's to have the conviction that philosophy isn't a matter

250 WHY DIDN'T NIETZSCHE GET HIS ACT TOGETHER?

of aesthetics, and be disinclined to look into the matter further. But either way, reconsidering the presuppositions of what one is doing *is* central to philosophizing, if anything is.

Thus neither the Dionysian nor the Apollinian response to that horrifying vision of the world is successful. The remarkable aesthetic innovation of Attic tragedy, in Nietzsche's view, was to execute the two simultaneously. In tragedy, or so his acknowledgedly controversial account has it, the Apollinian representation of lucid order is perceived—by the chorus, thus, within the staged material itself—as an illusion projected onto a underlying Dionysian reality, that is and *inter alia*, onto a nightmare of arational and uncontrollable disorder.[8] If the combination of these two points of view is carried off, and we have models for it in the works that have come down to us from the great Greek playwrights, the effect is to reconcile the theatergoer to the way that fate, working through and around him, is liable negligently to destroy not just him but everything that he cares about: seeing all of that, he is nonetheless willing to continue throwing himself into his life.

Nietzsche seems to have been reading the metaphysics of Schopenhauer's *World as Will and Representation* back into ancient Hellenic culture, and here's what you need to know about it for the moment. Schopenhauer took over from Kant the idea that the metaphysical structure of the perceived world is an artefact of our own cognitive processing. In particular, in his streamlining of Kant's categories of the understanding, the Principle of Sufficient Reason and the Principle of Individuation are both our own contribution; that is to say, both the structures—especially the causal structures— that support the various sorts of explanations we give to render our world intelligible, and even the way we parse the world into discrete individuals, are not there in the things "in themselves."[9] Where Kant, however, took it to follow that no one *could* tell you what the world, minus our structuring of it, was really like, Schopenhauer was not deterred. The picture emerges of a sea of roiling will, the will being something which Schopenhauer, making a clumsy mistake no clearheaded Kantian would have failed to call him on, thought we knew all about, from the inside.[10] In that boundless ocean, there are no divisions into particulars, no causation; that unindividuated will expresses itself by casting up what you perceive as endlessly reproduced creatures that struggle to devour one another, impelled from one moment to the next by the futile illusion that if they can only satisfy the last craving to have seized hold of them, they will somehow be satisfied and remain happy ever after. That world of distinct individuals, living lives that are either

WHAT WAS NIETZSCHE'S TRAGEDY? 251

catastrophically savage or dishearteningly tedious, but in any case threaded around one another in the environment which we experience as spatially and temporally structured, is an illusion: you yourself, as an individual, do not really exist; your own motivations are deceptions engendered upon you by that underlying sea of will, as ways of getting you to survive and reproduce. Whatever orderliness and intelligibility you perceive in the world is an illusion overlaid on an unthinkably horrible reality.

Once again, we're prescinding from the question of whether this is a reasonable take on the literary and dramatic productions of the ancient Greeks, and a metaphysical theory we ought to find convincing. What matters for our own purposes is what Nietzsche thought the response would be to apprehending the superposition of an artificially generated and illusory order and a chaos in which causal order and even the separation into discrete individuals fail to get a grip:

> *tragedy* . . . the quintessence of all prophylactic powers of healing . . . absorbs the highest ecstasies of music [and] places the tragic hero next to [the music], and he . . . takes the whole Dionysian world upon his back and thus relieves us of this burden. (1:134/BT 21)

Perhaps flipping back and forth between the two visions would merely mimic bipolar disorder, but if you can manage to bring them both into focus at the same time—the illusory order of things *as* illusory, spread over the underlying absolute lack of order—you'll experience a reconciliation with life. What you have to be reconciled with is precisely a universe that is too ungoverned to be conceptualized adequately and accurately. But watching the tragic hero being crushed by the indifferent universe displays to you the truth about it in a way that you can conceptualize. Although he's an individual with a name and backstory, he nonetheless figures as a generic representative of individuals, whoever they may be. Because you're watching it happen to someone *else*, it's not imminently and personally threatening to you; but the mythic aspect of the narrative (along with the musical cuing, when that's part of the work, as in, Nietzsche enthuses, Wagner's operas) allows you to perceive it as an allegory of *everything*: the content is metaphysical, but the Dionysian vision has been modulated in a way that enables you to take it in. The "Apollinian illusion . . . aims to deliver us from the Dionysian flood and excess" (1:138/BT 21); the symbolic representation allows you a kind of doublethink, which spares you from being overwhelmed by the

252 WHY DIDN'T NIETZSCHE GET HIS ACT TOGETHER?

horrific truth. In my own view, we still don't have a convincing psychological explanation for the juxtaposition producing the response Nietzsche expects, but there are justifications for it—another matter entirely—evidently waiting in the wings.

Briefly, the complaints you have about life have to do with the suffering that *you* undergo (or maybe, if you're altruistic, or you have friends, the suffering others undergo), the fact that *you* will die, and so on. But individuals are, on that Dionysian view, the projection of a cognitively tractable schema on a too-confusing background; as we saw earlier on, they're an aspect of a misrepresentation of your circumstances that makes those circumstances thinkable for you. But then, that "you" (an individual) are suffering, or that "your friends" (other individuals) are suffering, is simply a mistake. We can add to that a remark in *The Birth of Tragedy*:

> nor are we the true authors of this art world. On the contrary, we may assume that we are merely images and artistic projections for the true author [the Dionysian world itself], and that we have our highest dignity in our significance as works of art—for it is only as an *aesthetic phenomenon* that existence and the world are eternally *justified*—while of course our consciousness of our own significance hardly differs from that which the soldiers painted on canvas have of the battle represented on it.
>
> (1:47/BT 5)

Since the "you" you think exists is merely a painted soldier on the Apollinian canvas of the world, when you point at yourself, you point *past* the image and schema to what *is* there, namely, the underlying world of activity. (In the book we're now considering, following Schopenhauer, that was the activity of an amorphous will, and in Nietzsche's later rendering, will-to-power.) If you think "water" is a count noun, and you try to point at *a* water, you manage to point at *water*, the mass noun—what else could you be pointing at? And that's why you *should* identify yourself with the underlying, roiling chaos, allowing you to think of yourself, elatedly, as part of an endless, surging excitement.

Neither of these arguments is very good, or so it seems to me, and we can register in passing a better alternative, although it doesn't seem to have been in play in, at any rate, Nietzsche's early treatment.[11] The Apollinian order is not exactly an illusion: an evanescent order does appear on the surface of the disorder, in rather the way that shapes appear in the clouds. There can already be genuine delight in the very fact that these fluctuating, beautiful forms slip momentarily into place, and when they further represent the awful indifference and arbitrariness of the underlying shapelessness, that is something at which one can be brought to marvel—and that's why the world, as tragedy represents it, can be recognized as marvelous.

Be that as it may, Nietzsche's thinking his vision would induce either acceptance of or recommitment to one's own life is most likely accounted for by this being the response that *he* had, both to tragedy and to Schopenhauer. And that's the stepping stone we need in order to proceed, in our own assessment.

10.2

Let's now return to the portrait that's emerged of the author of the volumes we've worked our way through, starting with the official bio, which we can take to be the Apollinian cover story. Because we've already given this material extensive coverage, we won't need more than the most condensed synopsis.

Nietzsche's program had as its centerpiece the invention of values that were to be novel, personalized, and—although this was often enough belied by his own outbursts—no longer the expression of a deep-seated bitterness and resentment. The program was, by the lights of a metavalue that Nietzsche had himself introduced, enormously important; that metavalue was, precisely, the invention of such novel values, but he managed the setup so as to make this evaluation not (or not obviously) trivial by virtue of its circularity.

Values, we saw, must be filled in, made concrete, and applicable; this requires ongoing reality checks, and the socially available techniques for firming up and monitoring novel values—institutionalization, in one form or another—almost inevitably corrupt and ruin the idiosyncratic values that Nietzsche hoped for. In any case, institutional methods of stabilizing values are far too slow to meet the needs of an individual who is inventing a value for his own use, in his own lifetime. But occupying one after another perspective on a newly introduced value can substitute for institutional scaffolding; as you traverse perspectives, you're able to notice and correct your missteps and misreadings of the value you are crystallizing. Thus the person best suited to invent values is someone who is able to move between perspectives that he takes up on the values he invents.

254 WHY DIDN'T NIETZSCHE GET HIS ACT TOGETHER?

For these purposes, a perspective can be identified with a particular configuration of a human personality, and so Nietzsche's program requires a personality that reconfigures itself, and not just once, but over and over again; that is, the plan must be executed by a highly unstable psychology. A person who can't hold himself together in a stable psychological configuration is a decadent. In other words, it takes a decadent to bring off Nietzsche's enormously important contribution to our culture.

Now Nietzsche, we saw, *was* a decadent, and of just the right sort. It was a great affliction, but looking back on his life, from the tail end of the period in which it was still possible for him to make such judgments, the personal costs were absolutely worth it; only someone cobbled together in the way he was could have taken the step forward—a philosophical step, but not by any means confined only to philosophy—of making the self-aware invention of values an ongoing concern. The Eternal Return, a formulation within one of those perspectives of the demand that one retrospectively reaffirm the course of one's life, has returned; all of the awfulness notwithstanding, he would still do it over again: the return of the Eternal Return is Nietzsche's final Apollinian vision of his own life.

But now let's give an equally condensed recap of that great affliction, folding together the portrait we extracted from *Ecce Homo* with what we've seen in the course of traversing Nietzsche's perspectives, book by anguished book.

I do think that Pierre Klossowski has gotten something right in his reconstruction of how Nietzsche experienced what was happening to him, and we can entertain a somewhat adjusted version of his reconstruction.[12] Nietzsche had symptoms that would have suggested tertiary syphilis to just about anyone of his generation. Thanks to antibiotics, this is a stage of the disease with which we're no longer familiar; as a fatal sexually transmitted infection, the illness was morally and emotionally fraught, prompting more or less the attitudes widely evoked by the AIDS epidemic at the tail end of the last century. The cluster of symptoms included delusions of grandeur, and the lunatic asylums of France were packed with inmates who thought themselves to be Napoleon.

Did Nietzsche *believe* he was dying of syphilis? *Did* he die of syphilis? For too long, his fans and detractors took sides on these questions, meaning either to defend or attack the man himself; by this point, however, we should be past all of that. In any case, we're aware that the first of those questions doesn't necessarily admit of a straight answer; Nietzsche was frequently disorganized enough for even his very vivid thoughts not to count as beliefs.

WHAT WAS NIETZSCHE'S TRAGEDY?   255

And the medical diagnoses for which we have records—two of them—followed rather than preceded his breakdown.[13]

But the apprehensive idea that the spirochetes were eating his mind away from the inside would have been hard to avoid; once it had come up, it would have been constantly at the edges of his awareness. And then, one day, on one of his walks in the Swiss Alps, the thought of the Eternal Return came to him, as an *epiphany*. The obvious explanation for the revelation must have immediately occured to him: that he was finally going mad. Klossowski's conjecture is that Nietzsche's sketches for a cosmological proof of the Eternal Return, along with his abortive plans to go back to school and get a science degree, were driven by the need to convince himself that the Eternal Return might be real physics, and not just a symptom of oncoming insanity.

What Nietzsche experienced, starting with the epiphany of the Eternal Return, and culminating in the barrage of missives he sent out as he finally collapsed, closely matched that diagnosis: one note was signed "The Crucified," and others, summoning statesmen to meetings and announcing mass executions, were evidently composed by someone who, in the moment, imagined he was the dictator of the world. The downward spiral into insanity, paralysis, and eventual death was also the period when he produced the writings on which we have been focused, a period whose days consisted of recurrent migraines and rounds of vomiting.

Over and above the physical pain and the grim anticipation of what was in store, his academic career had been derailed, by the reception of *The Birth of Tragedy*, and then his debilitating illness. He was genuinely too sick to keep his job, but after several books that provocatively ignored the etiquette of scholarly publication, his administration agreed, no doubt with scarcely disguised alacrity, that he *was* too sick. Thereafter, Nietzsche lived in threadbare poverty, on funds scrounged out of contributions by fellow faculty. An indication of how bad it was: in the Swiss and Italian *pensions* he drifted between, heat in the winter—a stove and fuel for his room—was an optional extra he often could not afford. His publisher, he complained bitterly, was a fringe press known for its antisemitic tracts, whom he had to pay to print his books.[14] Today we call this vanity publishing, and before that final, completely incapacitated decade of his life, vanishingly few copies were sold; Hume's line about his *Treatise*, that it fell stillborn from the press, could well have described all of Nietzsche's output.[15] Desperately ill, grindingly impoverished, ignored by almost everyone, his situation was difficult by anyone's standards, but that was perhaps just the visible surface of it.

256 WHY DIDN'T NIETZSCHE GET HIS ACT TOGETHER?

Returning to his mental decline, we can see the lurching trajectory taken by his disunified agency—in his own vocabulary, his collapse, stage by stage, into ever deeper decadence—in the successive literary products we've surveyed, and let's remind ourselves of their implicit authors. On the assumption that the writing of these rapid-fire compositions was not controlled or deliberate in a way that would have let Nietzsche make up fictional characters from the ground up and out of whole cloth—that is, without repurposing his own state of mind and voice as raw material—they amount to a series of snapshots of Nietzsche's agential configuration, taken at regular intervals.

Starting with the volume that launches this phase of his working life, although the implicit author of *Zarathustra* doesn't purport to be a version of Nietzsche himself, its uncontrolled and self-indulgent writing provides such a snapshot indirectly: it's very hard to believe that it doesn't show Nietzsche himself being carried away, and losing all sense of restraint in regard to his own prose, as well as the ideas and their presentation more generally. Even at this relatively early stage of his gradual dissolution, this is someone who can't help letting go.[16]

There was the repackaging of Nietzsche's earlier French moralist phase into his Convalescent, which we suggested was a way of *just*—in a rather different sense—letting go; unable to stomach the world he is in, or himself, he allows himself to relax into something like a lover's daydream, in which everything he can't tolerate is covered over with gauzy fantasy.[17]

Then there was the authorial persona of the *Genealogy of Morals*, whom we've named Nietzsche's Genealogist: an intellectual, someone whose personality was configured around a dominant drive. We've been calling that drive a will to truth, but recall that this is only a convenient shorthand; part of the book's agenda was to tease out and put on display its complicated underlying motivational structure, which turned out to be thoroughly self-deceptive, giving rise to courses of action whose point the agent couldn't himself acknowledge. Nonetheless, even the superficial characterization of the drive, as the scholarly commitment to truth, marks an acknowledged demand for consistency, and it wasn't one he could live up to; we saw that this character was prone to emotional outbursts that induced sudden swerves in his train of thought, and which made him unable to remain consistent over even short stretches of text.

Nietzsche's Good European—that being the label we found for the implicit author of *Beyond Good and Evil*—was presented to us as a field of unregimented, quasi-independent drives successively seizing control of him for the duration of one or another ranting diatribe. And we saw those misogynist, antisemitic, and nationalist excesses disavowed, on the elaborately theorized grounds that this personality was unable to anchor the full-fledged attribution of opinions, choices, and attitudes generally.

Nietzsche's Psychologist—the author of *Twilight of the Idols*—appeared, like the Genealogist, to be someone unable to control his impulses sufficiently to manage moment-by-moment consistency. This authorial character had improvised a prosthetic, so as to keep himself on track. Meant to serve what was, very loosely, the function of Socratic hyperrationality, it deployed a new value contrast, between decadence and will-to-power; by poking and prodding himself with it, he could, if not exactly remain focused on his themes, keep himself returning to them, in more or less a constant spirit.

We saw his Antichrist, an implicit author configured around a dominant drive convincingly rendered as itself incoherent, in an extreme version of the way that the platforms of political parties normally are. Although the preoccupations of this character exhibited thematic continuity, it didn't project effective agency: the objectives it purported to set for itself, and to have achieved, weren't plausibly coordinated with the activity it motivated; we ended up using it as a case study of a drive that couldn't be made sense of teleologically.

We can consider what these snapshots show us along both the diachronic and synchronic axes. On the one hand, this isn't a personality that remains structurally stable over time. It's as though someone else, with the same name and the same memories, and many of the same ideas, writes each successive book, in a manner reminiscent of what used to be called multiple personality disorder. And on the other, we see each of its stages to be dramatically incoherent in one way or another.[18] Thomas Nagel once asked what it was like to be a bat, insisting that we could never know the answer to that question; in a draft of a book manuscript, Robert Nozick replied we could know a good deal: for instance, being a bat is a lot like being an F-15.[19] What must it have been like to be the disunified agent that Nietzsche portrays? Perhaps a lot like being the bread dough in a mixer; or like walking up to the very edge of a crumbling cliff, and gazing over its lip at the surf crashing on the rocks below; or like being drunk at the sort of party where guests get to call shots, and everyone has to line up for another round of cheap vodka; or like bipolar disorder; or like not being able to resist letting fly with a vicious rejoinder in the middle of an out-of-control quarrel; or like being

258   WHY DIDN'T NIETZSCHE GET HIS ACT TOGETHER?

a banana republic in which constitutions succeed one another with dizzying frequency, and competing claimants to the presidency duke it out with their respective militias.

As we see the sick and disintegrating former professor approach the brink of his remaining sanity, the scene is a psychological slice of the chaos that pervaded the Dionysian and Schopenhauerian apprehension of the world: the borders around the self and its parts that limn an articulated individual shift, blur, and blow away; the rationales and justifications which tie down beliefs, other attitudes, and activities, in ways that make them intelligible and allow an individual to lay claim to them, slip and slide along with the underlying psychic matter. Each temporary configuration of Nietzsche's personality had a story, which we saw to be sometimes quite elaborate, about what kind of character he was; but for each perspective—maybe invisibly to it, but not to the other perspectives—its own psychology doesn't fit the account it gives: odd bits and pieces stick out like sore thumbs. Perspectives truncate, abridge, and misrepresent more generally whatever they're looking at, and so they also truncate, abridge and misrepresent *him*, to himself. Just as, watching the ocean or the sky, you sometimes see momentary shapes in the waves or the clouds, you can see Nietzsche's personality taking on one or another of these forms, but the underlying reality is shapeless currents, flowing where they will.

As in Attic tragedy, on Nietzsche's reading of it, this violently inchoate field of psychological activity projects over itself the inspiring narrative which we rehearsed one lap back, on which all is literally in order, and the suffering and cacophany is redeemed through a magnificent accomplishment that is simultaneously the fated sacrifice of the drama's hero. Nietzsche brought his own life around to be a tragedy as he understood it, and whatever the merits of that early theory of tragedy, we observed that it tells us what *his* response to such tragedy was. The aesthetic payoff, so went the theory, was reconciliation to the horrors of the human condition, and one's own condition in particular. Let us do him the kindness of supposing that, as the philosopher transitioned to being a psychiatric patient, an invalid, and ultimately, to subsisting in a vegetative state, he had managed that reconcilation for himself.

11

What Is the Meaning of Life?

In Nietzsche's upending of values, the way to assess someone's philosophical view is to assess the person himself. We've worked our way to an overview of Nietzsche's philosophical enterprise, and the time has come to assess it. And if we take that enterprise seriously enough to think it worth engaging on its own terms, we ought to run that assessment as it suggests (without, of course, preempting others, conducted on other bases). Doing it his way would mean turning to an evaluation of Nietzsche, the man.

Moreover, evaluation, Nietzsche repeatedly insisted, is to be *personal*; time and again, we saw him invoking his own values and viscerally felt responses to pass judgment on this or that figure, and so, per his methodological stance, on their religious, philosophical, political, or social views. My own training has been to suppress such responses, but here I'm called upon to suppress that training, and come out with what *I* think of Nietzsche, on the basis of *my* evaluative commitments. I mean to be clear and up front about what those are, without assuming that my reader necessarily shares them; consequently, I won't be trying to twist your arm, but will leave to you what to make of my judgment, and whether you're ready to take it on board.

After which, returning to the Eternal Return, I'll ask how Nietzsche helps us to think about two closely related questions: what it is to succeed at life, and what the meaning of life might be.

11.1

As you might by this point expect, my own strongest evaluative commitments—at any rate, the ones that will be relevant here—are to philosophy, which in this connection we can treat as a value, as Nietzsche construed that notion. However, because I find myself seeing philosophy from, and here it's apt to retain his vocabulary, three very different perspectives, I have first to introduce them, at which point I can conduct evaluations of Nietzsche's person and endeavours from each.

Why Didn't Nietzsche Get His Act Together? Elijah Millgram, Oxford University Press. © Oxford University Press 2023.
DOI: 10.1093/oso/9780197669303.003.0011

260   WHY DIDN'T NIETZSCHE GET HIS ACT TOGETHER?

Philosophy is the machine tool industry of the mind: we philosophers are in the business of making the intellectual tools that are used to make the intellectual tools that we use day-to-day, but also those that we rely on for more exotic applications. If we take logic in its older sense, as telling us what it is to do reasoning right, philosophy of logic is first philosophy; all the rest of those philosophical subspecializations—epistemology, metaethics, even moral philosophy—stand to philosophy of logic in roughly the relation that applied ethics stands to ethics: the remainder of philosophy is applied logic. In particular, metaphysics is intellectual ergonomics; it's an engineering discipline, which fabricates the ontologies needed to support one or another logic.

In this way of seeing the guiding value of philosophy, strong philosophizing is exhibited in, especially, inventing a new way of thinking, and providing both the patterns of thought and the conceptual accessories needed to make those patterns effective in the real world. Aristotle might serve as an especially clear model. As a philosopher of logic, he originated our hylomorphic conception of logic: the idea that what makes an argument valid is its form, whose matter can be changed out without detriment to its correctness.[1] As a logician, Aristotle invented the syllogism, and exhaustively cataloged the variety of inference patterns of that type. As a metaphysician, he invented what we now call Aristotelian substances; these serve as the primary domain of application for those inference patterns; that is, substances are the accessories accompanying his logic, and needed to give it traction.[2] Aristotle was a paradigmatic philosopher in the first place in that he was a powerful and innovative philosopher of logic, and his metaphysics—what became the title of his book on the subject gives us that very word—fell into place to meet the demands of his logic.

That was one take on philosophy; here is another. To philosophize is to feel the full force of the Delphic oracle's command—"know thyself!"—and so to exhibit a distinctive mode of self-awareness in one's intellectual (and other) pursuits. We can see this specifically philosophical form of self-knowledge in play as early as Plato, who often enough uses the dramatic frames of his dialogues to register second thoughts about both the premises and the strategic presuppositions of the arguments they present. And, just to keep the relevant contrast vividly before us, we notice this absolutely essential awareness going missing when we come across philosophers who treat philosophy as though it were simply another science or scholarly field, one that just happens to have a subject matter other than, say, physical phenomena or English literature.

WHAT IS THE MEANING OF LIFE?   261

To do *that* is to be oblivious to a two-thousand-year-long track record: how can it be reasonable to proceed in this way, in a field in which *there are no results?*[3] Such obliviousness exemplifies the lack of self-awareness that makes the treatment of an apparently philosophical issue unphilosophical to its very bones.

And third and finally for now, philosophy—at any rate, this is a way of seeing it that I cannot help returning to—is anchored by a certain hard-to-delineate but vividly recognizable class of questions about life—one's *own* life. The question, thus Plato's Socrates, was: How is one to live? (On another occasion, Socrates described philosophy as preparation for death.) Not that long back, Albert Camus announced that our first order of business was the question: Why not commit suicide?[4] And nonprofessionals even today expect the meaning of life to be one of philosophy's central concerns; that the topic inadequately gestured at by that phrase largely appears only in the peripheral vision of the field ought to strike us as a collective failure on our part.

When a given value turns up, looking one way in one perspective, and another way in another, we'll usually be in the market for an account of how it did. So I'll touch on the topic below, but although I acknowledge that such an account is called for by the dramatically different renderings of philosophy I have just given, that's not what I'll be doing with it; we can leave that task for a further occasion. Right now, notice that on each of these conceptions of what philosophy is about and for, Nietzsche comes off remarkably well.

11.2

Nietzsche didn't advertise himself as a philosopher of logic, but we're belatedly equipped to recognize the engine of his perspectivism as a bounded-rationality reconception of logic and metaphysics. It followed, and this was a step we haven't assimilated even today, that our philosophical focus, in the cluster of concerns that in our analytic tradition was taken over by philosophy of language, should not be *accurate* representation—truth and how to understand it—but inevitable and strategic *mis*representation. (To remind you one more time: that isn't at all the lazy and sloppy disregard for truth that's come to pervade so many regions of the humanities; crafting falsehoods—approximations, idealizations, and even caricatures—that you can put to successful intellectual work is demanding, and perhaps

262   WHY DIDN'T NIETZSCHE GET HIS ACT TOGETHER?

paradoxically, requires the virtue of truthfulness ratcheted up to greater levels than does truth itself.) Where philosophers had sought to account for apriori and necessary truths, Nietzsche concluded that we had better be looking for a very different sort of explanation of what are actually the falsehoods we have to deploy, regardless. And if these strategic misrepresentations are accounted for by the limited cognitive and emotional resources of their users, which vary from person to person, we shouldn't assume that one and the same conceptual and metaphysical scheme will be shared by everyone.

Practical reasoning is deliberation directed toward choice and action, and so also falls within the scope of a philosopher of logic. And here, too, Nietzsche's innovations are muscular and important. The reconception of values as *to be invented* amounts to a reset for—as he perhaps too loudly insisted—ethical and moral thinking from top to bottom. If the values aren't facts, out there and the same for everyone, we can consider how different values would serve the needs of different clients; we can allow them to be temporary, and for a value to be superseded rather than refuted. And because bounded-rationality constructs are driven by prioritizing what is more important over what is less so, the different values can underwrite the choice of a metaphysics, along with the patterns of thought that deploy it; thus the reconception of value figures into the explanations that Nietzsche's philosophy of logic tells us to give for inferences.

Turning to the mode of self-awareness that is central to philosophy in the second of those perspectives on it, recall that we've been seeing Nietzsche displaying one after another configuration of his own personality, and throughout, we've seen him elaborately flagging for our attention the ways in which he's inconsistent, impulsive, and unable to control one or another unattractive drive . . . along with much more of the same. As we've seen over the last two chapters, having constructed a redemptive interpretation of his own life, he came to have unsettling second thoughts about it, seeing it as perhaps only an illusion projected by a collapsing personality. This is a philosopher who was fully attentive to what he was doing, and who didn't take its presuppositions—and especially not presuppositions about its merits—for granted.

And third and finally, this is a philosopher whose philosophical enterprise was in the service of his own life. Managing his disintegrating personality turned out to be the task of addressing the question of what his life was about, which turned out to require him to have thought-through views regarding what life, anyone's life, *could* be about—what that might amount to.

WHAT IS THE MEANING OF LIFE? 263

And that, in turn, required him to work up a response to most of the traditionally central questions of philosophy, for instance, those having to do with selfhood, and free will, and morality, and aesthetics, and epistemology and, as we reminded ourselves moments ago, logic and metaphysics. His remarkably inventive ideas on these topics coalesced into one after another gleaming vision that, like Goethe's "Eternal-Feminine," drew him ever onward. We've just been seeing how what would have formerly been described as a philosophical system, if it had but been more systematic, was marshaled to reconcile Nietzsche to the devastating collapse of his health, sanity, career, and personal relations, by allowing him to apprehend it as a tragedy.

In an unexpectedly Nietzschean moment, William James once remarked that truth "has to be measured by a multitude of standards," the "maximal combination" of which "is a many-dimensional term." Some of those standards, "for aught we know, may fail in any given case," and if they give conflicting answers, and if the standards prove to be, in the particular case, incommensurable with one another, it's not clear at all how to resolve them into a unified judgment.[5] We're lucky to be able to sidestep the Jamesian dilemma (or rather, polylemma); conveniently, all three of the evaluations I have just put on the table point in the same direction. I do need to reiterate that these are my own conceptions of philosophy and what I find to be central to it; your mileage may differ. But taking these conceptions as my frame, Nietzsche is an impressive figure, a deep and powerful philosopher, and someone that you have to take completely seriously, even when you're not about to sign onto one or another view or program. You owe it to yourself, as a philosopher, to think his ideas through, and more often than not, my own experience has it, doing so will change your mind about something you had thought was a settled matter.

11.3

Proceeding a bit further with that third way of seeing philosophy, how far should we be willing to adopt Nietzsche's attempts on the problem of the meaning of life?

Just for a moment, let's compare and contrast Nietzsche with another deservedly famous philosopher, John Stuart Mill. Mill mobilized his very highly organized, decision-driven personality around the utilitarian

264 WHY DIDN'T NIETZSCHE GET HIS ACT TOGETHER?

enterprise, which was at that time a many-sided radical political program aimed at making the world a better place for everyone. That is to say, his life made a very large, important project into its meaning, and so made him into a larger-than-life illustration of what is probably today's most popular view about what it takes to have a meaningful life.[6]

However that way of construing what it is for your life to have a meaning plays out, and whatever it has to be said for and against it, Mill *did* one thing after another to advance the utilitarian project. This is an approach to making your life meaningful that presupposes that you're an effective actor, in control of the steps you take, and reasonably confident that they're for the most part well chosen. As we've been seeing at length, this isn't a conception of the meaning of one's life that's suitable for everyone; Nietzsche was not nearly self-governed enough to have made it work, and someone in his predicament will be brought around to looking for very different spins to put on it.

We've encountered in passing other roles that taking on a meaning for one's life can play. In the reading of the Eternal Return which Alexander Nehamas and Lanier Anderson have done the most to refine, the objective is to interpret one's life so as assure oneself that in retrospect one wouldn't change anything about it at all.

This way of working up a meaning for your life is demanding in a different way than Mill's project-oriented version of meaningfulness. On the one hand, you don't have to get nearly as much done, and done to the specifications imposed by the project; rather, the emphasis is on finding an interpretation that covers what's already there. (To be sure, you produce the interpretation while you're still living, so there's an issue about getting the *rest* of your life to conform to what you say it's about.[7]) On the other hand, your interpretation is required to be responsible to what has actually happened; you're not allowed to make up stories in the manner of Terry Gilliam's *Adventures of Baron Munchausen* (1988). And the interpretation is supposed to lock down *everything* that has had a place in your life. So coming up with this sort of meaning for your life is likely to require remarkable doses of ingenuity.

Discussing a sonnet of Mallarmé's, Joshua Landy explains how the scattered contents of a room have been arranged into a poem that is so tightly composed that moving even a word, or any of the items in the room it describes, unravels the poem as a whole.[8] This makes the poem out to be a *tour de force*; Mallarmé was able to write a poem like that, but I certainly couldn't, and similarly, not just anyone can come up with the poem of their

WHAT IS THE MEANING OF LIFE? 265

life, where they can't move a single word or a single object, without throwing the whole thing out—which they won't do, because the composition is simply so *beautiful*.

We did see Nietzsche display that level of ingenuity in the interpretation he conjured up for his own life, which also, however, shows us that ingenuity is not enough: such an interpretation has to be *sustained*. We saw that when his personality reconfigured itself, as it did time and again, there was a slide from one interpretation to the next. We remarked that not everyone is in a position to muster up their life into a unified course of action—a project, in the apparently most straightforward version—and likewise, not everyone is equipped to have their life unified by a coherent and all-embracing self-interpretation.[9]

While these conceptions of what a meaning for a life comes to differ as to their purpose—in the former case, that was guiding ongoing action, and in the latter, it was reconciling you to a past that it's too late to change—each is extremely demanding, albeit in very different ways. But we've also seen a version of meaningfulness that required neither the level of executive control nor the interpretive ingenuity of those initial options. In *The Gay Science*, we encountered a recommendation for constructing an artistically rendered version of one's life, and because the model was Stendhal's crystallization— as you'll recall, the process by which lovers generate idealized fantasies of the objects of their romantic interest—the interpretation of one's life wasn't meant to be particularly responsible to what actually happened in it. And like daydreaming, although crystallization may induce action, the point wouldn't in the first place be to accomplish anything.

This mode of meaningfulness was, however, demanding in a different manner: if you're doing things this way, and you're at all self-aware about it, you have to be able not to care about whether your representation of yourself, and of the other parts of the world in which you've become emotionally invested, is accurate or fair. You arrive at that frame of mind when cynical realism bottoms out. A realist is revolted by the senseless awfulness of the way things turn out to work behind the scenes, once he takes the trouble to look; but he's also fascinated by what goes on behind the scenes, which is why he *does* look: realism is a self-destructive obsession. Eventually, realism turns on itself, driving the realist to the attitude that what goes on behind the scenes doesn't matter, after all: "Thinking of oneself yields little happiness: if one does experience a great deal of happiness in the process it is because basically one is not thinking of oneself but of one's ideal" (8:36/WEN 3[75]).

Once you're metacynical, you can entertain yourself with the set design and the costumes, and occupy yourself with staging your life. The invented "purpose of existence"—the meaning of life—is there to distract you from a horrific world by mounting a rose-tinted, radiant illusion.

We saw how a meaning for one's life can be put to work to bind together the parts of a not-yet-unified personality.[10] Values can catalyze the synthesis of drives with disparate orientations into a progressively more unified self. And then there were those personalities whose disparate psychic parts aren't integrated, and aren't going to be. At a late stage of his collapse, Nietzsche was brought face to face with being too far gone for anything to meld the fragments of his personality into a coherent person—much less into a hyperunified agent on the model of John Stuart Mill. So he invented a meaning to serve him as a sort of prosthesis: by repeatedly provoking the relatively independent parts of his personality to scrawl out one after another furious rant, or elated prophesy, or acerbic Rochefoucauldism, he kept himself producing one after another contribution to the collected works of their oh-so-discombobulated author.

And last for the moment, the meaning of your life can be that it's a tragedy—understood as *The Birth of Tragedy* explains it, an overlay of Apollinian illusion on Dionysian chaos—provided that you respond as Nietzsche anticipated, by becoming reconciled to the world and your life as they are.

What emerges even from this very short list is that the various senses we can give to a meaning for a life suit very different kinds of person. The sort of meaning that Mill oriented his life around is *for* someone who can control his own life, who takes decisions and gets things done. The program that Nehamas and Anderson find in Nietzsche is *for* someone who has had a very difficult time of it, needs to make himself alright with all of that retroactively, and let's emphasize that "needs to": we're talking about someone who can't just let the past go.[11] Not everyone *has* to make themselves okay with whatever it was that went down, and not everyone has to make themselves okay with *all* of it.

If we're reading Nietzsche correctly, making your life meaningful through Stendhalian crystallization is also for a very narrowly defined clientele, namely, people who are so preoccupied by cynicism that the best they can hope for is that their cynicism exhausts itself. When his Convalescent announces that he's recovering from his nihilism, he sounds like a character in one of Noël Coward's short stories (1985); supposedly recuperating from his surgery, he can't do much but lie back in the hospital bed, stare out at the snow on the mountains, and let his life drift before his eyes.

The next couple of versions of the meaning of life that we've just paged through were forms of personality management. When a meaning for your life merges your drives or other psychic components into larger, more stable personality structures, the job that it's doing is reshaping your personality. And when, as in Nietzsche's own case, no meaning you make up can repair the collapsing structure, then its job might be to keep it usable for the next while, by keeping the different pretty-much-independent psychological parts sufficiently on track to get what the person as a whole is doing . . . done. Here the meaning of life serves as a fix or a band-aid for a structural problem in someone's personality. Fixes like these are only *for* someone who has that sort of problem.

And then there was coming to see the catastrophic and ongoing collapse of your life as somehow inducing the brilliant illusion of there having *been* something that *was* a life, and a spectacularly successful one at that. Surely the meaning of life as tragedy—*this* type of tragedy—is only *for* someone whose life *has* collapsed, and catastrophically.

Evidently, when you find yourself inclined to ask what the meaning of your life is, you'd better first stop and ask yourself what you want it for; choose it thoughtfully; maybe it won't be one of the options we've seen him try out. Nietzsche was enormously inventive, but if you're lucky enough not to be coming apart at the seams, you might decide that you have no use for what he made of it.

A quick digression: If I'm recommending a cognitive function approach to understanding the meaning of life, but also identifying a number of different roles such a thing can play, don't I owe an account of what they have in common, to justify labeling them with the same phrase? Here isn't the place to lay out what I think, so this will just be a teaser. Maybe you have a sense of what your current agenda is, and of what you think is important, and of what sorts of things you want and would like; but consider where those resources, construed as a basis for practical inference, run out and leave you high and dry. (For instance, the ways you're liable to get confused when there are far too many directions you could reasonably be going in, given what you think matters and what you want.) And then ask how it would help to have a view as to what your life is *about*—what its subject matter is, so to speak.

But closing that parenthesis, you can be enormously impressed with what Nietzsche came up with when he took up the very personal problem of the meaning of life, without thinking that his attempts on it will suit you. The cognitive function that a meaning for your life can play depends on how your mental life is organized; Mill and Nietzsche seem to be out toward opposite extremes of how much in the way of organization a personality can exhibit. Most of us are much closer to the middle of the spectrum, and what those extremes demand and make feasible won't necessarily make sense closer in to the center.

11.4

Recall that Nietzsche announced the justification of existence—existence generally, and one's own existence—to reside in its uptake as an aesthetic phenomenon. Putting to one side the logical question—*how* can an aesthetic response constitute a justification?—let's take up the invitation to treat the aesthetics of Nietzsche's life and work as shouldering that role.

If we've been right in thinking he gave himself, and us, the wherewithal to see his life as a tragedy, we need first to notice a twist: perhaps tragedy reconciles one to life, but the one who is reconciled is normally the audience, not the tragic hero. Perhaps here it matters that in Nietzsche's reconstruction of Attic tragedy, the audience was supposed to identify with the chorus, who were construed as the voice of the Dionysian take on things. As Nietzsche came to see himself as more and more completely a disunified self, he would have felt himself to mingle with and take the point of view of the Dionysian world, in somewhat the manner of the ancient chorus.

But in any case, he himself was the intended target of this aesthetic justification: if we are right about it so far, seeing the Dionysian tumult of his own decadence behind the very neat narrative of his life infused it with emotion, in a way that rendered it fraught with significance, and an allegory of redemption. Now if I'm moved, when I contemplate the course of Nietzsche's life as a whole, but fail to conjure up the response he meant for himself, that doesn't impugn the success of the exercise: it's not as though it was staged for me.

Rather, and proceeding further with the very personal reaction that his life evidently calls for, I can come out with my own. How does Nietzsche's life strike me as an aesthetic phenomenon, from where *I* stand? And does it seem to me to surmount what is apparently deeply regrettable in a great many parts of that life?

WHAT IS THE MEANING OF LIFE? 269

Not that long ago, aesthetic assessments were confined to judgments of beauty and ugliness; at some point, the sublime entered the vocabulary; now we've become used to thinking in terms of a much wider range of effects, as for example when a Jeff Wall is praised for inducing a sense of the uncanny. Nietzsche was ahead of his time in this respect; recall that the real aim of the Alexandrian project was to make the universe seem knowable—where that was an aesthetic category. A few moments back, I suggested that meaningfulness was the impression Nietzsche aimed to have his own life bear, when he gazed on it himself. So with the breadth of those descriptors in mind, my own dominating aesthetic response to Nietzsche—jointly to the man and his body of work—is *inexhaustibility*, and let me explain what I have in mind by that.

Philosophy is a practice anchored by a canon of historical texts that share a remarkable feature. When a graduate student sits down in my office, and announces that she would like to write her dissertation on, say, Aristotle, or Plato, I don't try to close the project down, on the grounds that over the last two millennia (and some), generations of scholars have mined out that figure's writings; on the contrary, if the student is bright and hardworking, I can reasonably expect her to find something new and interesting to discuss in them. Philosophical work with this aspect is rare; it's not just strong philosophy. William Whewell's *Philosophy of the Inductive Sciences* (1847) is very strong philosophy, indeed a *tour de force*, and one that any philosopher would benefit from reading—once. Aristotle's work will bear repeated rereading, over the course of decades.[12]

It's too early to tell whether Nietzsche really is inexhaustible, in the way that the ancient philosophers I've just mentioned turned out to be, or Hume and Kant, after two or three centuries, seem like they will be. But he presents the *appearance* of inexhaustibility—that is, the *aesthetic* property. As you explore the body of writing he left us, around every corner, there's another Easter egg: always another big idea or deep move, which induces a shift in *how* you have to approach a problem or subject matter, and, not coincidentally, proves to be differently shaped than your first impression of it; always another neat point made in passing; always another bit of positioning that requires you to rethink what you had made of an argument; always another—as Williams memorably put it—booby trap.

Nietzsche invokes Stendhal's characterization of beauty, as the promise of happiness. The aesthetic impression of philosophical inexhaustibility, which Nietzsche manages so well, is the promise of actual inexhaustibility. If there

270   WHY DIDN'T NIETZSCHE GET HIS ACT TOGETHER?

is an aesthetic phenomenon that justifies Nietzsche's existence, not to him but to me, and perhaps to other philosophers as well, wouldn't it be that?

11.5

Having accepted as best I could the invitation to assess Nietzsche, I want to conclude by thinking about how to put him to *use*. We acceded to his insistence that we look back, from a position to the person who has it, but I think there is a different way of doing that, where we aren't simply taking someone as an object of evaluation. Some lives (not all of them) can be construed as arguments, and those arguments-by-biography are a philosophical resource: if a person instantiates a theoretical position, you can see what the position comes to by examining how it plays out within his life. In Plato's *Timeaus*, a divine craftsman sets out to fabricate a world on the model of the Platonic Form of a world, and what he ends up able to make, Plato shows you, is qualitatively different—indeed, inevitably wildly askew— from its model. Rather in this manner, even if someone doesn't manage to live up to a theory, but is doing not just his but anyone's very best to do so, the life may show you that what you had supposed the theory tells you to imagine isn't what the theory can come to in the real world. You may even discover that there could be nothing that counted as what the theory seemed to describe, and that you thought you had imagined. And so, by way of experimentation along these lines, I'm going to sketch a way of drawing a conclusion—one that Nietzsche no doubt would have resisted—from the life we examined.

We haven't yet quoted Nietzsche's dramatic introduction of the Eternal Return, and let's remedy that now:

> *The greatest weight.* —What, if some day or night a demon were to steal after you into your loneliest loneliness and say to you: "This life as you now live it and have lived it, you will have to live once more and innumerable times more; and there will be nothing new in it, but every pain and every joy and every thought and sigh and everything unutterably small or great in your life will have to return to you, all in the same succession and sequence... Would you not throw yourself down and gnash your teeth and curse the demon who spoke thus? Or have you once experienced a tremendous moment when you would have answered him: "You are a god and never

WHAT IS THE MEANING OF LIFE? 271

have I heard anything more divine." If this thought gained possession of you, it would change you as you are or perhaps crush you. The question in each and every thing, "Do you desire this once more and innumerable times more?" would lie upon your actions as the greatest weight. Or how well disposed would you have to become to yourself and to life *to crave nothing more fervently* than this ultimate eternal confirmation and seal?

(3:570/GS 341)

In part because there's been so much academic discussion of it, and consequently so many renderings, each controverted by the others, I have until this point pushed the Eternal Return out to the margins of our discussion. But we can direct our attention to the common denominator of the vast majority of those interpretations: that the question of whether you would receive with enthusiasm the news that you're going to relive your life, over and over again, exactly as it was, is a way of introducing a criterion of success for a life. That is, the underlying thought is that for your life to have gone well, you have to be able to affirm or endorse it, *all* of it, and all at once.

That way of putting it might make it sound like the sort of naive Romantic exuberance that grownups and twenty-first-century sophisticates know better than to lose themselves in, but the thought, expressed in a markedly lower-key manner, is a staple both of contemporary analytic moral philosophy and ordinary conversation. Who could disagree with meaning to avoid occasions for regret? And so wouldn't the ideal life be one about which you had no regrets at all?[13]

But now, let's consider what's involved in meeting this demand. In thinking it through, we'll want to use as much of Nietzsche's conceptual equipment as we can, and so let's deploy his many-sided conception of a value. One of the various functions a value serves is assessment, and to assess is to discriminate, between what lives up to the standard it imposes, and what doesn't. A putative value that in entirely indiscriminate fashion endorsed and affirmed anything that came its way would amount to the evaluative analog of a tautology: it would fail to have any content at all.

Taking our next step, everyone faces the same task, that of finding their way in life. And the hand that life deals you isn't up to you: you encounter one after another of a series of what you might as well see as found objects. You don't get to choose who your parents are, or who your children turn out to be; you don't get to decide what culture you'll grow up in, what opportunities the economy and your location in it will present you, or

272 WHY DIDN'T NIETZSCHE GET HIS ACT TOGETHER?

what sudden disasters—from mass shootings to wars, from drunken drivers to pandemics—will rocket over the horizon. And you also don't get to choose what you'll meet those external challenges with: who you are—your temperament, your abilities, how savvy or streetwise you turn out to be— is also part of the hand you are dealt. A value that you knew ahead of time would endorse everything that was going to appear in this stream of found objects would be a value that would endorse and affirm *anything*. But a putative value that *would* endorse just anything, we noticed, wouldn't be a value, after all. So you can't have a value, available ahead of time, that will let you unequivocally affirm all of your life.

Plausibly, if your objective is to give an enthusiastic thumbs up to every-thing in your life, you will have to effect that affirmation piecemeal. As one after another element of your life becomes visible, and as the issues they raise go live, you'll have to look for, and adopt, a mode of assessment that allows an affirmative response to the way they play out. For instance, come the pandemic, if you're the sort of person who can follow the public health guidance, and sit tight at home, you then take on, say, prudence and the importance of deferred gratification as your new—or perhaps, reaffirmed— value. But if you're uncontrollably restless, and find yourself unable not to board airplanes to exotic destinations, you make living dangerously, and living life in the moment to the fullest, into your guiding light. Your assent to how things have gone will take on the appearance of a patchwork quilt.

Perhaps most people are conventional enough for the menu of prepared values their culture provides them to cover all of the circumstances they happen to encounter. But someone's circumstances might prove unusual enough, and his internal constraints might be nonstandard enough, for bespoke values to be the only way to manage full coverage. This seems to have been Nietzsche's predicament; not only were his native gifts and the training that prepared him for that precocious classics professorship out of the ordinary, and not only did his intellectual and (let's just say) moral taste make the values he found on offer unpalatable to him, he found himself needing to cope with rapidly morphing forms of psychic and physical disintegration. And so he generated one remarkably original value after another: we noticed, among others, an over-the-top embrace of Stendhalian crystallization, a furious rejection of decadence in favor of will to power, and a mode of disparaging Christianity patterned after the political antisemitism of his day.

But there's a problem with that approach, one for which Nietzsche's own conceptual toolkit once more supplies a convenient shorthand. Values not

WHAT IS THE MEANING OF LIFE? 273

only induce perspectives, they require the appropriate perspective in order to be effectively applied. And we accordingly saw Nietzsche moving from one perspective to the next, as he wrote his way through one book after another; it appears to be not simply happenstance that the philosopher of the Eternal Return exhibited this sort of fluid personality, which evidently has the status of an implementation requirement. (Having already seen what Nietzsche's mode of disunified agency looked like, you may be wondering whether, in that case, the price you pay for the Eternal Return is too high. So don't let yourself get distracted; this isn't the line of argumentation we're pursuing.)

However, the perspective, with its embedded value (or values), from which you can appreciate and affirm one aspect of your life will generally be blind to other aspects—or they may seem out of focus, or even perverse. We have a suitably straightforward illustration on hand in my earlier review of the different takes I've come to have on philosophy. Not only is it unobvious how they fit together; it's not even clear that they are so much as compatible with one another. Just to remind you, on one way of looking at it, philosophy is the machine-tool industry of the mind; on another, it responds to the command of the Delphic oracle, *Know thyself!* And on the third, it's anchored by such questions as: What is the meaning of life? But if philosophy first and foremost is the art—that is, the craft—of developing and debugging new methods of reasoning, why should the craftsman need to be self-aware? Why should his logic have anything to do with what would popularly be called his existential crises? It shouldn't be at all obvious that worries about the meaning of life are to be assuaged by designing better logical tools, and moreover, self-awareness isn't obviously always a good thing, when it comes to fielding urgent concerns of this sort; as Bernard Williams once remarked, "the question of life being desirable . . . gets by far its best answer in never being asked at all."[14]

The illustration suggests that although the piecemeal approach to the Eternal Return perhaps allows you to affirm each element in your life, as it comes into view, there's nowhere—no perspective, that is—from which you can affirm your whole life, all at once. Nietzsche seems to run those differently ordered quantifiers together in the passage we quoted a moment back. But even if, for every element of your life, there is a value and a perspective from which to affirm it, it does not follow that there is a value and a perspective from which you can endorse everything in your life. And that was the demand expressed in the Eternal Return.

The escape hatch is evidently the move to a metaperspective, where what you affirm and endorse is in the first place that ability to switch from perspective to perspective, and from operative value to operative value, so as to be able to affirm each of the elements in your life, every one in its turn. And we saw Nietzsche make this move, which at this point seems nonoptional: the value of inventing values—caricatured in the Overman, but not-at-all-disingenuously promoted elsewhere—shaped the metaperspective from which all those transitions from perspective to perspective, and value to value, could be enthusiastically affirmed. Although the matter was far too fraught for him to have thought of it this way, when more relaxed agents step into this sort of metaperspective, it will often be characterized and valued as *playfulness*.[15]

At second glance, however, the demand whose satisfaction we're considering looks to have a unity requirement built into it that the very form of agency it forces us to assume doesn't allow us to meet. The hard-to-avoid problem is not that internalizing the standards in the metavalue—again, in Nietzsche's case, the value of inventing values—undercuts the various lower-order and so to speak more substantial values.[16] Rather, it's that, as we remember Nietzsche putting it, "it is only as an *aesthetic phenomenon* that existence and the world are eternally *justified*"—and whether or not that's correct across the board, it goes for the Eternal Return, as Nietzsche is asking us to sign onto it.

That you say "*Yes!*" to an element of your life, or to your life as a whole, and see it as something not to be given up—that affirmation is a response, in Nietzsche's vision of it, that is logically of the same type as apprehending something as beautiful, or as sublime, or as having the appearance of knowability, or inexhaustibility.[17] There are various turns to be given to that realization, and the one relevant just now is that you have to be present and accounted for during your affirmation. I mean, when it's a matter of building up your theory of the world around you, or even a matter of making decisions, of course you should delegate much of your fact-finding, or collecting the inputs to your choices, or even the choices themselves to others—to your agents, in the ordinary rather than the philosophers' sense of the word.[18] However, when it comes to appreciating a gorgeous Botticelli, say, you don't delegate the task to anyone else, no matter how much of an expert they are, and no matter how similar you think their tastes are to yours. "Go to the concert for me, and let me know how it was" is not a substitute for listening to the music yourself, and someone who acts as though it were is mistaking aesthetic response for transmissible information.[19] The affirmation Nietzsche is

WHAT IS THE MEANING OF LIFE? 275

asking us for is like that: because you're supposed to be *appreciating* your life and its contents, you can't pass the task of affirming it off to anyone else; you have to in be attendance for the affirming yourself.[20]

Just as it cannot be handed off to others, that sort of appreciation cannot be delegated to earlier or later iterations of yourself. To agree that you were probably right, when your earlier self responded to the performance with a feeling you cannot now recapture or even make sense of, is not to now be appreciating—even retrospectively—the play. The affirmation Nietzsche is asking us for has to be produced on the spot, in one's apprehension of what one is affirming, or not at all.

That entails that you can only affirm what is apprehended within a perspective you are currently occupying. So you can't affirm everything in your life, all at once, by delegating the affirmation of large parts of it to previous selves with differently configured personalities, that is, to responses from perspectives that you formerly occupied.[21] We acknowledged that many different components or elements of a life make sense from differing perspectives, and reminding ourselves that we can see perspectives as expedients serving boundedly rational agents, since perspectives compete for limited cognitive resources, they will normally exclude one another. It follows that there's no perspective from which you can appreciate and so affirm everything in your life, and so that you can't affirm all of your life in the manner demanded by the Eternal Return.

Ascent to a metaperspective, it becomes evident, isn't an escape hatch after all. We can see how this plays out in Nietzsche's own retrospective survey of his literary career in *Ecce Homo*. Looking back on his earlier books, the metaperspective of his autobiography allows him to appreciate directly only the revaluings of values that the central value of the metaperspective highlights. The effects and substantive contents of the values he invented— the way those values see the world—go missing. Just for instance, a single page discussing *The Gay Science* is devoted to the verse that bookends the volume, and seems to have nothing to say about the body of the work itself; he quotes some of those rhymes so as to imply that he was, at the time he wrote it, feeling "ever healthier and brighter" (6:333f/EH III.GS)—which we saw to be a claim that ought to bring us up short. Or again, a close reading of *Zarathustra* will find it advancing one evaluative innovation after another; while his somewhat longer reminiscence of the work in *Ecce Homo* starts off with the Eternal Return, and does eventually circle back to it, almost all of it is enthusing about how he was "building mountain ranges" and "draw[ing] circles and sacred boundaries"—the actual evaluative content of *Zarathustra* goes almost entirely missing.[22]

I'm uncertain whether that lack of sympathetic projection into his former perspectives was intentional or an inadvertent but telling side effect; in either case we should add a warning for Nietzsche's readers and interpreters. The temptation to treat his late-on pronouncements about his own writings as somehow authoritative is to be resisted. What they display is rather the unavailability, from the inside, of various perspectives that he had occupied, to that tail-end metaperspective. It may have seemed to Nietzsche, as various moments in his writing suggest, that he had affirmed all of his life, all at once, but only because he was missing what, in those moments, he was unable to see. In other connections, Nietzsche emphasized the importance of forgetting, and how it allows you to seem coherent to yourself (how, adapting a Kantian concept, memory loss supplies the illusion of transcendental unity of apperception). We can now see how large it figures as well in allowing you to think that you'd do it all over again, and wouldn't change a thing.

I suggested that the story that Nietzsche told himself, about why it was he could will the Eternal Return, must not have looked right to him (and I speculated that it would have seemed too *pat*—again, a specifically aesthetic criticism). We can now see why the too-neat account was not believable, and notice that the emotional posture to which Nietzsche fell back, that of tragic reconciliation, is not by any means the wholehearted *there's-nothing-I-would-change* of the Eternal Return. If Nietzsche's demon were to steal into the last act of *Hamlet*, and ask the dying protagonist if he would like to have done anything differently, the only reasonable answer would be *Of course!* If Nietzsche's demon were to offer Oedipus a do-over, is there any question but that he'd take it?

Nietzsche was, it seems, living out an argument, one that amounted to a *reductio* of one his most famous evaluative innovations, and since the point was to illustrate how arguments-by-biography can go, that should be our own landing and disembarkation point. It's remarkable that when you look at his life, what stands out starkly is that what he most wanted, or at any rate thought he wanted, is convincingly unattainable—and that's the sort of thing that lives are useful for, philosophically. Let's just very tersely register the sorts of questions the *reductio* invites us to take on.

Early in the history of Western moral philosophy, Aristotle began his course of lectures on ethics by soliciting his audience's agreement that we

WHAT IS THE MEANING OF LIFE? 277

all want a well-lived life; the real question on the table accordingly was what that would be. But we've just run up against an implicit argument against a success criterion for a life as a whole. Surely a global success criterion would have to draw on—and so depend on—more partial assessments, of different elements or components or aspects of a life. Although that dependence need not be particularly mechanical, it would be unreasonable for the global assessment to pull free of the local ones. But then in that case, the comprehensive assessment requires the partial assessments to be jointly available. And if there are ways of relaxing the aesthetic immediacy requirement we invoked one lap back, into requirements of the coaffirmability of one's standards of assessment, they're not: the lesson of Nietzsche's life is very plausibly that there is no single vantage point from which it's reasonable to assess everything in a life, and so, the life as a whole.[23]

Why did we want to assess our lives as wholes? There was a practical promise, that having an overall take on how you're doing will make your decision-making more tractable. And then there's an idea we've encountered repeatedly, that the thought that things have gone well overall, on balance, *altogether*, is comforting, and allows you to accept the difficult, apparently bad, and even straight-out awful parts of your life. For my own part, I'm not convinced that these are compelling reasons, and here I'll focus just on that need for comfort.[24]

Why *do* you have to accept and affirm the tedious or disheartening or awful sides of your life—allowing that you have to put up with them? Why not rather acknowledge that there's the bad, but also the good, and not try to convince yourself that, somehow, the bad is, really, good? When you do try, you end up giving a great deal of attention to the bad, whether in the currently popular mode of making a past trauma or present impairment into the center of your self-conception, or in Nietzsche's manner, of seeing his life as a tragedy, or in the reading we saw Anderson give to Nietzsche, in which you retroactively reinterpret and "transfigure" those ugly and difficult experiences. Why isn't it better to turn your attention away from the bad bits and aspects, to the better parts? I'm not myself all that sure that regrets are always a bad thing, and that a life that contains them is thereby regrettable. And I agree with Nietzsche that much of life is the small stuff. Hasn't something gone wrong when I'm trying to make out all that small stuff— from the morning grooming ritual, to taking out the trash at night—into something wonderful? If Nietzsche's demon came around and told you that you could do it all over again, except that next time you wouldn't have to

278 WHY DIDN'T NIETZSCHE GET HIS ACT TOGETHER?

take out the garbage—well, who would say no to *that*? Once we allow that affirming every element of a life doesn't entail the ability to affirm all of it, we should have second thoughts about that insistence on affirming each and every element of it, in the first place.

And now we can turn back to the question that has repeatedly come up over the course of our discussion of Nietzsche: What is the meaning of life?

If we've surrendered the aspiration for a criterion of success for a life, we'll see that turning out to be a trick question: there should not generally be anything that counts as *the* meaning of a life. Think of the way one reads a richly complex work of literature: one attends to one theme or aspect after another, and one doesn't—or rather, one shouldn't—insist on there being a unified, comprehensive, all-inclusive meaning that it conveys, one that somehow synthesizes all those different threads.[25] The work will offer many meanings, but no one overall meaning, rather as the different perspectives that Nietzsche occupied on his own life generated one after another meaning of that life, each different from the others, and not in any way coalescing into what would be *the* meaning of his life. And although Nietzsche's life and personality strike most of us as unusual in their levels of fragmentation, in this respect, the lesson we're able to draw from it about the meaning of life is a lesson for us all.

Notes

Notes to Chapter 1

1. Nietzsche was a fan of Ralph Waldo Emerson, and the latter line may be derived from his "Compensation": "In general, every evil to which we do not succumb, is a benefactor" (1971–2013, vol. II, p. 69).
2. You can find the image reproduced at Sluga, 1993, p. 187.
3. And as before, that was just starting in on a much longer list; see Aschheim, 1992, and Thomas, 1983, for more of the early twentieth-century uptake. Encapsulating that uptake, in Bely, 2009, p. 113, a Russian novel first published in 1916, but set in 1905, we find a character announcing that "at that time I was a desperate Nietzschean. We are all Nietzscheans: you, too, you know . . . are a Nietzschean; only you will never admit to it."
4. Under the heading of familiar, just for instance, the Nietzsche of Clark, 1991, advances what are recognizably the doctrines of middle-period Hilary Putnam (1981). Or again, Hales and Welshon, 2000, pp. 42–44, and ch. 3, purport to find in some of Nietzsche's apparently conflicting pronouncements about logic a hazy anticipation of our contemporary syntax/semantics distinction, and place his metaphysics in a family of views which we associate with, say, Bertrand Russell, on which objects are "bundles" of less tangible items. Or yet again, Katsafanas, 2013a, takes Nietzsche to be a constitutivist, that is, someone who thinks that there are features that are essential to being an agent, and that what you have reason to do can be read off those features; see Millgram, 2005b, sec. 3, for a summary.
5. Solomon and Higgins, 2000.
6. I earlier mentioned that there's a specifically Foucauldian understanding of Nietzsche's genealogies; I'll bring you up to speed on it in those interludes also.
7. See, e.g., Nehamas, 1985, Nehamas, 1988, and on the idea that the author of a text—its "postulated" author—is an interpretive artefact, and something entirely different from the human being who actually wrote it, see especially Nehamas, 1981, as well as Nehamas, 1987, and Nehamas, 1986.

   The nontriviality qualification is intended as follows. If a postulated author is shown to be a hodgepodge of inconsistent intentions, a fragmented personality, and so on, it is possible to protect the "regulative ideal" of "critical monism" by insisting the text coherently projects *that*. But I take it that only more demanding notions of coherence are worth our attention. And Nehamas's reading pursues the sort of integration of character exhibited by protagonists of the classic nineteenth-century novel.

280 NOTES

I'll eventually argue against the distinctness of the implicit author and the flesh-and-blood writer in Nietzsche's own case, but for reasons to balk at always making that distinction, see Millgram, 2002.

8. Why? I explain how I think it's a dead end in this problem space in Millgram, 2019, sec. 12.1.

9. Why the hedge? For complaints about this conception of desires, see Millgram, 1997, ch. 2, and for objections to giving this role to beliefs, Millgram, 2009a, ch. 6.

10. Millgram, 2019.

11. And why *can't* we appreciate art at second hand? Nguyen, 2017, gives a straightforward and plausible explanation.

12. "Any but a handful": there are a few philosophers who concern themselves with "philosophy as a way of life," e.g., Nussbaum, 1994, Nehamas, 1998, Hadot, 1995, Anderson and Cristy, 2017, or Anderson and Landy, 2001. Millgram, 2002, discusses that tradition and takes up a recent addition to it by Robert Nozick (1989).

Notes to Chapter 2

1. 5:258f, 260f/GM 1.2, 3; the view being criticized is evidently paraphrased from Rée, 2003, pp. 98, 120–123, 160–162. (Janaway, 2007, p. 25n15, provides a catalog of the points on which Nietzsche ended up differing with Rée.) However, Paul Rée was a German of Jewish extraction, and so I take it that Nietzsche is using him merely as a representative of British Empiricism; the repetition of "English psychologists" (by my count the Preface and first Essay contain five variants on it) is quite emphatic. The core of British Empiricism, in the nineteenth century, was associationism, and Nietzsche picks out "the *vis inertiae* of habit" and "a blind and chance mechanistic hooking-together of ideas" as preoccupations of "English psychologists" (5:257/GM 1.1); at 5:343/GM 3.4 he glosses the phrase "*psychologischer* contiguity" as "speaking with the English" (Kaufmann footnotes the use of the English word as an allusion to David Hume, but it was common property of the later Empiricists). Rée enthusiastically quotes Mill on "the primary law of association" (p. 101), and seems to be familiar with Hume and Bain as well (p. 104); he devotes much of *The Origin of the Moral Sensations* to explicitly associationist explanations of—in addition to the sense of "good" and "bad"—the retributive theory of punishment (p. 114), the feeling of justice (p. 145), and wanting to be admired (pp. 128, 130, 134f).

2. The problem is noticed by Bittner, 1994. You might wonder whether division of labor is a way out of the problem: the priests do the inventing for the slaves (so they know the afterlife is invented, but don't need to find the revenge satisfying), and the slaves consume the priests' invention (so they find the revenge satisfying, but never knew that it was a fantasy). Or you might suspect that unconscious or self-deceiving invention would do (Leiter, 2002, p. 203n14), or perhaps just suspension of disbelief. If this is a cluster of issues you want to pursue, let me point you to Millgram, 2007, p. 94n3, and p. 100n15.

3. This problem is noticed by Leiter, 2002, ch. 6, and others. For the masters' view of the slaves' dishonesty, see 5:263/GM 1.5. Nietzsche doesn't tell us outright that

NOTES   281

the masters take the priests to be untrustworthy, but he puts in place claims that entail that they should have: contemplative and thus unwarlike characters arouse the suspicions and mistrustfulness of a militarized society (5:359/GM 3.10). The nobility's accepting the deliverances of a priestly class requires explanation.

4. I'm grateful to David Dick for pointing this out to me. Still, could Nietzsche be relying on a retained bodily aversion to painful experiences—that is, on something less than memory? In that case, we'd need a Nietzschean account of memory that explains why the aversion doesn't count; that distinction seems to lean on a further distinction, between mind and body. Nietzsche doesn't take that latter distinction for granted.

"Soul," we're told elsewhere, "is only a word for something about the body," where the view is that what you think of as your mental life, with all of its first-person aspects, is projected by your body, as a way of mobilizing and directing your body itself—that is, *you* (4:39f/Z I.4). Memory is an aspect of your first-person mental life; but then, why presume that your body will duplicate its own device for learning and retaining the lessons of experience? (Indeed, that presumption looks to be a version of the fallacy of reduplication, which we'll discuss shortly.)

5. Nietzsche is not unique in adopting this tactic; as, for instance, Bayard, 2000, esp. ch. 3, points out, the murder mystery genre requires that the clues be available to the reader, which means that concealing the solution requires making the reader not notice, or forget, the clues, and Bayard provides a very suggestive list of techniques used to this effect.

6. 5:293, 295, 307, 319, 327/GM 2.2–3, 9, 14, 19; compare the longish quote from *Daybreak* at 5:359/GM 3.9: its subjects are "half-animals" (5:322, 324/GM 2.16f) and "man-beasts" (5:332/GM 2.22).

7. However, perhaps Nietzsche is also intentionally providing incoherent chronological cues, in which case we can't take his timelines at face value. For that suggestion, with supporting argument, see Gemes, 2006.

8. Williams, 2006b, p. 300; William James remarks on the tendency as well: living through the 1906 San Francisco earthquake, and understanding very well that "earthquake is simply the collective *name* of all the cracks and shakings and disturbances that happen," he nonetheless felt that "*the* earthquake was the *cause* of the disturbances" (1987a, pp. 1216f).

9. Kaufmann isn't consistent in his translation of this distinctly academic term, and in the note at the end of the first Essay, does render it as "treatise." That note titles itself an *Anmerkung*, and so is a further allusion to academic prose forms.

10. I'm grateful to Candace Vogler for bringing my attention back to this aspect of Nietzsche's writing. Janaway, 2007, pp. 51f, 96, 99–101, 105, 111–113, 209–211, 219, 250, 252, offers somewhat different explanations for it than the one I'm going to be developing. First, "the personal affects, and Nietzsche's deliberate rhetorical evocation of them," are a way of showing you how your concepts and values arose out of, and perhaps even today still have built into them, "gut allegiances, fears, admirations, and ambivalences." Second, Nietzsche is using your affective responses to convince you that you have within you not one morality, but an overlay of both aristocratic good/bad ethics and Christian morals: that you're morally ambivalent.

282 NOTES

And third, "our feeling shocked, embarrassed, disgusted, or attracted by some phenomenon *tells us something about* that phenomenon."

The idea that seems to be moving Janaway is that values can be investigated by prompting affective responses, and that line seems promising to me. However, in my view the approach needs to be less straightforward than in his treatment. Furthermore, because many—even most—of the prompts to affective response in the *Genealogy* are missing from that treatment, the patterns that tell us what Nietzsche is up to are also being missed.

We shouldn't imagine the relation between value and affect to be uncomplicated in the manner of old-fashioned emotivism, where you could just read the value off the affect, and vice-versa. (In the emotivists' illustrations, "lying is wrong" was equivalent to "lying [insert expression of disgust here].") Just to gesture at part of the problem, Nietzschean values have histories. On the one hand, conceptual coinage tends to get worn down over time—a point Nietzsche made in an early essay that will come in for discussion in the appendix to ch. 9. We should expect values to keep their conventionalized inferential shape even when a good part of their affective force has become etiolated. When values are old, they will have originated in affective responses that are very unlike our own; on this point see, just for instance, 3:389f/GS 18, 3:412/GS 47 or 3:495/GS 152. Moreover, as we'll see in the next chapter, the normal trajectory of a value involves its intensification, refinement, and self-overcoming. But in that case, we mustn't expect that we can understand our present values by provoking and recreating the affects out of which they arose.

Affects do plausibly play a role in knowledge; however, Janaway never supplies a convincing Nietzschean explanation of their "cognitive potency." On the assumption that affects are functionally integrated into values, and that perspectives fall into place around—are induced by—values, we will have preliminaries for the requisite account in ch. 9.

We'll start looking at places where Nietzsche is trying to get a rise out of his reader in a few moments; most of them don't fit into Janaway's account, but over and above that problem, and for the record, the emotional reactions he claims you're meant to experience aren't those I have myself.

11. Not that every *Streit* is necessarily academic: compare the *Karikaturenstreit* of a few years back—the brouhaha that erupted when cartoons depicting Mohammed were run in a Danish newspaper.

12. 5:247/GM P.1; at 5:398/GM 3.24 he reiterates the self-identification. Elsewhere in the third Essay he speaks of "us psychologists" (5:385, 387/GM 3.19, 20), which you might take to be giving us a tighter fix on the kind of "knower" he takes himself to be—but that's a topic to which I'll return in chs. 5–6.

13. There are at least two ways of using the resources of the Nietzsche corpus to answer this question, but because I want to allow this particular text to direct the interpretation right now, I'm going to stick to the one that can be made out using only what the *Genealogy* provides. If I'm right, they're in any case compatible.

The other reason, which raises issues we'll take up in later chapters, has to do with the way thinking (*any* thinking) requires what in science we regard as idealization and approximation, which involves, on Nietzsche's view, forgetting that things aren't as you represent them. Compare the announcement, at 5:400/GM 3.24, that "forcing, adjusting, abbreviating, omitting, padding, inventing, [and] falsifying... [are] of the *essence* of interpreting." To have a mind—to think—*is* to forget that things are not as you represent them. And consequently any mind at all will have forgetting as "an active and in the strictest sense positive faculty of repression... responsible for the fact that what we experience and absorb enters our consciousness as little while we are digesting it (one might call the process 'inpsychation') as does the thousandfold process, involved in physical nourishment—so-called 'incorporation'" (5:291/GM 2.1).

14. But see ch. 5, note 50, below.

15. 5:382/GM 3.18; we need to mark another undischarged and Cartesian metaphor here, of the mind as something like a room or a stage.

16. I'm grateful to Ken Gemes for this last point.

17. What's Nietzsche trying to distract us from at this juncture? A number of possibilities come to mind, one of which is the surfeit of explanations for freedom of the will. Later in the same section, Nietzsche informs us that free will was invented to make divine interest in human life plausible; earlier on, we were told that the free agent was invented to allow slaves to blame their "evil" masters (5:280f/GM 1.13).

18. Because the postwar reception of Nietzsche in the United States involved a great deal of defensiveness vis-à-vis his (actual or alleged) antisemitism, I'd better not postpone being explicit about just what I am suggesting at this point. I'm claiming that Nietzsche is self-consciously shifting into a markedly antisemitic register (something he does at much greater length elsewhere, as I'll show in ch. 7), and I'm suggesting that he is, also self-consciously, presenting his own psychology as containing (what he thinks of as) an antisemitic drive. However, by describing these as tactical choices, I'm also implying that it would an interpretative mistake to take up the topic of antisemitism in Nietzsche by launching into argument about whether he was or he wasn't. (Apropos, but under the heading of tensions built into the text, notice that Nietzsche subsequently goes out of his way to insult antisemites, at 5:309, 370, 407/GM 2.11, 3.14, and 3.26.) I'll address this question more directly, and reconstruct Nietzsche's principled take on it, in ch. 4.

Nietzsche's remarks about the Jews provide a further instance of a contradiction in the text from which the reader needs to be distracted. The actions of the Jews are described in the language of intentional action: e.g., they "dared to invert," they "were ultimately satisfied with nothing less...," they produced "this most fundamental of all declarations of war...". Only a few sections later, Nietzsche, we've seen, makes the methodological point that reifying a natural, psychological, or social process into an agent who lies behind the effect isn't just a metaphysical mistake, but to be explained as motivated self-deception (5:278–281/GM 1.13).

19. There are a handful of exceptions, of which perhaps the most interesting is Donald Davidson. His argument for using the Principle of Charity depends, in its developed form, on the view that theories of meaning have to have the form of Tarski-style truth theories, and that the evidence to which a theory of meaning must consequently be

284 NOTES

responsible consists in Tarski-style T-sentences. These have to be collected more or less from observation, and to do this, without already drawing on a theory of meaning, requires supposing the subjects of the theory to be more or less correct in their utterances. (See Davidson, 1984, and Millgram, 2009a, sec. 9.2, for a less compact rendering; for a different reconstruction of Davidson's reasons, see Sorensen, 2001, pp. 132f.) Two points matter for our purposes. The first is that this argument for Charity deploys a great deal of theoretical baggage, and you have to be a die-hard Davidsonian to find the argument persuasive. The second is that almost no one, I've found, is aware that Davidson *does* have an argument.

20. I'm grateful to Renée Baernstein for explaining the history to me.

21. The correction to the Principle of Charity can be broadened from texts constructed to exhibit contradictions to texts whose authors wouldn't have concerned themselves about them. Apropos the Bible, Walter Kaufmann remarks that

> Anyone who has ever written with any feeling for literary form must have felt a real regret at having to eliminate one of two inconsistent statements or passages, assuming that both were exceedingly well put and that each also said something worth saying. A modern philosopher will generally feel that he must do something to eliminate the inconsistency; a modern preacher or poet may not consider it necessary; and the assumption that the author of Genesis should have felt any such constraint is downright fantastic. (1972, p. 386)

22. The latter option wouldn't be philosophically unprecedented; Wittgenstein's *Tractatus* is a prominent example.

23. See, e.g., Solomon, 1994, pp. 96f, Solomon, 1996. The term "argument *ad hominem*" has more than one sense; the one I have in mind here involves conflating personal aspersions cast on one's opponent with a refutation of his view. The worry here isn't just that it would be uncharitable to ascribe a fallacy to Nietzsche, but that he himself insists that one ought to disregard the producer when assessing the work (at any rate when we're considering artists, but it's hard to see why the point wouldn't generalize: 5:343/GM 3.4). The analogous concern about genetic fallacies can be anchored in what's sometimes cast as Nietzsche's discussion of genealogical methodology at 5:313–318/GM 2.12–13, where he insists that "the cause of the origin of a thing and its eventual utility, its actual employment and place in a system of purposes, lie worlds apart." And in a notebook entry from 1885–1886, he explicitly recites the point that the genetic fallacy *is* a fallacy: "Questioning the origins of our valuations and tables of values is by no means the same thing as criticising them—however much it's true that for our feelings, understanding some pudenda origo reduces [its] value . . . (WLN 12:160/2[189]).

24. We'll encounter this proposal in ch. 6, and consider what could make it seem sensible in ch. 7. That special class is discussed at Millgram, 2002, p. 182.

25. 5:259/GM 1.2; "utility" translates *Nützlichkeit*, and notice the immediately subsequent paraphrase as *berechnende Klugheit*. For both of the suggestions I've just entertained, see Reginster, 1997. Reginster takes his second suggestion—that this particular form of self-deception engenders self-frustrating agency—to underwrite the first, and so to save it from the charge of moralism.

NOTES 285

26. There may be individual exceptions; "with noble men cleverness can easily acquire a subtle flavor of luxury" (5:273/GM 1.10), and surely intellectual pursuits might be taken up as an upper-class hobby.

27. Recall Nietzsche's remark, at 5:311/GM 2.11, to the effect that the reactive man is bound to take a false and prejudiced view of the object before him.

Notice, however, that the argument I'm now sketching doesn't require the premise that *all* the priestly knowledge workers of the past were intellectually incompetent in the ways we've had on display; it suffices that, in the course of the collective enterprise of fabricating, transmitting, and reappropriating values, *enough* were to guarantee (or almost guarantee) a product that is shoddy by the standards of contemporary intellectuals.

28. However, Solomon, 1996, p. 190f, takes a move with this formal shape to be a way legitimizing *ad hominem* arguments, rather than an alternative to them.

29. To return to our examples of moralistic interpretation: when Reginster claims that Nietzsche's critique of *ressentiment*-driven morality has bite because such morality turns out to involve self-deception, he doesn't pause to consider who's going to care about self-deception; but people who've been raised to value intellectual cleanliness might well care.

30. Compare the passage at 5:378f/GM 3.17 where Nietzsche explains why he's going to ignore the philosophers' struggle against the feeling of displeasure.

Given how dismissive Nietzsche can be about consciousness, why think that his philosophical therapy is intended to operate in ways of which his readers will be aware? (I'm grateful to Ken Gemes for raising this concern.) Here's one reason: the elaborately constructed booby traps I've been displaying won't be effective if they're not appreciated, and appreciating them requires noticing them.

31. Nietzsche describes an instance of the problem in the guise of autobiography. As a child he was preoccupied with the Problem of Evil (5:249/GM P.3); the Problem looks like a straightforward contradiction; religious academics treat it as an occasion for theory; Nietzsche thinks that he needs to explain his own youthful resolution of it by way of his personal predispositions.

32. This is a good place to say straight out, for those who need the signaling, that you're not being given a Straussian reading: although Nietzsche is quite aware that not all of his readers will follow his train of thought or cotton onto what he's doing, it's not, it should by now be apparent, that there's an esoteric content meant for the privileged few, under the misleading surface doled out to the masses.

Notes to Chapter 3

1. "Seems to," because we shouldn't assume that we can always take what we're told for granted. 6:343/EH III.Z.6, for instance, has the look and feel of booby-trapping: Nietzsche's announcements that Goethe, Shakespeare, and Dante aren't up to writing like *Zarathustra*, that "there is no wisdom, no investigation of the soul, no art of speech before Zarathustra," and that, "measured against [the concept of the 'Dionysian'

286 NOTES

presented there], all the rest of human activity [!] seems poor and relative"—these are the sort of bragging we expect from rappers and television tag-team wrestlers and, if we're going to get anything from reading Nietzsche, must be treated as themselves a puzzle. (Compare 6:154/TI 10.1: "even in my *Zarathustra* one will recognize a very serious ambition for a *Roman* style, for the *aere perennius* in style"—what is one to make of *that*? In ch. 6, I'll advance a suggestion, and I'll return to the topic in sec. 9.4.)

2. Raz, 1999, pp. 274f, and the cluster of claims that fall under this heading often includes a further commitment, to the bottom-line equality of human beings. As Buss, 2023, p. 1, puts it, "to treat some human beings as less worthy of concern and respect is to lose sight of their humanity." Nietzsche doesn't share this view, either: "men are *not* equal: thus speaks justice" (4:162/Z II.16, and there's a very similar remark at 4:130/Z II.7); or elsewhere, compare 6:217/AC 43 on "the poison of the doctrine of '*equal* rights for all'" (restoring Nietzsche's emphasis), 3:477/GS 120, looking forward to a future in which "we abjure the dogma of the 'equality of men,'" and see similar remarks at 6:150/TI 9:48. Here I'll leave to one side Nietzsche's view that the value of humanity, when it has any, is unevenly distributed.

  In such discussions, respect is standardly distinguished from esteem; for a representative instance, see Neuhouser, 2008, pp. 62f. Since Nietzsche thought the distinction as intended perverse, "respect" will be used here in the broader, ordinary sense.

3. Why sometimes? To anticipate ch. 9, Nietzsche worked very hard at exhibiting what he called "perspectivism" in his own writings. Central concepts, such as, in this case, 'nihilism,' are accordingly very differently inflected as they travel from perspective to perspective: hence the qualification.

4. Higgins, 1988, p. 132; the friend almost certainly had in mind Gibran, 2004.

5. To be sure, not everyone has this reaction by any means; for instance, Hayman, 1984, p. 273, tells us that "it would be pointless to deny that *Also sprach Zarathustra* is one of the finest pieces of prose in the German language." But then, Hayman has not been a professional academic philosopher; here is Brinton, 1940, p. 139, with the contrary assessment: "even in the German original the book seems to many (including the present writer) forced in its rhetoric, false in its taste, off-key throughout."

6. 3:571/GS 342, which duplicates and functions as a segue to the beginning of *Zarathustra*.

7. For biblical usage, see, e.g., Jer. 2:1, 6:9, 16, 21, 22, 7:3. For Nietzsche's, see 4:50/Z I.7, 54/I.8, 57/I.9, 60/I.10, etc.

8. For what was being signaled by the higher/lower distinction, see Benne, 2005, pp. 75, 77f.

9. Wellhausen, 1883; for the convenience of readers of the English translation, I'll generally refer to Wellhausen's *Prolegomena* by chapter, section, and subsection; however, when discussing Nietzsche's own marginal annotations, references will be to the page numbers of the 1883 edition. (I was first alerted to Nietzsche's having read Wellhausen by Yovel, 1998, p. 160.) Coppens, 1952, is a useful overview of the Higher Criticism.

NOTES   287

10. Let me lay out some back and forth about that. Nietzsche started writing *Zarathustra* at the outset of 1883, and the *Prolegomena* presumably wouldn't have been available for its early stretches; however, the writing wrapped up only some two years later, which gives him time to have taken a look (for the chronology, see Hayman, 1984).

Ahlsdorf, 1997, p. 56, dates Nietzsche's "intensive" reading of Wellhausen to 1888; he's going by the allusions to Wellhausen in later works (which we'll get to momentarily), and the fact that explicit mentions of Wellhausen in Nietzsche's journals almost all postdate Nietzsche's composition of the initial segments of *Zarathustra*. Ahlsdorf's primary concern is Wellhausen's portrayal of Judaism and the ancient Hebrews, apparently prompted by the entanglement of nineteenth-century Orientalism and Bible Studies with the political antisemitism of the period.

I'm not sure the *Nachlass* shows that the *Prolegomena* can't be figuring into the design of Nietzsche's book. Not to compare myself to Nietzsche, but I keep a journal, and the books I read often enough come in for discussion only months or even years later; you generally can't tell when I've read something by looking at my notebooks. So should we assume that we can tie a timeline of Nietzsche's reading to his handwritten notes? That would make sense only if he were a particular type of reader, and one he discusses in *Ecce Homo*:

> Scholars who at bottom do little nowadays but thumb books—philologists, at a moderate estimate, about 200 a day—ultimately lose entirely their capacity to think for themselves. When they don't thumb, they don't think. They *respond* to a stimulus (a thought they have read) whenever they think—in the end, they do nothing but react. Scholars spend all their energies on saying Yes and No, on criticism of what others have thought—they themselves no longer think.... I have seen this with my own eyes: gifted natures with a generous and free disposition, "read to ruin" in their thirties—merely matches that one has to strike to make them emit sparks—"thoughts."   (6:292f/EH II.8)

Given how dismissive Nietzsche is of this sort of reactive intellectual, it would be a mistake to rely on exegetical inferences that presuppose a stimulus-response workflow. I wouldn't be surprised to have it turn out that Nietzsche had been reading the *Prolegomena* during the later stages of writing *Zarathustra*—though for present purposes, namely, putting in place a crisp picture of how the Higher Critics approached Biblical texts, we don't need to have a view about that.

11. Strauss, 1892; on his encounter with Strauss, see Janz, 1981, vol. i, p. 146. Ernest Renan wasn't a typical member of the movement, but he wrote a biography of Jesus that, shockingly for the time, treated him as an ordinary human being (1955); Nietzsche was familiar with it (e.g., 6:111f/TI 9.2). We also have reason to believe that Nietzsche had been exposed to Bruno Bauer's view, roughly that Christianity is mostly recycled Stoicism and the theologizing of the politics of the early Roman Empire; however, it's unclear whether Nietzsche ever read the volume in which those ideas received their fullest exposition (2015).

The suggestion that *Zarathustra* is a parody isn't unprecedented, and Meier, 2017, pp. 12f, understands it to be a takeoff on the life and teachings of Jesus. But note that Nietzsche does not seem to be taking any *particular* religion as his

288 NOTES

reference point. I'll be emphasizing Old Testament allusions because we still have a book, from Nietzsche's personal library, that tells us how to read them. As I've just remarked, we know that he owned and read a very similar book, directed to the New Testament; Ben-Menahem, n.d., observes that a large number of *Zarathustra's* chapter headings are lifted from the Koran; the title and protagonist are obviously a gesture at Zoroastrianism; finally for now, Janz, 1981, vol. ii, pp. 221f, mentions reasons for taking one of Nietzsche's models to be Buddhist writings, and indeed Meier also notices an allusion in this category (p. 29).

12. For instance, early on in Wellhausen, 1883, ch. 5, it's argued that authors of *Deuteronomy* and the "Priestly Code" progressively altered earlier rules to specify that priests were to receive, as their dues from a sacrifice, first the shoulder, cheeks and maw of the animal, and subsequently the right leg and breast. When Nietzsche writes that "the priest formulated once and for all, down to the large and small taxes he was to be paid (not to forget the tastiest pieces of meat, for the priest is a steak eater), what he wants to have, 'what the will of God is'" (6:196/AC 26), we know to which page his copy of Wellhausen is open. (Note the extensive underlining at vol. 1, p. 159, of that copy, for instance of "*eine unverschämte Forderung*," the demand being for "*roher Fleischstücke*"; for this and further illustrations, see Ahlsdorf, 1997, pp. 156f.)

    Over and above his penchant for iconoclasm, there are textual reasons for wondering whether Nietzsche flat out believed Wellhausen's narrative; at 5:66/BGE 45, for instance, Nietzsche complains about the quality of work in religious studies, and concludes that "in the end one has to do everything *oneself*." And discussing Strauss, 1892, Nietzsche suggests that only the immature can take this sort of scholarship at face value (6:199/AC 28; compare 6:104/TI 8.2, where it's dismissed as merely "*clever*"). (He means: A youth who was raised in a religious environment might take the question of whether Jesus performed the miracles that were attributed to him to be addressed by a close reading of some text; once you're all grown up, stories involving miracles are obviously confabulations, and you don't need involved and complicated textual arguments to decide that.)

13. Nietzsche seems to have paid close attention to this motif in Wellhausen's exposition. See, for instance, the marginal emphasis at vol. 1, p. 168; Wellhausen is remarking that the Exile had left the Hebrews' collective memory the sort of tabula rasa that made such misrepresentations feasible. Or again, at p. 233, Nietzsche underlines Wellhausen's characterization, "*die Judaisierung der Vergangenheit*" (the Judaization of the past); see also his emphases on pp. 243 and 245: "*Kurz, was man so eigentlich für das Theokratische in der Geschichte Israels ausgiebt, das ist durch die Bearbeitung hineingebracht.*" Again, at p. 256, he underlines Wellhausen's dictum, "*je näher die Geschichtschreibung ihrem Ursprung ist, desto profaner ist sie.*" There are many further emphasized passages of this sort.

14. In due course, starting in sec. 3.13, I'll take up the question of whether we're in a position to call any view properly Nietzsche's own. In the meantime, however, you might be worried that, since the protagonist of the book is its title character rather than Nietzsche himself, we shouldn't assume the views being turned upside down to be Nietzsche's. If you are, as we proceed, keep track of the points at

NOTES   289

which "Zarathustra's" various dicta are compared to pronouncements drawn from Nietzsche's other writings.

15. The first two are adduced by Wellhausen in his introduction, the last in VIII.I.3; compare also Wellhausen's discussion of 1Sam. 12, in VII.II.1. In Nietzsche's copy of the *Prolegomena* we find him giving unusually heavy emphasis (both underlining and marginal markings) to *"Abenezra's und später Spinoza's Aufmerksamkeit"*—followed by a list of such Biblical passages that they had noticed (p. 10).

16. Kaufmann's translation of the section title at 4:33/I.2 as "On the Teachers of Virtue" is unfortunate.

17. Or perhaps Schopenhauerian (1966, vol. ii, pp. 374f).

18. At 4:381–385/Z IV.16.2; compare the shift from "thus spoke Zarathustra" to "thus sang Zarathustra" at e.g. 4:221/Z III.6.

19. Is it plausible that a nineteenth-century author was writing science-fiction *avant la lettre*? I don't think we should be incredulous on this score: just for instance, William Whewell, the early nineteenth-century philosopher of science, penned an account of a visit from an inhabitant of the moon (Todhunter, 1876, pp. 380–405).

If Nietzsche is appropriating the doctrines of the secular Bible scholarship of his day as a stylistic model, how is it not already widely known? I suppose a fast version of the answer would be another question: how could it have taken as long as it did for the likes of Ibn Ezra, Spinoza, and Wellhausen to have noticed those markers of the composition of the Old Testament?

A slower version of that answer might go as follows. The Bible is hard for us to read in good part because we've lost the literature and forgotten the literary conventions of the time in which it was written. In rather a similar manner, *Zarathustra* is hard for us to read because by the time it started to receive serious attention from philosophers, the Higher Criticism had receded into our cultural past. Of early uptake of *Zarathustra*, Thomas, 1983, p. 3, finds it "remarkable how often, when it is quoted, the references are to the earlier ... parts of the book, as if that was as far as the reader had got"; and I scarcely ever find that a member of our academic tribe today has any familiarity with the Higher Criticism at all.

20. To be sure, "Zarathustra's" pronouncements can be brought to bear on a reconstruction of what Nietzsche himself thought, but only when they're read as inflected, so to speak, by the genre exercise in which Nietzsche has embedded them. We can be fairly confident that this approach to his texts is licensed, since his models— Wellhausen, Strauss *et al.*—took themselves to be able to reconstruct the true history of ancient Israel or of Jesus from the later misrepresentations. Here the attitude of the village atheist on which I earlier remarked is in play; the Higher Critics adopted a breathtakingly condescending attitude toward the authors of the texts they were reading, treating them as incompetent writers and editors who would be simply unable to cover their tracks.

21. Redfield, 1993. That characterization is in a way misleading, because some of the "secrets" the protagonist discovers will strike most academic readers as flat-out goofy; the Jungian notion that coincidences are significant is probably the most innocuous of them. But the characterization is nonetheless on-target for my purposes, because

290 NOTES

the audience of the book is the New Age community, and *they* already take the more-or-less magical pronouncements for common knowledge: that people have auras is, for *them*, a truism.

22. Heidegger, 1979–1987, vol. ii, ch. 5.

23. There are many variations. Danto, 1980, p. 212, presents it as Nietzsche's Categorical Imperative: "So act (or so be) that you would be willing to act exactly the same way (or be exactly the same thing) an infinite number of times over." Clark, 1991, ch. 8, "compare[s] Nietzsche's question—would you be willing to live this same life eternally?—with a question people do in fact ask each other: if you had it to do all over, would you marry me again? The way in which members of a couple respond to the latter question is usually taken to reflect their true feelings about their marriage" (p. 269). Nehamas, 1985, ch. 5, ties the test of whether your life is regret-free to Nietzsche's anti-essentialist metaphysics, and to the ideal of a maximally coherent character and life. Anderson, 2009, very interestingly argues that the key to affirming one's past is changing its aesthetic properties by reframing it. Reginster, 2006, ch. 5, however, takes the Eternal Return to be Nietzsche "exhorting us to recognize a certain substantive value, namely the value of 'becoming,'" and "that there are perfections to which impermanence might actually be essential" (pp. 225f). When discussing previous interpretations, Reginster notices a version of the problem we are raising: "Who would find novel or controversial the exhortation to live life so as to have no regrets about it?" (p. 221) But his own proposal makes Nietzsche's views out to be merely the recycled platitudes of German Romanticism (and when the time comes to illustrate the view, Reginster turns to Goethe's *Faust*).

An older group of interpretations made Nietzsche out to be attempting bad apriori cosmology; see, e.g., Zuboff, 1980, and Soll, 1980. These have largely dropped out of view in the current literature, and I won't discuss them here. However, the cosmological notion was familiar enough at the time. Just for instance, John Stuart Mill points out that on his view, "if any particular state of the entire universe could ever recur a second time, all subsequent states would return too, and history would, like a circulating decimal of many figures, periodically repeat itself"; he then goes on to quote Virgil, before reassuring the reader that "things do not really revolve in this eternal round" (1967–1991, VII:347).

24. Remembering that its being truistic doesn't make it true, or particularly good advice. Kundera, 1984, pp. 3–6, and Windelband, 2015, p. 296, entertain perceptive second thoughts.

25. You can find a version of that second worry in Danto, who remarks of what he takes to be "an ancient, vaguely pagan ideal, the passions disciplined but not denied," that, "divorced from the extravagant language and the rushing cadences of Zarathustra's singing, [it] turns out to be a bland and all-too-familiar recommendation" (1980, p. 199).

Danto does find a side of the Eternal Return that would perhaps be worth prophecy, if we could attribute it to Nietzsche: that because the world has no final state, it has no meaning, and so it's up to us to supply its meaning (pp. 211f). Even if the conclusion is Nietzsche's, however, it would be uncharitable to attribute this train

NOTES 291

of thought to him. Presumably the transition from "no final state" to "no meaning" is to be managed by trading on the ambiguity of "end": the meaning, i.e., the attained purpose, comes last. But Nietzsche, whom Nehamas singles out as preoccupied with literary models of understanding, is unlikely to be crude enough to endorse that transition: the meaning of a novel is not its climax, and the meaning of an essay is not its last line.

26. 4:274/Z III.13.2; 4:201/Z III.2.2; 4:125/Z II.6 (restoring Nietzsche's emphasis of "*nöthig*"); 4:19/Z P.5. Compare Nietzsche's characterization of the proper object of pity at 5:160f/BGE 225: "we see how *man* makes himself smaller ... Well-being as you understand it ... soon makes man ridiculous and contemptible ..."

27. Anything as valuable as *that* would be something you wouldn't trade in for any amount of *anything* else, and as undergraduates in classes on Mill's higher pleasures are easily brought to acknowledge, there is nothing in the real world of which this is true; evidently, our standards are balanced enough so that no one sort of thing can have the requisite priority over all the others.

Of course, the Christian system of evaluations purports salvation to be valuable in just this way. But Nietzsche insists both that the Christian world-behind-the-world, i.e., heaven and hell, is a fiction, and that the values it supports are themselves a large part of the problem that he's trying to solve.

28. Nietzsche's account of the process, in the section "On Self-Overcoming," makes it out to be a side effect of enforcing standards on oneself: "whenever the living ... commands *itself* ... it must become the judge, the avenger, and the victim of its own law." The motivation for pressing towards ever more rigorously construed versions of one's ideals, standards, and so on is put down to "will to power" (4:147f/Z II.12), a Nietzschean notion that we'll return to in chs. 6 and 8.

29. The canonical but overinvoked model is the self-overcoming of the will to truth, as recounted in the *Genealogy*. "All great things bring about their own destruction through an act of self-overcoming" (5:410/GM 3.27); once the will to truth has been sufficiently refined, the question of the value of truth becomes unavoidable. The upshot is to free up the scientific and intellectual discipline developed in its service for other uses. And in the same work, Nietzsche tells us that justice overcomes itself also, into mercy (5:309/GM 2.10). Another brief but representative treatment can be found at 6:129/TI 9.28: being impersonal, evenhanded, sympathetic, and emotionally restrained, when pressed to an extreme, prompts that impersonal person, presumably so as not to come out unsympathetic and holier-than-thou, to develop one or another idiosyncratic personal emotional investment.

30. 4:248/Z III.12.3, where "overcome" renders "*überwunden.*" However, it's almost certain that Nietzsche in fact picked up the word "overman" from Ralph Waldo Emerson's essay on "The Over-Soul" (1971–2013, vol. ii, pp. 157–175). Once our discussion is farther along, it may be useful for the reader to compare and contrast the regulative functions served by the respective constructs. Emerson famously calls on you to, as a recent idiom went, tell it like it is—that is, tell it like it seems to you that it is, whether or not you agree with others, or for that matter with what you've insisted on previously. That the Over-Soul is speaking through you assures

292 NOTES

you, as much as that's possible, that when you speak your truth, it will be recognized as truth by others, and will prove to be more than an expression of your merely personal proclivities and illusions. But there's no account of how the Over-Soul works through you, and why it expresses itself consistently across persons; Emerson is giving a placeholder for an explanation—an explanation by magic—rather than a philosophical argument. As we'll see, the Overman is being positioned as a supremely important value, one that's in the business of regulating what it vouches to be a supremely important activity; you may want to consider whether we are told enough about the Overman to make it any more than just another explanation by magic.

31. Mackie, 1977, ch. 1; to be sure, metaethicists do their very best to propose alternatives, but since in doing so these options are taken, seemingly inevitably, as their foils, it's hard to avoid the sense that this is how philosophers today (and not just philosophers) *do* think about values.

32. E.g., "good and evil that are not transitory, do not exist" (4:149/Z II.12).

33. Let me mention a category of standards in order to put it to one side: if I already have a standard available, I may use it to frame a derivative standard. For instance, once we have ways of measuring temperature, along with a specification of a range of temperatures, given in degrees Farenheit, that an oven is supposed to stay within, we can produce a new standard for the European market; rendered in degrees Celsius, it sets tighter bounds on fluctuations in oven temperature. Following Nietzsche, we're interested in independent standards: standards conformity to which can't be specified in terms of the standards and standards-related techniques that one already has available. (If this is your home philosophical vocabulary, here we're interested in standards that aren't *reducible* to other standards.)

34. Both illustrations are filled out in Millgram, 2015a, pp. 44–48, 271f.

35. The exercise at the moment isn't to reconstruct Nietzsche's objections to moral realism, but it's worth registering how different they'll be from those that figure into today's back and forth, and here is a passage that encapsulates the contrast:

> *Historical refutation as the definitive refutation.* —In former times, one sought to prove that there is no God—today one indicates how the belief that there is a God could *arise* and how this belief acquired its weight and importance: a counter-proof that there is no God thereby becomes superfluous. —When in former times one had refuted the 'proofs of the existence of God' put forward, there always remained the doubt whether better proofs might not be adduced than those just refuted: in those days atheists did not know how to make a clean sweep.   (3:86f/D 95)

Showing how moral realism would be the side effect of memory loss is, in this way of thinking, its definitive refutation.

36. For a quick illustration, presented however as a way common law might develop, see the "series of imaginary judicial decisions" at Fuller, 1958, pp. 96–99.

37. To invent a value isn't to have a light bulb go on over one's head, as in a cartoon, and in the somewhat different form that Wittgenstein gave it (1958, e.g., Part I, §§143–146, 151–157), this point received a good deal of attention during the late twentieth century. Presented with a novel rule or concept (thus, with a novel criterion

for successful performance or concept application), the student's feeling that *now he has got it* counts for little or nothing in determining whether he *has* got it. What *does* matter is the student's ability correctly to apply the rule or concept in an indefinitely extensive range of further somewhat different cases.

The importance of this thought for understanding the form that Wittgenstein chose to give his own polished writing is insufficiently appreciated. He tells us in his Preface that "the very nature of the investigation . . . compels us to travel over a wide field of thought criss-cross in every direction . . . The same or almost the same points were always being approached afresh from different directions . . ."—the reason being that, on the views he's developing, only this sort of display of competence shows us that there is geniune understanding. The feeling that one has followed a single argument, say, the so-called Private Language Argument, and even the ability to recite it to a classroom of students, is, if Wittgenstein is correct, not enough to tell us that there is a philosophical insight one has understood—and therefore, that there is so much as a philosophical insight to *be* understood. (I'm grateful to Brooke Hopkins for discussion of these passages.)

I don't think that Nietzsche anticipated Wittgenstein's Private Language Argument, but he was quite aware of the more informally put version of the problem that I'm posing. And to get ahead of our story, if the reading we're starting to put in place is correct, the literary form given to his later works, taken as a group, is motivated by closely related considerations.

38. 5:47f/BGE 29; compare the insistence, at 6:148/TI 9.45, that innovators experience themselves as untouchables, "because they themselves feel the terrible cleavage which separates them from everything that is customary or reputable."

39. Pippin, 2010, p. 82, registers the point this way:

> if the most important deed is the legislation of values, what *actually* is legislated cannot be fixed by the noble man's strength of resolve *alone* or guaranteed by his "pathos of distance." There is a difference between actually legislating values, that is, succeeding in doing so, and, on the other hand, engaging in a fantasy of self and value creation.

40. 3:422/GS 58, amending Kaufmann's misleading translation of "Wahrscheinlichkeiten" as "probabilities." Perhaps the most famous extended discussion of the role of value terms in crystallizing values is to be found in the first Essay of the *Genealogy*.

In a note from 1885, Nietzsche remarks, of "tyrannical spirits capable of *tying fast* the meaning of a concept . . . who know how to turn the most fluid thing, the spirit, to stone for long periods and almost to eternalise it," that "they are sculptors—and the rest . . . are, compared to them, only *clay*" (11:449/WLN 34[88]).

41. As Nietzsche puts it elsewhere, apropos another Strauss-influenced discussion, the doctrine of the religion ends up being "the opposite of that which was the origin" (6:208/AC 36). Again, whatever Nietzsche is, he's not a latter-day Zoroastrian; nonetheless, he chooses to appropriate the figure who was the first to insist that both good and evil are built into the metaphysics of the universe, and to make of him a character who denies precisely that claim.

294 NOTES

These iconic examples don't stand alone; although our agenda just now isn't to trace out the pattern of inversions in *Zarathustra*, here are two more, just to make it more plausible that there *is* a pattern. First, in *Zarathustra*, we're given the sort of paeans to Life—two "Dancing Songs"—that have led to misclassifying Nietzsche as an especially uninteresting Romantic (4:139–141, 282–284/Z II.10, III.15). Whereas in *Twilight of the Idols*, we come across the dry pronouncement: *"the value of life cannot be estimated.* Not by the living, for they are an interested party . . . not by the dead, for a different reason" (6:68/TI 2.2); compare also Nietzsche's much earlier approach to the question at 2:51–53/HTH I:32f.

And second, we have internal reversals, of the sort that Higher Critics claimed were present in the Bible. For instance, "On Free Death" (4:93–96/Z I.21) recommends that you opt for suicide or euthanasia, rather than hanging on past your time, and becoming that demented resident of an assisted living facility. (I'm told that the German concept, "Freitod," is derived from this passage; thanks to Margaret Battin for the observation.) The "Freitod" recommendation does get echoed at 6:134f/TI 9.36, but notice the contrast with 4:20/Z P.5, where Zarathustra, complaining about the "last man," condemns them for preferring "much poison in the end, for an agreeable death."

42. 4:105f/Z II.1—and notice the conspiracy-theory dress given to what the Higher Criticism makes out to be in large measure a side effect of impersonal sociological forces and constraints.

43. 3:607f/GS 360; of course, we should probably not expect the heavy-handed priesthood of *Thus Spoke Zarathustra*'s imagined future to track Nietzsche's subtle criticism of what we would now think of as Anscombean action theory. We'll take up that criticism in sec. 8.6.

44. The worry that the Overman, as an objective deferred to the distant future, is an underhanded way of devaluing the present crops up in the literature, but accompanied by attempts to read the awkward entailment away; e.g., Creasy, 2020, p. 36, and esp. n. 13, raises the issue, and then suggests that since the "overman [is not] one pre-established standard . . . we see the importance of actively justifying existence through the creation of *new* values situated in one's own interests and engagements."

45. In Zarathustra's way of putting it, "as if there were but a single path to the future" (4:119/Z II.4); see, just for instance, at 5:155f/BGE 221—although notice the qualification at the end of the section. Compare a remark in his notebooks from 1887–1888: "The idea that mankind has a total task to fulfil, that as a whole it is moving towards some kind of goal, this very obscure and arbitrary idea is still very young. Perhaps we'll rid ourselves of it before it becomes an 'idée fixe' . . . It's not a whole, this mankind" (13:87/WLN 11[226]).

46. The rhetorical question fairly represents the relevant step in Nietzsche's reasoning, it seems to me, but we shouldn't treat the question as rhetorical ourselves. Recent philosophical discussions of liberal institutions have had as an ongoing theme the extent of their ability to handle a stream of different and perhaps unanticipated evaluative postures. (For an entry representative of the post-Rawlsian phase of the debate, see Gaus, 2016.)

NOTES 295

47. 4:243f/Z III.11.2; cf. 4:388f/IV.17. Relatedly, when he looks back on his own life, Nietzsche pronounces: "I do not want in the least that anything should become different than it is; I myself do not want to become different." But when he says so, he has just announced how seriously he takes the "imperative...to say *No as rarely as possible*" (6:292-295/EH II.8-9). The self-mocking pose he strikes in this section of *Ecce Homo* indicates that he's displaying one more way *not* to affirm things, an indication reinforced by the reason he doesn't want anything different: "'Willing' something, 'striving' for something...I know none of this from experience." Coming from the pen of the philosopher of will to power, we have to understand that as making the author of Nietzsche's autobiography convict himself of failure out of his own mouth; we'll return to this point in sec. 8.4.

48. 3:463f/GS 106; it will be convenient to present the parts of the relevant passage out of order.

49. This seems to have been a persisting thought; already in 1866, in a letter to Carl von Gersdorff, we find him experimenting with it (Nietzsche, 1969, p. 18): "Art is free, also in the domain of concepts. Who would refute a phrase by Beethoven, and who would find error in Raphael's *Madonna*?"

50. For background, see Liébert, 2004, and Perrakis, 2011; see also Janz, 1981, vol. ii, pp. 211-220.

51. The phenomenon seems to have been anticipated by his earliest readers; see the excerpt from Otto Erich Hartleben's diary reproduced in Wunberg, 1978, vol. i, p. 68. Bloom, 2012, pp. 148-156, 198-214, 226, 228f, complains that something of this sort has also taken place in the popular reception of Nietzsche's ideas in the United States.

52. Not that Nietzsche himself had much patience for it; in what seems to have been unused draft material for *The Birth of Tragedy*, he announces that "phantoms such as the dignity of man or the dignity of labour are the feeble products of slavery hiding from itself"; "the slave...is forced by his nature to describe all his circumstances by deceptively glamorous names in order to be able to live" (7:336/WEN 10[1]). But perhaps it nonetheless counts as part of the "*historia abscondita*" he foresees at 3:404/GS 34.

53. For an overview, see Becker, 2013.

54. Can we take seriously the supreme value of the Overman, and the absolute rigor of the Eternal Return, as these notions have traditionally been construed? (That is, that the Overman will be valuable enough to redeem *all* of his past, the upshot being that we regret *nothing*?) After all, we can be enthusiastic about the prospect of making up new values, of personalizing them, of embedding them in one's life or profession and so on without taking the activity to be overwhelmingly important in the way that Nietzsche's character makes the Overman out to be. And we can look forward to the invention of values putting us in a position to assess our world much more positively, without insisting that every last snippet of one's life, of humanity, and its past will end up worthy of respect.

Here is one reason to allow that to suffice. You only do have to insist on this sort of rigor in your positive thinking when you're one of those people who can't simply nod when their friends tell them not to sweat the small stuff: when you can't just

296 NOTES

let things go. Nietzsche has an account of those people—they're eaten away by *ressentiment*—and perhaps relatedly, Clark, 1991, p. 275, has suggested that Zarathustra's ideal of the Overman is supposed to be motivated by the character's need for revenge. Whatever the correct interpretation of his view, we surely don't want to adopt, as our own, a benchmark of success tailored to clients who are psychologically sick. Nietzsche is committed to the idea that different values are suited to different clients; the rigorist reading of the Eternal Return is not, you should hope, suited to *you*.

55. "Conventionally": a convention of Nietzsche's translators, since "*Umwertung*" is not a word in the normal German lexicon.

56. There's a further question to address: Nietzsche seems to have thought that *The Antichrist* was going to serve as the first volume of his *magnum opus*. But if the *Umwertung* of all values is as just described, how could that book be the first lap of it? I'll defer an answer to a full-dress treatment of the book itself, in ch. 7.

57. E.g., 3:467f, 570/GS 109, 341; 6:313, 345/EH III.BT.3, III.Z.6; 10:645, 11:224f, 11:556f, 12:205, 11:536f, 13:43, 13:374–376, 11:610f/WP 1057, 1060–1067. Not nearly all of what are on their face discussions of the Eternal Return or the Overman deploy those labels, which seem to be largely but not exclusively reserved for the use of the fictitious priestly authors of *Zarathustra*.

58. Gen. 1:27; the coinage metaphor comes with unwelcome implications—for instance and especially, money is fungible—and Mishnah Sanhedrin 4:5 is a rabbinic attempt to forestall them and bring this way of explaining the value of humanity into line with our own more recent attitudes: "the King of kings . . . has stamped every man with the seal of the first man, yet not one of them is like his fellow. Therefore every one must say, For my sake was the world created" (Danby, 1933, p. 388).

59. For some discussion, but in a non-Nietzschean accent, of how we manage moral standing, in both senses of the verb, see Millgram, 2009b.

Notes to the First Interlude

1. The usage isn't entirely unprecedented, however; see, e.g., Rousseau, 2013, p. 28. And Nietzsche's own use of the word has in some overly enthusiastic circles broadened the scope of the term to allow for genealogies of, well, almost anything.

2. Nehamas, 1994; I'll be offering a different meta-genealogy than Nehamas, but we can leave for another occasion the question of how far they are compatible.

3. Clark, 2015, pp. 31, 40, and from the Continent: "Die *Genealogie der Moral* ist eine historische Studie. Eine geschichtsphilosophische Arbeit will sie gerade nicht sein" (Benne, 2005, p. 132).

4. 5:313–318/GM 2.12–13, but I also need to say something about how I can just tell you what the Foucauldian uptake of Nietzsche is; if you look at his explicit pronouncements on the topic, you'll find them to be unhelpful.

   Here I think a remark by the late Stanley Cavell, on one of the differences between analytic and continental philosophy, is apropos. Analytic philosophers attempt to achieve clarity by paraphrasing what they are concerned is unclear into

NOTES 297

an antecedently clear vocabulary; continental philosophers, who don't believe there *is* such a thing as an antecedently clear vocabulary, strive for clarity in *use*. I don't know about the broad generalization, but it does fit Foucault; consequently, you best discern his take on things by watching what he *does*, and charitably overlooking the accompanying commentary.

You'll see the procedure as I describe it executed in *Madness and Civilization* (1988) and, writ large, in his treatment of panopticism, of which I'll give a terse sketch in note 6.

5. Under this heading, Nietzsche mentions Eugen Dühring (5:310/GM 2.11), whom we'll encounter in a different connection in ch. 7.

6. Returning briefly to Foucault, he noticed that the skeptical argument doesn't turn on the *temporal* succession of interpretations. In an ambitious series of treatments, he identified an underlying drama, *panopticism*: within an institution, the pervasive micromonitoring and control of small-scale behavior. (The label is a gesture at Jeremy Bentham's plan for a model prison; see Bentham, 1995.) The arrangements and techniques appear and reappear in a great many apparently very different institutional structures: prisons, hospitals, military bases, psychiatric wards, and so on. In each institutional context, the interpretation given to the panoptical procedures is local; for instance, when it's hospitals, the patients are monitored for *medical* reasons. (I could add that sometimes the reasons purport to be educational, and the sort of panopticism that my students experience is likely to be quite familiar to my readers: grades are given for exams, quizzes, term papers, many further small assignments, and perhaps also for classroom performance; they're entered into a spreadsheet, to produce a further grade that is sent to the registrar, to be compiled along with similarly produced grades into a transcript, and so on.) The techniques are invariant; the Foucauldian conclusion we're being invited to draw is that we shouldn't believe the justifications we're given for those panoptical procedures.

This isn't the place to assess the Foucauldian argument; suffice it for now that we see what it looks like to take very seriously a method one thinks one finds in the *Genealogy*.

7. If we look back somewhat earlier, we find startlingly different forms of detention, which is why the model genealogy is confined to the recent era for which the main lines of the procedure are a constant. Just for instance: Hugo Grotius, you will recall, was smuggled out of prison in a trunk of what were supposed to be his books—which meant not only that he was allowed large quantities of reading matter, and that he was able to use his quarters as a study, but that his activities were only very lightly monitored. That was not the sort of prison we know.

8. How airtight is the argument? The phenomenon is apparently real enough, but does it always work its way to the same endpoint? Why can't a ruthless reappropriator scrape away all of the rough edges, down to the very last of them?

We don't have to insist that Nietzsche was right on this point, but there is this to say on his behalf: when a locus of agency *is* powerful enough to override the inertia and sluggish persistence of an already-existing practice or institution, the upshot is

298 NOTES

likely to strike us not as its repurposing, but rather as sweeping it away and replacing it with a different structure entirely.

9. Bernard Williams held that 'thick ethical concepts'—both 'punishment' and 'prison' are presumably examples—cannot be peeled apart into their descriptive and prescriptive components. (Williams, 1985, pp. 140f; for an overview of the early discussion, see Millgram, 1995.) Here we're being shown where some of the most important such concepts come from, in a way that explains why Williams's claim would be true of them.

   You sometimes find analytic philosophers calling what are roughly state-of-nature arguments by the name "genealogy"; Williams himself subtitles his *Truth and Truthfulness* "An Essay in Genealogy" (2002), and Robert Nozick's *Invariances* includes a chapter on "The Genealogy of Ethics" (2001). A state-of-nature argument is a functional analysis of its subject, one that purports to legitimize it by showing what job it does, and both Williams's and Nozick's treatments match this pattern. But if anything like Foucault's understanding of the concept is on target, this is a misuse of the term: a genealogy shows its subject to *resist* functional analysis, and that there is *no* job it does.

10. Kaufmann, 1972, pp. 377–386, complains about imputing this sort of editorial process to the individuals responsible for the Bible as we have it, because it makes them out to have been, as Corngold, 2019, p. 203, summarized it, "idiot forgers"— but such unvarnished assessments of the Higher Critics are even now still outliers.

   For the version of the complaint (not quite Kaufmann's) that's relevant to us, let me draw on the academic employment of many readers: when you're grading papers, you often enough encounter clumsy student plagiarism, where even though you don't necessarily recognize the source, you can tell that the naive freshman has cut and pasted a stretch of text into his essay. To Wellhausen, the "redactors" of the Old Testament exhibit that level of clumsiness.

   Now, this take on biblical composition is quite implausible. In the pre-Gutenberg era, if a book was not recopied, by hand, in each generation, it simply disappeared; so the persistence of the books that were eventually canonized, over the course of, for the most part, many centuries, witnesses ongoing enthusiasm that, over time, only literary masterpieces sustain. Nothing on the order of that all-thumbs exercise in freshman plagiarism would plausibly have summoned up the effort to copy and recopy and recopy a text.

11. How could Wellhausen's treatment of the texts he worked with have gone largely unnoticed for as many decades as it did? And how is it that Wellhausen is still regarded as a respectable academic, albeit one whose field has moved on? My best guess is that, while partly it's a matter of how students were trained, and a complicated interaction of prejudices and agendas, to a large extent it was also a matter of linguistic competences: you have to have a full command of Hebrew to notice what Wellhausen is doing, and most of the scholars in the field have only a shaky grip on the language. Here's the tell: even today, remarkably frequently, you'll hear someone say that they read biblical Hebrew, but not modern Hebrew, and they'll say something that implies that they think it's possible to speak modern Hebrew without being able

NOTES 299

to read the Bible. Now, these variants of the language are actually quite close, and not coincidentally; modern Hebrew was, for ideological reasons, revived from biblical Hebrew. To have someone say that they can read one but not the other is rather like encountering students who can't read Shakespeare; if you're a native English speaker and you can't read Shakespeare, it's not that there's a different language you haven't learned: you don't control your *native* language, and you're plain and simple semiliterate.

But we should not expect that Nietzsche's command of Hebrew was inadequate; he had been studying it anyway since high school (Nietzsche, 1959, p. 27), and we know how full his mastery of other ancient languages became. Indeed, there are indications that his Hebrew was good enough to correct Luther's translation of the Bible; when *Zarathustra* riffs on 1 Kings 19:11–13, the episode in which Elijah hears—in the King James version—"a still, small voice" (and in German, "ein stilles, sanftes Sausen"), Nietzsche renders the phrase much more literally, as a "silence" (4:187–190/Z II.22, and for discussion of how best to render the phrase literally, see Millgram, 2014, pp. 110f).

12. Amusingly, when Benne, 2005, p. 109, comes to realize just what Nietzsche is insisting interpretation amounts to—"*verschiedenen Katagorien von Textkorruptionen!*"—the horror in his summary is audible, and is even italicized for emphasis: "*Das Wesen der Interpretation liegt in der Missachtung des Textleibes.*"

However, while Benne exhaustively documents Nietzsche's philological training and the academic traditions to which he was exposed in that field, his treatment is motivated by the presumption that Nietzsche would take over the methodological directives of a tradition into which he was raised, rather than treating them as raw materials to be repurposed. Here I'm suggesting that that training does account for his awareness of what scholars like Wellhausen were doing with their texts—Nietzsche had learned to notice such things when he did his reading—without endorsing the idea that Nietzsche would have retained the objectives and ideals promulgated by his mentor, Friedrich Ritschl.

More generally, as we're starting to see, Nietzsche was an intellectual magpie, someone who picked up and drew on a great many sources—and a very independent thinker, who hardly ever simply adopted what they said or did as was; instead, he remade almost everything he found into the materials that his own uses required.

Notes to Chapter 4

1. Nehamas, 1988, pp. 48, 51f, 59; we've seen his term "postulated author" introduced in Nehamas, 1981.
2. See the references in ch. 1, note 7; the "intentional fallacy" is announced in Wimsatt and Beardsley, 1954, a manifesto that despite its enormous influence will strike a properly trained philosopher as remarkable for its lack of cogent argumentation.

To be fair, a great deal of earlier author-centered literary criticism was weak, and that may have accounted for the alacrity with which the purported fallacy was

300 NOTES

rejected; Proust, 1988, can give you a sense of that sort of impatience with those quality issues—although it also advances an atypical reason, that there has to be a "dividing-line between real life (the one which is not so, in my opinion) and the life of [the writer's] novels (which alone is real for [him])" (p. 59).

3. For some occasions on which it isn't in place, see Millgram, 2002.

4. Nehamas, 1985, e.g., at pp. 230–234.

5. You'll recall from ch. 2 that the first sentence of the *Genealogy* announces that "we are unknown to ourselves, we men of knowledge" (5:247/GM P.1)—identifying its author, right from the get-go, as an intellectual, and likely a scholar or academic. We saw in the previous chapter that *Thus Spoke Zarathustra* introduced the implicit author less directly.

6. Each of the further self-descriptions flags an important move; one of the book's Parts is titled "We Scholars," and I'll take up the question of what his scholarliness tells us about the Good European in sec. 4.14.

7. Nehamas, 1988, p. 51.

8. Clark and Dudrick, 2012; here I won't register my point-by-point disagreements, which will be evident enough, but we'll shortly put to use an article by one of those authors which I think is very much on the right track.

9. 5:26f, 34f/BGE 12, 20; the complaint predates Nietzsche, and he gestures at Lichtenberg's famous objection to Descartes: that his *cogito* should properly be rendered "*it* thinks," where that has the grammar of "it's raining" (5:30f/BGE 17). Lange, 1950, vol. i, p. 262, reproduces Lichtenberg's objection, and credits the deeper point to Kant. (See Brobjer, 2008, pp. 32–36, for documentation that this was a book that Nietzsche read closely.) The transcendental unity of apperception need not reflect the unity of an underlying substance, and in fact is to be accounted for via the synthesis of cognitions. Nietzsche's appropriation of the concept of synthesis will turn up below, in secs. 4.4 and 7.5.

   The label, "atomism," is perhaps misleading. Nietzsche is appropriating it from what was then a debate within both physics and philosophy, conducted during a period in which atoms were highly speculative theoretical entities. Nietzsche's discussion leans heavily on Lange, 1950, Book II, sec. ii, ch. 2 (on "Force and Matter"): n.b. the discussion of Boscovich (in vol. ii, p. 364; cf. 5:26/BGE 12); reliance on picturable theoretical models (vol. ii, pp. 371, 375f, 389; cf. 5:28/BGE 14); substances as a reification of subject-predicate grammar (pp. 379f; cf. 5:34f/BGE 20); and the shared features of material substances and selves or egos (p. 380; cf. 5:27/BGE 12). Nonetheless, what Nietzsche makes of it is a good deal more general, and atomism should be regarded as a thesis in philosophy of logic. For some very perceptive uptake, couched however as an argument that Nietzsche's position is unsustainable, see MacIntyre, 1990, ch. 2.

10. One theme of those latter passages is that these aren't *merely* mistakes one can get past, and we'll take that issue up in ch. 9.

11. Of course, there's no metaphysical coathook, and no actual box to contain our weakly attributed mental states; so it's easy to wonder whether the right explanation for these two versions of soul isn't, after all, a variation on the error of metaphysical

NOTES 301

reduplication that Nietzsche renders for us in the *Genealogy* (5:278–281/GM 1:13; see sec. 2.2, above). We want to talk about people's psychologies, but we don't understand how the psychology can belong to the person; so we imagine a self, which is just the person over again, but thought of as distinct from the person in front of us, to be the owner. And because we want two different forensic strengths of belonging, we imagine that self twice over.

12. Nietzsche's remark, "*l'effet c'est moi*" (5:33/BGE 19) alludes to the perhaps-apocryphal pronouncement, "*l'etat c'est moi*"; in former times, that identification had been official ideology, of which Kantorowicz, 1957, remains the classic treatment.

13. Other theses built into the picture would include, it seems to me, what Aristotle called "separability"—that the mind has delimiting boundaries—and what Nagel, in a related context, termed "whole-number countability": roughly, there being always a definite answer, which will be a positive integer, to the question of how many people there are in a room. (See below, ch. 9, note 17.)

14. But even if we grant that free will has to do with the operation of one's inner bureaucracy, we needn't agree that Nietzsche has picked out the organizational feature that lies behind our phenomenology. When John Stuart Mill went looking for the personality structures that would account for the experience of free will, he settled on a state of motivational balance, one in which no single component of one's personality has the final say-so, and called it "moral freedom"; Millgram, 2019, ch. 7, is an overview.

15. Anderson, 2013, secs. 2.A and 2.D, briefly rehearses the relevant moves as a frame for interpretations of Nietzsche's views on autonomy; for discussion of a recent and representative contribution to this debate, see Millgram, 2015a, ch. 10.

16. For a noteworthy exception, in certain respects in the spirit of Nietzsche's attempt to rethink attribution-based representational conventions in psychology, see Dennett, 1991.

17. We'll return to this topic in our second Interlude.

18. Compare the description of "We who are homeless... too manifold and mixed racially and in our descent," summarized, "in one word... *good Europeans*" (3:630f/GS 377). The idea isn't original to Nietzsche: for instance, Lange, 1950, vol. i, pp. 162f, note 1, opines that "the subjection and fusion of numerous and utterly different peoples and races brings confusion not only into the specific forms of morality, but also into its very principles."

19. The main lines of this story are derived from the very helpful contributions of Lanier Anderson; however, I've departed from and smoothed out a good deal of the contouring of his nuanced and textually sensitive account. I can recommend Anderson, 2006, as an entry point into the discussion.

20. For a quick overview of the variety in Nietzsche's psychological Lego set, see Anderson, 2012, pp. 209f.

21. Richardson, 1996, sec. 1.4; his own example involves hunger and a drive to socialize; if the latter drive recruits the former, we now have a single but more complex drive, in which eating subserves socializing: what one now wants to do, again and again and again, is make lunch and dinner dates, or perhaps invite people over for dinner

302 NOTES

parties. The model seems to have taken shape gradually; in the early notebooks, we find an entry about "thinking in images," to the effect that "the stronger image consumes the lesser ones" (7:448/WEN 19[87]).

22. That last move is roughly that of Frankfurt, 1999, ch. 8, deploying his notion of satisfaction to underwrite attitude attribution.

23. I'll supply a review in the Appendix to this chapter.

24. Longuenesse, 1998, esp. pp. 3–14, provides context for that last observation. An alert reader will be concerned that drive recruitment and synthesis can only be accounted for by invoking a coherence-hungry, already-synthesized mind—the very thing the process was supposed to explain. Part of Nietzsche's alternative account leans on his doctrine of will to power, which we'll take up in ch. 8; I'll return to those aspects that we can make sense of using local resources in sec. 4.12.

25. At the tail end of his Preface, the Good European describes himself as not "even German enough," the point being that he doesn't want to let go of accumulated spiritual capital, in particular, the inner state of high tension produced by the Enlightenment. Nonetheless, the Good European *is* a German: German is the language he's speaking, and as we'll see, he makes a point of speaking *as* a German. So when he goes out of his way to tell us that "the German soul is above all manifold, of diverse origins, more put together and superimposed than actually built," we could take him to be describing himself. The etiology is that of Europeans more generally: "As a people of the most monstrous mixture and medley of races ... the Germans ... elude *definition*" (5:184/BGE 244).

Nonetheless, our question rearises: is the character merely a "mixture and medley," or is he perhaps one of the exceptional individuals who has synthesized his drives into an integrated and unified personality?

26. "Almost": in a segment I've left out, the narrator suggests that antisemites be kicked out of the country. For background on the role that such views played in German nationalist discourse, see Rose, 1990.

27. For a quick introduction to the Paradox, see Millgram, 1994.

28. Thus I'm in agreement with Clark, 1994, that "the misogyny of Part VII of [*Beyond Good and Evil*] is not the simple and straightforward matter it appears to be," and that, as she claims, "the misogyny exhibited there is on the level of sentiment, not *belief*" (p. 4). This essay is laudable as one of the very few in the analytic literature that attends to the textual surface of Nietzsche's writing. Still, I'm unconvinced by Clark's further claims, in particular, that "Nietzsche's comments about 'woman as such' ... [are] overcoming what he would like to believe about women, out of his commitment to truth" (p. 10), and that the misogyny is "used by Nietzsche to illustrate points he is trying to make about philosophy and the will to truth" (p. 4). The misogynistic opinions fall short of belief in that full-fledged belief requires a level of agential integration which the Good European is unable to manage, and *that* is what his diatribes are there to illustrate.

29. Bratman, 2007, e.g., at pp. 24 and 60.

30. Katsafanas, 2013b; in more recent work, he adjusts the view slightly: "Drives are dispositions that token evaluative orientations, and Nietzsche's claims about drives

constituting organisms should be understood as claims about how drives impact the organism's cognitive, perceptual and motivational states" (2016, p. 199). This strikes me as a philosopher responding to pressure to clean up the notation in which Nietzsche's discussion is being conducted, and it's important to bear in mind that the philosophically deep point being made by Nietzsche's critique of soul-atomism is that we don't *have* a worked-out, usable alternative to attribution-based representational conventions; that's why we keep lapsing back into them. If we don't want our efforts to be wasted, we should postpone this sort of smoothing out until we've come up with a candidate.

31. Katsafanas's treatment is derived from Freud (2013b, p. 746—who did read Nietzsche), from Iris Murdoch (p. 742), from Schopenhauer (sec. 2.2, and cf. Katsafanas, 2016, sec. 4.2.1; Nietzsche did indeed read him closely), and from discussions in the biological literature of the time (sec. 2.1; cf. Katsafanas, 2016, pp. 89–91). The pattern of swerves, away from Nietzsche's own writings to other well-known—or lesser-known—views, should prompt second thoughts, for we shouldn't assume that Nietzsche, who is of interest to us today precisely because he was on so many points an original thinker, would adopt his understanding of a central concept, unchanged, from his intellectual environment—or for that matter that Freud, who was also an original thinker, would have adopted his own understanding of drives unchanged from Nietzsche.

32. Perhaps in more integrated agents drives do give rise to out-in-the-world activity. Moreover, as J. L. Austin reminded us, when properly positioned, speech itself can constitute out-in-the-world action. But the drives we are being shown seem not to bother with that kind of positioning. (I mean, while Nietzsche is trying to be, say, provocative, *provoking* is not an Austinian speech act: it is not like making a promise.) The utterances being emitted by these drives are merely expressive.

Anticipating a model I'll begin using in just a moment, you'll have seen the politically engaged public go in for group displays, generally of emotions such as outrage; these amount to a default activity, regardless of whether they will plausibly result in policy changes. Revealingly, these events are called "demonstrations" (and similarly, in French, "*manifestations*"). I've found that if you ask a participant whether the activity counts as an effective instrumental means to an end, normally they will affirm that it is, even when they cannot say how; *expressive* activity gets naively construed as calculatively selected action, and we should be skeptical when we're told that drives are directing achievements and accomplishments.

33. There's a supporting argument to be made, turning on the way that, in his other writings, Nietzsche exhibits drives with incoherent aims. An incoherent aim or object can't be represented propositionally, and accordingly doesn't give us the descriptive leverage we would need to individuate a particular drive. I'll return to this point in ch. 7.

34. Nietzsche seems never to have been particularly interested or invested in democratic politics—on the contrary. Thus he overlooked an alternative to the form of self-government that we saw him using to account for unified agency, recall, absolute control of the psychological machinery by a single component. Parliamentary

304 NOTES

democracies are frequently governed by coalitions of parties, and when suitable political norms are in place, such coalitions can regulate the activity of a political state quite effectively. Although he would almost certainly have rejected the suggestion, in thinking through Nietzsche's ideas for ourselves, we should ask how a self managed by a governing coalition of drives would function, and consider to what extent we already operate this way.

35. Have we? The character repeatedly implies that he produces his various blurts *at will*. Recall the several pairs of bookends, and in addition he pronounces:

> To have and not to have one's affects, one's pro and con, at will; to condescend to them, for a few hours; to *seat* oneself on them as on a horse, often as on an ass—for one must know how to make use of their stupidity as much as of their fire. (5:231/BGE 284)

You might think that if the rants are under his control, their contents can perhaps be attributed to him, after all.

There are two points to register here. First, although the character is suggesting that he does produce these eruptions at will, we have to think twice about whether to *believe* him. Nietzsche's theoretical views elsewhere indicate that we shouldn't, and I'll introduce his criticism of what we now tag as Anscombean action theory in the next section, with a followup in sec. 8.6.

Second, the ability to turn one's ranting on and off, more or less at will, and Frankfurt-style identification with the contents of such a rant are two very different matters. As a philosopher who can work himself up into a heated defense of almost any philosophical view, pretty much on the spot, but solely in the mode of trying it on for size, I can vouch for the distinction personally. We'll shortly see the Good European's own explanation for his being able to do much the same.

36. As we'll see in ch. 8, it's an important part of Nietzsche's enterprise to display the matter of his personal psychology in his writings.

37. Nehamas, 1981, p. 144f; Nehamas, 1986, pp. 686, 689, and at p. 687 we are told: "interpretation...is...to ask, Why?...and to expect answers appealing to agents, to intention and rationality."

We can notice in passing a further drawback of Nehamas's reconstruction. On his view, the text as we have it is motivated by something like the following train of thought. Perspectivism (which centrally includes the thought that any picture of the world is an interpretation, from a particular point of view) is being opposed to dogmatism (i.e., insisting that such-and-such is the *truth, and that's that*). You can either advance a view (with perspectivism itself as a special case) as "only an interpretation" or just assert the view. But if you advance a view as "only an interpretation," you're inviting your interlocutor to dismiss it out of hand. On the other hand, if you simply assert a view, your interlocutor won't treat it correctly, i.e., as an interpretation—and if the view is perspectivism itself, it will seem to be self-refuting. In short, the trap is this: if you advance the perspectivist position, it will either get dismissed out of hand, or get treated incorrectly, or get rejected as self-refuting.

Nietzsche's way of avoiding the trap, thus Nehamas, is to script rambling monologues; these induce an implicit and fictional character. Since what you read is a transcription of the voice of the character, perspectivism is being presented as (just) *his* point of view, *his* perspective, *his* interpretation. The response to a presentation of a character is a "*decision* to accept him as a whole" (Nehamas, 1988, p. 64)—or to reject him—rather than, say, to draw the conclusion of an argument.

We'll take up Nietzsche's perspectivism in ch. 9; in the meantime, the most striking problem with the proposal is the way that this particular would-be script turns out to be a hard-to-refuse invitation to dismiss Nietzsche's character and his view jointly. If you try to hear *Beyond Good and Evil* as a monologue, you recognize the scenario and your interlocutor immediately: he's the crank who sits down at your table in the coffeeshop, who won't let you work or read, who goes on about conspiracies, his nutty politics, and so on, until eventually you abandon your cappucino and flee. Even if presenting you with a character *was* formally a plausible path between the horns of Nehamas's perspectivist dilemma, it would be hard to imagine a less effective persona for the job than the one we're supposedly given.

38. Nehamas, 1981, p. 145; for overviews of the relevant models of action, see Millgram, 2005b; Millgram, 2010a. We'll distinguish two ways of construing that explanatory priority in ch. 8, where we can briefly consider the merits of Nehamas's move to his fallback position in note 29.

39. Nehamas, 1981, p. 147; compare Nehamas, 2018: "in the ideal case . . . no 'piece' of one's life is independent of any other: Every action casts light on every other, and to remove one would cause all the rest to collapse. And to specify their interrelations in as much detail as possible is to gradually reveal the *one* intention, the unified character, of their agent."

40. Frege, 1970, p. 54. But, you might be wondering, who—or what drive—is responsible for the arrangement of the text of *Beyond Good and Evil*, as we now have it? I'll return to this issue in sec. 8.6.

41. Just as a reminder, here's a typical expression of the picture, from Creasy, 2020, p. 148: "the integrated nature of her will indicates that she has been able to recruit drives *other* than the dominant drive/s in service of her highest value and task (that is, the bulk of her drives has been successfully incorporated into the end/s and purpose/s of her dominant drive or set of drives)."

42. Then why isn't the right approach to *pare down* the agent, by extirpating the uglier drives? Remember that "unchangeable 'This is I' ": in Nietzsche's view, and possibly this will emerge from his conception of drives, there's no reason to expect that to be feasible.

43. Notice in particular that you can accept the suggestions that morality has a function and that its assessment should be client-driven, while thinking that Nietzsche has gotten both the functions and the effects on the clientele wrong. Although the former and more formal moves are fairly dramatic departures from mainstream moral theory, for my own part I am sympathetic, whereas work in the vein of Elias, 2000, has made me skeptical about the more substantive claims.

306 NOTES

44. Compare 3:529f/GS 289, but you might be wondering how a value one invents for oneself can be intended to be used by—and even compel—others over the long term. Nietzsche had given this some thought while he was living and working in Genoa; observing the mansions built onto the hillsides, he noted that they were "a way to express [someone's] superiority . . . Each once more conquered his homeland for himself by overwhelming it with his architectural ideas and refashioning it into a house that was a feast for the eyes"; but they also "wished to live on . . . their houses [were] built and adorned to last for centuries and not for a fleeting hour" (3:531f/GS 291). The passage appears just after the demand for idiosyncratic values and for stylistically regimented characters, and we shouldn't assume that Nietzsche's remarks on the local architecture are changing the subject.

While there are anticipations in Hume, in Kant, and perhaps elsewhere, it was a real innovation on Nietzsche's part to ask a question that no one had asked before— at any rate, in his fully practical register—namely, What is the value of values? (5:253/GM P.6) You are interested in *assessing* values because what values to have is a practical question: a *choice*. Since it is a choice, rather than a matter of fact to be discovered, it can be made in many ways; you can be deliberate and thoughtful about it, or not; creative, or plodding; and so on.

Said a bit differently: Nietzsche's metaethical position is that understanding values isn't a matter of understanding what kind of fact they metaphysically are, but rather, making sense of the workings and effects of such assessment tools and of the form of guidance they provide—so as to arrive at a view as to which of them belong in your decision-making toolkit. That makes Nietzsche out to have anticipated by about a century the general direction of the turn to what's now called constructivism, only with this difference: where Rawls's "Kantian constructivism" is directed towards providing uniform guidance (the CI-procedure is supposed to be used by *everyone*, and the outputs of Rawls's Original Position are meant to be acknowledged by all citizens of his "well-ordered society"), Nietzsche's turn to the practical is meant to guide different people differently. (Rawls, 1989; for a non-Nietzschean practical metaethics that allows interpersonal variation, see Millgram, 2015a, ch. 5.)

If this is correct, attempts to place Nietzsche within the old-school map of the space of metaethical positions (are values metaphysically real? or rather, expressions of our attitudes? etc.) are deeply misguided. For a review of that recent back-and-forth, see Hussain, 2013.

Just in case you're experiencing it yourself, I should perhaps register a response that today's philosophers tend to have to such a proposal: that if the values are invented thoughtfully and deliberatively, they must be chosen in light of already available values, so must be reducible to them, and consequently cannot be genuinely novel. (You can see what it looks like to wrestle with this train of thought, in this case trying to split the difference, in Raz, 1999, pp. 208f.) We've already sketched some of how Nietzsche resists this way of thinking in ch. 3, and we'll take up the matter further in ch. 7.

45. Nehamas, 1988, pp. 59, 61, quoting 5:146/BGE 212.

46. There are further values that Nietzsche marks in this book, and one of these, "nobility," has the status of a necessary precondition of the possibility of value invention: that is to say, we can see in the background something on the order of a transcendental argument for it. Especially when the novel values are ambitious, you need a kind of confidence that allows you to dismiss the nay-sayers. That personality trait—which Nietzsche talks about using metaphors of distance, views from above, and so on—is the subject of the final stretch of *Beyond Good and Evil*.

    Lest we construe nobility as familiar, recall that on Nietzsche's view, when basic evaluations are nonreactive, the primary and positively valenced value term will be a word for the value legislating class, and its substantive content will prove to be what centrally matters for sustaining that class. For instance, chivalry, a value term that descends to us from a ruling class of knights, is derived from *cheval* (see White, 1964, ch. 1, for an account of the central role of horsemanship in crystallizing medieval hierarchies). To be sure, over a period of time, the values of those landed-proprieters-on-call-as-human-tanks underwent the very Nietzschean process of self-overcoming, and we now caricature chivalry as exaggerated deference to, especially, upper-class women.

    "Nobility" is a generic term for aristocracy; until we know what the central or defining feature of *this* elite is, we don't know what value Nietzsche has in mind when he invokes it. The ordinary connotations of the word are uninformative, and we have to let him tell us. Fortunately, once we know that the new nobility that Nietzsche has in mind are philosophers of the future, that is, value inventors, we're equipped to consider what the value, "noble," must come to.

47. Only pretty much, because of course not all of my drives were integrated. I seem to have had a doodling drive, which absorbed much of my time in high school and which didn't respond to the value of philosophy by folding itself into these other drives—unsurprisingly, because philosophy as we have it doesn't demand doodling. In the Nietzschean conceptual scheme, an isolated drive of this sort is likely to be repressed by its heftier and more articulated neighbors.

    Huddleston, 2019, p. 86n23, picks a related example out of *Twilight of the Idols*: "Socrates . . . takes his agonistic and erotic impulses (of the sort, Nietzsche says, that would be more healthily discharged in a 'wrestling match between young men and youths') and brings them into the service of a rational activity suited to his overgrown logical faculty—dialectical argument."

48. And motivational over-integration can easily become a pathway to nihilism. Let's go back to Richardson's example of drive recruitment: my sociability drive assimilates my drive to eat, producing a new drive to social eating, addressed by lunch dates, dinner parties, and so on. But now, suppose I also have a moviegoing drive, and suppose moviegoing is now to be motivationally integrated with social eating. At this point, the original appetites are likely to be fatally compromised: I am reduced to munching cardboard-like popcorn drenched in artificial butter flavoring; sitting silently in a dark theater is not satisfying social interaction; there are too many movies (think *Vertical Features Remake*) that none of my friends will ever want to see. Each of the component drives is being addressed, but none of them is getting what it

308 NOTES

needs; that combination, of seeming to oneself to be satisfying one's desires, while remaining thoroughly unsatisfied, is something of a recipe for what Creasy calls "affective nihilism."

49. Here I've confined myself to issues of fit, but there's a more important issue to be broached. The late Vicki Hearne, who came to philosophy from training dogs and horses, once remarked:

> I used to wonder why trainers existed; giving an animal to someone else to train for you seemed to me as queer a business as giving your spouse to a surrogate husband or wife for training in the conversation that is marriage. It's not clear to me what you would want a spouse *for* under such circumstances. (1987, p. 174)

You might well wonder, in rather a similar manner, about people who are willing to go through life taking direction entirely from values handed down to them by others, what their stake in living their life *is*.

50. 5:157f/BGE 223f; of a slightly different list—"the order of rank of the valuations ... the relationship of these valuations to the conditions of life; the relation between the authority of the values and the authority of the forces that are at work"—Nietzsche says in a note that "being able to *reproduce* all this within oneself constitutes the historical sense" (11:509/WLN 35[2]).

51. I'm very grateful to Michael Million for explaining the branding process, not to mention a facility tour.

52. Both of these can be found at 5:144/BGE 211, where Nietzsche allows that "it may be necessary for the education of a genuine philosopher that he himself has also once stood on all these steps," and demotes systematizers of extant values—he gives Kant and Hegel as examples—to mere means and tools.

53. But *could* it work? That is, could there *be* an underlying condition that allows you to live through and benefit from arbitrary illnesses? Maybe not: for a model argument, see Millgram, 2022.

54. This is a good place to mark a Nietzschean response to the thought that since the intelligent, thoughtful choice of values must be made on the basis of already-present values, the new value cannot after all be new. Now of course inventions cannot generally be derived from or reduced to their inventors' aims or priorities; the successful inventor's ingenuity at which we marvel is not usually cleverness in the choice of means to established ends. But recall also that Nietzsche thinks of the values we start out with as typically the products of those Lamarckian racial histories. If we could only produce new values that conformed to those we had inherited, we would be victims of racial determinism, and Nietzsche would be left without an audience capable of acting on his recommendations. But although our parents' values reside in our bodies, Nietzsche thinks, they also overcome themselves; we can deploy them in different ways, incorporate them into novel constructions and much more of the same.

55. See also Hussain, 2004.

56. This is Book II, Sec. iii, ch. 4, pp. 202–230; n.b.: the single-volume third English edition has highly nonstandard pagination, inherited from the three volumes of the original—you'll need both the Book, etc. and the page to find references in this work.

NOTES 309

57. See Schopenhauer, 1966, vol. ii, pp. 174, 195, 216, 245, 249–251, 256, 258f, 271, 273, 285f, 322f.

Notes to the Second Interlude

1. Camus, 1977, pp. 57–71; the quote is at p. 68. Under the heading of popular expressions of the same thought, you'll find a cover of *Der Spiegel*—Germany's equivalent of what *Time* magazine used to be, reproduced at Aschheim, 1992, fig. 17— with copy reading (rendered into English) "Perpetrator [or: Doer] Hitler, Thinker Nietzsche," the suggestion being that Hitler was merely carrying out Nietzsche's program.
2. Brinton, 1940, pp. 132, 150; Alfred Bäumler, especially prominent in this connection, is reviewed by Whyte, 2008, and Baeumler, 1966, an abridged but representative essay, will give English-speaking readers a sense of how Nietzsche was made to sound. Bernasconi, 2013, p. 48, remarks that "for those within Nazi Germany who were sympathetic to Nietzsche, his name served almost as a surrogate for the National Socialist movement itself," but he proceeds to complicate the identification: "that simply means that there was no standard Nazi assessment of Nietzsche any more than there was a uniform understanding of National Socialism." The course of lectures I just mentioned—prudently expurgated—is published as Heidegger, 1979–1987, although his affiliation with and commitment to Nazism has been controversial and contested in rather the manner that Nietzsche's own relation to it is.
3. For the former move see Aschheim, 1992; for the latter, Sluga, 1993.
4. Kaufmann, 1974; for a journalistic account of the failed colony, see Macintyre, 1992. Although *The Will to Power* is indeed selections from Nietzsche's *Nachlass*, Förster-Nietzsche tampered with other documents, turning some of them into outright forgeries. And it is hard to know what to think about *My Sister and I*, a book that was for quite some time accepted as one of Nietzsche's works: a disturbing melange of antisemitic rants, turn-of-the-twentieth-century pornography, and effusive expressions of confidence in Nietzsche's sister as an intellectual intimate. A late-in-life photograph of Förster-Nietzsche meeting Hitler can be found at Aschheim, 1992, fig. 16.
5. Kaufmann was himself a Jewish émigré; he had experienced the Nazi regime as a teenager, managing to escape Germany in 1939—that is, just in the nick of time. Working at a university that at the time was only still in the process of accepting Jewish faculty into its community made this a delicate issue for him.
6. Although it's important to keep in mind that making Nietzsche out to be innocuous— as though that were the sole alternative—will bump up against a great many recalcitrant stretches of text:

    > We simply do not consider it desirable that a realm of justice and concord should be established on earth ... we think about the necessity for new orders, also for a new slavery—for every strengthening and enhancement of the human type also involves a new kind of enslavement. (3:629/GS 377)

310 NOTES

Once morality is swept away, we can look forward to "breakdown, destruction, ruin, and cataclysm... [a] monstrous logic of terror... an eclipse of the sun whose like has probably never yet occured on earth" (3:573/GS 343)—a prophecy that seems to have been borne out by twentieth-century history. Or again, the reader is directed to 3:609f/GS 362; there is no shortage of blood-curdling remarks in Nietzsche's corpus. Corngold, 2019, pp. 578ff, reviews a series of complaints directed against Kaufmann, to the effect that his presentation of Nietzsche's corpus suppresses its unsavory sides.

Furthermore, the Nazis' uptake was not just a matter of seeing things that weren't there. Antisemitism was a central component of the ideology, and we've already seen Nietzsche presenting his own personality as containing an antisemitic drive. In ch. 7, we'll return to that aspect of his self-portrait, and see what they were responsive to from a different angle.

7. If the phrase "direction of fit" is useful philosophical shorthand for you, as I think of it, an interpretation properly has the direction of fit of a belief, not that of a desire or wish. For a standard presentation of that concept, see Searle, 1983, pp. 7f; the notion was introduced by Anscombe, 1985, sec. 32.

Notes to Chapter 5

1. Nietzsche calls the main divisions of the volume "Books," and as I've already started to, I'll capitalize those mentions.

2. 3:623f/GS 372, and Nietzsche rested so much weight on the claim that a health issue could be psychological—that is, on the notion of mental illness—that one of his most famous disciples took it upon himself to criticize his master, by producing a Nietzschean genealogy of that very concept Foucault (1988). We'll want to keep our own criticisms on this point at the ready as well.

3. For representative and sophisticated attempts in our own analytic tradition to articulate realism as a metaphysical claim, see Putnam, 1981, Dummett, 1991, Boyd, 1983.

4. Pippin, 2010, Pippin, 2006. It's worth taking a look at Nietzsche's attempt to put his finger on the common denominator of the category, at 2:647/HTH II.2.214; twice he trails off into an "I am at a loss to finish the definition," or an "I am again at a loss to complete my list."

5. Chamfort, 2014, is a typical selection, and for a similar selection in English, see Chamfort, 2003; the copy in Nietzsche's personal library (Chamfort n.d.) is lightly marked up. Nietzsche's library ended up with *four* different versions of La Rochefoucauld's *Maxims* (1976). (See Campioni *et al.*, 2003, p. 630; one entry is to be found under "Vauvenargues.")

6. Rée, 2003; Nietzsche himself affiliates Rée with "Larochefoucauld and the other French masters of psychical examination" at 2:59/HTH I.36. For background, see Small, 2005.

7. That's the default, but Nietzsche seems to treat Stendhal (that being the pen name of Marie Henri Beyle), whom we think of as a novelist, Ferdinand Galiani, known

NOTES 311

for his correspondence and for a dialogue on the wheat trade (1984), and Michel de Montaigne, who wrote (and originated the category of) "essays" (2001) as in that category.

Nietzsche subsequently purported to demo for his audience how one should read an aphorism (5:255f/GM P.8), and that display has generated some controversy in the secondary literature (Janaway, 2007, ch. 10). It's part of what now seems to be the popular view that 5:340/GM 3.1, a passage which is about two-thirds of a page long, counts as an aphorism. The *Genealogy* was written some time after the work we are now considering, so I won't need to take a stand on this question, other than to register that the section looks rather different from paradigms you're about to see. Nehamas, 1985, pp. 18f, is a valuable corrective to the familiar and too-casual description of Nietzsche's writing as "aphoristic": Nietzsche penned aphorisms *sometimes.*

8. Maxims 220, 223, 247, and 254 in Rochefoucauld, 1976; 1871 English rendering by J. W. Willis Bund and J. Hain Friswell.

9. "Stendhal...may well have had more thoughtful eyes and ears than any other Frenchman of *this* century" (3:450/GS 95, and compare 6:147/TI 9.45 on Dostoyevsky, as well as 2:22/HTH I.P.8). Resa von Schirnhofer reported that "she heard a great deal from [Nietzsche] about Henri Bayle [i.e., Stendhal]," and apropos another figure we'll mention shortly, "Emerson, for whom he nourished a great sympathy," that he had read not just the latter's own writing, but Hermann Grimm's book about him (Janz, 1981, vol. ii, pp. 275, 278).

10. A slightly different but standard view of the content: "With remarkable virtuosity La Rochefoucauld demonstrates pride to be the perpetual motion of the human soul, casting its decisive lot in almost every action. At times it seems that the *Maximes* are one kaleidoscopic variation on the theme of vanity" (Donnellan, 1982, p. 75). Compare also 6:157/TI 10.3, where the "psychologist" that its author claims to carry within himself sees through the calm, balanced nobility of the ancient Greeks to their overbearing drive for power.

11. For a run of straight Rochefoucauldisms, see, just for instance, 2:239–247/HTH I.293–335. And Nietzsche claims the category for himself, although he delegates to you the task of putting the entailments together. In the work titled "Human, All Too Human," he straight out tells us "that reflection on the human, all too human" is otherwise called "psychological observation," that it allows you to formulate "useful maxims," and that "the great masters of the psychological maxim" are "Larochefoucauld [and] those related to him in style and spirit" (2:57f/HTH I:35).

12. That argument was a representative sample, but there is much more of the same. Just so you don't have the impression that the argument from custom is the sole basis for Nietzsche's correction of earlier French moralists, here are a couple of further points from *Daybreak*: First, at 3:91/D 103, Nietzsche allows that you can "deny morality" by being, roughly, a traditional French moralist, someone who insists that the apparent, moral motives aren't the *real* ones—*or* by arguing that the "moral" motives, which may indeed give rise to action, have mistaken presuppositions. Nietzsche takes his

312 NOTES

stand on the latter, reminding you, however, that to debunk a motivation is not necessarily to debunk the types of action that have been performed on its account.

Next, in another and nearby section (3:92f/D 105), Nietzsche informs you that although people tend to think they act on the basis of their own perceived interests, in fact they largely act on the basis of opinions and attitudes they perhaps picked up as children (in the manner described in 3:92/D 104) or by the by. Their guiding lights are generally distorted, simplified copies of their sources, and not particularly integrated into a coherent view of anything, much less their interests.

This sort of cynicism was subsequently kept in play; we're familiar with the role that *ressentiment* plays in the later works. A motivation that clouds one's perceptions, reconstruing one's circumstances so as to fit a narrative of grievance, it is backward-rather than forward-looking and, consequently, it rarely comports with self-interest.

13. And he does seem to have been self-aware about it, as indicated by a remark-in-passing in his journal from 1885–1886: "Critique of egoism, e.g., La Rochefoucauld" (12:149/WLN 2[165]).

14. Williams, 2006b, pp. 307, 302, 309f; as Nietzsche put it, apropos a different but related topic, in 2:129/HTH I.135: "a certain false psychology, a certain kind of fantasy in the interpretation of motives and experiences is the necessary presupposition for becoming a Christian and for feeling the need of redemption. With the insight into this aberration of reason and imagination one ceases to be a Christian."

Philosophers these days are often enough inclined to describe Nietzsche as naturalistic—see, just for instance, the title of Janaway and Robertson, 2012—and Williams, who however was much less crude than the norm in how he thought of naturalism, held that, despite everything, there was something they were getting right: "naturalistic moral psychology explains moral capacities in terms of psychological structures that are not distinctively moral" (301). That is to say, naturalistic moral psychology, and naturalism more generally, are the insistence, and the attempt to show, that when it comes to a prop for one's dignity, there's far less than meets the eye. So in our terms, naturalism, as Williams construes it, has the debunking *function* of behindology.

15. Giving you just a bit more background, the view that the Cathar heresy influenced the troubadours has been disputed (see, for instance, Gere, 1955, esp. ch. 5), and it's been argued somewhat more recently that the very existence of the Cathars was a figment of the imagination: that they were a fictitious enemy conjured up to satisfy the needs of the persecutors (the view taken by Pegg, 2008; Sennis, 2018, is an overview of the debate). I am myself disinclined to take sides in this debate, and fortunately, we don't have to; we're not after the history of romantic love in the middle ages, but rather, how that history was thought about in the nineteenth century. You can get a sense of how the Cathars were talked about at the time from Schmidt, 1849, vol. ii, pp. 1–173, and on the topic at hand, esp. 87–89.

16. de Rougemont, 1974; to fill out the picture, I'll be folding in material as well from Elias, 2000, vol. 2.

17. For a dated but still useful overview of the tradition, see Chaytor, 1912. Even so, a would-be knight *could* end up literally singing for his supper; after all, if you're a

NOTES 313

houseguest, the least you can do is be entertaining. You can find an illustration in Stendhal, whom we'll take up shortly; he reproduces a twelfth-century Provençal account of "the son of a poor knight of the château Cabstaing... [who] took to fashioning pretty, gay little couplets... and for this he was much admired, not least by the lady for whom he sang" (1975, pp. 169f).

For complaints about the "two cardinal tenets of received literary history, namely the beliefs that the ladies whom the Provençal troubadours loved were the wives of other men, and that they were superior in social rank to the poets," see Paden, 1975. The propagation of the alleged mistake during the eighteenth and nineteenth centuries is, conveniently for us, being documented by those very complaints.

18. For the military and political history, see Wakefield, 1974; the passage I just quoted, at p. 246, is from testimony to the Inquisition regarding the conversation of someone subsequently excommunicated for heresy, with a relative who successfully entrapped him. Pegg, 2008, is a retelling that frames the course of events as a sort of early dress rehearsal for episodes such as the Spanish Inquisition or the Holocaust.

19. You can get a sense of the impression one is left with from descriptions provided by up-to-date historians (up-to-date, that is, in no longer uncritically accepting that the *cansos* concealed suspect theological content): "total submission... places the fate of the troubadour in the hands of a superhuman lady"; "the addressee of [a troubadour love song] is not a real lady but an idealised abstraction, *la domna*... The qualities ascribed to the *domna* are not the individualized traits of an existing person but those superlative virtues which any woman would presumably like to hear attributed to herself"; the *domna* "incarnate[s] or substitute[s]... a total scheme of ideals" (Gaunt and Kay, 1999, pp. 91, 201, 116; in the essays by G. Gourian, D. Monson, and T. Sankovitch, the last adapting a quote from Marianne Shapiro).

20. For pushback, which provides a sense of how the ideas circulated, see Boase, 1977, p. 38; also pp. 21–23, 25, 77–81, 119, and 126. In another volume, in which Nietzsche again assumes the posture of a "psychologist," one of the maxims informs us that "man has created woman... [o]ut of a rib of his god—of his 'ideal' " (6:61/TI 1.13). To reiterate, it's hard to be precise about Nietzsche's image of the troubadours, and in particular, about whether it included the assimilation of Cathar theological descriptive conventions. Nietzsche may well have thought of the objects of troubadours' romantic interest as impossibly idealized, without having that backstory for it.

21. Although we no longer have Nietzsche's copy of De l'Amour, there's sufficient evidence that he read it; for instance, the commentary of Nietzsche, 1988, vol. 14, p. 249, identifies a couple of lines at 3:440/GS 84 as adapted from the book.

22. Stendhal, 1975, at, respectively, pp. 128, 116n1, and 111; the visit to the mine is retold at pp. 284–292. Introducing the concept, he tells us "that by *crystallization* I mean a certain fever of the imagination which translates a normally commonplace object into something unrecognizable" (p. 64n1). Stendhal's extended discussion of twelfth-century "courts of love" can be found at pp. 275–283; as Boase, 1977, pp. 12, 21, notes, his belief that there really had been such courts apparently derived from an undependable source.

314 NOTES

23. 3:424f/GS 60, and compare journal entries that rephrase Stendhal's take on crystallization still more directly, and make it clear that he was responding to it:

> what's called love ... gets the better of reality in such a way that, in the consciousness of the lover, the cause seems obliterated and something else located in its place—a quivering and a sudden gleam of all the magic mirrors of Circe ... (13:299/WLN 14[120])
>
> once the aesthetic drive has started to work, a whole abundance of other perfections, originating elsewhere, crystallise [*krystallisirt sich*] around 'the particular beauty'. It's not possible to remain *objective*, or to uncouple the fabricating force that interprets, supplements and fills out (the force which is itself that concatenation of the affirmations of beauty). The sight of a 'beautiful woman' ... the judgment of beauty ... *heaps* upon the object stimulating it a *magic* conditioned by the association of many different judgements of beauty— but which is *quite alien to the nature of that object.* (12:555/WLN 10[167])

24. 3:421f/GS 57, emph. deleted.
25. Using the term in its older sense, Stendhal calls his treatment an "ideology" of love— "a detailed description of ideas and of all the parts into which those ideas can be analyzed"—i.e., what we understand as a conceptual analysis (1975, 49n1).
26. At pp. 230, emphasis deleted, 175n2, 246, 220.
27. Pp. 35, 209, 63, 208, and here's a sampling of similar passages: "once it was only pleasant things which had the right to please, and the pleasure they gave was no more than momentary; but now all that has any bearing on the woman one loves, even the most irrelevant object, moves one deeply" (102); "in love everything is a *symbol*" (131); "every day brings forth a new blossom" of happiness (51).

One can come away with a very different impression of Stendhal, as when de Beauvoir, 2011, pp. 252f, "return[ing] to Stendhal ... [and] leaving behind ... carnivals where Woman is disguised as shrew, nymph, morning star, or mermaid ... find[s] it reassuring to approach a man who lives among flesh-and-blood women." But we want to distinguish between how Stendhal depicts the characters who populate his novels, and what he recommends as a way of improving one's life.

We should also notice the life lessons he offers in some of his fiction: in *Armance* (which we know Nietzsche read), we find one character cynically telling another that "love ... always implies a certain amount of illusion," and the two of them, he insists, "know each other too well to feel for each other that sort of sentiment"; the speaker has made the bitter and disillusioned rejection of crystallization into the centerpiece of his own self-conception (Stendhal, 1946, p. 163). The novella puts on display the destructive consequences of that way of regarding it; crystallization, we're being shown, is to be embraced, not disdained.

Again, in *The Charterhouse of Parma*, its protagonist falls in love with a young woman he can only see through an aperture in the window of his prison cell, a romance that becomes the center of gravity of the remainder of his life. The narrator comments, "out of what nothings does love not create its happiness!" (Stendhal, 2006, p. 324)—this being a further advantage of crystallization, namely, that one isn't particularly disadvantaged by a paucity of raw materials.

NOTES 315

28. For the background on Mead, see Freeman, 1999.
29. I.e., it's no accident that he wraps up his thoughts about reforming the divorce laws with: "But enough of these fancies" (203). It's not that Stendhal necessarily believed those tall tales about other European countries, or for that matter, took his odd and fortunately brief excursion into what must have been the pornographic register of his time for reporting (269f).

    In his discussion of Stendhal, de Rougemont, 1974, p. 225, describes the view as "pessimistic"; this is evidently a confusion.
30. Nietzsche's uptake of the lesson we just elicited from Stendhal is almost certainly mediated by yet another philosophical and literary appropriation, this time, of Ralph Waldo Emerson, whom you'll find on a (very short) list of people whose writing Nietzsche really admires (3:448/GS 92).

    Emerson has a penchant for stating his epistemological views using sexual metaphors, and we're about to see Nietzsche follow him in that. For instance, when Emerson wants to describe the correct epistemological stance, he tells us that "the universe is the bride of the soul"; "the constructive intellect... is the generation of the mind, the marriage of thought with nature"; "the art of life has a pudency, and will not be exposed" (1971–2013, III:44, II:198, III:40).

    Second, Emerson imports *practical* concerns into his epistemology, and we're about to see Nietzsche follow him in that, also. What matters is what your epistemological stance does *to you*. Is your materialism, your insistence on stripping away the appearances to see the naked truth underneath, turning you into a sleazy patron of strip joints and peep shows? "I see not, if one be once caught in this trap of so-called sciences, any escape for the man from the links of the chain of physical necessity. Given such an embryo, such a history must follow. On this platform, one lives in a sty of sensualism, and would soon come to suicide" (III:32).
31. Pippin, 2010, pp. 42–46; he is relying on Devereux, 2011.
32. 6:59/TI 1.5; for the literary history of the "unveiling of truth," see Hadot, 2006, pp. 234–249, 265–272, 284–299, and there is, just perhaps, an alternative and less prudish construction to put on the shocked reaction we're led to anticipate: Nature had traditionally been depicted (including by Goethe, with whom Nietzsche was familiar) as a female figure possessing multiple breasts.

    As we'll see, the author of that book also describes himself as a "psychologist," and starts off his volume with a series of maxims, in the style of a French moralist. So it's not unreasonable to take this pronouncement to be telling us where a French moralist will end up. If I'm right, the characters we're presented with in *The Gay Science* and *Twilight of the Idols* also differ from one another in important respects, and we need to handle our materials with caution. But they touch many of the same bases. We've already noted that the Stendhalian take on the troubadours is given a nod at 6:61/TI 1.13, and the metaphor from the two prefaces we've just been discussing reappears at 6:61/TI 1.16: "*Among women*: 'Truth? Oh, you don't know truth! Is it not an attempt to assassinate all our *pudeurs*?'" Compare also 3:426/GS 64; I'll return to what distinguishes the authors of *The Gay Science* and *Twilight of the Idols* in ch. 6.

316 NOTES

33. 3:485/GS 130; in Nietzsche's day and age, the old contrast between the supernatural and the natural was still alive, and naturalism meant—was *about*—the rejection of the supernatural. As I've just noted, that behindology was itself adopted as a way of devaluing real life, but nonetheless, it had made life meaningful, and the naturalism of Nietzsche's day, as he understood it, was a way of disposing of the only thing that had made the order of things in the universe look *less* hateful.

34. However, we ought ourselves to complicate Nietzsche's diagnosis. Certainly within analytic philosophy, realism is normally a way of reaffirming some doctrine which the philosopher happens already to hold; it commits what we saw Nietzsche identify in the *Genealogy* as the fallacy of redoubling or reduplication. Just as when you imagine that there are two things, the flash of lightning, and the lightning bolt behind it (but there's just the lightning), so you insist that behind your moral imperative lies a moral fact, or behind your theoretical construct is a *thing* that looks just like it.

    Realism in this key is not generally in the service of disconnecting from the life one is about to surrender. Rather, the tone of voice is typically bluff, hearty, unthinkingly confident; realism for *us* is mostly a way of going on doing and thinking the things one is already thinking and doing. Perhaps, we will want to say, realism of this sort is not a mode of behindology at all.

    As Nietzsche indeed recognized—recall those remarks on abstraction at 3:623f/GS 372—a given doctrine can mean very different things, depending on whose doctrine it is, and why they are sticking to it. That will be true of realism as well.

35. Maudemarie Clark and David Dudrick read the Prefaces we've been discussing as marking Nietzsche's resistance to "naturalistic" accounts of humanity, as we find them in his middle-period writings, and keeping in mind our remarks about naturalism in earlier footnotes, we can now allow that that is right as far as it goes (2012, pp. 114–116). It is, however, also clear that the story Clark formerly told about the evolution of Nietzsche's metaphysical views must be mistaken: that Nietzsche started out identifying truth with correspondence to the things-in-themselves behind the appearances, and that when he dismissed the noumena as a metaphysical mistake, he moved on to a different account of truth, more or less what Hilary Putnam later dubbed "internal realism." When the clothes are removed from the hapless women in those Prefaces, what has gone wrong—and this was taken to be what had gone wrong with metaphysical realism—is quite evidently not that there was no one there under the dress.

36. Lange, 1950, was an influential work in this tradition that we know Nietzsche to have read, and it's available in English; Schopenhauer, who importantly influenced Nietzsche's philosophical development, although he looks to be an exotic sort of Idealist, nonetheless had his own very distinctive account of the noumenal realm, and seems to have thought that the Kantian synthesis of the manifold was a process taking place in the brain, one that was amenable to empirical investigation. A couple of typical remarks: "this perceptible and real world is obviously a phenomenon of the brain . . . time, space, and causality, on which all those real and objective events rest, are themselves nothing more than functions of the brain"; Schopenhauer, 1966,

vol. ii, pp. 5, 8; there are many similar passages, e.g., at pp. 3, 6, 20, 46, 191, 195, 214, 245, 285, 500.

37. For a sketch of the argument pattern, see Anderson, 2001; for an elegant rethinking of that story, in the intellectual idiom of mid-twentieth-century analytic philosophy, see Strawson, 1971, esp. chs. 1–2.

38. Nietzsche was quite aware of the problematic issues faced by this program; you'll remember that we've spelled them out in the appendix to ch. 4.

39. For that account of modality, see Nozick, 2001, pp. 120–155.

40. 3:607/GS 359, and the latter phrase is lifted from 3:582/GS 347. Let me remind you that we shouldn't expect a definitive and univocal rendering of the concept. If I'm right about how Nietzsche's perspectivism is supposed to work, each of the perspectives exhibited in the later works will construe the nihilism differently, as it were from another angle. However, if you'd like to see how it comes out when a commentary treats Nietzsche's concept as something you can have in focus all at once, Creasy, 2020, is in the mainstream of recent work.

41. 3:576/GS 344, and compare 3:581/GS 346, where Nietzsche equates abolishing yourself with one form of nihilism.

42. 3:431f, 558f, 590–593/GS 76, 333, 354.

43. 3:538/GS 299; cf. 3:434/GS 78 on "the art of viewing ourselves as heroes—from a distance and, as it were, simplified and transfigured." But then recall that at 3:563f/GS 335, under the slogan "*Long live physics!*," we're reminded that you can't make intelligent decisions about what person to become unless you know how things really work.

That "I rather think that in themselves they never are" is not just Nietzsche copping an attitude; you'll remember from the previous chapter the hard-to-take drives which Nietzsche found within himself. Having looked behind his own socially and personally respectable presentation, inspected the ugliness close up, and put it out for his readers to see, he is now in a position to swallow hard and give us that assessment. Thus in *Beyond Good and Evil* Nietzsche is disregarding the joint recommendation of the two prefaces—we could call this his *Paradox of the Prefaces*—and we will want to know why.

44. 3:530f/GS 290; however, if you *can't* manage it, there's a different recommendation—a point to which we'll return.

45. 3:573, 574, 579, 612, 613, 616, 622, 623, 626, 627, 628/GS 343, 344, 346, 364, 365, 368, 371, 372, 374, 375, 376, 377 (italics deleted throughout).

46. But as a reminder, and to anticipate a point we'll press in the next chapter, an intellectual doctrine or approach can serve more than one need or type of person; at 3:374/GS 3, we're told how realism sometimes is (not nihilistic but) merely plebian.

47. 3:477/GS 120, but you'll want to keep in mind that the process of "convalescence" and the repackaging of the material to exhibit a convalescing persona are two very different things. The turn to metacynicism starts as early at 3:433f/GS 78, it seems to me, where it is still mixed in with advanced French-moralist debunking (as in 3:439–443/GS 84 and 85). The realism-about-realism is driven by the dialectic of French moralism, as Nietzsche insistently presses it ever deeper; the shift of focus, to

318 NOTES

the person who has lived through that turn, could take place only once it was possible to see it in retrospect—that is, once Nietzsche was able to stand back from the first edition of his book and see what had been happening in it.

48. 3:574–577, 581–586, 588f, 624–627/GS 344, 347–349, 352, 373–374.

49. "I no longer breathe easily once this music begins to affect me...does not my stomach protest, too? my heart? my circulation? my intestines? Do I not become hoarse as I listen?" (3:617/GS 368) "It is our habit to think outdoors—walking, leaping, climbing, dancing..." (3:614/GS 366). And relatedly—there is *some* enacting of the character—we're shown how his mind slides from topic to topic: from his account of actors, which is roughly race-theoretic in the sense of *Beyond Good and Evil*, to women, who are actors (3:608f/GS 361), then from women, to how the sexes or genders differ (3:610–612/GS 363), then to a show of misanthropy—of refined disgust with the men and women he has just been discussing (3:612–614/GS 364f).

50. Commentators find that it's not obvious what Nietzsche's contrast between strength and weakness means, or even if there is anything it can be intelligibly made out to mean; for some back and forth on the question, see Anderson, 2006, Staten, 1990, and for an amusing alternative, Kaufmann, 2017, p. 94. These are the terms in which he tries to understand what is happening to him, or to his authorial character, but here too, it seems to me, we're being offered a promissory note: a value whose content has yet to be put in place.

Notes to Chapter 6

1. I'm not alone in finding it unobvious; for instance, you come across remarks like this: "I am *not* going to be attributing to Nietzsche some sophisticated meta-axiological view. For my part, I am doubtful that he has one" (Huddleston, 2019, p. 128).

   Sometimes it *has* seemed obvious what the proposal amounts to, and then complaints have not been far behind; for some of these cast in a popular register, see Bloom, 2012.

2. And why my squeamishness about the term? See Millgram, 2015a, sec. 6.1.

3. 6:57/TI P, deleting Nietzsche's emphasis. Compare the variant, "*Werte umdrehn*," in his 1886 Preface to *Human, All-Too-Human* (2:17/HTH I.P.3).

4. *Others'* revaluations sometimes come across this way; in *The Antichrist*, composed at about the same time, the "theologians'... *value judgments* have been stood on their heads and the concepts of 'true' and 'false'... reversed: whatever is most harmful to life is called 'true'; whatever elevates it... is called 'false' " (6:176/A 9).

5. Underscoring that point, towards the end of *Twilight*, we see Nietzsche's first book described as "my first revaluation of all values" (6:160/TI 10:5); when we get around to discussing *The Birth of Tragedy*, in ch. 10, we'll see that there also it is not simply older dicta being replaced with newer ones.

6. This initial "upending" doesn't go entirely unargued; we're instructed to watch out for "Cornarism," the error of accepting as a universal panacea a regimen that was recommended because it suited someone else's likely idiosyncratic metabolism

NOTES 319

(6:88f/TI 6.1). But this can't underwrite the explanatory inversion in anything like its full generality; Nietzsche is quite clear elsewhere that, for instance, religious leaders often enough lay down lifestyle dictates of the form he's rejecting, without having themselves experienced the payoffs they are supposed to produce—that is, whether the lifestyle suited them or not.

We're given supporting arguments for other special cases. Religious and moral claims are so obviously literally nonsensical vestiges of cultures that lack a concrete grip on the distinction between real and imaginary that the only thing you can plausibly use them for is cultural analysis (6:98/TI 7.1). Or, perhaps more interestingly, judgments of the value of life cannot ever be taken at face value: a credibly fair such judgment could be produced only by someone who had seen the question from all its different sides—that is, who had been both living and dead, and who had had all or many of the different sorts of lives there are—and no one could be in that position. So once again, the only use to be made of such judgments is diagnostic (6:86/TI 5.5; for discussion of a related passage, construing it as an anthropic argument, see ch. 8).

We'll take up the question of what could motivate the shift to this form of argumentation below, in secs. 6.8, 7.9, and 9.4.

7. For thick ethical concepts, see the first Interlude, note 9.

8. 6:78f/TI 3.6, and while the assessment is not confined to *Twilight*, it's worth noticing how it is differently cast in Nietzsche's various works. See, e.g. the "Attempt at a Self-Criticism," where Nietzsche tells us that "faith in 'another' or 'better' life ... [is] at bottom a craving for the nothing, for the end, for respite, for 'the sabbath of sabbaths' " (1:18/BT A.5)—the emphasis being on a pervasive death wish, rather than rancor directed against the real but unsatisfactory world.

9. And to remind you, this complaint has been repeatedly leveled by Nietzsche's readers; for instance, here's Dannhauser, 1974, p. 208: "Nietzsche is on solid ground when he insists that agreement about a proposition does not establish its truth. But neither does the decadence of a man establish the falsity of the proposition he advances."

10. Considering Nietzschean arguments that apparently share this form elsewhere, Solomon (1994; 1996, at pp. 97–98 and 189–193, respectively), attempts to parry the charge, arguing that by our present lights, we do and should accept properly constructed *ad hominem* arguments. Be that as it may, here they're being endorsed as part of what's announced to be an exemplary upending of values.

11. 6:27/CW 7; the characterization is adapted from the discussion of Baudelaire at Bourget, 1901, p. 20. (I'm grateful to Matt Potolsky for pointing this out to me.) For directions to earlier discussion of the sourcing, see Huddleston, 2019, p. 89n28. "Disgregation" in Nietzsche's German means, as in English, "separation of the molecules of a substance by heat or other agency" (Lueger, 1904); however, the reader should be aware that while the word still belongs to today's chemistry lexicon, its sense has shifted substantially.

12. That is, with a very mainstream conception, today, of unity of agency; see, e.g., Korsgaard, 1996, ch. 13, and compare Nietzsche's complaint, at 6:143/TI 9.41, that "today the individual still has to be made possible by being *pruned*: possible here means *whole*" (restoring Nietzsche's emphasis). The pruning is his recommendation for

320 NOTES

"instincts [that] contradict, disturb, destroy each other," amounting to "physiological self-contradiction"; but recall the objection we've touched on in ch. 4, note 42.

13. 6:133f/TI 9.35; if I'm right that decadence is being fielded as a basic and overarching value concept, renderings like Huddleston's (2019, p. 87), which confine it to the Socratic strategy we'll discuss below, are evidently mistaking an unusual but important special case for a paradigm.

14. If decadence in our vocabulary is, more or less, disunity of agency, will to power should correspondingly amount to (some version of) unity of agency, again, treated in the first place as a central value concept. We'll return to the concept, viewing it however in another perspective, in ch. 8.

15. It does appear at 6:124, 139, 157/TI 9.20, 38; 10.3.

16. Dannhauser, 1974, p. 193.

17. Reminding ourselves again of points of agreement and disagreement with the recent discussion of Nietzsche's work, Pippin, 2006, discussing Nietzsche's appropriation of that tradition, argues that he *was* a French moralist. My own view, you'll recall from the previous chapter, is more nuanced: at one stage of his career, Nietzsche meant to place himself in that tradition, but later on, he developed *characters* who assign themselves to it.

   For the novelists, see such remarks as this: "Dostoyevski, the only psychologist, incidentally, from whom I had something to learn; he ranks among the most beautiful strokes of fortune in my life, even more than my discovery of Stendhal" (6:147/TI 9.45). Notice also that Bourget, 1901, which discusses literary figures such as Baudelaire, Renan, Stendhal, and Flaubert, and which Nietzsche apparently read, titles itself "*Essais de psychologie contemporaine.*"

18. 6:108/TI 8.6. "Involuntary" renders "*unfreiwillig,*" which we saw Nietzsche explain in sec. 6.2, above, and within a few short sentences he cross-references that discussion: "the essential feature [of a strong will] is precisely *not* to will—to *be able* to suspend decision."

19. 6:111ff/TI 9.1; the list of targets is lengthy, including Seneca, Rousseau, Dante, Schiller, Kant, Renan, George Eliot, Emerson, and Carlyle, among others, but gradually the author's attention drifts away from individuals, and towards aesthetics, modern moral sensibilities, and various other topics. The latter stretches of the "Skirmishes" do even out a good deal from its choppy beginning.

   While I think you ought to be somewhat taken aback by the beginning of this part of *Twilight*, it has prompted rather different responses in other readers. For instance, Dannhauser, 1974, p. 230, sees it as "a display of Nietzsche's self [where] the splendor of that self is meant to be a voucher for the validity of what he says." That is, the imperative to look behind the text to its author is being respected, but what is seen there is something quite other than decadence.

20. For that final point, thanks to Kasen Scharmann.

21. Much more, but right now I'll just give a brief sampling. Here is Nietzsche's Psychologist praising Sallust's prose style (6:154/TI 10.1):

   Compact, severe, with as much substance as possible, a cold sarcasm against "beautiful words" and "beautiful sentiments"—here I found myself. And even

NOTES 321

> in my *Zarathustra* one will recognize a very serious ambition for a *Roman* style, for the *aere perennius* in style.

As anyone who has read *Zarathustra* will recall, it's overloaded with beautiful words and sentiments, and is very low density when it comes to substance; "cold sarcasm" is the last thing it manages, or even tries for. To describe *Zarathustra* as aiming for a Roman style, one that is "even more long lasting than bronze," if it is not some sort of a joke, has to be an author speaking impulsively—that is, it is the utterance of someone who is unable to pause and consider whether what he feels himself inclined to say is plausible enough to proceed with. When Nietzsche's Psychologist denounces "that physiological overexcitability which is characteristic of everything decadent" (6:137/TI 9.37), that pronouncment is issued by one of the more overexcited characters you'll ever encounter in your reading.

Or again, here is Nietzsche distributing pieces for his reader to assemble: at 6:117/TI 9.10, we're informed that "the essential feature" of "the Dionysian state" is "the inability *not* to react," and in case the reader had not noticed the elaborate displays of that inability, at almost the very end of the book, its author identifies himself, following on a discussion of the "psychology of the orgiastic," as "the last disciple of the philosopher Dionysus" (6:160/TI 10.5).

Or again, Nietzsche's Psychologist condemns Sainte-Beuve, for his "plebian" "*ressentiment*," as "a genius of *médisance*, inexhaustibly rich in means to that end; no one knows better how to mix praise with poison" (6:112/TI 9.3); you'd think that, in the name of consistency, the author would suppress the impulse to produce that very mixture of fluffing and slander himself. But the passage wraps up by complimenting its target's "fine, well-worn taste," and—to pick just one further instance—within a few pages, following on fulsome but hard to parse praise ("he simply does not know how old he is already and how young he is still going to be"), Nietzsche shifts into Latin to describe Emerson as not only impotent, but complacently so (6:120/TI 9.13).

22. 6:90f/TI 6.3, and you can find draft material working through some of the ideas at 13:274–276/WP 551—not that this lap is likely to convince his readers. Just for instance, John Dewey, who was a careful reader of Mill, Kant, and Nietzsche, remarks:

> Extraordinary and subtle reasons have been assigned for belief in the principle of causation. Labor and the use of tools seem, however, to be a sufficient empirical reason ... They are more adequate grounds for acceptance of belief in causality than are the regular sequences of nature or than a category of reason, or the alleged fact of will. (1958, p. 84)

23. 6:91/TI 6.3; compare 6:77/TI 3.5 on the "crude fetishism" of the ego and will being "projected by thought" onto the surrounding world. ("Ego" is the perhaps unfortunately Freudian rendering of "Ich," that is, the plain and simple "I.") For Nietzsche's complaints about the I and the will, see, e.g., 5:26f, 29–34/BGE 12, 16–19.

24. 6:92–95/TI 6.4–6. Perhaps the most interesting part of this passage is an aside, in which Nietzsche seems to be debunking physicalism, and perhaps naturalism more generally. Recapping his argument, an "explanation" derives something unknown from something familiar; "the first representation that explains the unknown as

322 NOTES

familiar feels so good that one 'considers it true' "; a feedback loop is liable to be created where a particular kind of explanation which is somewhat more familiar (therefore more pleasant) is selected for new phenomena; that makes it still more familiar, until it has become fully habitual. "Consequence: one kind of positing of causes predominates more and more, is concentrated into a system, and finally emerges as *dominant*, that is, as simply precluding other causes and explanations" (6:93/TI 6.5). Nietzsche gestures at Christian views of sin as one of his illustrations, but the obvious target is the position, popular within twentieth-century philosophy, but also in the neo-Kantian school of his own day, that all explanation must be, at bottom, physical. (For the neo-Kantian materialism, see, e.g., Lange, 1950.)

25. For further discussion of the Principle of Charity and its application to Nietzsche, see Interlude 3, below.

26. If decadence is the inability not to respond, how can Socrates—whom Plato, in the *Symposium*, represents as able to turn down Alcibiades' sexual invitation with a deliberate weighing of the considerations at hand—be both hyperrational *and* decadent?

    In Nietzsche's view, decadence is evidently a matter of degree, and I can invoke my own work practices as an analogy. (Apologies if this is more than you want to know.) I regulate myself by using side bets; for instance, this week, if I fail to write twenty pages in my journal, I owe my partner a substantial amount of money. I turn to side bets because I'm weak-willed; if simply deciding to write those twenty pages was enough to make me do it, I wouldn't bother with the commitment device. That is, I am to some degree a disunified agent. However, the effectiveness of a side bet presupposes agency that is at least somewhat unified: if the penalties failed to motivate me, they wouldn't work, and when I tell people about the stratagem, they frequently enough respond by asking me, "Then why don't you just lie?" (I'm *enough* of a unified agent so that I don't.)

    That is, we have to construe Nietzsche's Socrates as *enough* of a unified agent for his arguments to move him, but not enough so that he can dispense with those arguments.

27. For a turn in this direction, in our own philosophical tradition, see Stich, 1990.

28. The value isn't being invented out of whole cloth; it has differently valenced antecedents in, for instance, Baudelaire. But to remind the reader once again, while inventions are never creations *ex nihilo*, that doesn't entail that they're reducible to their predecessors. In a few moments I'll help myself to Steve Jobs's iPod, as my example of invention, and so let me jump the gun now. It was a device which assembled many already available components: hard drives, already developed file systems, digitized music, and much else. But the iPod was nonetheless an innovation, and likewise, a value that assembles and incorporates older evaluative materials can be more than a mere redeployment of those already-available values.

29. If we were reading Nietzsche's Convalescent correctly, there was no such prosthesis in play; that character—Nietzsche's other French moralist character—had just *given up*. That his Psychologist turns to this device is as much as to say that *he* hasn't given up.

30. E.g., Swanton, 1998, Solomon and Higgins, 2000, ch. 6, or Welshon, 1992.

NOTES 323

31. For this way of putting it, see Millgram, 1998.
32. The objection to virtue ethics has become familiar once again, although the underlying picture and the reasons given for it today are different; see Doris, 2002.
33. This very chapter, in asking the question of its title, does as its putative author insists. Is its own argument *ad hominem*, and has it committed what is supposed to be the characteristic fallacy of such argumentation in the course of developing it?
34. The example is somewhat in the spirit of 6:131/TI 9.33: "Self-interest is worth as much as the [physiological worth of the] person who has it: it can be worth a great deal, and it can be unworthy and contemptible."
35. And for much the same point made with regard to cruelty, see 12:74/WLN 2[15].

Notes to the Third Interlude

1. Kaufmann, 1980, p. 58, Goethe, 1981, vol. 3, p. 52.

Notes to Chapter 7

1. E.g., at Nietzsche, 1954, p. 565; cf. Corngold, 2019, p. 633n18. Nietzsche's other authorial characters do occasionally describe themselves as "Antichristians" (e.g., at 6:84/TI 5:3).
2. 6:191f/A 24; "clunky," because of course there was more to the shift in values than that; just as a for-instance, the "bad" weren't supposed to be in the business of reforming themselves, but the "evil" were, and the *Genealogy* sketches additional structural differences in the psychologies of the people governed by the value systems.
3. 6:176, 250/A 9, 61, deleting Nietzsche's emphasis in the former quotation.
4. Why the temporal restriction? On the one hand, we've started to see new types of metaethical view—in particular, constructivism and constitutivism—that don't fully fit the characterization I am about to give, and that in some ways take steps in the direction of Nietzsche's much more radical position. On the other, the two branches of the debate that I'm about to describe began to converge towards the end of the twentieth century: each camp attempted to accommodate the points made by their opponents inside ever-more-contoured theoretical constructions. (And so the two camps recapitulated the history of the consequentialism-deontology debates earlier in the century; that is, they ended up with, as Adrian Piper put it in that connection, "a distinction without a difference.")

I'm going to shortly be invoking the Nietzschean evaluative turn we were discussing in the previous chapter, from the view back to the person who has and needs it. And so for our purposes, what matters is that the kind of person—or so it seems to me—who devotes himself to reconstructing the theater of moral realism using the intellectual toolkit of noncognitivism (or the other way around) is driven by rather different underlying needs than, say, Moore or Ayer or Stevenson. That newly prominent personality type deserves its own treatment, which I'll defer to a further occasion.

324   NOTES

And why am I confining the comparisons to our own tradition? For one thing, I'm not sure how to locate mid-century French existentialism, as we find it for example in de Beauvoir, 2018, on this map.

There's an emerging literature that attempts to place Nietzsche within the theoretical option space of contemporary metaethics; scholars disagree as to whether he was a moral realist, a relativist, an error theorist, a constitutivist, and so on, paging through what they take to be the available options. (See Hussain, 2013, for a recent overview.) Now, it's not as though we lack passages to marshall on behalf of one or another identification; just for instance, Nietzsche tells us of "an insight which [he] was the first to formulate: that *there are altogether no moral facts*" (6:98/TI 7:1). But let's pause to ask what Nietzsche's own response to this activity of classification would be.

To remind ourselves of a passage from *The Gay Science* which we had occasion to examine in sec. 4.3, in what's intended as a rebuttal of Kant, Nietzsche remarks:

> When the sons of clerks and office workers of every kind, whose main task it has always been to bring order into diverse materials, and in general to schematize things, become scholars, they manifest a tendency to consider a problem almost as solved when they have merely schematized it ... for them the formal aspect of their fathers' occupation has become content.
>
> (3:584/GS 348)

Given the fairly elaborate map of what are taken to be all the possible positions in logical space that a metaethicist could occupy, we have a cadre of historians who take it that their task is to assign Nietzsche to one of those slots in the diagram. And presumably Nietzsche thinks that it suffices to observe that this shows them to have inherited from their no doubt undistinguished parentage the souls of filing clerks.

Leave aside the worry that we don't learn much of philosophical interest by deciding that a dead philosopher has some position that's familiar and that we already understand. Surely any such exercise ought to accommodate Nietzsche's own very personal, very in-your-face take on exercises of this kind; a historian has to make room, in the view he ascribes to Nietzsche, for Nietzsche's thinking that *this* sort of response is on point, and as far as I can see, none of the positions on the standard metaethical menu do that.

5. Looking closer, you might not find that obvious, because throughout the twentieth century, metaphysics took on many different guises. For instance, the logical positivists insisted that they weren't in the business of metaphysics at all—what in retrospect clearly was metaphysics being presented as philosophy of language. Over the following decades, the moves were couched as moral psychology and epistemology, among other things. But recall the logical positivists' own view, that there are assertions that can be advanced in different "modes"; for instance, if you say that numbers exist, that's in the "material mode," but you could also say that our language contains terms for numbers, and that would be in the "formal mode"; either way, they thought, you'd be saying the same thing. In rather that manner, metaphysical claims about values are often advanced in a psychological mode (they

present as claims in philosophy of mind), or as semantics (so, much like the positivists' formal mode), or in an epistemological mode ... but like the assertions the positivists were considering, they're interconvertible, and despite surface differences, say the same things. (For an illustration, see Millgram, 2005a, pp. 47f.) So I'm sure the characterization of metaethics as the metaphysics of ethics will get protests, but I think it's fair nonetheless.

6. For a representative in-period sampling, see Sayre-McCord, 1988. Of course, the fine grain of the dialectic of twentieth-century metaethics is complicated. A case in point might be Hare, 1961, one of the classics of that literature, and a canonical member of the noncognitivist camp, where it is however unclear that Hare's prescriptivism, which makes moral judgments out to be concealed commands, requires you to defer to something or someone else: some of the commands, Hare thinks, you give yourself, and as for the others, who's to say where they come from, and how you're to respond to them? But for present purposes, that very rough rendering of the field suffices, in which, as Nietzsche put it in another connection, *"was nimmt ab? Der Wille zur Selbstverantwortlichkeit"* (13:66/WLN 11[142], emph. deleted).

7. A tip of the hat to MacIntyre, 1981, ch. 2; this observation follows the lead of his discussion of emotivism.

8. And, once again, within metaethics, I think turn-of-the-millennium constructivists, expressivists, and so on may well take a different diagnosis: the field, and the people who occupy it, have to some extent moved on.

9. For background, see Katz, 1980. Harrison, 2020, distinguishes social from political antisemitism: the former is a matter of antipathy towards Jews, stereotyping them, and treating them with contempt as one's social inferiors, whereas the latter is centrally the fantastic belief that "the Jews" are a demonically effective conspiracy that secretly runs the world to the disadvantage of its gentiles. We'll see both aspects of the phenomenon in play in Nietzsche's production.

10. Dühring's book has been rendered into English by a translator who is unfortunately an enthusiast (1997); while I'm unable to vouch for its respectability, academic or otherwise, it can supply a sense to those who don't read German of what this sort of writing was like. de Lagarde, 1878, was influential enough to have gotten, post-World War II, some concerned historical attention; see Lougee, 1962, and Sieg, 2013. Reminding us of the prominent role of academics in the crystallization of the ideology as we see it still, the subtitle of the latter work is "Paul de Lagarde and the Origins of Modern Antisemitism."

11. And recall that the two of them actually moved to Paraguay to found a racially pure Aryan colony; see Interlude 2, above (p. 109). Nietzsche's brother-in-law, Bernhard Förster, had "gained a certain amount of notoriety by being involved ... in a disturbance on a tramcar in which a Jewish businessman was beaten up" (Pulzer, 1964, pp. 94f); he gifted Nietzsche copies of his books, but they apparently were never opened.

12. Bauer, 1958, and 6:317/EH III.UM.2 describes "the old Hegelian, Bruno Bauer," as "one of my most attentive readers"; Janz, 1981, vol. ii, pp. 104, 567; Katz, 1980, pp. 164–170, 214–218.

326 NOTES

13. It is, however, not the only genre Nietzsche is drawing upon: the insistence on contrasting Christianity unfavorably with some Eastern religion, on the flaws of Christianity having been inherited from Judaism, and on recovering the historical Jesus hidden from us by Christian tradition were all standard Enlightenment themes. That last was also a staple of the Higher Criticism, which was contemporaneous with Nietzsche and, as we've already seen in ch. 3, being put to use in *The Antichrist*. In the interest of keeping our discussion as focused as possible, I am going to for the most part set these other elements of the work to one side here.

14. Recall our discussion of what the central assumptions are from ch. 4. But against the whitewashing reflex that seems so often responsible for professional scholars' initial responses, compare, taking passages almost at random, the following notes from Nietzsche's *Nachlass*:

> The *profound contempt* with which the Christian was treated in the noble areas of classical antiquity is of a kind with the present instinctive aversion to Jews: it is the hatred of the free and self-respecting orders for those *who are pushing* and combine timid and awkward gestures with an absurd opinion of their worth. (12:511/WP 186, restoring Nietzsche's emphases)
>
> People of the basest origin, in part rabble, outcasts not only from good but also from respectable society, raised away from even the *smell* of culture, without discipline, without knowledge, without the remotest suspicion that there is such a thing as conscience in spiritual matters; simply—Jews . . .
> (12:360/WP 199)

These are not-unrepresentative journal entries, thus, raw material rather than carefully shaped, ready-to-ship finished product. (*The Will to Power*, you'll recall, is a selection from his journals assembled by Nietzsche's sister.) If we see those displays of the quasi-antisemitic drive in *The Antichrist*, Nietzsche is no doubt able to produce them so fluently because it is easy for him to muster up what he experiences as the antisemitic drive within himself.

15. "Tend": there are exceptions, for instance, Brewer, 2009. And "most of them": desires can be specified as having objects that can't be fully attained, e.g., a desire always to be swimming.

16. For the foregoing, see especially Katsafanas, 2013b; the view is further developed in Katsafanas, 2016.

17. See especially Anderson, 2012, Anderson, 2006.

18. The illustration, along with some of the vocabulary, is borrowed from Richardson, 1996, p. 47, and *passim*.

19. We're gradually seeing why, but for right now, here's a motivating train of thought, one that fits the mainstream reading of drives fairly well. Decadence is, again to a first approximation, disunified agency. (One way it's *just* a first approximation: in *The Antichrist*, Jesus is described as a decadent, and is presented as a limiting case of failed agency, someone who no longer tries to do anything at all.) Disunified agency is paradigmatically exhibited when an agent initiates and tries to follow through on mutually frustrating courses of action. While Nietzsche sometimes seems to think that a traditional culture can populate personalities with independent but

smoothly coordinated drives, in societies in flux, such as our own, drives that operate independently of one another will be prone to produce just that sort of paradigmatic disunity of agency. However, if one of a person's drives is able to assimilate or to override the others, won't those self-undermining courses of action be preempted?

20. We can already anticipate that this will mirror antisemitic activity; when antisemitism gives rises to action as opposed to speech, "sometimes," as Pulzer observes, "the destruction is quite vicarious and borders on fetishism, such as the destruction of Jewish cemeteries" (1964, p. 64n).

21. 6:239/AC 56, and the Antichrist reiterates the point two sections later: "Indeed, it makes a difference to what end one lies" (6:245/AC 58). The conversational implicature is that the author is in the course of lying to you, the reader, but that *his* lies are justified, and as though to emphasize this point, the intervening section contains Nietzsche's variation on Plato's "noble lie," one endorsing a three-layer caste system very similar to that of the *Republic*.

22. The Persian monarch Xerxes appears as Ahasuerus in *Esther*; for step-by-step contextualization of the narrative, see Millgram, 2008, Part II. Nirenberg, 2014, documents the transformations of antisemitism, starting with Alexander's successor-states, and through the Christian and Islamic traditions. Nirenberg is giving a history of ideas, in which each successive adaptation and readoption of antisemitic memes is to be accounted for via the tactical—thus, the rational—considerations motivating each successive historical actor. Thus, by Nietzsche's lights, he is missing the spontaneous, arational, and expressive character of drives, a topic we'll return to in sec. 7.9. (Relatedly and more abstractly, by those lights, Nirenberg is assuming a form of reductionism, of the activity of a drive to a different explanatory basis; Nietzsche did find reductionism about drives plausible anyway early on; cf. 8:406/WEN 23[9], 1876–1877.) However, he does, again by Nietzsche's lights, get this right about how drives operate: Nirenberg insists that antisemitic ideation has very little to do with Jews themselves, and is rather to be explained as something which, e.g., Christians at particular times and places found it convenient to take on. Returning to the most usual example of a drive in our own philosophical environment, appetite is not explained in the first place by what is placed in front of one, but by how hungry one is.

23. The other wing's variation on Holocaust denial is discussed by Yakira, 2006, Essays 1 and 2. Although some quite influential radicals on the left have thrown themselves under the train insisting that Jews weren't actually being exterminated at Auschwitz, the focus of this sort of discourse on the progressive left is the insistence that the Holocaust is no more than an excuse used to legitimize the much greater horrors allegedly committed by the state of Israel. So here the characteristic incoherent combination of ideas is that the Holocaust wasn't so bad—it's often suggested that, as far as genocides go, it was nothing special—*and* that, horror of horrors, the Israelis are perpetrating a second Holocaust.

24. E.g., Heyen, 1983, pp. 108f, compare the facing pages; and there are similarly oxymoronic thoughts on display throughout: Jews are "plutokratisch-bolschewistischen," and in 1941, at the height of waging the war that Hitler had begun, the Jews were the warmongers (e.g., pp. 91, 94).

328 NOTES

25. See, e.g., Katz, 1980, pp. 161, 163, 215f; Pulzer, 1964, p. 51; Nirenberg, 2014, p. 342, although in this case, the opposing characterizations were largely adopted by political opponents; Netanyahu, 2001. And notice that the pattern of incoherences doesn't seem to run out: the drive seems to generate ever more of them. During World War II, the leader of the Christian Front in Boston argued "that Jews were both trying to rope America into war in their own defense and to ensure that America was too enervated to fight" (Gallagher, 2021, p. 167); in the US today, Jews are told (by, respectively, voices on the left and on the right, but at the same time) that they're white, and need to check their privilege, and also that they're the bane and enemy of the white race, so, definitely not white—and one could extend this list indefinitely. Indeed, a recent linguistic analysis of antisemitic hate mail sent to Israeli and Jewish institutions, primarily in Germany, found it necessary to devote a section to "Contradictions and Paradoxes," which they found to pervade their corpus of some 14,000 missives (Schwarz-Friesel and Reinharz, 2017).

26. Other observers of the phenomenon have noticed this aspect of it as well. Harrison, 2020, pp. 23, 26, 241f, observes that the claims at the center of antisemitic conspiracy theories are "deluded [not just] in the sense that [one] believes something that might have been true but happens not to be true . . . [rather, one] believes something that could not possibly be the case"; he concludes: "Such claims deal in dreamwork." The observation is not all that distant from Nietzsche's way of thinking; when Kaufmann takes up a remark in *Daybreak*, to the effect that "between waking and dreaming there is no *essential* difference" (3:113/D 119), he glosses it, not implausibly, as meaning that "our experiences are fictions not different in principle from our dreams" (2017, pp. 56f, his translation).

27. Lang, 2003, pp. 39f, 202n40, takes the policy to show that, of the competing priorities, the destruction of the Jews was more important than victory—presupposing a coherent preference ordering. However, he almost immediately proceeds to catalog ways in which "the history of anti-Semitism has been . . . gripped by inconsistency . . . Jews were excoriated becuse they were clannish and refused to assimilate, but also as cosmopolitans; because they were wealthy and powerful, but also as dependent and parasitic; because they represented a weightless modernity, but also because they were committed to an obdurate past." Once it is allowed that "the contradictions are not the result of thoughtlessness but are themselves expressive . . . implying knowledge and an impulse to act that must be concealed from others but from oneself as well," why assume that views about what is a cause for or means to what else must be themselves coherent?

28. See, e.g., Katz, 1980, pp. 205, 212, 225f, 303; Hertzberg, 1968, pp. 73, 314, 358, observes: "Two antithetical positions . . . arose . . . often held by the same thinker": Jews were to be shifted to new economic roles, but had to be prohibited from occupying new economic roles; Jews would be endangered by being given civic equality, and if given civic equality, would end up "own[ing] the whole province and the people would be miserable."

29. "Elsewhere": in ch. 4, for instance, we saw him putting on display misogynist and German nationalist drives, each of them forcing themselves on the reader's attention

NOTES 329

by their way of talking. But neither drive seemed oriented toward objectives or, for that matter, to be seriously considering the means of achieving anything in particular.

30. Davidson, 2004, chs. 2–4.

31. The received view of Nietzschean drives sees him to be taking over Schopenhauer's conception of them, and so here's a reminder that we'd want to have second thoughts about that: "I regret now [Nietzsche is looking back on his first book] . . . that . . . I tried laboriously to express by means of Schopenhauerian and Kantian formulas strange and new valuations which were basically at odds with Kant's and Schopenhauer's spirit and taste!" (1:19/BT A:6)

32. For discussion of such platforms, and the philosophical lessons to be drawn from them, see Millgram, 2005a, ch. 8.

33. Perhaps Pulzer's (1964, p. 58) characterization of the object of antisemitism could be adapted here: "tribal purification through a perpetual cathartic riot of intolerance."

34. Sartre, 1995, whose treatment is as far as I can tell not directly influenced by Nietzsche's, categorizes antisemitism as a passion—or rather, "at one and the same time a passion and a conception of the world" (17), rather than simply a collection of political opinions, and similarly observes that the apparently theoretical and factual claims the antisemite makes are products of the passion, not its justification. So this is a good place to mark a difference between Sartre's and Nietzsche's takes on the phenomenon.

Sartre accounts for antisemitism as satisfying deep-seated psychological needs: for instance, the need to feel superior to others at the same time that one opts for thoroughgoing mediocrity (28); the need to feel that one is an agent of a systematically ordered social world, which licenses one's actions, even as one lapses into anarchic and uncontrolled activities (31f); access to a "fireside of social warmth and energy" (51); the need to avoid thinking about what the good would be, and what it would take to achieve it (44f). That is, like Nirenberg (see note 22, above), antisemitism is accounted for as a strategic or tactical choice. But from the point of view of drive theory, to take drives to be strategically motivated is to be unable to let go of the model of rationality that Nietzsche is trying to displace; it is too easy for what the *Genealogy* called "men of knowledge" to be so committed to rationality that, for them, even irrationality has to come with reasons.

Drives induce needs, and are not adopted to serve them—with a delicate qualification. As we see in the *Genealogy*, values can be invented and adopted strategically; for instance, out of the need to feel superior to one's oppressors, one can adopt Christian values. And those values can catalyze new drives, for instance, a drive to self-abasement. But the path to the new drive is indirect; if someone needs motivation to do his work, he cannot, just by deciding on it for tactical reasons, come to have a passion for excellence, and the people who say they do are mostly just pretending during a job interview. The pattern here is familiar from discussions of belief: just as you can't choose to believe something at will, but you can take steps to make yourself believe something by, say, reading up on it, so you can't choose to have a drive and thereby have it, but you *can*, perhaps, work on sculpting a value that might induce a drive within you. And generally, drives are a justificatory bottom line;

330 NOTES

you can give historical and sometimes biological explanations for their presence, but it's a mistake to look for their *justifications*.

35. The point is closely related to one we find in MacKinnon, 2005, p. 321f, although her discussion is shaped by the goal of finding a legal category that will serve to prohibit pornography.

36. However, he sometimes seems to think of those who produce them as on a par with wind-up toys; see 5:20/BGE 6.

37. Does this capture the full extent of the use that Nietzsche thought we should make of *ad hominem* argumentation? To see why we've only taken a first step, consider Paul de Man, who along with Jacques Derrida briefly turned deconstruction into an orthodoxy in literary studies and a byword in the culture at large. In her biography, Barish, 2014, makes him out to be a sort of high-class intellectually oriented grifter: someone who not only concealed his collaborationist past, but had been sentenced to prison for fraud; someone who never paid rent, who pretended he had finished college, who committed bigamy—in short, someone who got away with things.

Now, the ideas for which he became famous included the insistence that biographical narratives can't be trusted; and that there are deep tensions between what texts say and what they do. If we turn to his treatment of Nietzsche in particular (de Man, 1979, chs. 4–6), we find the reiterated insistence that, whenever you examine a linguistic production closely enough, it will point out, or point you to, the way that some rhetorical device is illegitimate, while it uses and depends on that very rhetorical device. For instance, it's held to be "characteristic for all deconstructive discourse [that] the deconstruction states the fallacy of reference in a necessarily referential mode" (p. 125). Certainly there are texts of which this is a fair description—the *Tractatus* comes to mind—but de Man repeatedly slides from purporting to identify these moments in particular writings to insinuating that they must be there in all of them.

Indeed, his reading of a passage in the *Nachlass* is something of a model for his own procedure. In 12:389–391/WP 516, Nietzsche is experimenting with treating Aristotle's Principle of Non-Contradiction as a rule governing Kantian synthesis. The consequence de Man gestures at is that the consistency isn't there in whatever you're thinking about (since you added it in later, yourself); but of course an argument—or just a theoretical position—only makes sense if it's consistent: that is, if *it* is consistent. And of course that goes for de Man's own position and his arguments for it. Though we notice de Man analogously adopting deconstruction as *his* rule, governing the synthesis of the understanding of a text: in a startling reversal of Aristotle, it must be made out to be a pragmatic contradiction, and so, necessarily, all interpretations show texts to undercut what they say by what it is they do—and vice-versa.

Putting the ideas side by side with the person, it's easy to find yourself saying: of course, these are the sort of views someone like this *would* have. It's not simply that the mode of living is mirrored in the theoretical position; there is a longing for, as de Man evocatively puts it, "the feeling of liberation and weightlessness that characterizes the man freed from the constraints of referential truth" (1979, p. 114). And de Man himself got through life—again, if we can believe Barish—by having other people assume him consistent: his consistency was an artificial imposition,

NOTES   331

introduced in the course of other people's syntheses of their representations of Paul de Man.

Now, Nietzsche often enough seems to look at people and their intellectual commitments in the manner of this capsule diagnosis of de Man's views: the view is explained by its emotional convenience, via the "*backward inference*...from [the] way of thinking and valuing to the commanding *need* behind it" (3:621/GS 370, restoring Nietzsche's emphasis). But that isn't the same thing as looking to the source of the worthless emissions of a drive; de Man's writing seems to be remarkably clean in this regard.

38. 6:27/CW 7; and why not obviously equivalent? Take *The Antichrist*, where an organism is said to be decadent when it "chooses [which implies that it is capable of choice]...what is disadvantageous for it" (6:172/AC 6); we've also seen that Jesus, who is said to scarcely choose anything at all, is framed as the most extreme possible form of decadence.

39. If you're interested in filling out that picture see, in addition to the references in ch. 1, note 7, Binion, 1968, and Nin, 1994.

Notes to Chapter 8

1. Under the first and second headings, Christine Korsgaard has assembled an ambitious argument to the effect that being a unified agent means being a Kantian practical reasoner, with pieces of the argument distributed throughout Korsgaard, 2008, and Korsgaard, 2009. Frankfurt, 1988, develops a well-known version of the third move, and Bratman, 2007, works up similarly motivated analyses of full-fledged action attribution and of self-government.

2. So the "anthropic" part of the label is meant to highlight structural similarities to the anthropic arguments deployed in cosmology and elsewhere. See Smart, 1987, Barrow and Tipler, 1986, pp. 18, 251ff, and Millgram, 2009a, sec. 4.5, for examples; for framing discussion, see Roush, 2003.

3. Etymologically, the word is derived from a special case of such monitoring: verification by duplicate register (Onions et al., 1966). Clark and Dudrick, 2009, notice that what I'm calling control isn't just a matter of what *does* happen, but in part of what is *supposed* to happen: in an older vocabulary, that the notion straddles the distinction between descriptive and prescriptive.

4. Richardson, 2004, pp. 18ff and esp. n. 26, lists relevant passages.

5. Here I'm disagreeing with Richardson, 2004, as to what's at the bottom of Nietzsche's views.

6. But see ch. 9, note 36 for second thoughts.

7. See, e.g., Anderson, 1994, pp. 729f: "the will to power appears to be incompatible with perspectivism... [which] claims that every view is only a view, that all our theories are partial and provisional... To all appearances, the will to power is a claim about the unique underlying essence of the world."

332 NOTES

8. 11:611/WP 1067; of course, the program of maintaining and extending the pattern of control that constitutes oneself does not actually amount to a guiding aim or a directive unless one can also tell what would count as a continuation or extension of the relevant pattern of control. So there must be additional content to the conception of will to power that guides an organization. We've had one such conception in the background of our discussion, which can give us a sense of what these patterns might come to in practice: the view attributed to Nietzsche by Nehamas (1985, 1988), on which a self is roughly the protagonist in a narrative, archetypally, the central character of a nineteenth-century novel. To maintain a self of this sort is to stay in character, that is, to act (but not just to act, because not everything that constitutes a character is an action) in a way that is consistent with one's character. Notice that staying in character doesn't necessarily mean taking the character for granted, as opposed to exploring it, deepening it, and bringing out hitherto unexpected aspects of it; thus this notion of *same pattern* has some flexibility to it, which for this application is a desideratum.

9. The point gives us a low-key explanation for what might seem like an implausible Nietzschean doctrine, that a thing is the "sum of its effects" (13:275/WP 551). It's implausible if it's construed (with Nehamas, 1985, ch. 3) as committing Nietzsche to a modally flat understanding of our world; when we can't distinguish, roughly, essential from accidental properties, we lose the wherewithal to talk about change, and that's an intellectual competence that neither we nor Nietzsche are equipped to bypass. However, the imposition or construction of a perspective is in large part a matter of what one pays attention to, and what one ignores. Control exhibits itself in effects, and so if you're interested solely in control, when you think about an object, you're thinking pretty much solely about achieving effects. So if you're occupying the privileged will to power perspective, any feature of an object that isn't exhausted by its effects is cognitively irrelevant to you, and can be ignored. To revert to our ongoing example: perhaps there are features of scholarship—exquisiteness of treatment, say— that don't make a difference to measures of academic productivity (such as rates of publication, or citation indexes), that don't affect the national ranking of the author's department, that don't make a difference to enrollments, and so on—i.e., features that have, as far as an administrator is concerned, no effects. Then a dean doesn't need to concern himself with such features as exquisiteness of treatment, and in fact he would be better off simply disregarding them.

10. One concern we raised in ch. 4 was that we have only one notation, as it were, in which to describe a psychology. Peter Strawson once argued that the notion of a disembodied soul was parasitic on the notion of an embodied soul (1971, pp. 115f); if we're confined to that notation, we may likewise be able to identify decadents only by understanding them as continuations of (or more generally deviations from) priority-guided homeostatic patterns of control—hence the concessive "no longer."

11. The phrase is of course an allusion to John 19:5. Although I'm not the only reader to classify the book this way (e.g., Pippin, 2006, p. 37), I've found that the genre doesn't always strike readers as obvious; recall, however, that he starts it off by announcing: "and so I tell my life to myself" (6:263).

NOTES 333

12. 6:266/EH 1.2. A quick sampling of the flurry: In the course of discussing his early essay, "Richard Wagner in Bayreuth," he tells us that "in all psychologically decisive places I alone am discussed—and one need not hesitate to put down my name or the word 'Zarathustra' where the text has the word 'Wagner'" (6:314/EH 3.BT.4; for discussion, see Liébert, 2004, pp. 95–100). In that essay we're given the picture of a character who vividly conforms to the will-to-power characterization we've already seen, and are introduced to "the *ruling idea* of [Wagner's] life—the idea that an incomparable amount of influence, the greatest influence of all in the arts, could be exercised through the theatre." We're also given his response to it: "Influence, incomparable influence—how? over whom?—that was from now on the question and quest that ceaselessly occupied his head and heart. He wanted to conquer and rule as no artist had done before" (1:472/UM 4.8). Elsewhere he takes Wagner to task for being, precisely, a decadent, and admits to his reader at the outset that he is "no less than Wagner, a child of this time; that is, a decadent" (6:11/CW P).

13. As before, I've deleted the paragraph breaks, adjusted the punctuation, and restored emphases to better match the German. I've allowed Kaufmann's rendering of "Weiblein" and "Weib" as "woman," although that doesn't capture the derogatory sound of the choice of words. However, I've adjusted his translation of "Gymnasial-Bildung" to "high-school education"; a *Gymnasium* is an academically oriented high school.

14. Compare Nietzsche on the strength to discard (6:267/EH 1.2)—a strength he claims while taking pains to exhibit his inability to do so.

15. Anderson, 2009, distinguishes two modes of interpretation that might be deployed in the service of Nietzsche's famous demand, that one will one's life, and the world as a whole, eternally to recur. On the Compensation Model, you judge that your life is worth reliving, on balance, because the good parts outweigh the bad parts. On the Transfiguration Model, the bad parts are "transfigured" by your reinterpretation of them, and you judge that your life is worth reliving because each part of it is worth reliving—as when you come to see an excruciatingly embarrassing experience as, in retrospect, hysterically funny. (The example is due to Joseph Jarone.) Anderson argues for attributing the Transfiguration Model to Nietzsche.

When can these models be expected to *work*? Who can decide to live with an ugly, painful, humiliating experience now, in order to have a pleasant or beautiful or sidesplitting experience later? The Compensation Model evidently requires a unified agent, someone who can command his psychic parts to take the hit, and take it because he says so: the drive sentenced to the painful experience (perhaps by being prevented from producing its characteristic mode of activity) is going to have to cooperate. And who can contemplate painful past experiences without being derailed by the responses of the drives that found them most frustrating? Once again, it's the unified will-to-power agent that is able to suppress the unruly drive's reaction to unpleasant memories. Decadent agents, however, must have recourse to the Transfiguration Model: when they decide to go ahead with ugly, painful experiences, those experiences must be rewarding for the drives that undergo them, at the time they undergo them, because if the drive isn't on board, it won't chip

334 NOTES

in, and the agent as a whole can't *make* the drive cooperate. And because decadent agents can't suppress a drive's reaction to what for the drive counts as past frustration, transfiguration is the only way for such an agent to avoid *ressentiment*.

16. As a Kantian moral philosopher who hopes to use the inescapability of agency as an anchor for the moral duties, I imagine that Korsgaard counts it as auspicious that "plight" and "Pflicht" are etymological relatives, and here are a few remarks that display the tenor of her view. She reminds us of "the things we say to people when it is time for them to stop dithering and bring deliberation to an end: *Make up your mind*, or even better, *Pull yourself together.*" Characterizing failure to constitute oneself: "If you have a particularistic will, you are not one person, but a series, a *mere heap*, of unrelated impulses." Motivating the specifically Kantian turn to principle: "a formal principle for balancing our various ends and reasons must be a principle for unifying our agency, since that is so exactly why we need it: so that we are not always tripping over ourselves when we pursue our various projects, so that our agency is not incoherent" (Korsgaard, 2009, pp. 58, 76, 126).

17. Korsgaard's argument is anchored by the claim that there are no alternatives to unified agency, and there has been some back and forth as to whether she's in a position to rule putative alternatives out (Millgram, 2005b, Enoch, 2006, Ferrero, 2009, and Tubert, 2010). We can speak to this debate, since Nietzsche, as he presents himself, is all-too-obviously such an alternative. However, in fairness to Korsgaard, the participants too often misconstrue her point as turning on the metaphysics of agency, and as bottoming out in a series of interlocking definitions. (Quickly: only agents act; so if you're deciding what to do, you're an agent; so anything that is true of agents must be true of someone who is making a choice.) The objections to her view are right about this much: a series of interlocking definitions, purporting to show that you have no alternative to acting—because nothing you *choose* will *count* as an alternative to action—don't give anyone a reason not to live like a slacker. But the discussion is misunderstanding Korsgaard's position, which sees the necessity that sustains an agential constitution as practical rather than metaphysical.

The apparently entailed regress—every instance of agency is reconstituted from a prior instance of agency—means that Korsgaard owes an account of how agency originates, which will presumably be a story about bootstrapping. For preliminary groundclearing by a former student, see Schapiro, 1999. For a critical reconstruction of Korsgaard's argument that your commitment to your agency is not contingent, see Millgram, 2011.

18. His best-known composition is the *Hymn to Life*; for its early publication history, see Schaberg, 1995, pp. 140–149. The books are of course *The Case of Wagner*, *Nietzsche Contra Wagner* (which consists of selections from previous works), *Richard Wagner in Bayreuth* (now usually folded into the *Untimely Meditations*, but originally printed as a separate volume), and the *Birth of Tragedy*, whose 1872 title continues: *Out of the Spirit of Music*. His doctrine of the Eternal Return clearly has a musical model; Nietzsche sums it up with a "*da capo*," i.e., with a bit of musical notation. For general discussion, see Liébert, 2004; see also Perrakis, 2011.

NOTES 335

19. See, e.g., the story of Midas and Silenus at 1:35/BT 3, and the remarks about "metaphysical comfort" at 1:56/BT 7.

20. We can find Nietzsche expressing related views elsewhere also; he says, for instance, of the opposing demands of sensuality and chastity that "it is precisely such 'contradictions' that seduce one to existence" (5:341/GM 3.2 [= NCW 7.2]).

Perrakis, 2011, pp. 53, 143, takes the intended dissonance to have to do with the clash between Dionysian and Apollonian artistic sensibilities, which seems to me to be a reach; but he does go on to attribute to Nietzsche a view that has points of contact with ideas I'll take up in ch. 11: that insofar as man is dissonance incarnate, the human animal is infinitely interpretable.

21. Since drives can have, as far as I can see, arbitrary foci, the decadent's will to power might be the focus of one of numerous drives—in the terminology drawn from Katsafanas, 2013b, its aim. Indeed, John Dewey argued that this does sometimes happen, attempted to characterize the conditions in which the will to power emerges as the aim of a distinct drive, and suggested that, when it does, it's normally a guise taken by *ressentiment*. (Dewey, 2008, pp. 97–99; the criticism which Dewey is making of Nietzsche is that he has the explanatory order backwards; instead of explaining *ressentiment* as an expression of will to power, he ought to be explaining will to power as an expression of *ressentiment*.)

However, we don't have to assume that the agent has such a drive. Earlier, I introduced the will-to-power perspective as the metaphysics of the org chart. Now, recall that Nietzsche devotes much of the early stretches of *Beyond Good and Evil* to arguing against atomism, which is in part a matter of treating the items in one's ontology as lacking internal structure: in the will-to-power metaphysics, when you click on a box in the org chart, it opens up to reveal yet another org chart... presumably, all the way down. (You may remember 5:31–34/BGE 19, which gives us a first-pass sense of what that looks like, when we're considering volition in particular.)

Thus we can ask what we see when we look inside a drive, and what holds the drive together; when we do, we recapitulate a variant of the Nietzschean anthropic argument. Drives are extremely complex patterns of control; so complex, indeed, that a recurring scholarly worry has been that drives look too much like intentional agents to be philosophically kosher. If drives themselves have something like governing priorities, those priorities must be centered on or include will to power: here, the priority of extending the scope of control of the drive. So we can also understand the decadent's interest in his own existence as the expression of one or another of his drives' will to power. (I'm grateful to Margaret Bowman for helping me out with this point; the view I now think is correct is quite close to that of Richardson, 1996, p. 26.)

22. Nietzsche objects to the ascetic priest's insistence on prescribing the same medicine to everyone, so we don't need to suppose that dissonance will work for us, too. His treatment was tailored to his own "physiology"—not all that successfully, as we'll see over the final two chapters, since he collapsed while completing and revising *Ecce Homo* itself. (For a description of the collapse, see Hollingdale, 1999, pp. 237–239.)

336 NOTES

23. Nehamas, 1981, Nehamas, 1987. The primary motivation for the distinction between "writer" and "author" seems to have been the desire to avoid committing the so-called intentional fallacy (which, recall, we quickly introduced in ch. 4, note 2). Because Nehamas's postulated author is a "regulative ideal," rather than an actual person, its intentions don't count as biography, and this allowed Nehamas to sidestep one of the academic McCarthyisms of his day. We'll shortly consider whether these motivations are in place in a reading of Nietzsche.

24. I'm grateful to Ian Anthony for reminding me of this.

25. Can this be right? What do we make of the third Essay of the *Genealogy*, which as Lanier Anderson has reminded me, looks like it's written to an outline given in its first section? To be sure, disintegration and loss of control can wax and wane, so even if this Essay looks less assembled than fully intentionally written through, that remains compatible with the description we're giving of Nietzsche as a writer during his later period. However, there's also what is perhaps signaling that suggests we should think twice about this, although it's just slightly involved to explain what it is.

     I indicated earlier on (ch. 5, note 7) that there's been a controversy as to what aphorism that third Essay is supposed to be explicating: On the one hand, an epigraph from *Zarathustra* appears at its head, and quite pointedly, because the other Essays do without. On the other, it makes much more sense to construe the first section—or better, its final assertion—as what is being spelled out below, and moreover, the Essay and pointer to it seem to have been completed before that quotation was prepended. So the latter view has come to be the near-consensus.

     But we might recall that Nietzsche's Genealogist has made a very big deal out of the theme of forgetting, which he has also very elaborately displayed. If you'd forgotten what you were in the middle of doing (or if you wanted to make a show of having forgotten), *wouldn't* you prepend a superfluous epigram to your demo of how to explicate an aphorism?

26. Vogler, 2002, and Thompson, 2008, pt. ii, are recent and sophisticated expositions; they're in the business of developing the views of Anscombe, 1985, which readers are however likely to find obscure.

27. Nehamas, 2018; the idea that goals can evolve over time is developed in the specificationism literature; for a survey, see Millgram, 2008. The shift addresses a tension internal to the Anscombean picture: on the one hand, the view is antipsychologistic, in that it anchors reasons in the structure of actions, and not in the mental states that are imagined as constituting one's inner life; on the other hand, when the structure of an action is traced out via a series of "Why?"-questions, of the sort we saw a couple of paragraphs back, the agent is clearly aware of the trajectory of his action, and so its structure does seem to be tied to his inner life. Nehamas's fallback position, to allow actions for which those questions cannot be answered until the action is over and done, defuses that conflict; we can think of this as a motivation for decaf-strength Anscombeanism that is independent of container-shipping similes and of the intentional fallacy.

     As we've seen, Nietzsche's interpreters have for the most part tried to understand his drives, and Nietzschean valuing, teleologically. GS 360—that container-ship passage—reminds us that we need to think of drives as Nietzsche's attempt at an *alternative* to end-directed forms of explanation, rather than a complicated implementation of end-directedness.

28. Notice that the analogy highlights a further and mostly unnoticed option in the logical space of options. Sometimes coalition governments succeed one another, retaining the objectives of the former administration, while shifting to a different plan for realizing them; for long-term policy goals, this can take place many times before the goal is finally attained (or abandoned). We don't see this quite as vividly or quite as often in the lives of individual human beings, but there's an amusing science-fiction portrayal of the strategy in Dick, 2012: in order to keep their opposition off-balance, the operators of an assassin switch off with each other, retaining the objective of executing their target, but changing the plan for doing so. That is, the caffeinated assumption that, when the end *is* selecting the means, the upshot *will* be a well-formed Anscombean action proves to be insufficiently cautious.

29. I mentioned above, in note 23, that Nehamas's insistence on the distinction between "writer" and "author" seems to have been motivated by the need to avoid the intentional fallacy. So this is an occasion to push back against that motivation.

    Recall that one of Nietzsche's characteristic moves is to interpret religious, moral, and other doctrines as symptoms of underlying sickness—that is, to read texts through the biographies of their producers, and often, through their unavowed intentions. Consequently, if you are convinced that the intentional fallacy really *is* a fallacy, you should find Nietzsche so thoroughly and persistently wrong-headed as not to be worth your exegetical time and attention. Conversely, if you find that Nietzsche is worth careful and close reading, you had better proceed on the working assumption that the intentional fallacy is not a fallacy after all. (I'm very grateful to Carolina Allen for this observation.)

    Given how his view has adjusted, I am myself puzzled by Nehamas's continued loyalty to the doctrine of the intentional fallacy and its consequences; gesturing at Wimsatt and Beardsley, 1954, he affirms the faith: "I believe their argument, which I won't reproduce here, is conclusive" (2018, p. 690). As I mentioned earlier on (and I encourage you to confirm this for yourself), there isn't any argument; when Nehamas does his best belatedly to provide one for them, its target—something of a straw man—is an especially crude notion of intention, as a little mental act prior to acting. On the notion of intention he would like to keep, it's a mode of description of an action-in-context; but with this notion in play, we no longer have a reason to restrict the context. That is, Nehamas claims that you can't just look at the little mental act, but doesn't show why an interpreter shouldn't look to anything in the context that helps him make out what's going on in a text. And with no reason to exclude the biography and personal life of an author from the context, there's no reason to manufacture a substitute anchor for the intention—and so, no reason to insist on distinguishing the postulated author from the flesh-and-blood writer. Sometimes real live biographical context can help make sense of someone's writing, and with any luck this discussion is itself an illustration.

30. Compare Millgram, 2002, p. 177.

338 NOTES

31. I'm embarrassed to admit that I once made this move myself (1997, p. 175). It now rings hollow.

32. And what could be a more definitive condemnation of Kantian moral theory? So Korsgaard attempts a reply: the disunified agent is a defective agent (but still an agent), in something like the way a house with holes in the roof is a defective house, but a house nonetheless (2008, pp. 112f). So far Nietzsche agrees; the decadent is *sick*. But she concludes that the standards we apply to the nondefective item apply to the defective item also. The problem with this strategy is not just that it's obsolete metaphysics: that in the twenty-first century, nothing has a medieval essence determining it to be really a house, rather than, say, a gazebo. It's that if the standards aren't something you can use to guide your behavior, they're practically irrelevant. There's no point telling a decadent to buck up, pull himself together, and conform to the standards we apply to fully functioning agents: he *can't*.

33. Having contrasted the attitudes involved in *amor fati* with those of the will-to-power agent, we can see Nietzsche's preferences on display in the self-mocking attitude he takes towards the former. The posture of *amor fati* has its ridiculous side, which Nietzsche goes out of his way to emphasize. He tells us that his painful eye problems, his severe (and he anticipates terminal) illness, his very disintegration (i.e., his decadence) were each, as we would colloquially put it, the best thing that ever happened to him (6:326/EH 3.HTH.4; 6:265f/EH 1.1; for his "Dreiviertelblindheit," see Janz, 1981, vol. 2, p. 500). He evidently toyed with insisting that Christianity itself (formerly condemned as nearly two millennia of contemptible lies, self-mortification, and on and on) was justified as a necessary precondition of . . . himself (13:641/Nietzsche, 2000, p. 799). And in a section that he did end up trying to replace with a vitriolic diatribe against his closest relatives, he implied that he had chosen the date of his own birth. (The former can be found as Kaufmann's rendering of EH 1.3; the latter in the *Studienausgabe* version of the same section.) Nietzsche had a wonderful ear for style, and it is implausible that he was unaware of just how comic this sounded.

34. Nagel, 1991b. You might think that there's no need to wonder about it: if Nietzsche is right, this *here* is what it's like to occupy the will-to-power perspective. But that's to assume that one is the sort of creature for whom the Nietzschean anthropic argument goes through, and we've just seen that that assumption isn't always allowable.

35. Coscarelli, 2004.

36. My own guess is that the extremes can be approached, perhaps quite closely, but not actually occupied. This is obvious enough at the fragmented end of the spectrum, but I think it's also, albeit less obviously, true at the will-to-power end. Imagine an agent that is fully governed by a dominant drive. When we open up the drive—in our earlier metaphor, when we click on that box in the org chart—we'll either find structure that is in turn fully governed by one of its components, or we'll find disorganization and disunity. If we find the latter, we must expect the control of the drive to lapse sooner rather than later, and in any case, we've identified a residuum of decadence that prevents us from assigning this agent to the endpoint of the spectrum. But if we find the former, we can open up that governing component as well . . . and now it's obvious that we're embarked on a downward regress.

NOTES 339

Notes to Chapter 9

1. E.g., Putnam, 1981, p. 119, which credits Alan Garfinkel for an amusingly West Coast way of putting the point. For what it's worth, my own view is that thoughtfully formulated relativist positions aren't refuted in this way; see Millgram, 2013. For a recent collection that provides a sense of how relativism is engaged nowadays, see Hales, 2011, with discussion at Millgram, 2012. MacFarlane, 2014, is an attempt to differentiate relativism from contextualism.

2. E.g., as when Arthur Danto asks (1980, p. 80), "Does Perspectivism entail that Perspectivism itself is but a perspective, so that the truth of this doctrine entails that it is false?" Nehamas, 1985, pp. 2, 35–37, 65–68, tries to peel perspectivism apart from relativism, and parry the problem of self-refutation, largely by invoking the ways that some readings of a text are better than others; interpretations aren't all on a par, and the best one wins. For a persuasion-oriented variation of the self-refutation problem, see Nehamas, 1988, pp. 62f; the argument is spelled out above, in sec. 4.8, note 37. Or again, Hales and Welshon, 2000, ch. 1, respond to the problem by weakening the relativist claim to allow for some claims to come out true for just anyone; here what matters is that they see it as a *problem*.

3. Herbert Simon is usually counted as a founding figure, and Simon, 1957, collects some of his influential early work. Conlisk, 1996, reviews the first few rounds of discussion, and Gigerenzer *et al.*, 1999, Bendor, 2010, Morton, 1991, and Rubenstein, 1998, sample the range of styles in which work on these ideas is being conducted.

   To give you an initial feel for that contrast between well- and less well-defined problems: On the one hand, there's a determinate answer to whether a number is prime; since for large numbers, the computation can be too difficult, Rabin, 1980, offers instead a form of proof that has a very high probability of giving the correct answer. On the other, consider problems that require you to select an option from a choice set with no maximal elements; no matter what you choose, there will always have been a better alternative. (Such problems have come in for occasional discussion in the philosophy literature; see, e.g., Schlesinger, 1964, Fehige, 1994, or Landesman, 1995.) In these cases, there's no in-principle-correct solution with which heuristic techniques such as satisficing are to be contrasted.

4. I'm grateful to Sarah Childs, who some time back made the transition herself, for consultation here.

5. See Espeland and Sauder, 2016; the complaint is complicated by the phenomenon of value capture (Nguyen, 2020, ch. 9), in which rankings like these are internalized by the parties themselves. If you come to care only about attending the law school with the highest *USNWR* ranking, the heuristic suits your overt preferences precisely.

6. The presumption is vividly on display in Kahneman *et al.*, 1982, a famous early collection of empirical work documenting ways in which subjects deviate from the supposedly gold-standard procedures.

7. Carroll, 1976, p. 617, emphasis and exclamation marks deleted; Borges, 1999, is a variant of the story.

340 NOTES

8. 3:471f/GS 111, and in his *Nachlass* we find remarks such as these: "in our conscious mind there must be *above all* a drive to *exclude, to chase away*, a selecting drive...Our logic, our sense of time, sense of space are prodigious capacities to abbreviate...A concept is an invention which nothing corresponds to *wholly* but many things *slightly...this intellectual world, this sign-world, is pure 'illusion and deception'*" (11:464/WLN 34[131]; cf. 11:561/WLN 36[23]).

9. A couple of characteristic remarks from the notebooks: "Logic is tied to the condition: *assuming that identical cases exist.* Indeed, in order to think and conclude logically, the fulfillment of this condition *must* first be feigned. That is: the will to *logical truth* cannot realise itself until a fundamental *falsification* of all events has been undertaken" (11:633f/WLN 40[13]). "In *our* thinking the *essential* thing is the fitting of the new material into the old schemata (= Procrustean bed), *making* it alike" (11:688/WLN 41[11]).

   Nietzsche may in addition have been aware of Hermann Lotze's variation on the thesis, to the effect that what are apparently repeated instances of the same predicate are made qualitatively deeply different by the different subjects in which they inhere: "gold is not yellow simply, but golden yellow, the rose rosy red, and this particular rose only this particular rosy red"; when you say of someone that, my, his face was red, a rose that exhibited the very same shade would *not* count as red, which is to say that in normal usage, our predicates exhibit systematic ambiguity, which Lotze in turn takes as continuous with our practice even when the subjects to which a predicate is applied are of the same type (Lotze, 1888, vol. i, pp. 60, 140).

10. Putting the point a little more abstractly, logic is formal: on one way of understanding that notion, an argument is valid when you can change out the nonlogical vocabulary without affecting whether, if the premises are true, the conclusion is true. (For our menu of constructions to put on the formality claim, see MacFarlane, 2000.) In this trivial syllogism, you can replace "Socrates" throughout with "The Duke of Wellington," and if the premises are true, the argument goes through, just as before; you can replace "are mortal" with "are ducks," and the argument stays valid; and so on. The slots in a valid argument form generally occur more than once, and substitutions into the same slot have to be made uniformly; for instance, in the toy syllogism, "Socrates" occurs twice, "...is/are mortal" occurs twice, and "...is a man" occurs twice. So again, logic is useless if you can't use the same name or the same predicate more than once.

11. To be sure, there are many points in the argument at which to push back. Among others: Constructing an argument does require being able to mention things more than once; is that the same as finding them again, in a different way? Isn't the entire point of predication to pick out, not the very same, unchanged item again, but something that's the same in *a particular respect*? (For a protest in this neighborhood, see Poellner, 1995, pp. 193–195.) How does Nietzsche know that it's all really Heraclitean flux? I'll return to this latter issue in ch. 10, note 10, but here we're trying to put Nietzsche's picture in place, rather than to defend it, and so I won't pursue the back and forth.

12. McCloud, 1994, p. 66; Breathed, 1990, p. 92, amusingly explains the way comic-book artists represent the aspect of causation that Hume insisted we could not see, and something like it is presumably, in Nietzsche's view, another aspect of perspective construction.

13. William James's pragmatist variation on this train of thought is a good deal more optimistic, and the comparison is illuminating; see, e.g., James, 1987b, p. 900.

14. 3:471f/GS 111, adjusting the punctuation; when Arthur Danto remarks, "This is of course a weird argument" (1980, p. 89), we can put that down to the unavailability, back in the 1960s, of the bounded-rationality perspective: without that, it is unnatural to construe subsumption under a predicate as error and making things up.

15. Tooby and Cosmides, 1992, p. 70, and *passim*.

16. For a very hands-on warning about coping with this particular misrepresentation in the context of preserving natural habitat, see Hilty *et al.*, 2006, pp. 130–132.

17. Recall the discussion in sec. 4.2; the point Nietzsche is pressing is very closely related to a well-known but insufficiently assimilated reflection of Thomas Nagel's. As he lamented, "the idea of . . . a single subject of experience and action," what Nietzsche called a soul, that cannot come in degrees, and that in any and all cases exhibits "whole number countability," is one that perhaps "we shall be unable to abandon . . . no matter what we discover" (1991a, pp. 146, 164). However, because we aren't empty boxes—"atoms"—but rather composed of complex internal machinery, we find that its performance can be degraded in ways that undercut the descriptive practice. On the one hand, we're deeply committed to highly simplified representations; on the other, the ways they caricature us mean that we can't help getting the most intimate and important aspects of *ourselves* simply wrong. (Warren, 1991, pp. 152–158, thoughtfully elicits some of the political consequences of this point.)

18. McCloud, 1994, pp. 28–31, stepping readers of comic books through the process, emphasizes "amplification through simplification," and the way that it underwrites generality and universality: "the more cartoony the face is, for instance, the more people it could be said to *describe*." As we are starting to notice, the perspective of comics and graphic novels is a further very helpful point of view from which to make sense of Nietzsche's ideas.

19. 3:593/GS 354, and from the notebooks: "experiences . . . that have all been simplified, made easy to survey and grasp, thus *falsified*" (11:578/WLN 37[4]).

20. And what is incommensurability taken to be? Bernard Williams, focusing on the attitudes that figure into decisions, and extending an approach he had launched early on (1973b, chs. 10–12), found himself considering cases in which, standing outside another culture, "to raise seriously questions in the vocabulary of appraisal about this culture considered as a concrete historical reality will not be possible for a reflective person" (1981, pp. 141f). Or again, Rovane, 2011, p. 37, restricting herself to purportedly factual claims, highlights the idea that "logical relations do not run everywhere, among all truth-value-bearers . . . [a] truth-value-bearer [that] is 'normatively insulated' from our beliefs . . . wouldn't provide any basis for revising our standing beliefs in any way" (emphasis deleted).

21. Clark, 1991, pp. 3f; here is Danto's version of the concern:

342 NOTES

> Strictly, [Nietzsche's philosophy] should almost have been impossible to understand. How are we to understand a theory when the structure of our understanding is itself called into question by the theory we are asked to understand? Would it not follow from the fact that we had understood it at all that we had misunderstood it?   (1980, p. 97)

For a further variant, see Hales and Welshon, 2000, p. 191. And for yet another, Nehamas, 2009, p. xxviii.

22. And what sort of thing am I leaving out? Just for instance, while it's straightforward enough to account for interpolation as a bounded-rationality technique, much of what we do along those lines is more like conjuring up entire scenes—details, overall import, substantive content, phenomenology—out of practically nothing. Nietzsche gives this sort of confabulation extended discussion at 5:113f/BGE 192, a passage I recommend to the reader, but just because it *is* extended, it's too long to quote now. Instead, here's Wittgenstein evoking the phenomenon:

> It is as if a snapshot of a scene had been taken, but only a few scattered details of it were to be seen: here a hand, there a bit of a face, or a hat—the rest is dark. And now it is as if I knew quite certainly what the whole picture represented. As if I could read the darkness.   (1958, §635)

Again for instance, a central aspect of any perspective is its implicit sense of normalcy, which is also best dealt with from a different perspective than the one we're invoking now.

And again for instance, the stylistic aspects of perspectives are best dealt with from a literary perspective—but I'll introduce some of those below.

23. For an example of the former, see the citations in note 3; and for two of the latter, Millgram, 2009a, secs. 5.2–5.3, 8.3.

24. Perhaps one of the ways it might be overstated is motivated in a way that should be familiar to us. Nietzsche seems to overassimilate the partial truths—approximations, for example—to flat-out falsehoods, in something like the way that today's philosophers, who are largely committed to bivalence, treat the alternative to full-on truth as plain and simple falsity. However, as was remarked even at the time,

> to repeat the old Stoic paradox *omnia peccata esse aequalia,* or to go on preaching that even the smallest error is still not truth but error and nothing else, is but to waste time in tedious assertions which as they contain only half-truths may on this very principle be called errors and nothing else.
>
> (Lotze, 1888, vol. i, p. 242)

25. And what *would* it mean today? See, e.g., Douglas, 2009.

26. In draft material he seems not to have used, Nietzsche tried out a different condition: "how much of the *truth* [a man] can endure without *degenerating*" (11:540/WLN 35[69]).

Perspectives have recently become a keyword in the philosophy literature, and I haven't been marking either conceptual overlap or divergence. For the reader who would like to compare and contrast Nietzsche's perspectivism with what's sometimes called "perspectivalism," Camp, 2013, sec. 3, is a respectable starting point.

NOTES 343

27. Notice that if you thought about each of these issues separately, you could reasonably come up with many different combinations of views on them: they're *logically* independent of one another. Since we can nonetheless normally predict what opinion a member of the citizenry will hold on one of these from his opinion on any other, it follows, as I've argued elsewhere (2005a, ch. 8), that these positions aren't held for reasons at all—and I take this to be typical of political opinions across the board. In political discourse, the arguments and reasons don't account for the positions.

   Like political parties, Nietzschean drives can be focused on remarkably many issues—apparently, almost anything. Hales and Welshon, 2000, pp. 160f, assemble a list, wrapping up with the comment that "a more heterogeneous mixture is hard to imagine."

28. As Nietzsche puts it in the *Nachlass*, "It is our needs *which interpret the world*: our drives and their for and against. Every drive... has its perspective, which it would like to impose as a norm..." (12:315/WLN 7[60]). And there *was* something, it will be recalled, that the aim-directed model of drives seemed to get right: that a drive doesn't run out, but rather induces its characteristic motivation and pattern of activity again and again and again. A perspective requires rendering ever more objects, in particular categories, in the manner required by the heuristics those renderings support, as well as continually suppressing ever more objects in other categories, so as to remove them from one's field of attention. This fits the *again and again and again* aspect of drives nicely.

29. From the notebooks: "the mental sorting and storing" "does *not* enter our consciousness" (13:67f/WLN 11[145], deleting emphases and rearranging); "what presents [a] selection to our intellect, what has simplified, assimilated, interpreted experiences beforehand, is at any rate not that intellect itself" (11:578/WLN 37[4]).

30. It's worth noting in passing a possible shortcoming of the perspectives that are culturally available for appropriation in this manner: that they won't so much as notice, or anyway will fail to bring into focus, whatever it is you're most concerned with. Whereas a perspective that originates with you, and so is anchored to your own concerns, is less likely to overlook them.

31. "Paradigm": although not all perspectives, as we've been reminding ourselves, are individuals' psychologies, if I'm seeing it right, the ones that aren't are best made sense of by starting out with the ones that are—for instance, by thinking about coping strategies that respond to human cognitive limitations.

32. In his notebooks, for instance, we find remarks to the effect that "the *dominating passion*, which even brings with it the co-ordination of the inner systems and their operation in the service of one end... is almost the definition of health... a multiplicity of 'souls in one breast' [is] very unhealthy, inner ruin" (13:342/WP 778, restoring Nietzsche's emphasis); however, per 3:477/GS 120, 'health' is properly an *idiosyncratic* concept; it's not the same thing for everybody, and it's hard to see how the formal point can be compatible with the dominant-drive model of psychological health. (I'm grateful to Rachel Bottema for pressing this point.)

33. I'm putting to one side one of the minor diatribes, *Nietzsche contra Wagner*, partly for this reason as well. I'm not at all sure that it's the kind of exercise we've been

344 NOTES

considering, but as a hasty collage of hostile remarks on Wagner from his other publications, perhaps it would turn out to be: how decadent does one have to be, for authorship to collapse into mere editing?

34. In one version of its subtitle, "Turinese Letter of May 1888," the identification is taken care of very early on. (The other version is "Ein Musikanten-Problem.") The second Postscript also starts off by referring to the piece as "my letter."

35. Recall our recap of one of his arguments in sec. 5.2; for some further backup to the rhetorical question, see the Appendix to this chapter.

36. But sometimes it is: Clark, 1991, pp. 213–217, catalogs both complaints within *Beyond Good and Evil* itself, and the objections from the Psychologist's "Four Errors." However, Nietzsche does seem at points to have entertained some of these ideas and found them plausible (e.g., 7:469, 471/WEN 19[159], 19[165]).

   For contrast, a promising straight reconstruction of the ideas in this passage can be found in Doyle, 2017, pp. 216f: because there's no self demarcated in advance of the outcomes of synthesis, synthesis must be out there in the world as well as within the mind.

37. 6:93/TI 6:5, again with some abridging; we noticed in ch. 6, note 24, that we're being given a further account of physicalism, one which the perspective of *The Gay Science*—that of *another* "psychologist"—seems to have missed.

   On Anderson's reading of the passage from *Beyond Good and Evil*, what it's invoking is not a single type of cause or entity, but rather "that the *methodology* of science, and particularly our commitment to the ideal of explanatory economy, demand that we make the attempt to unify total science under a single explanatory framework, and to unify that framework under a single principle" (1994, p. 736). We can allow that possibility, while still taking the Psychologist's perspective to offer a debunking account of our commitment to the methodological principle—even if it's supposed to subsume many different kinds of causes.

38. It's not just that the Bible is claimed to be a cobbled-together hash of older documents; it's so ineptly assembled that a nineteenth-century German academic, one to whom the cultural context of the volume he's reading is completely unfamiliar, can tell, *just by looking*, which bits and pieces came from which source documents—even when those bits and pieces are no more than scraps a few words long. As we noted in our first Interlude, note 10, on this view, the redactor has nearly no control of his own prose.

39. The King James Version can especially seem like a miracle: it was "a Bible ... designed by committee" (Ferrell, 2008, p. 91), and committees don't normally produce literary masterpieces. Ferrell's description of the KJV registers the status it now holds: as is currently standard, she tells us it is "now considered a masterpiece of English prose" (p. 88), and mentions "its ravishing flights of language and sonorous, rhythmic cadence" (p. 92). Nietzsche expresses the usual view about the Luther translation at 5:191/BGE 247:

   > The masterpiece of German prose is ... the masterpiece of the greatest preacher: the *Bible* has so far been the best German book. Compared with Luther's Bible, almost everything else is mere "literature" ...

However, we should keep in mind that there are mixed reviews elsewhere. At 5:72/BGE 52, he suggests that the Old and New Testaments have very different styles, and seems to prefer the Old to the New. And at 5:393/GM 3:22 he complains about the New Testament:

> I do not like the "New Testament," that should be plain; I find it almost disturbing that my taste in regard to this most highly and overestimated work should be so singular (I have the taste of two millennia *against* me): but there it is! [He continues, quoting Luther:] "*Hier stehe ich, ich kann nicht anders.*"

40. Ridley, 1998, p. 154, worries about interpretations of Nietzsche that conflate recommending an ideal with realizing it. If I'm right, Nietzsche himself was all-too-aware of the difference, and went out of his way to display it.

   A helpful point of comparison in the recent philosophical literature might be the discussion, in Nussbaum, 2001, of what it would be like to adopt the hedonism of the *Protagoras*. As Nussbaum portrays the personalities that make up her Socrates' hedonist utopia—unable to appreciate tragedy, able to see other human beings only as bearers of an entirely fungible good, emotionally shallow—we're supposed to find ourselves having second thoughts. Just what sort of choice is Socrates offering us?

41. Compare the Preface to the *Antichrist*, which describes itself as "belong[ing] to the very few. Perhaps not one of them is even living yet. Maybe they will be the readers who understand my *Zarathustra*: how *could* I mistake myself for one of those for whom there are ears even now? Only the day after tomorrow belongs to me. Some are born posthumously" (6:167). At 4:298/Z IV:1, Zarathustra is made to say that "we do not speak to the Today, nor do we speak to the Never . . . one day it must yet come . . . our great distant human kingdom, the Zarathustra kingdom of a thousand years." (This is not of course the only proposed gloss. For instance, here is Cavell, 1979, p. 390: "a book for all and none, i.e., for the no one anyone may be.")

   However, this way of accounting for *Zarathustra*'s style seems to require construing Nietzsche's letter to Erwin Rohde as a proleptic assessment:

> From you, however, as a *homo literatus*, I will not keep back a confession—it is my theory that with this *Z* I have brought the German language to a state of perfection. After *Luther* and Goethe, a third step had to be taken—look and see, old chum of mine, if vigor, flexibility, and euphony have ever consorted so well in our language . . . My line is superior to his [Goethe's] in strength and manliness, without becoming, as Luther's did, loutish. (1969, p. 221)

42. 6:89f/TI 6.2; as Nietzsche put it elsewhere, "in the past one said of every morality: 'By its fruits shall ye know it'; I say of every morality: it is a fruit by which I know the *soil* from which it grew" (13:256/WLN 14[76]).

43. See sec. 6.1, note 10; recall that we've put in place a backstop of this kind ourselves, in sec. 2.5, but also since deepened the move.

44. We're also familiar enough, in our day-to-day life, with values adopted in the name of consequences that are desired independently, for instance, institutional convenience (D'Agostino, 2003); in these cases, there's a noticeable and worrisome tendency for them to flatten out the classes of items they're used to assess.

346 NOTES

45. But we don't want to forget that perspectives are valuable in other ways as well. We'll consider inexhaustibility as an aesthetic property in the final chapter, but for the moment, a sense of elusive further significance and meaning can be produced by different perspectives on something remaining askew from one another. (We say that stereoscopic vision allows for depth perception, and a device in a well-known track by Elastica, "2:1," can serve as an audible icon of the effect; in two of its three verses, its voices simultaneously sing lyrics that are strikingly different in both attitude and tone. We'll take up a more elaborate instance of this sort of double vision in the next chapter.) Here we have a further reason to resist the suggestion that what one ought to be aiming for is the completed synthesis of one's various drives and other motivations into a single drive that will turn out to be oneself: the merger of the associated perspectives, in producing coherent and fully visible objects of engagement, is likely to flatten them out, in a way that makes the engagement harder to sustain. In yet another way, fully unified agency is a pathway to nihilism. (For this last point, I'm grateful to Svantje Guinebert.)

   The comparison to maps is by now frequently made and familiar; see, e.g., Young, 2010, p. 475.

46. And you might think there were yet easier shortcuts. As Nguyen, 2019, emphasizes, when you learn to play a new game, you can immerse yourself in its world quite rapidly. Moreover, there's a long and mythologized tradition of artists, writers, and musicians not quite switching perspectives, but loosening or blurring them with the help of alcohol and other narcotics.

   While there is no doubt something to these techniques, fully mastering a demanding game—think of chess or go—can occupy a substantial part of one's life. Nguyen, 2020, argues that games attract us in part because they offer us artificially simplified versions of real life, and indeed, they are far more stripped down than even the thinned-out contents of perspectives that we have been considering. You may be less inhibited when you're drunk, but that's not the best state to be in when you're looking for errors in something you've done; you don't drink when you're trying to debug your code, for instance. So it's not clear to me how far these observations suggest we can speed up the reality checks we want, for the judgments we make within a perspective we fully occupy.

47. Clark, 1991, ch. 3; compare Nehamas, 1985, pp. 42f, or Williams, 2006a, p. 323. However, it wasn't that Nietzsche didn't notice Schopenhauer's ineptness even early on; for instance, Schopenhauer thought that we were intimately acquainted with the will as it is in itself, from the inside, and in a journal entry from Spring 1871 Nietzsche already corrects him: "I must insert here contrary to Schopenhauer . . . even Schopenhauer's 'will' is nothing but the most universal form of appearance of something, for us, totally indecipherable" (7:360f/WEN 12[1], adjusting the translation). For other sources on which Nietzsche seems to have drawn, see Mattioli, 2017, pp. 78–80.

48. A point I learned myself from Stanley Cavell.

49. In "Truth and Lie" Nietzsche seems to have shared the assumption—note the mention of coins whose reliefs have been worn away—but as we know, he subsequently argued that genealogies show the items that have them to be indefinable.

NOTES 347

50. Recall the "Four Errors" in *Twilight of the Idols*, which we discussed in sec. 6.4, as well as Nietzsche's stiff corrections of our misunderstanding of the will in *Beyond Good and Evil*, which we reviewed in sec. 4.2.
51. Not that this is the place to survey the menu of options, but just to point you to one of them, meme selection approaches have been argued to filter randomness into exquisite functionality; see, e.g., Boyd and Richerson, 1985.

Notes to Chapter 10

1. 3:347/GS P.2; 1:47/BT 5, and compare his reiteration at BT 24/1:152; however, 8:530/WEN 30[51] seems to register second thoughts.
2. 5:382, 397f/GM 3:18, 23, and the response can be even more visceral, as in these remarks about historians:

> The "contemplatives" are a hundred times worse: I know of nothing that excites such disgust as this kind of "objective" armchair scholar... who betrays immediately with the high falsetto of his applause what he lacks, *where* he lacks it, *where* in this case the Fates have applied their cruel shears with, alas, such surgical skill! (5:406/GM 3:26)

To be impersonal is to be a spiritual eunuch, and that was enough, apparently, to turn Nietzsche against the very last people who were willing to put up with him. Here is vituperation directed, presumably, at Overbeck and Köselitz:

> My acquaintances include several guinea-pigs who illustrate for me different reactions to my writings—different in a very instructive manner. Those who want no part of the contents, my so-called friends for example, become "impersonal"... (6:303/EH 3.3)

Impersonality in matters philosophical makes a friend no more than so-called.
3. Murdoch, 1970, p. 87.
4. 7:69/WEN 3[32], but we might wonder if this is a place for a more radical response: why isn't it begging the question against the Dionysian approach to insist on living that coherent human life? And in any case, if the inchoate underlying reality preempts a coherent human life, then it *is* preempted: the problem is not that, at the end of the week, Burning Man is over, but that, no matter what you think, it's *never* over. (I'm grateful to Madeleine Parkinson and Sarah Buss for pressing these points.)
5. Not that I would know for myself, but so I have been told by someone who should— Amanda Johnson has been an author of murder mysteries.
6. 1:101/BT 15; he subsequently glosses the observation: "Kant and Schopenhauer... destroy[ed] scientific Socratism's complacent delight in existence by establishing its boundaries"; they "make use of the paraphenalia of science itself... to deny decisively the claim of science to universal validity" (1:128, 118/BT 19, 18).
7. 5:626/GS 373; on Nietzsche's encounter with the historical Alexandrian tradition, see Benne, 2005, ch. 2.
8. The controversy famously started early, with Wilamowitz-Möllendorff, 2000.

348 NOTES

9. Schopenhauer, 1966, and he laid out the different forms he thought those explanations could take in Schopenhauer, 1974; for the Kantian version, the best exposition I know, but one which is probably only accessible to specialized readers, is Anderson, 2022.

10. Is Nietzsche making that same mistake? Not necessarily; even though there's no text I know of to hang this on, his perspectivism, it seems to me, gives him a way to say that things in themselves are chaotic. Allow that perspectives are formed by deleting, omitting, truncating, abridging, and similarly misrepresenting the slice of the world seen within that perspective. Allow that these truncations and so on are visible from *other* perspectives—though of course not all of them, from any given perspective, or even from as many perspectives as you could ever occupy. And suppose you're able to survey perspectives, switching perspectives as you do so; we've seen that Nietzsche represents himself as someone who can't help flipping from one perspective to another.

    Eventually, if the pattern is borne out, you're going to be able to draw an inductive inference: you'll be able to say that each perspective omits, truncates, abridges, and so on in indefinitely many ways, so that from any perspective, the way things are is deeply and pervasively misrepresented. And you can flip that characterization around, turning it into a characterization of the world. Say that something is *chaotic* if you can't accurately represent it, regardless of which perspective you're in. And call it *roiling* if, in particular, representing it as containing or composed of definite individuals or properties won't be correct, either. Then you can conclude inductively that the world is chaotic and roiling.

    We've already seen a number of reasons to think that the charity shown by readers like Nehamas and Clark, in supposing Nietzsche to have given up the ideas in his early essay on "Truth and Lie," was misplaced; here is another.

11. I'm indebted to Madeleine Parkinson for the following suggestion.

12. *Something* right, but Klossowski, 1997, gives such an obscurely continental rendering of Nietzsche's own sense of urgency that I'm not sure I'm fairly representing it.

13. However, if that *was* what Nietzsche thought his malady to be, would he have been correct? Retrospective medical diagnoses are always problematic, but recent discussion has picked out a carcinoma on the brain as a leading candidate (Sax, 2003; for a recent overview of the topic, see Huenemann, 2013). We should however bear in mind that this was the period during which our contemporary concept of syphilis was taking shape (Fleck, 1981); we shouldn't read all of it back into Nietzsche's thinking.

14. Janz, 1981, vol. ii, pp. 423, 513.

15. For details, see Schaberg, 1995.

16. I suggested earlier on that there's a philosophical point to the stylistic lapses that one finds throughout the work, so we can observe once again that it's compatible with Nietzsche's scarcely being able to control himself as the words gush out onto the page.

17. The stance is captured in one of his notes: "Restless knowledge leads to the bleak and ugly. —*To be contented* with the world as seen through art!" (7:465/WEN 19[145])

NOTES 349

18. Though these inconsistencies take more than a moment to exhibit themselves, so when we assess their synchronic consistency, we have to do so over the duration of a personality configuration.

19. Nagel, 1991b; the F-15 is a 1970s combat aircraft, still in production and in use at the time of writing. This passage was unfortunately omitted from the published version of Nozick, 2001, but its point was that Nagel couldn't have given an argument for his impossibility claim without having first spelled out what would count as imagining something, which he did not do. Instead, Nagel evidently leaned on a naive conception of imagination as mental picturing, and seemed not to notice our sizable repertoire of literary technique.

Notes to Chapter 11

1. For the point spelled out, see ch. 9, note 10.

2. Since this last is not always a familiar idea, let me gesture very briefly at what I mean. If all horses are mammals, and all mammals are warm-blooded, then all horses are warm-blooded: that inference can be as cut-and-dried as it is only because there are crisp yes-or-no answers to whether something is a horse, and whether it is a mammal. It was Aristotle's realization that we can insist on certain concepts always having that yes-or-no answer; as he explains in the *Categories*, a starving, underweight horse is no more or less of a horse than a sleek, well-fed steed, or for that matter, than a month-old foal: each is exactly 1.0 of a horse, no more and no less. Not everything can be construed as a substance; Aristotle's contrasting category was "heaps," and it is very easy, by running slippery-slope arguments on heaps, to arrive at wildly false conclusions.

   For more leisurely passes over this train of thought, see Millgram, 2009a, ch. 12, Millgram, 2018, or Millgram, 2015b.

3. For the necessary qualifications to that very bald claim, see Millgram, 2013.

4. Camus, 1991, p. 3.

5. James, 1976, pp. 128, 134; I'm uncertain, however, how sensitive James was to the problem of incommensurability lurking in his account of truth.

6. I've done my best to spell that out in what you can regard as a companion volume to this treatment of Nietzsche, in Millgram, 2019.

7. Briefly: since, as we'll shortly emphasize, you don't control what circumstances you'll subsequently encounter (or realistically, even what your own reaction to them will be), and since you're trying to produce a highly coherent rendering of your life, new circumstances are likely to require radical revisions of the story you're telling—one after another after another. It's not at all clear how the pursuit of coherence can avoid a series of sudden swerves that looks like the very opposite of coherence; however, I won't attempt to get to the bottom of this concern here.

8. Landy, 2012, pp. 77–89.

9. Why the qualification? Let me reserve the term "project" for courses of action with two features. First, they're instrumentally structured, that is, the justifications that

350 NOTES

tie elements of the course of action together are uniformly means-end. (You execute one subplan as a way of getting to the next subplan, and so advancing the larger plan in which they are embedded.) And second, unlike the pursuit of a goal, which comes to an end when it's attained (Vogler, 2002), projects are openended; as in Mill's utilitarian life project, there's always something further to do to promote, in his case, the Greatest Good of the Greatest Number.

With that construction put on the notion of a project, we can see that there will be alternative ways one might attempt to turn a life into a unified course of activity. For instance, by changing out the means-end reasons for aesthetic justifications, one might try to make of one's life—as Oscar Wilde did—a work of art.

10. The reader will recall from secs. 4.7 and 4.4 how this conception of meaningfulness fit nicely into an emerging reading of Nietzsche due, mostly, to Anderson and Katsafanas.

11. As we registered in ch. 3, note 54.

12. In literary studies, an analogous phenomenon has come in for notice, and the proliferation of interpretations has been put down, by critics such as Kermode (1979) and Fish (1980), to institutional incentive structures. No doubt there is some truth in this explanation, but it's a matter of disciplinary experience—and here the craft knowledge of the philosophers may diverge from that of the literary critics—that there are not many texts to which this sort of treatment can be given.

13. Of course one *can* disagree: how would you ever grow up? Without regrets, wouldn't you be condemned to immaturity? And regret avoidance can lead you to surprising places; Oscar Wilde famously has one of his characters announce that the only things one never regrets are one's mistakes. We won't pursue these trains of thought here, however.

14. Williams, 1973b, p. 87.

15. For this last point, I'm grateful to C. Thi Nguyen.

16. Although, as analytic moral philosophers will be aware, that can well happen; Williams pointed this out as the fate of utilitarianism. In that approach to moral theory, the higher-level perspective assesses everything solely as a bearer of utility; utility arises out of meeting the concerns of actual people, concerns that are local and whose intelligibility turns on seeing them as important in their own terms, that is, not merely as bearers of utility. So invoking the higher-level perspective undercuts the satisfactions it collates, and on which it depends. Williams ended up concluding, with a shrug, that either utilitarianism was mistaken, or we shouldn't believe it. (See Williams, 1973a, and Millgram, 2015a, sec. 4.1, for a summary.)

17. This isn't a lone moment in the history of philosophy; John Stuart Mill's teenage epiphany, in which he took on the utilitarian project as fully his own, was of this kind (Millgram, 2019, ch. 3). We observed in ch. 4 that analytic moral psychology has, like Nietzsche, seen full-fledged attribution of attitudes and actions to bottom out in the structure of a personality. Such accounts don't appear to accomodate the aesthetic mode of owning an event in one's life, and this strikes me as a reason to rethink them.

18. There is by now a large epistemological literature on testimony; Millgram, 1997, ch. 7, discusses practical testimony and the need to rely on it; Millgram, 2015a, ch. 2, identifies pitfalls.

19. Nguyen, 2017, is a very plausible attempt at an explanation, and can serve as a guide to earlier discussion.

20. A closely related observation: as Nietzsche is thinking about it, your acceptance of the Eternal Return is neither a decision on your part nor something under your control. (For this point, I'm grateful to Svantje Guinebert.) However, the observation is subject to a number of qualifications and caveats, closely paralleling hedges to the impossibility of voluntary belief and desire in Millgram, 1997, ch. 2.

21. Once again, there's a contrast to be highlighted: Ferrero, 2010, argues for treating earlier versions of yourself as decision-makers whom it's reasonable to trust, and to whom you may delegate your choices.

22. 6:335–349, and those phrases are from 343/EH III.Z.6; the "circles" are likely an allusion to Emerson (1971–2013, II:177–190).

23. What do I mean by "not mechanical"? See Millgram, 2010b. Svantje Guinebert has pointed out to me that the problem I'm focusing on is a sort of miniature of the social problems posed by extreme specialization, in which the points of view of the many experts can't be merged into single, all-encompassing overview; for those issues, see Millgram, 2015a.

24. But here's a sketch of how I think about the former issue. Indeed, we do need to be able to make decisions when different ways of seeing and assessing things jockey for position in our lives. But that's not the same thing as resolving those competing ways of seeing things into a unified and comprehensive mode of assessment. As D'Agostino, 2003, argues, we see in the practices of large bureaucracies how easily this goes badly wrong. If you're an academic, you no doubt have an administration that has adopted an index of scholarly productivity which merges together ways of counting the various academic activities in which you engage. When that number is used as a basis for decision-making, not only does it generate perverse incentives, but the faculty come to see everything in the evaluatively flat manner themselves. Now, do you really want to take the risk of ending up living as though you were a lumbering *Dilbert*-like corporation or university administration?

25. Here I'm disagreeing with a view of interpretation we've had in the background of our discussion, defended by Nehamas, on which interpretation is supposed to provide exactly that; this seems to be bad reading practice.

Bibliography

Ahlsdorf, M., 1997. *Nietzsches Juden: Ein Philosoph formt sich ein Bild*. Shaker Verlag, Aachen.

Anderson, R. L., 1994. Nietzsche's will to power as a doctrine of the unity of science. *Studies in the History and Philosophy of Science, 25(5)*, 729–750.

Anderson, R. L., 2001. Synthesis, cognitive normativity, and the meaning of Kant's question, 'How are synthetic cognitions a priori possible?' *European Journal of Philosophy, 9(3)*, 275–305.

Anderson, R. L., 2002. Sensualism and unconscious representations in Nietzsche's account of knowledge. *International Studies in Philosophy, 34(3)*, 95–117.

Anderson, R. L., 2006. Nietzsche on strength and achieving individuality. *International Studies in Philosophy, 38(3)*, 89–115.

Anderson, R. L., 2009. Nietzsche on redemption and transfiguration. In Landy, J. and Saler, M., editors, *The Re-enchantment of the World*, pages 226–258, Stanford University Press, Stanford.

Anderson, R. L., 2012. What is a Nietzschean self? In Janaway, C. and Robertson, S., editors, *Nietzsche, Naturalism, and Normativity*, pages 202–235, Oxford University Press, Oxford.

Anderson, R. L., 2013. Nietzsche on autonomy. In Gemes, K. and Richardson, J., editors, *The Oxford Handbook of Nietzsche*, pages 432–460, Oxford University Press, Oxford.

Anderson, R. L., 2022. Transcendental idealism as formal idealism. *European Journal of Philosophy, 30(3)*: 899–923.

Anderson, R. L. and Cristy, R., 2017. What is 'The meaning of our cheerfulness'? Philosophy as a way of life in Nietzsche and Montaigne. *European Journal of Philosophy, 25(4)*, 1514–1549.

Anderson, R. L. and Landy, J., 2001. Philosophy as self-fashioning: Alexander Nehamas's art of living. *Diacritics, 31(1)*, 25–54.

Anscombe, G. E. M., 1985. *Intention (Second Edition)*. Cornell University Press, Ithaca.

Aschheim, S., 1992. *The Nietzsche Legacy in Germany 1890–1990*. University of California Press, Berkeley.

Baeumler, A., 1966. Nietzsche and National Socialism. In Mosse, G., editor, *Nazi Culture: Intellectual, Cultural and Social Life in the Third Reich*, pages 97–101, University of Wisconsin Press, Madison. Translated by Salvatore Attanasio and others.

Barish, E., 2014. *The Double Life of Paul de Man*. W. W. Norton, New York.

Barrow, J. and Tipler, F., 1986. *The Anthropic Cosmological Principle*. Clarendon Press, Oxford.

Bauer, B., 1958. *The Jewish Problem*. Hebrew Union College–Jewish Institute of Religion, Cincinnati. Translated by Helen Lederer.

Bauer, B., 2015. *Christ and the Caesars: The Origin of Christianity from the Mythology of Rome and Greece*. Xlibris, Bloomington. Translation of the second German edition (1879) by Helmut Brunar and Byron Marchant.

354 BIBLIOGRAPHY

Bayard, P., 2000. *Who Killed Roger Ackroyd?* The New Press, New York. Translated by Carol Cosman.

Becker, A., 2013. *Wols: Die Retrospektive*. Hirmer Verlag, Munich. Exhibit catalog produced by Kunsthalle Bremen and the Menil Collection.

Bely, A., 2009. *Petersburg*. Pushkin Press, London. Translated by John Elsworth.

Ben-Menahem, H., n.d. Nietzsche's *Thus Spoke Zarathustra* and the Quran. Unpublished manuscript.

Bendor, J., 2010. *Bounded Rationality and Politics*. University of California Press, Berkeley.

Benne, C., 2005. *Nietzsche und die historische-kritische Philologie*. de Gruyter, Berlin.

Bentham, J., 1995. *The Panopticon Writings*. Verso, London. Edited by Miran Božovič.

Bernasconi, R., 2013. Heidegger, Nietzsche, National Socialism: The place of metaphysics in the political debate of the 1930s. In Raffoul, F. and Nelson, E., editors, *The Bloomsbury Companion to Heidegger*, pages 47–53, Bloomsbury, London.

Binion, R., 1968. *Frau Lou: Nietzsche's Wayward Disciple*. Princeton University Press, Princeton.

Bittner, R., 1994. *Ressentiment*. In Schacht, R., editor, *Nietzsche, Genealogy, Morality*, pages 127–138, University of California Press, Berkeley.

Bloom, A., 2012. *The Closing of the American Mind*. Simon and Schuster, New York.

Boase, R., 1977. *The Origin and Meaning of Courtly Love*. Manchester University Press, Manchester.

Borges, J. L., 1999. On exactitude in science. In *Collected Fictions*, page 325, Penguin, New York. Translated by Andrew Hurley.

Bourget, P., 1901. *Essais de psychologie contemporaine, vol. i*. Librarie Plon, Paris.

Boyd, R., 1983. On the current status of the issue of scientific realism. *Erkenntnis, 19*, 45–90.

Boyd, R. and Richerson, P., 1985. *Culture and the Evolutionary Process*. Chicago University Press, Chicago.

Bratman, M., 2007. *Structures of Agency*. Oxford University Press, Oxford.

Breathed, B., 1990. *Classics of Western Literature: Bloom County 1986–1989*. Little, Brown, and Company, Boston.

Brewer, T., 2009. *The Retrieval of Ethics*. Oxford University Press, Oxford.

Brinton, C., 1940. The National Socialists' use of Nietzsche. *Journal of the History of Ideas, 1(2)*, 131–150.

Brobjer, T., 2008. *Nietzsche's Philosophical Context*. University of Illinois Press, Urbana.

Buss, S., 2023. Introduction. In Buss, S. and Theunissen, N., editors, *Rethinking the Value of Humanity*, pages 1–23, Oxford University Press, New York.

Camp, E., 2013. Slurring perspectives. *Analytic Philosophy, 54(3)*, 330–349.

Campioni, G., D'Iorio, P., Fornari, M. C., Fronterotta, F., and Orsucci, A., 2003. *Nietzsches persönliche Bibliothek*. de Gruyter, Berlin.

Camus, A., 1977. *The Rebel*. Penguin, New York. Translated by Anthony Bower.

Camus, A., 1991. *The Myth of Sisyphus and Other Essays*. Vintage, New York. Translated by Justin O'Brien.

Carroll, L., 1976. Sylvie and Bruno concluded. In *Complete Works*, pages 504–794, Vintage, New York. Introduction by Alexander Woollcott.

Cavell, S., 1979. *The Claim of Reason*. Clarendon Press, Oxford.

Chamfort, S. R. N., 2003. *Reflections on Life, Love and Society*. Short Books, London. Translated and edited by Douglas Parmée.

BIBLIOGRAPHY 355

Chamfort, S. R. N., 2014. *La Pensée console de tout*. Flammarion, Paris. Edited by Frédéric Schiffter.

Chamfort, S. R. N., n.d. *Pensés – maximes – anecdotes – dialogues*. M. Lévy Frères, Paris, new edition. Edited by P. J. Stahl; includes Mirabeau's letters to Chamfort.

Chaytor, H. J., 1912. *The Troubadours*. Cambridge University Press, Cambridge.

Clark, M., 1991. *Nietzsche on Truth and Philosophy*. Cambridge University Press, New York.

Clark, M., 1994. Nietzsche's misogyny. *International Studies in Philosophy, 26(3)*, 3–12.

Clark, M., 2015. Nietzsche's immoralism and the concept of morality. In *Nietzsche on Ethics and Politics*, pages 23–40, Oxford University Press, Oxford.

Clark, M. and Dudrick, D., 2009. Nietzsche on the will: An analysis of BGE 19. In Gemes, K. and May, S., editors, *Nietzsche on Freedom and Autonomy*, pages 247–268, Oxford University Press, Oxford.

Clark, M. and Dudrick, D., 2012. *The Soul of Nietzsche's* Beyond Good and Evil. Cambridge University Press, Cambridge.

Conlisk, J., 1996. Why bounded rationality? *Journal of Economic Literature, 34*, 669–700.

Coppens, J., 1952. *The Old Testament and the Critics*. St. Anthony Guild Press, Patterson. Translated by Edward Ryan and Edward Tribbe.

Corngold, S., 2019. *Walter Kaufmann: Philosopher, Humanist, Heretic*. Princeton University Press, Princeton.

Coscarelli, D., 2004. Bubba Ho-tep. Produced by Don Coscarelli, Jason R. Savage, Ronnie Truss, and Mark Wooding. Metro-Goldwyn-Mayer.

Coward, N., 1985. Me and the girls. In *The Complete Stories*, pages 467–498, Methuen, London.

Creasy, K., 2020. *The Problem of Affective Nihilism in Nietzsche*. Palgrave Macmillan, Cham.

D'Agostino, F., 2003. *Incommensurability and Commensuration*. Ashgate, Aldershot.

Danby, H., 1933. *The Mishnah*. Oxford University Press, Oxford. Translated by Herbert Danby.

Dannhauser, W., 1974. *Nietzsche's View of Socrates*. Cornell University Press, Ithaca.

Danto, A., 1980. *Nietzsche as Philosopher*. Columbia University Press, New York, Morningside edition.

Davidson, D., 1984. *Inquiries into Truth and Interpretation*. Clarendon Press, Oxford.

Davidson, D., 2004. *Problems of Rationality*. Clarendon Press, Oxford.

de Beauvoir, S., 2011. *The Second Sex*. Vintage, New York. Translated by Constance Borde and Sheila Malovany-Chevallier. Introduction by Judith Thurman.

de Beauvoir, S., 2018. *The Ethics of Ambiguity*. Open Road, New York. Translated by Bernard Frechtman.

de Lagarde, P., 1878. *Deutsche Schriften*. Dieterichsche Verlagsbuchhandlung, Göttingen.

de Man, P., 1979. *Allegories of Reading*. Yale University Press, New Haven.

de Rougemont, D., 1974. *Love in the Western World*. Harper, New York, revised edition. Translated by Montgomery Belgion.

Dennett, D., 1991. *Consciousness Explained*. Little, Brown and Company, Boston. Illustrated by Paul Weiner.

Devereux, G., 2011. *Baubo, la vulve mythique*. Éditions Payot & Rivages, Paris.

Dewey, J., 1958. *Experience and Nature*. Dover, New York.

Dewey, J., 2008. *Human Nature and Conduct*. Southern Illinois University Press, Carbondale. Edited by Jo Ann Boydston and Patricia Baysinger.

356 BIBLIOGRAPHY

Dick, P. K., 2012. *Solar Lottery*. Houghton Mifflin Harcourt, New York.

Donnellan, B., 1982. *Nietzsche and the French Moralists*. Bouvier Verlag Herbert Grundmann, Bonn.

Doris, J., 2002. *Lack of Character*. Cambridge University Press, Cambridge.

Douglas, H., 2009. *Science, Policy, and the Value-Free Ideal*. University of Pittsburgh Press, Pittsburgh.

Doyle, T., 2017. The Kantian roots of Nietzsche's will to power. In Brusotti, M. and Siemens, H., editors, *Nietzsche, Kant and the Problem of Metaphysics*, pages 205–232, Bloomsbury, London.

Dühring, E., 1997. *On the Jews*. Nineteen Eighty Four Press, Brighton. Translated by Alexander Jacob.

Dummett, M., 1991. *The Logical Basis of Metaphysics*. Harvard University Press, Cambridge, Mass.

Elias, N., 2000. *The Civilizing Process*. Blackwell, Malden, revised edition. Translated by Edmund Jephcott.

Emerson, R. W., 1971–2013. *Collected Works of Ralph Waldo Emerson*. Harvard University Press, Cambridge, Mass.

Enoch, D., 2006. Agency, schmagency: Why normativity won't come from what is constitutive of action. *Philosophical Review, 115(2)*, 169–198.

Espeland, W. N. and Sauder, M., 2016. *Engines of Anxiety*. Russell Sage Foundation, New York.

Fehige, C., 1994. The limit assumption in deontic (and prohairetic) logic. In Meggle, G. and Wessels, U., editors, *Analyomen 1*, de Gruyter, Berlin.

Ferrell, L. A., 2008. *The Bible and the People*. Yale University Press, New Haven.

Ferrero, L., 2009. Constitutivism and the inescapability of agency. *Oxford Studies in Metaethics, 4*, 303–333.

Ferrero, L., 2010. Decisions, diachronic autonomy, and the division of deliberative labor. *Philosophers' Imprint, 10(2)*, 1–23.

Fish, S., 1980. What makes an interpretation acceptable? In *Is There a Text in This Class?*, pages 338–355, Harvard University Press, Cambridge, Mass.

Fleck, L., 1981. *Genesis and Development of a Scientific Fact*. University of Chicago Press, Chicago. Translated by Fred Bradley and Thaddeus Trenn; foreword by Thomas Kuhn.

Foucault, M., 1988. *Madness and Civilization: A History of Insanity in the Age of Reason*. Random House, New York. Translated by Richard Howard.

Frankfurt, H., 1988. *The Importance of What We Care About*. Cambridge University Press, Cambridge.

Frankfurt, H., 1999. *Necessity, Volition, and Love*. Cambridge University Press, Cambridge.

Freeman, D., 1999. *The Fateful Hoaxing of Margaret Mead*. Westview Press, Boulder.

Frege, G., 1970. On concept and object. In Geach, P. and Black, M., editors, *Translations from the Philosophical Writings of Gottlob Frege*, pages 42–55, Basil Blackwell, Oxford.

Fuller, L., 1958. A rejoinder to Professor Nagel. *Natural Law Forum, 3*, 83–104.

Galiani, F., 1984. *Dialogues sur le commerce des blés*. Librairie Arthème Fayard, Tours.

Gallagher, C., 2021. *Nazis of Copley Square*. Harvard University Press, Cambridge, Mass.

Gaunt, S. and Kay, S., editors, 1999. *The Troubadours: An Introduction*. Cambridge University Press, Cambridge.

Gaus, G., 2016. *The Tyranny of the Ideal*. Princeton University Press, Princeton.

BIBLIOGRAPHY 357

Gemes, K., 2006. 'We remain of necessity strangers to ourselves': The key message of Nietzsche's *Genealogy*. In Acampora, C., editor, *Nietzsche's* On the Genealogy of Morals: *Critical Essays*, Rowman and Littlefield, Lanham.

Gere, R. H., 1955. *The Troubadours, Heresy, and the Albigensian Crusade*. PhD thesis, Columbia University.

Geuss, R., 1994. Nietzsche and genealogy. *European Journal of Philosophy*, 2, 275–292.

Gibran, K., 2004. *The Prophet*. Alfred A. Knopf, New York.

Gigerenzer, G., Todd, P., and the ABC Research Group, 1999. *Simple Heuristics That Make Us Smart*. Oxford University Press, Oxford.

Gilliam, T., 1988. The adventures of Baron Munchausen. Columbia Pictures. Adapted from the stories by Rudolf Erich Raspe and Gottfried August Bürger.

Goethe, J. W., 1981. *Werke*. Insel, Frankfurt a. M.

Hadot, P., 1995. *Philosophy as a Way of Life*. Blackwell, Oxford. Translated by Michael Chase.

Hadot, P., 2006. *The Veil of Isis*. Harvard University Press, Cambridge, Mass. Translated by Michael Chase.

Hales, S., editor, 2011. *A Companion to Relativism*. Wiley-Blackwell, Oxford.

Hales, S. and Welshon, R., 2000. *Nietzsche's Perspectivism*. University of Illinois Press, Urbana.

Hare, R. M., 1961. *The Language of Morals*. Clarendon Press, Oxford.

Harrison, B., 2020. *Blaming the Jews: Politics and Delusion*. Indiana University Press, Bloomington.

Hayman, R., 1984. *Nietzsche: A Critical Life*. Penguin, New York.

Hearne, V., 1987. *Adam's Task: Calling Animals by Name*. Random House, New York.

Heidegger, M., 1979–1987. *Nietzsche*. Harper and Row, San Francisco. Translated by David Farrell Krell.

Hertzberg, A., 1968. *The French Enlightenment and the Jews*. Schocken, New York.

Heyen, F.-J., 1983. *Parole der Woche: Eine Wandzeitung im Dritten Reich 1936–1943*. Deutscher Taschenbuch Verlag, Munich.

Higgins, K., 1988. Reading *Zarathustra*. In Solomon, R. and Higgins, K., editors, *Reading Nietzsche*, pages 132–151, Oxford University Press, Oxford.

Hilty, J., Lidicker, W., and Merenlender, A., 2006. *Corridor Ecology*. Island Press, Washington. Foreword by Andrew Dobson.

Hollingdale, R. J., 1999. *Nietzsche: The Man and His Philosophy (Revised Edition)*. Cambridge University Press, Cambridge.

Huddleston, A., 2019. *Nietzsche on the Decadence and Flourishing of Culture*. Oxford University Press, Oxford.

Huenemann, C., 2013. Nietzsche's illness. In Gemes, K. and Richardson, J., editors, *The Oxford Handbook of Nietzsche*, pages 63–80, Oxford University Press, Oxford.

Hussain, N., 2004. Nietzsche's positivism. *European Journal of Philosophy*, 12(3), 326–368.

Hussain, N., 2013. Nietzsche's metaethical stance. In Gemes, K. and Richardson, J., editors, *The Oxford Handbook of Nietzsche*, pages 389–414, Oxford University Press, Oxford.

James, W., 1976. *Essays in Radical Empiricism*. Harvard University Press, Cambridge, Mass.

James, W., 1987a. On some mental effects of the earthquake. In Kuklick, B., editor, *William James: Writings 1902–1910*, pages 1215–1222, Library of America, New York.

358 BIBLIOGRAPHY

James, W., 1987b. A word more about truth. In Kuklick, B., editor, *William James: Writings 1902–1910*, pages 897–908, Library of America, New York.

Janaway, C., 2007. *Beyond Selflessness*. Oxford University Press, Oxford.

Janaway, C. and Robertson, S., editors, 2012. *Nietzsche, Naturalism, and Normativity*. Oxford University Press, Oxford.

Janz, C. P., 1981. *Friedrich Nietzsche, Biographie*. Deutscher Taschenbuch Verlag, Munich.

Kahneman, D., Slovic, P., and Tversky, A., 1982. *Judgment under Uncertainty: Heuristics and Biases*. Cambridge University Press, Cambridge.

Kant, I., 1998. *Religion within the Boundaries of Mere Reason*. Cambridge University Press, Cambridge. Translated and edited by Allen Wood and George di Giovanni.

Kantorowicz, E., 1957. *The King's Two Bodies*. Princeton University Press, Princeton.

Katsafanas, P., 2013a. *Agency and the Foundations of Ethics: Nietzschean Constitutivism*. Oxford University Press, Oxford.

Katsafanas, P., 2013b. Nietzsche's philosophical psychology. In Gemes, K. and Richardson, J., editors, *The Oxford Handbook of Nietzsche*, pages 727–755, Oxford University Press, Oxford.

Katsafanas, P., 2016. *The Nietzschean Self*. Oxford University Press, Oxford.

Katz, J., 1980. *From Prejudice to Destruction*. Harvard University Press, Cambridge, Mass. Translated by the author with the assistance of Arthur Super and others.

Kaufmann, W., 1972. *Critique of Religion and Philosophy*. Harper and Row, New York.

Kaufmann, W., 1974. *Nietzsche: Philosopher, Psychologist, Antichrist*. Princeton University Press, Princeton, fourth edition.

Kaufmann, W., 1980. *From Shakespeare to Existentialism*. Princeton University Press, Princeton.

Kaufmann, W., 2017. *Nietzsche, Heidegger, and Buber*. Routledge, New York. Introduction by Ivan Soll.

Kermode, F., 1979. Institutional control of interpretation. *Salmagundi*, *43*, 72–86.

Klossowski, P., 1997. *Nietzsche and the Vicious Circle*. University of Chicago Press, Chicago. Translated by Daniel Smith.

Korsgaard, C. M., 1996. *Creating the Kingdom of Ends*. Cambridge University Press, New York.

Korsgaard, C. M., 2008. *The Constitution of Agency*. Oxford University Press, Oxford.

Korsgaard, C. M., 2009. *Self-Constitution*. Oxford University Press, New York.

Kundera, M., 1984. *The Unbearable Lightness of Being*. Harper and Row, New York. Translated by Michael Henry Heim.

Landesman, C., 1995. When to terminate a charitable trust? *Analysis*, *55(1)*, 12–13.

Landy, J., 2012. *How to Do Things with Fictions*. Oxford University Press, Oxford.

Lang, B., 2003. *Act and Idea in the Nazi Genocide*. Syracuse University Press, Syracuse.

Lange, F. A., 1950. *The History of Materialism*. Humanities Press, New York, 3rd edition. Originally published in 1865. Translated by Ernest Chester Thomas; introduction by Bertrand Russell.

Leiter, B., 2002. *Nietzsche on Morality*. Routledge, London.

Liébert, G., 2004. *Nietzsche and Music*. University of Chicago Press, Chicago. Translated by David Pellauer and Graham Parkes.

Longuenesse, B., 1998. *Kant and the Capacity to Judge*. Princeton University Press, Princeton. Translated by Charles Wolfe.

Lotze, H., 1888. *Logic*. Clarendon Press, Oxford, 2nd edition. Translation edited by Bernard Bosanquet; translators include R. Nettleship, F. Peters, F. Conybeare, and R. Tatton.

Lougee, R., 1962. *Paul de Lagarde, 1827–1891: A Study of Radical Conservativism in Germany*. Harvard University Press, Cambridge, Mass.

Lueger, O., editor, 1904. *Lexikon der Gesamten Technik*. Deutsche Verlags-Anstalt, Stuttgart.

MacFarlane, J., 2000. *What Does it Mean to Say that Logic is Formal?* PhD thesis, University of Pittsburgh.

MacFarlane, J., 2014. *Assessment Sensitivity*. Oxford University Press, Oxford.

MacIntyre, A., 1981. *After Virtue*. University of Notre Dame Press, Notre Dame.

MacIntyre, A., 1990. *Three Rival Versions of Moral Enquiry*. Notre Dame University Press, Notre Dame.

Macintyre, B., 1992. *Forgotten Fatherland*. Farrar Straus Giroux, New York.

Mackie, J. L., 1977. *Ethics: Inventing Right and Wrong*. Penguin, New York.

MacKinnon, C., 2005. *Women's Lives, Men's Laws*. Harvard University Press, Cambridge, Mass.

Mattioli, W., 2017. The thought of becoming and the place of philosophy: Some aspects of Nietzsche's reception and criticism of transcendental idealism via Afrikan Spir. In Brusotti, M. and Siemens, H., editors, *Nietzsche, Kant and the Problem of Metaphysics*, pages 71–102, Bloomsbury, London.

McCloud, S., 1994. *Understanding Comics*. HarperCollins, New York.

Meier, H., 2017. *Was ist Nietzsches Zarathustra?* C. H. Beck, Munich.

Mill, J. S., 1967–1991. *Collected Works of John Stuart Mill*. University of Toronto Press/Routledge and Kegan Paul, Toronto/London.

Millgram, E., 1994. An apprentice argument. *Philosophy and Phenomenological Research*, *54(4)*, 913–916.

Millgram, E., 1995. Inhaltsreiche ethische Begriffe und die Unterscheidung zwischen Tatsachen und Werten. In Fehige, C. and Meggle, G., editors, *Zum moralischen Denken, vol. i*, pages 354–388, Suhrkamp, Frankfurt a.M.

Millgram, E., 1997. *Practical Induction*. Harvard University Press, Cambridge, Mass.

Millgram, E., 1998. Review of Iris Murdoch, *Existentialists and Mystics. Boston Review*, *23(1)*, 45–46.

Millgram, E., 2002. How to make something of yourself. In Schmidtz, D., editor, *Robert Nozick*, pages 175–198, Cambridge University Press, Cambridge.

Millgram, E., 2005a. *Ethics Done Right: Practical Reasoning as a Foundation for Moral Theory*. Cambridge University Press, Cambridge.

Millgram, E., 2005b. Practical reason and the structure of actions. In Zalta, E. N., editor, *The Stanford Encyclopedia of Philosophy*, Stanford Metaphysics Laboratory.

Millgram, E., 2007. Who was Nietzsche's genealogist? *Philosophy and Phenomenological Research*, *75(1)*, 92–110.

Millgram, E., 2008. Specificationism. In Adler, J. and Rips, L., editors, *Reasoning: Studies of Human Inference and its Foundations*, pages 731–747, Cambridge University Press, Cambridge.

Millgram, E., 2009a. *Hard Truths*. Wiley-Blackwell, Oxford.

Millgram, E., 2009b. The persistence of moral skepticism and the limits of moral education. In Siegel, H., editor, *Oxford Handbook of Philosophy of Education*, pages 245–259, Oxford University Press, New York.

Millgram, E., 2010a. Pluralism about action. In O'Connor, T. and Sandis, C., editors, *A Companion to the Philosophy of Action*, pages 90–96, Wiley-Blackwell, Oxford.

Millgram, E., 2010b. Virtue for procrastinators. In Andreou, C. and White, M., editors, *The Thief of Time*, pages 151–164, Oxford University Press, New York.

360 BIBLIOGRAPHY

Millgram, E., 2011. Critical notice: Christine Korsgaard, *Self-Constitution* and *The Constitution of Agency. Australasian Journal of Philosophy, 89(3)*, 549–556.

Millgram, E., 2012. Review of Steven Hales, *A Companion to Relativism. Notre Dame Philosophical Reviews.*

Millgram, E., 2013. Relativism, coherence, and the problems of philosophy. In O'Rourke, F., editor, *What Happened in and to Moral Philosophy in the Twentieth Century?*, pages 392–422, Notre Dame University Press, Notre Dame.

Millgram, E., 2015a. *The Great Endarkenment*. Oxford University Press, Oxford.

Millgram, E. 2015b. The ministry of truth. https://aeon.co/essays/orwell-was-wrong-doublethink-is-as-clear-as-language-gets.

Millgram, E., 2018. Hypophilosophy. *Social Philosophy and Policy, 35(2)*, 138–157.

Millgram, E., 2019. *John Stuart Mill and the Meaning of Life*. Oxford University Press, New York.

Millgram, E., 2022. Bounded agency. In Ferrero, L., editor, *Routledge Handbook of Philosophy of Agency*, pages 68–76, Routledge, London.

Millgram, H., 2008. *Four Biblical Heroines and the Case for Female Authorship*. MacFarland, Jefferson.

Millgram, H., 2014. *The Elijah Enigma*. MacFarland, Jefferson.

Montaigne, M., 2001. *Les Essais*. Le Livre de Poche, Paris. Edited by Denis Bjaï, Bénédicte Boudou, Jean Céard, and Isabelle Pantin.

Morton, A., 1991. *Disasters and Dilemmas*. Basil Blackwell, Oxford.

Murdoch, I., 1970. *The Sovereignty of Good*. Routledge Kegan Paul, London.

Nagel, T., 1991a. Brain bisection and the unity of consciousness. In *Mortal Questions*, pages 147–164, Cambridge University Press, Cambridge.

Nagel, T., 1991b. What is it like to be a bat? In *Mortal Questions*, pages 165–180, Cambridge University Press, Cambridge.

Nehamas, A., 1981. The postulated author: Critical monism as a regulative ideal. *Critical Inquiry, 8*, 133–149.

Nehamas, A., 1985. *Nietzsche: Life as Literature*. Harvard University Press, Cambridge, Mass.

Nehamas, A., 1986. What an author is. *Journal of Philosophy, 83*, 685–691.

Nehamas, A., 1987. Writer, text, work, author. In Cascardi, A. J., editor, *Literature and the Question of Philosophy*, pages 267–291, Johns Hopkins, Baltimore.

Nehamas, A., 1988. Who are "The philosophers of the future"?: A reading of *Beyond Good and Evil*. In Solomon, R. and Higgins, K., editors, *Reading Nietzsche*, pages 46–67, Oxford University Press, Oxford.

Nehamas, A., 1994. The genealogy of genealogy: Interpretation in Nietzsche's second *Untimely Meditation* and in *On the Genealogy of Morals*. In Schacht, R., editor, *Nietzsche, Genealogy, Morality*, pages 269–283, University of California Press, Berkeley.

Nehamas, A., 1998. *The Art of Living*. University of California Press, Berkeley.

Nehamas, A., 2009. Introduction. In Geuss, R. and Nehamas, A., editors, *Writings from the Early Notebooks*, pages ix–xxxvii, Cambridge University Press, Cambridge.

Nehamas, A., 2018. Nietzsche, intention, action. *European Journal of Philosophy, 26*, 685–701.

Netanyahu, B., 2001. *The Origins of the Inquisition in Fifteenth Century Spain*. New York Review Books, New York, 2nd edition.

Neuhouser, F., 2008. *Rousseau's Theodicy of Self-Love*. Oxford University Press, Oxford.

Nguyen, C. T., 2017. The uses of aesthetic testimony. *British Journal of Aesthetics, 57(1)*, 19–36.

Nguyen, C. T., 2019. Games and the art of agency. *Philosophical Review, 128(4)*, 423–462.

Nguyen, C. T., 2020. *Games: Agency as Art*. Oxford University Press, New York.

Nietzsche, F., 1954. *The Portable Nietzsche*. Penguin Books, New York. Edited and translated by Walter Kaufmann.

Nietzsche, F., 1959. *Unpublished Letters*. Philosophical Library, New York. Edited and translated by Kurt Leidecker.

Nietzsche, F., 1969. *Selected Letters*. University of Chicago Press, Chicago. Edited and translated by Christopher Middleton.

Nietzsche, F., 1974. *The Gay Science*. Vintage Books/Random House, New York. Translated by Walter Kaufmann.

Nietzsche, F., 1982. *Daybreak*. Cambridge University Press, New York. Translated by R. J. Hollingdale; introduction by Michael Tanner.

Nietzsche, F., 1988. *Sämtliche Werke (Kritische Studienausgabe)*. Deutscher Taschenbuch Verlag/de Gruyter, Berlin. 15 vols., edited by Giorgio Colli and Mazzino Montinari.

Nietzsche, F., 1996. *Human, All Too Human*. Cambridge University Press, New York. Translated by R. J. Hollingdale.

Nietzsche, F., 2000. *Basic Writings of Nietzsche*. Modern Library, New York. Edited and translated by Walter Kaufmann; introduction by Peter Gay.

Nietzsche, F., 2003. *Writings from the Late Notebooks*. Edited by Rüdiger Bittner. Cambridge University Press, Cambridge. Translated by Kate Sturge.

Nietzsche, F., 2009. *Writings from the Early Notebooks*. Edited by Raymond Geuss and Alexander Nehamas. Cambridge University Press, Cambridge. Translated by Ladislaus Löb.

Nin, A., 1994. *The Diary of Anaïs Nin, vol. I*. Harcourt, New York.

Nirenberg, D., 2014. *Anti-Judaism: The Western Tradition*. W. W. Norton, New York.

Nozick, R., 1989. *The Examined Life*. Simon and Schuster, New York.

Nozick, R., 2001. *Invariances*. Harvard University Press, Cambridge, Mass.

Nussbaum, M., 1994. *The Therapy of Desire*. Princeton University Press, Princeton.

Nussbaum, M., 2001. The *Protagoras*: A science of practical reasoning. In Millgram, E., editor, *Varieties of Practical Reasoning*, pages 153–201, MIT Press, Cambridge, Mass.

Onions, C. T., Friedrichsen, G. W. S., and Burchfield, R. W., 1966. *The Oxford Dictionary of English Etymology*. Clarendon Press, Oxford.

Paden, W., 1975. The troubadour's lady: Her marital status and social rank. *Studies in Philology, 72(1)*, 28–50. With the collaboration of Mireille Bardin, Michèle Hall, Patricia Kelly, F. Gregg Ney, Simone Pavlovich, and Alice South.

Pegg, M. G., 2008. *A Most Holy War: The Albigensian Crusade and the Battle for Christendom*. Oxford University Press, Oxford.

Perrakis, M., 2011. *Nietzsches Musikästhetik der Affekte*. Karl Alber, Munich.

Pippin, R., 2006. *Nietzsche, moraliste français*. Odile Jacob, Paris. Translated by Isabelle Wienand, with a preface by Marc Fumaroli.

Pippin, R., 2010. *Nietzsche, Psychology, and First Philosophy*. University of Chicago Press, Chicago.

Poellner, P., 1995. *Nietzsche and Metaphysics*. Oxford University Press, Oxford.

Proust, M., 1988. *Against Sainte-Beuve and Other Essays*. Penguin, New York. Translated by John Sturrock.

362 BIBLIOGRAPHY

Pulzer, P., 1964. *The Rise of Political Anti-Semitism in Germany and Austria*. John Wiley and Sons, New York.

Putnam, H., 1981. *Reason, Truth and History*. Cambridge University Press, Cambridge.

Rabin, M., 1980. A probabilistic algorithm for testing primality. *Journal of Number Theory*, *12(1)*, 128–138.

Rawls, J., 1989. Themes in Kant's moral philosophy. In Förster, E., editor, *Kant's Transcendental Deductions*, pages 81–113, Stanford University Press, Stanford.

Raz, J., 1999. *Engaging Reason*. Oxford University Press, Oxford.

Redfield, J., 1993. *The Celestine Prophecy*. Warner, New York.

Rée, P., 2003. *Basic Writings*. University of Illinois Press, Urbana. Translated and edited by Robin Small.

Reginster, B., 1997. Nietzsche on *ressentiment* and valuation. *Philosophy and Phenomenological Research*, *57(2)*, 281–305.

Reginster, B., 2006. *The Affirmation of Life: Nietzsche on Overcoming Nihilism*. Harvard University Press, Cambridge, Mass.

Renan, E., 1955. *The Life of Jesus*. Modern Library, New York. Introduction by John Haynes Holmes.

Richardson, J., 1996. *Nietzsche's System*. Oxford University Press, Oxford.

Richardson, J., 2004. *Nietzsche's New Darwinism*. Oxford University Press, Oxford.

Ridley, A., 1998. *Nietzsche's Conscience: Six Character Studies from the 'Genealogy'*. Cornell University Press, Ithaca.

Rochefoucauld, F., 1976. *RÉFLEXIONS ou sentences et maximes morales suivi de RÉFLEXIONS diverses*. Gallimard, Paris, 2nd edition. Edited by Jean Lafond.

Rose, P. L., 1990. *German Question/Jewish Question*. Princeton University Press, Princeton.

Roush, S., 2003. Copernicus, Kant, and the anthropic cosmological principles. *Studies in History and Philosophy of Modern Physics*, *34*, 5–35.

Rousseau, J.-J., 2013. Letter to Beaumont. In Kelly, C. and Grace, E., editors, *Letter to Beaumont, Letters Written from the Mountain, and Related Writings*, pages 21–101, Dartmouth College Press, Lebanon.

Rovane, C., 2011. Relativism requires alternatives, not disagreement or relative truth. In Hales, S., editor, *A Companion to Relativism*, pages 31–52, Wiley-Blackwell, Malden.

Rubenstein, A., 1998. *Modeling Bounded Rationality*. MIT Press, Cambridge, Mass.

Sartre, J.-P., 1995. *Anti-Semite and Jew*. Schocken, New York. Translated by George Becker, with a Preface by Michael Walzer.

Sax, L., 2003. What was the cause of Nietzsche's dementia? *Journal of Medical Biography*, *11*, 47–54.

Sayre-McCord, G., 1988. *Essays on Moral Realism*. Cornell University Press, Ithaca.

Schaberg, W., 1995. *The Nietzsche Canon: A Publication History and Bibliography*. Chicago University Press, Chicago.

Schapiro, T., 1999. What is a child? *Ethics*, *109*, 715–738.

Schlesinger, G., 1964. The problem of evil and the problem of suffering. *American Philosophical Quarterly*, *1(3)*, 244–247.

Schmidt, C., 1849. *Histoire et doctrine de la secte des Cathares ou Albigeois*. J. Cherbuliez, Paris.

Schopenhauer, A., 1966. *The World as Will and Representation*. Dover, New York. Translated by E. F. J. Payne.

BIBLIOGRAPHY   363

Schopenhauer, A., 1974. *On the Fourfold Root of the Principle of Sufficient Reason*. Open Court, La Salle, IL. Translated by E. F. J. Payne, Introduction by Richard Taylor.

Schwarz-Friesel, M. and Reinharz, J., 2017. *Inside the Antisemitic Mind: The Language of Jew-Hatred in Contemporary Germany*. Brandeis University Press, Waltham.

Searle, J., 1983. *Intentionality*. Cambridge University Press, Cambridge.

Sennis, A., editor, 2018. *Cathars in Question*. York Medieval Press, York.

Sieg, U., 2013. *Germany's Prophet: Paul de Lagarde and the Origins of Modern Anti-semitism*. Brandeis University Press, Waltham. Translated by Linda Ann Marianiello.

Simon, H., 1957. *Models of Man*. John Wiley and Sons, New York.

Sluga, H., 1993. *Heidegger's Crisis*. Harvard University Press, Cambridge, Mass.

Small, R., 2005. *Nietzsche and Rée: A Star Friendship*. Oxford University Press, Oxford.

Smart, J. J. C., 1987. Philosophical problems of cosmology. *Revue Internationale de Philosophie*, *41(160)*, 112–126.

Soll, I., 1980. Reflections on recurrence: A re-examination of Nietzsche's doctrine, *Die ewige Wiederkehr des Gleichen*. In Solomon, R., editor, *Nietzsche: A Collection of Critical Essays*, pages 322–342, Notre Dame University Press, Notre Dame.

Solomon, R., 1994. One hundred years of *ressentiment*: Nietzsche's *Genealogy of Morals*. In Schacht, R., editor, *Nietzsche, Genealogy, Morality*, pages 95–126, University of California Press, Berkeley.

Solomon, R., 1996. Nietzsche *ad hominem*: Perspectivism, personality and *ressentiment*. In Magnus, B. and Higgins, K., editors, *The Cambridge Companion to Nietzsche*, pages 180–222, Cambridge University Press, Cambridge.

Solomon, R. and Higgins, K., 2000. *What Nietzsche Really Said*. Schocken Books, New York.

Sorensen, R., 2001. *Vagueness and Contradiction*. Clarendon Press, Oxford.

Staten, H., 1990. *Nietzsche's Voice*. Cornell University Press, Ithaca.

Stendhal, 1946. Armance. In *The Shorter Novels of Stendhal*, vol. I, pages 7–282, Liveright Publishing, New York. Translated by C. K. Scott-Moncrieff.

Stendhal, 1975. *Love*. Penguin, New York. Translated by Gilbert and Suzanne Sale, with an Introduction by Jean Stewart and B. C. J. G. Knight.

Stendhal, 2006. *The Charterhouse of Parma*. Penguin, New York. Translated by John Sturrock.

Stich, S., 1990. *The Fragmentation of Reason*. MIT Press, Cambridge, Mass.

Strauss, D. F., 1892. *The Life of Jesus Critically Examined*. MacMillan, New York. Second edition, translated from the fourth German edition by George Eliot.

Strawson, P. F., 1971. *Individuals*. Methuen, London.

Swanton, C., 1998. Outline of a Nietzschean virtue ethics. *International Studies in Philosophy*, *30(3)*, 29–38.

Thomas, R. H., 1983. *Nietzsche in German Politics and Society 1890–1918*. Open Court, La Salle, IL.

Thompson, M., 2008. *Life and Action*. Harvard University Press, Cambridge, Mass.

Todhunter, I., 1876. *William Whewell, Master of Trinity College, Cambridge*. Macmillan and Co., London.

Tooby, J. and Cosmides, L., 1992. The psychological foundations of culture. In Barkow, J., Cosmides, L., and Tooby, J., editors, *The Adapted Mind*, pages 19–136, Oxford University Press, Oxford.

Tubert, A., 2010. Constitutive arguments. *Philosophy Compass*, *5*, 656–666.

364 BIBLIOGRAPHY

Viereck, P., 1965. *Meta-Politics: The Roots of the Nazi Mind.* Capricorn Books, New York.

Vogler, C., 2002. *Reasonably Vicious.* Harvard University Press, Cambridge, Mass.

Wagner, R., 1973. Judaism in music. In Osborne, C., editor, *Richard Wagner: Stories and Essays*, pages 23–39, Peter Owen, London.

Wakefield, W., 1974. *Heresy, Crusade and Inquisition in Southern France, 1100–1250.* University of California Press, Berkeley.

Wallace, D. F., 2016. *The Broom of the System.* Penguin, New York.

Warren, M., 1991. *Nietzsche and Political Thought.* MIT Press, Cambridge, Mass.

Wellhausen, J., 1883. *Prolegomena zur Geschichte Israels.* G. Reimer, Berlin.

Welshon, R., 1992. Nietzsche's peculiar virtues and the health of the soul. *International Studies in Philosophy, 24(2)*, 77–89.

Whewell, W., 1847. *The Philosophy of the Inductive Sciences.* John W. Parker, London.

White, L., 1964. *Medieval Technology and Social Change.* Oxford University Press, Oxford.

Whyte, M., 2008. The uses and abuses of Nietzsche in the Third Reich: Alfred Baeumler's 'heroic realism'. *Journal of Contemporary History, 43(2)*, 171–194.

Wiggins, D., 1991. Truth, invention, and the meaning of life. In *Needs, Values, Truth (2nd edn.)*, pages 87–137, Blackwell, Oxford.

Wilamowitz-Möllendorff, U., 2000. Future philology! *New Nietzsche Studies, 4(1/2)*, 1–33. Translated by G. Postl, B. Babich, and H. Schmid.

Williams, B., 1973a. A critique of utilitarianism. In Smart, J. J. C. and Williams, B., *Utilitarianism: For and Against*, pages 75–150, Cambridge University Press, Cambridge.

Williams, B., 1973b. *Problems of the Self.* Cambridge University Press, Cambridge.

Williams, B., 1981. *Moral Luck.* Cambridge University Press, Cambridge.

Williams, B., 1985. *Ethics and the Limits of Philosophy.* Harvard University Press, Cambridge, Mass.

Williams, B., 2002. *Truth and Truthfulness.* Princeton University Press, Princeton.

Williams, B., 2006a. Introduction to *The Gay Science*. In Burnyeat, M., editor, *The Sense of the Past*, pages 311–324, Princeton University Press, Princeton.

Williams, B., 2006b. Nietzsche's minimalist moral psychology. In Burnyeat, M., editor, *The Sense of the Past*, pages 299–310, Princeton University Press, Princeton.

Wimsatt, W. K. and Beardsley, M., 1954. The intentional fallacy. In *The Verbal Icon*, pages 3–18, University Press of Kentucky, Lexington.

Windelband, W., 2015. History and natural science. In Luft, S., editor, *The Neo-Kantian Reader*, pages 287–298, Routledge, London.

Wittgenstein, L., 1958. *Philosophical Investigations (Second Edition).* Basil Blackwell, Oxford. Translated by G. E. M. Anscombe.

Wunberg, G., 1978. *Nietzsche und die deutsche Literatur, Band 1: Texte zur Nietzsche-Rezeption 1873–1963.* Deutscher Taschenbuch Verlag/Max Niemeyer Verlag, Munich/Tübingen.

Yakira, E., 2006. *Post-Tzionut, Post-Shoah.* Am Oved, Tel Aviv.

Young, J., 2010. *Friedrich Nietzsche: A Philosophical Biography.* Cambridge University Press, Cambridge.

Yovel, Y., 1998. *Dark Riddle: Hegel, Nietzsche, and the Jews.* Pennsylvania State University Press, University Park.

Zuboff, A., 1980. Nietzsche and eternal recurrence. In Solomon, R., editor, *Nietzsche: A Collection of Critical Essays*, pages 343–357, Notre Dame University Press, Notre Dame.

Index

abstraction 113, 129 n.34
action
  intentional 6, 23 n.18, 88–90, 145, 225
  theory, Anscombean 50 n.43, 88 n.35,
    89–90, 206–7
ad hominem argument 25–6, 78, 141,
    150 n.33, 151–3, 155, 179–81,
    235–6, 245, 259
aesthetic justification 245, 249, 252, 258,
    268–70, 274–5
agency 89, 106
  disunity of 4–6, 80, 86, 141–2, 155,
    159–60, 169 n.19, 182, 209 n.32,
    210, 239, 266
    reasons suitable to 188, 202
    see also decadence
  unity of 4, 8, 76–7, 87 n.34, 143, 146,
    159, 187, 202, 209, 212 n.36, 237
    n.45, 264
    see also will to power
    as precondition for value invention 96
akrasia 5, 76, 142, 146, 147 n.26
Albigensian crusade 121
Alcibiades 147 n.26
Alexandrianism 248–9, 269
amor fati 200, 204, 210 n.33, 212
analysis
  conceptual 8, 124 n.25, 182
  cognitive-function 8–9, 267–8
Anderson, R. L. 264, 266, 277
Anscombe, G. E. M., *see* action theory,
  Anscombean
anthropic argument 187–94, 201–2,
    204 n.21, 209, 210 n.34
antisemitism 23, 35 n.10, 82–3, 87–8, 91,
    156, 159, 164–7, 169, 174–5, 255
  Nietzsche's 166
  political tracts 159
aphorisms 115–6, 143, 205 n.25
Apollonian 204 n.20, 250–4, 266
apriori 131–2, 220, 262

Aristotle 177, 181 n.37, 260, 269, 276–7
ascetic ideal 22
astrology 243
atomism 74–6, 86 n.30, 105, 145,
    204 n.21, 220
attribution 62, 73, 80
  of actions 75–7
  default (weak) 75, 84
  failure of 82–5, 89, 155, 257
  of psychological states 4–5, 75–7, 90
  superlative (strong) 75, 81, 87–8, 92
Austin, J. L. 87 n.32

Baubo, *see* truth, naked
Bauer, B. 35 n.11, 165
Beethoven, L. 81
behindology, *see* realism
Bible 24, 38
  King James 70 n.11, 233–4
  see also New Testament, Old Testament
Bonaparte, N. 81, 254
Bond, J. 163
branding 101
Bratman, M. 86, 187 n.1
Brinton, C. 109–10
British Empiricism 15–6
Bubba Ho-tep 211

Camus, A. 108, 261
Carroll, L. (Charles Dodgson) 216
cartoon, *see* comic strips
Cathars 120 n.15, 121
causation 119, 130, 168, 217–8, 243, 250
  as projection 145
Cavell, S. 67 n.4
Celestine Prophecy 40, 53
Chamfort, S. 115, 143, 164
channeling 154–5
Clark, M. 66, 86 n.28, 129 n.35, 221–2
comic strips 218, 220, 222, 227
Comte, A. 64, 145

366 INDEX

consciousness 133, 219–20
consistency 21–2, 27–9, 146, 148, 171–7,
    200, 205, 256–7
constitutions 76, 87, 178
Cornarism 140 n.6, 145
Coward, N. 266
crystallization 122–5, 127, 132–5, 138,
    256, 265–6, 272
custom 116–7
cynicism, *see* realism

Davidson, D. 24 n.19, 177, 227
decadence 139, 141–4, 146–8, 151–2,
    160, 169 n.19, 173, 175–6, 184,
    195, 200–2, 204–5, 254
  defined 141–2, 181–2, 194, 229
  supporting value invention 238
  as value concept 142, 272
    prosthesis 139, 148, 257, 266
de Lagarde, P. 164
Delphic oracle 260, 273
de Man, P. 181 n.37
de Rougemont, D. 120
desire 4, 8, 167
Descartes, R. 74 n.9
Dewey, J. 145 n.22, 204 n.21
Dionysian 31 n.1, 144 n.21, 197, 204
    n.20, 247–8, 250–2, 258, 266, 268
Dostoyevsky, F. 116, 143, 173
drives 21, 167–8, 203
  aims vs. objects of 86, 159, 167, 177
  analogs of political parties 87, 178–9,
    207–8, 224—5
  articulateness of 87, 178
  ateleological 207 n.27, 224, 257
  coherence of 159, 177–8
  dominant 79, 169, 225, 228–9
  illustrations
    cleaning 86
    doodling 97 n.47
    fashion 81
    glamour 183
    grooming 167
    hunger 81 n.21, 98 n.48, 169,
      174 n.22, 177
    moviegoing 98 n. 48
    reading 97
    shopping 81, 86

sociability 81 n.21, 98 n.48,
    167–9, 183
  for social status 98
  will to truth 44 n.29, 170, 256
  inexhaustibility of 167, 174, 225 n.28
  perspectives induced by 224–5
  recruitment 98 n.48, 169, 171, 178–9
    limit of 91
  responsiveness of to incoherence 204
  synthesis of 81–2, 91–2, 168–9,
    232 n.36, 237 n.45
    mediated by values 96–7, 183–5,
    266–7
  see also antisemitism, German
    nationalism, misogyny
Dühring, E. 67 n.5, 164

egoism 15–6, 152, 175, 197
Emerson, R. W. 1 n.1, 44 n.30, 116 n.9,
    126 n.30, 129, 144 n.19, 144 n.21,
    241–2
end in oneself, *see* value of humanity
Eternal Recurrence, *see* Eternal Return
Eternal Return 13, 34, 40–2, 47, 59–62,
    108, 134, 154, 203 n.18, 212, 264,
    270–6
  Compensation Model vs.
    Transfiguration Model of
    201 n.15, 277
  Idea of Reason 58
  as metavalue 43, 49
  meaning vs. doctrine 211–2
  in Nietzsche's life 237–40, 254–5
  as success criterion for life 52, 271
Europeans, psychology of 79–80
explanatory monism 145 n.24, 232

forgetting 16–7, 22, 28, 46, 195–6, 276
Förster-Nietzsche, E. 109–10, 165,
    166 n.14, 196–7
Foucault, M. 1–2, 67, 68 n.6, 70 n.9,
    113 n.2, 156
Four Errors 145–6, 148
Frege, G. 91
French moralists 115–7, 127 n.32, 128–9,
    132–3, 135, 138, 143, 148 n.29,
    153, 198, 232, 256
Freud, S. 87 n.31

Galiani F. 115 n.7
genealogy 2, 46 n.35, 65–71, 113 n.2, 156
genetic fallacy 26–7
German nationalism 83–4, 91, 150,
    177 n.29
Geuss, R. 66, 71
Gibran, K. 32
Gilliam, T. 264
goals 50
God 162
    death of 13, 34, 48, 63–4, 137
    man made in image of 63, 242
    union with 121
Goethe, J. 31 n.1, 40 n.23, 81–2, 123, 127
    n.32, 154, 263

Hare, R. M. 161 n.6
health 146, 188, 210, 228
    great 103, 135–7, 153
Hearne, V. 99 n.49
Hegel, G. 101 n.52
Heidegger, M. 1, 40, 109
Heine, H. 81
Heraclitus 217
Herbert, F. 44
heuristic misrepresentation 215–23, 230,
    236–7, 252, 261–2
Higgins, K. 32
Higher Criticism 33–9, 47, 51, 59–60, 70,
    233, 238
higher pleasures 42 n.27
Hitler, A. 1, 108, 156
Hulk, Incredible 118–9
Hume, D. 16 n.1, 94 n.44, 162, 218 n.12,
    255, 269

illness 93, 136
    idealism as 113
    love as 124
    Nietzsche's 3, 204 n.22, 228, 239, 254–6
    see also syphilis
implicit author, see postulated author
Impressionism 57, 236
inconsistency 18–20, 21, 23, 28–9,
    171–7, 200
    see also consistency
inexhaustibility, see interpretation,
    infinite

insanity 117, 154, 254–5
intentional fallacy 73, 75, 205 n.23,
    208 n.29
interpretation 17–8, 88, 134, 264–5
    active vs. passive 200–1
    attribution of views to Nietzsche
        61–2
    infinite 133, 204 n.20, 269–70
    methods suitable to Nietzsche's
        texts 2–3, 5, 20, 25, 39, 53, 55, 61,
        65–6, 153–7, 208, 211–2, 276
    Nietzsche's view of 5, 68, 70–1, 110–1
    vs. truth 213
iPod 147 n.28, 151, 179

James, W. 19 n.8, 218 n.13, 263
Jesus 35 n.11, 172–3, 182 n.38
Jews, see antisemitism

Kant, I. 51, 78, 81, 94 n.44, 101 n.52, 108,
    113, 128–30, 145 n.22, 154, 168,
    220, 241, 249–50, 269, 276
Katsafanas, P. 86–7
Kaufmann, W. 12, 109–10, 140, 154, 159,
    196, 227
Klossowski, P. 254–5
knights 96 n.46, 120–1
Koran 35 n.11, 234
Korsgaard, C. M. 89, 187 n.1, 202,
    209 n.32
Kundera, M. 1

Landy, J. 264
Lange, F. 74 n.9, 80 n.18, 107, 130 n.36
law school rankings 215–7, 241, 243
Lehrer, T. 206
Liar Paradox 19, 25, 150
Lichtenberg, G. 74 n.9
life
    as argument 270, 276
    as work of art 134–5
    meaning of, see meaning of life
    project 8
    value of 48 n.41, 140 n.6, 190
logic 131–2, 216
    formality of 217 n.10, 260
    philosophy of 260–1
Lotze, H. 217 n.9

368 INDEX

Louis XIV 76
Luther, M. 70 n.11, 233

Madison, D. 101, 104
Mallarmé, S. 264
Mann, T. 109
Marr, W. 175
materialism, *see* physicalism
maxim, *see* aphorisms
meaning 211
  vs. priority 201, 204, 210, 212
  of life 7–9, 40 n.25, 113, 137–8, 263–4,
    266, 273, 278
metaethics 9, 59–60, 104, 159–62
  constitutivist 2 n.4, 161 n.4
  constructivist 94 n.44, 161 n.4, 163 n.8
  expressivist account of 162–3
  see also noncognitivism, moral realism
metaphor 241–3
  productivity of 242
Mill, J. S. 8, 16 n.1, 40 n.23, 42 n.27,
    76 n.14, 144, 145 n.22, 263–4,
    265 n.9, 266, 268, 274 n.17
Miller, H. 91
misogyny 78, 84–8, 91–2, 137 n.49, 150,
    177 n.29, 180, 198–9
monologue 72, 74, 88 n.37
Montaigne, M. 7, 115 n.7
Moore's Paradox 85
moralism 26, 27 n.29, 132, 161, 197
  see also French moralists
moral realism 46, 48 n.41, 49, 59, 94
    n.44, 104, 139, 161
morality 55–6, 117 n.12
  one size fits all 92–3
  slave 16, 142, 151, 160, 162–3
  system 119
  theories of 149
Murdoch, I. 87 n.31, 149, 247
music 54, 203–4, 251

Nagel, T. 210, 220 n.17, 257
National Socialism, *see* Nazis
naturalism 119 n.14, 128 n.33, 145 n.24
Nazis 1, 77, 108–11, 156
Nehamas, A. 6, 31, 39, 40 n.25, 72–3, 75,
    82, 88–90, 96, 105, 143, 184, 193

    n.8, 193 n.9, 205, 207, 208 n.29,
    264, 266, 278 n.25
  on genealogy 66, 71
neo-Kantians 106–7, 127, 130, 145 n.24
New Testament 35–6, 171–2, 233 n.39
nihilism 31, 98 n.48, 113, 132, 136, 210,
    237 n.45, 266
Nin, A. 184
nobility 96 n.46
noncognitivism 20 n.10, 45, 94 n.44,
    104, 161
noumena, *see* things in themselves
Nozick, R. 70 n.9, 131, 257

objectivity 44 n.29, 100, 157,
    225, 237
Old Testament 34–36, 48,
    233 n.39, 234
Orwell, G. (Eric Blair) 48
Overman 34, 40, 50–1, 59–61, 233, 238
  meaning vs. doctrine 211–2
  as metavalue 44, 49

panopticism 68 n.6
Paradox of the Prefaces 134 n.43
perspective 6, 48, 60, 63, 66, 87, 88 n.37,
    111, 132 n.40, ch. 9, *passim*
  of art criticism 236
  of bounded rationality 221–2, 227,
    236–7
  as bounded-rationality device 230
  correction through switching 31 n.3,
    237–8, 250 n.10, 253
  of literature 227
  privileged 192–3
  voluntary adoption of 225–6, 239
philosophers of the future 43, 47, 50, 72,
    93–4, 100, 185
philosophy 7, 10–1 , 259–61, 273
  analytic 4, 101, 129 n.34, 240, 246, 261
  and the meaning of life 7
  as a value 97, 101, 259
physicalism 119, 128, 130, 145 n.24
Pippin, R. 115–6, 153
Plato 5, 45, 46, 113, 144, 147, 170 n.21,
    178, 260, 269–70
Poirot, H. 248

Pooh-Bah 66
postulated author 6–7, 31, 33, 39, 72–3,
    88, 90–1, 112, 143, 163–4, 205,
    207–8, 233
  coherence of 82
practical reasoning 187, 202–3, 262
Principle of Charity 17–8, 20, 24–5,
    146, 154
Principle of Individuation 250–1
Principle of Sufficient Reason 250
priority 189–94, 200, 204
prisons 67–9
psychologist 116, 143–4, 198

Quine, W. V. O. 227

race 23
  theory of 77–80
racism 87–8, 150
rationality 133, 180 n.34
  bounded 130–1, 214–20, 227, 230,
    236–7, 261
  consequentialist assessment of 147
  means-end 169, 176–7
  as prosthesis 146–8
Rawls, J. 94 n.44, 227
Raz, J. 31
reactive 152, 156
realism 113–5, 117–9, 123, 127–30,
    140–1
  about realism 132–3, 136, 265–6
redoubling 17 n.4, 19, 49 n.42, 75 n.11,
    129 n.34, 235–6
reduplication, see redoubling
Rée, P. 18, 115, 164
relativism 213, 221, 237
Renan, E. 35 n.11, 143 n.17, 144 n.19
repetition 217, 220
ressentiment 19, 26, 29, 59 n.54, 93,
    117 n.12, 142, 156, 195, 204 n.21,
    234, 253
revaluation 23, 59, 136, 139–41, 158–62,
    182–3
  argument for 163
  first example of 119, 140–41, 162,
    179–80, 235
    see also ad hominem argument

Ritschl, F. 71 n.12
Rochefoucauld, F. 115–6, 129, 132–3,
    143–4, 164

Salome, L. 184
Sartre, J.-P. 175, 180 n.34
satsificing 215–6
scholars 21–4, 26–7, 38, 53, 55–6, 80,
    100–2, 157, 162, 246, 249
Schopenhauer, A. 13, 38 n.17, 87 n.31,
    108, 130 n.36, 178, 230, 241, 246,
    250, 252–3, 258
scientific method 231–2
selection
  anthropic 187
  cultural 219, 244 n.51
  natural 131, 191, 218
self 62, 75–6, 81, 91, 134, 145, 197, 243
  see also atomism
self-interest 116–7, 152
self-overcoming 44, 96 n.46, 185
  of nihilism 113
  of realism 133–6, 138
  of the will to truth 105
sexism, see misogyny
Sierra Club 224
skepticism, see will, paralysis of
slacker 201–2
Socrates 97 n.47, 139, 144, 146–7, 217,
    234 n.40, 248, 261
state of nature argument 70 n.9
Stendhal (Marie-Henri Beyle) 81, 115
    n.7, 116, 120, 122–5, 133, 138, 143,
    265, 269
Strauss, D. 35, 48
Strawson, P. F. 154, 194 n.10
Streitschrift 20–1, 29–30
strength 22, 96, 137 n.50, 208
style 32–3, 134, 144, 164, 199, 233–4
substance 119, 216, 243, 260
suicide 48 n.41, 201–2, 247
synthesis
  of cognitions 81, 168–9, 181 n.37
  as empirical process 130
  of drives, see drives, synthesis of
  incomplete 91–2
syphilis 239, 254

370 INDEX

things in themselves 38, 114, 129–30,
    168, 243–4, 250
troubadours 120–2
Tour of the Workshop 19–20
tragedy 203, 250–1, 258, 263,
    266–8
truth 55, 261
    analytic 131
    -for 213, 221
    naked 126, 129 n.35
    necessary 130, 262
    partial 222
    see also drives, illustrations, will to
        truth

universities 47, 188–91, 193
utility 15–6, 26, 274 n.16

value
    of dignity of labor 56–8
    of humanity 31–2, 37, 41–2, 50–2,
        58, 63–5
    inversion 47–9, 51–2, 55–6, 65,
        160, 238
    polarities 142–3, 151–2
values 27–8, 93
    as facts 162
    as ideals 45, 58
    idiosyncratic 26, 28, 50, 63, 94, 183,
        238, 253, 272
    illustrations
        cuisines 100–1, 104
        doodling 57
        writing voice 94–5
        philosophy 97
        see also Impressionism
    institutionalization of 36, 39, 47–51,
        53–5, 62, 64–5, 182, 233–4,
        238, 253
    invention of 32, 42–7, 56–8, 139, 182,
        212, 253, 262, 274
        difficulty of 33–4, 46–7
        inadvertent 19, 57, 182
        motivation for approach 42
        motivating particular invented
            values 58, 151, 179
    meta- 43, 44, 49, 51, 58, 96, 104, 237,
        253, 274

niche-marketed 98–9
objects of drives 179, 183
perspectives, role of in 48, 223–25, 273
queer 45
reducibility of 45 n.33, 57–8, 94 n.44,
    95, 101, 104 n.54, 147 n.28
stabilization of 47–8, 51–3, 63
as standards 42, 45–6, 57, 94–5, 271
    of schools of art 57
upending of, see revaluation
value of 94 n. 44
virtue ethics 149–50

Wagner, R. 3, 81, 137, 165, 195 n.12,
    229, 251
Wall, J. 269
Wallace, D. F. 192
Waters, A. 100
Wellhausen, J. 35–8, 48, 64, 70, 233
Whewell, W. 39 n.19, 269
whole-number countability 76 n.13,
    220 n.17
Wiggins, D. 210
Wilde, O. 265 n.9, 271 n.13
will 145
    free 23 n.17, 76, 86, 118–9, 145, 187, 220
    strength of 96, 142, 144 n.18
    paralysis of 77, 80
    weakness of, see akrasia
will to power 44 n.28, 52 n.47, 68, 95,
    133, 139, 142, 147, 152, 188–94,
    210, 212, 231
    as object of a drive 204 n.21
    matter of the world 230–1, 250
    perspective 192–3, 204 n.21, 210
    as priority 189–92, 200–1, 233
Williams, B. 19, 70 n.9, 118–9, 127, 269,
    273, 274 n.16
Wittgenstein, L. 46 n.37, 221 n.22, 227
Wolfgang, A. O. (Wols) 57
women 121–3, 126–7, 137 n.49, 197–8
    see also misogyny
writer, see postulated author

Xerxes 174

Zarathustra, ch. 3, passim
Zoroastrianism 35 n.11, 48 n.41